If mere survival, mere continuance, is of interest, then the harder sorts of rocks, such as granite, have to be put near the top of the list as most successful among macroscopic entities. . . . But the rock's way of staying in the game is different from the way of living things. The rock, we may say, <u>resists</u> change; it stays put, unchanging. The living thing escapes change either by correcting change or changing itself to meet the change or by incorporating continual change into its own being.   —Gregory Bateson, *Mind and Nature* (New York: E. P. Dutton, 1979)

Pintupi Country, Pintupi Self

Sentiment, Place, and Politics among Western Desert Aborigines

Fred R. Myers

SMITHSONIAN INSTITUTION PRESS
Washington and London

AUSTRALIAN INSTITUTE OF ABORIGINAL STUDIES
Canberra

For My Parents,
Bernice Myers and Robert Myers

FRONTISPIECE: Kim Napurrula and her son on a cold winter day.
(*Warlungurru, 1983*)

Library of Congress Cataloging in Publication Data

Myers, Fred R. (Fred Ralph), 1948–   .
  Pintupi country, Pintupi self.

  Bibliography.
  Includes index.
  ISBN 0 85575 171 1(AIAS).
  ISBN 0 87474 690 0(Smithsonian).

  1. Pintupi (Australian people). 2. Ethnology—Australia.
  I. Australian Institute of Aboriginal Studies. II. Title.

306′.0899915

∞ The paper used in this publication meets the minimum
requirements of the American National Standard for Permanence
of Paper for Printed Library Materials Z39.48–1984.

Table of Contents

Maps and Diagrams

ORTHOGRAPHY

The following orthography (after Hansen and Hansen 1969) has been used in transcribing Pintupi phonemes:

Point of Articulation	Stops	Nasals	Laterals
Bilabial	p	m	
Apico-Alveolar	t	n	l
Apico-Domal	rt	rn	rl
Lamino-Alveolar	tj	ny	ly
Velar	k	ng	

	Vibrants	Semiconsonants
Apico-Alveolar	rr	
Bilabial		w
Lamino-Palatal		y
Apico-Domal		r

Vowels	Short	Long
High front unrounded	i	ii
High back rounded	u	uu
Low central unrounded	a	aa

Preface

My field research with the Pintupi has always been both joyous and exhausting—and for the same reason, namely that the Pintupi have expected me to take on the obligations appropriate to community membership. This has been true from the beginning.

I arrived in Australia's Northern Territory in June 1973 to ask the Pintupi for permission to conduct my study in Yayayi, a small breakaway community they had just established twenty-six miles west of Papunya. These people from the Gibson Desert had been coming east to Northern Territory settlements for the past forty years. That they had at last set up their own community, largely isolated from government supervision, provided a novice anthropologist with an opportune situation. I hoped to learn how the Pintupi organized themselves and their own destiny, in terms of their concerns and values.

Even with this aim, I must confess that a long time passed before I began to comprehend what my Pintupi friends were telling me. Once I understood that they were indeed trying to explain themselves to me in a Pintupi fashion—and that there *was* a Pintupi fashion—my confusion and struggles became more directed. None of this would have been possible without the friendliness and warmth of the Pintupi and their acceptance of me into the community as a member, as a "one-countryman" with my own responsibilities to them. This interaction and the difficult but rewarding emotional awareness I gradually gained of a Pintupi way of life inform the explanations and interpretations I offer in this book. I came to see that the "feel" of Pintupi life was central to any understanding.

Throughout my field stays I have struggled with the problem of imposing my ideals and expectations on the people I studied. I felt this all the more deeply because the Pintupi remain in a semicolonial situation that still emphasizes the values and expectations of the white Australian majority. This conflict and its anthropological significance forced me to come to grips with the continuity and persistence of Pintupi cultural concepts.

Since my initial twenty-one months at Yayayi, I have lived for intervals with Pintupi people as they have shifted their residence further and further west toward their own country. These stays—at Yayayi and Yinyilingki for two months in 1979, at New Bore and Papunya for eight months in 1980–81, and short visits to Balgo in

1982, Balgo and Kintore in 1983, and Kintore and Kiwirrkura in 1984—have renewed the personal relationships that define my status as a "relative" and have maintained a sense of the moral basis for the ongoing conversation that is ethnography. Once "back from the field," it is all too easy for anthropologists to forget their accountability to local mores. In returning to the Pintupi, I have sought not only to justify their trust and acceptance but also to retain contact with what matters to them. My own life has been deeply affected by their awareness of people as persons, and I hope that their enduring respect for persons in the *concrete*, as Kierkegaard once wrote, will be matched by my respect for them.

Pintupi sociality is anything but anonymous. In fact, the presence of particular individuals defines Pintupi society itself, yet the properties of one's identity are quite personal. Thus, I have tried to represent individuals in their concrete identities, only substituting pseudonyms to protect their privacy and also to avoid using names that might become taboo through death. The Pintupi themselves will know the characters I describe. Likewise, photographs help to maintain the immediate reality of Pintupi life, but readers should be aware that pictures of deceased relatives can cause great pain to Aboriginal people. Out of politeness and consideration, it would be appropriate to request permission from some knowledgeable member of the Pintupi communities before showing these photographs.

Finally, in Aboriginal society, access to some kinds of information is restricted. This limitation holds especially true for religious matters, including men's and women's rituals. As a male, I was taught a great deal about men's religious life with the understanding that I would not make it public. In accordance with this restriction, I have written only of matters that were considered public knowledge in the community.

In no sense does an anthropologist work alone. Many people took part in the ongoing conversation that has worked itself out in this study. The degree to which I have made sense of the experience should be seen as testimony to the friendship and patience of the Pintupi—to whom I here express my enormous debt and my gratitude. For their continuing help throughout the years, I am particularly grateful to Shorty Lungkarta, Freddy West, George Yapa Yapa, Ginger Tjakamarra, Kanya Tjapangarti, Ronnie Tjampitjinpa, Yanyatjarri Tjakamarra, and Yumpurlurru Tjungurrayi. These people made me their kinsman and their friend.

I am indebted also to a number of others, especially to Jane Goodale, who first interested me in Aboriginal culture and taught me how to be a fieldworker. In Australia, Nicolas Peterson initially helped me choose a field location; throughout the years, he and his wife Roz have kept me in touch with Aboriginal studies through letters, hours of discussion, and the warm hospitality of their home. My fellow Western Desert researchers, Robert and Myrna Tonkinson, have generously provided me with support, much-needed conversation, and rest and recreation on my way into and out of the field. The list of others in Australia is extensive and, although I cannot name them all, I would like to thank Diane Barwick, Jeremy Beckett, Jeremy Long, and Judith Wilson.

In the Centre, my gratitude to Ken and Leslie Hansen is great, extending beyond my use of their grammar of Pintupi before it was published. I would like to thank particularly Jeff Stead, who has provided understanding, insight, and moral support first as community adviser to the Pintupi and now as research officer at the Central Land Council. David and Lyn Bond and Carolyn and David Cann have helped me in every imaginable way at Papunya.

My research in the field was supported by NSF Dissertation Improvement Grant No. GS 37122, NIMH Fellowship No. 3FOIMH7275-01, and the Australian Institute of Aboriginal Studies. I am particularly grateful to the Institute for its graciousness and support through the years. By providing me with a Presidential Fellowship to complete this book, New York University made it possible to bring a long project to fruition.

I would also like to thank the following people who provided comments and constructive criticism on various parts of the manuscript: Tom Beidelman, Don Brenneis, Dan Goodwin, Ivan Karp, Terry Turner, Annette Weiner, and Randy White. Finally, my gratitude to Bette Clark, who has shared not only in the struggle to clarify the subtleties of Pintupi life but also in the difficult times of fieldwork and self-doubt.

I gratefully acknowledge the permission of the editor of *Mankind* to use material from my articles "The Cultural Basis Politics in Pintupi Life" (*Mankind* 12 [1980]: 197–213) and "A Broken Code: Pintupi Political Theory and Contemporary Social Life" (*Mankind* 12 [1980]: 311–26). The University of Queensland Press has given permission to draw on my paper "Ideology and Experience: The Cultural Basis of Pintupi Politics," published in M. Howard, ed., *Aboriginal Power in Australian Society* (1982), and Westview Press has done so for "Always Ask: Resource Use and Landownership among the Pintupi of Central Australia," published in N. Williams and E. Hunn, eds., *Resource Managers* (1982). Thanks are also due to Heidi Knecht for preparing maps and charts.

FRED MYERS
New York, New York
June 1985

Introduction

The true locus of culture is in the interactions of specific individuals and, on the subjective side, in the world of meanings which each one of these individuals may unconsciously abstract for himself from his participation in these interactions. (Sapir 1970: 151)

The Pintupi were among the last Aboriginal people in Australia to abandon an autonomous hunting-and-gathering way of life, a last family moving in from the remote stretches of the Gibson Desert in 1984. Had we the "double vision" of poets, we could—perhaps—read their history in the landscape itself, in the Gibson Desert of Western Australia and the adjacent plateau of central Australia to the east, at the edge of the magnificent Macdonnell Ranges.

The sight of these ranges—hills of quartzite that change color from red to blue to purple as the sun moves through the sky—suggests the haunting unreality of a watercolor that remains in a viewer's mind longer than the original subject. It is a stark country, known to Europeans as an arid and dangerous place, but its red sand, flat scrubby plains covered with a sparse pale greenery, and craggy, long-eroded hills lie in muted beauty beneath an awesomely blue sky. One cannot escape its immensity and its calm. The paleness of its colors seems always to be a kind of ghostly habitation of color, barely corporeal. White gum trees (the "ghost gums" of the early settlers) line the dry creeks, and the vast stretches of desert have been bleached to an austere beauty under the searing sun. In the enduringness of this landscape, Aborigines see a model of the continuity they aim to attain in social life, a structure more abiding and real than their transitory movements on its surface.

In Aboriginal Australia the relation of past with present poses an unusual problem for an ethnography. A brief trip to the tin shanties of today's Aborigines in central Australia invites the unaccustomed visitor to interpret their lives as irrevocably dominated, if not destroyed, by Western civilization. Ironically, the eyes of the concerned see mainly poverty and deprivation, rather than the structured social world Aboriginal people continue to maintain. With a view to the imposing, apparently unchanging landscape, the nostalgic may reflect sadly on the intervention of history in a timeless world. But these reactions would be mistaken.

For all its trappings of worldliness and hard knowledge of history's inexorable laws, such a dichotomous "before and after" view reflects a rather shallow grasp of society as human action. Focusing on outward form alone makes it impossible to see the past in the present. Hunting-and-gathering bands, it is true, no longer exist for observation. Yet their substance, if not their material form, remains here: as part of the structure with which the present encounters the future.

When I first came to work with the Pintupi in 1973, my intention was to study the individual and territorial organization. The problem of local organization remained central to my research, but what I encountered in the field expanded my sense of the issue. I came to understand that the organization of people in space is itself a manifestation of what is called by some a "deeper structure" or an "inner logic" and by others a "total system." To treat this dimension of organization as an autonomous institution, however hallowed by the history of anthropological inquiry, would be mistaken.

The Problem of Ethnography

At the heart of the anthropological enterprise lies the idea that what is learned in fieldwork at a particular time and place has meaning that transcends the immediate moment. This notion, after all, is what underlay the Boasian concept of culture. The difficulty ethnographers face is in deciding how to apply this intuition. Although the narrative convention of the continuous ethnographic present simplifies the difficulty, it does so by obscuring the process through which one constructs a "society" from data. For better or worse, the current situation in Aboriginal Australia makes this impossible. The moment of observation cannot be simply generalized into a description of a set of social arrangements enduring through time. Instead, the current politics surrounding the movement for land rights and the Aboriginal control of local institutions make us aware of people struggling to maintain an order of being and action that they value. What moves through time can be found in our data, but it cannot be located simply in outward behavior itself. However distressing the consequences of time, an awareness of this dimension of action draws our attention to the inner logic of social systems. Persisting despite apparent transformations of societal form, the internal contradictions of this structure continue to set the limits of social life. Recognizing the past in the present forces upon us the realization that these small-scale societies exist in time and reproduce themselves through it. *Pintupi Country, Pintupi Self* represents my attempt to articulate this view.

Ethnography is a product of a special sort of dialectic. An ethnographer with a past and cultural background that focuses his or her attention on particular issues encounters the reality of other human subjects. Part of this background, inevitably, are the problems that anthropology currently defines as its subject matter. These issues make up the culture we share with our audience. Thus, for example, Malinowski's justly famous ethnography was drawn to the issue of whether or not the "family" was universal. One of the enduring anthropological issues concerning hunter-gatherers has been the question of territoriality. My own analyses of these issues are defined in relation to those of my predecessors.

Malinowski, however, not only brought his special sense of problem to the Trobriand Islanders; his experience made him aware of issues salient to *them*. The sexuality of these Melanesians, for example, was not simply his preoccupation. No less has the Pintupi definition of human relations in terms of compassion, sympathy, and sorrow shaped my own conception of what analytic frameworks are viable.

Ethnographic accounts reflect the working out of this process of assimilation, these dialogues between concept and evidence (Thompson 1979: 31). Beyond the author, however, are the people he or she has known, and anyone trained in ethnography soon learns that one reads an account to look *through* the construction to a reality it attempts to represent.

The Question of Meaning

My ethnography is informed by a general theoretical interest in the relationships between cultural meaning and the processes of social life—the very old problem of consciousness and society. Understanding the significance of cultural form itself seems inevitably to bring us face to face with the idealism/materialism controversy, and it is only appropriate that I should own up to how I have been influenced.

On the whole, literary approaches and sociological approaches to meaning have opposed each other. The former, especially as exemplified in the Anglo-American New Criticism and the Continental emphasis on hermeneutics, emphasizes the freedom of the individual subject to find or construe meaning in his or her world. A classic example is the continual reinterpretation of the Bible to find meaning for the present, and the Boasian commitment to the autonomy of cultural meaning takes its place in this range of cultural theory. The sociology of knowledge, contrastingly, focuses on the superindividual processes and structures that constrain or elicit the individual's activities. This approach suggests that the concrete realities that human beings confront shape the interpretations they produce. The problem of the individual is, to some extent, our own, but it is also an issue for the Pintupi.

One of the main themes of most current anthropological theories of meaning is to resolve this long-standing opposition between creativity and constraint. It is the earmark of the influential trend represented by Bourdieu (1976), Giddens (1979), and R. Williams (1977). For my own part, the influence of the Boasian tradition of Boas, Radin, and Sapir has proven as significant as my reading of recent phenomenologically inspired work. When Sapir (1938) pointed out the implications of one informant's (Two Crows) denial of another man's account, he suggested that individuals have the capacity to drastically transform and reinterpret cultural tradition. This analysis was part of Sapir's own brilliant and prescient attack on the reification of culture; it has been taken up again by Geertz (1973), Frake (1974), and others in the past decade.

The solution I adopt to the opposition between constructive activity and determination is to analyze the relationship between cultural meaning and social action by placing social life in a temporal perspective, similar to that embodied in the concept of "social reproduction" (cf. Bourdieu 1976, Comaroff and Roberts 1981, Giddens 1979, Sahlins 1981, T. Turner 1979a, Weiner 1976, R. Williams 1977). This perspective establishes a mediation of the individual/society opposition by granting to social actors an awareness or intuition of some properties of the sociocultural systems on which they draw in acting and which they reproduce in their activities.

If cultural constructs are, as R. Williams (1977) maintains, forms of "practical consciousness," the problem becomes locating them in relationship to domains of experience. Therefore, cultural analysis consists of properly situating people's cultural constructs in relationship to their social reality. Ethnography becomes the premier instrument for the investigation of social reality thus conceived, a means through which to situate culture within the processes of social activity.

At the same time, one must recognize that cultural constructs are not "transparent" to their use. As an instrument of intersubjectivity, culture is necessarily a "false consciousness" or "alienation" in a technical sense. T. Turner (1984b) captures this dimension of cultural form when he writes that cultural symbols not only represent, they also misrepresent. Culture cannot simply embody an individual's intentions or consciousness; it also creates him or her. This was Marx's great insight. Only a systemic analysis can come to terms with this quality of culture that escapes the individual's control.

My choice of these issues is not simply a theoretical one. It represents, rather, a result of the movement back and forth between concept and evidence. The ethnography of hunters and gatherers raises three particular theoretical questions.

Negotiation: Rules and Processes

My own connection has never been to the Pintupi as a group, but instead to various individuals who have considered me to be a "relative." To say so is to indulge neither in self-promotion nor in self-revelation. The concrete qualities of being are as central to my learning as to Pintupi lives.

As Margaret Mead once said, anthropology has informants, not objects of study. People teach us. The condition of my living in Pintupi communities has always been my participation as a "relative." Their acceptance has never been based on my research, which they have never been much interested in once they decided I was a friend (despite my sincere and lengthy attempts to explain my work). Rather, what they expect from me is my human commitment to them as fellow people. This condition has set the tone of my whole research. Since the Australian government's policy of "self-determination" began, the Pintupi have insisted that those who live in their communities must "help Aboriginal people."

Their willingness to provide me instruction in Pintupi culture has followed a similar course in making me part of their lives. The Pintupi I know have emphasized my learning through participation and have been reluctant to submit to the sort of "white room" formal sessions of inquiry of which, in frustration, I have occasionally dreamed. It is neither polite nor productive to ask a lot of questions. When individuals have sponsored me with their help, we have worked by my spending the day in participant-observation, waiting for opportune moments to ask questions. In this way I learned gradually to identify certain Pintupi symbolic constructs with realms of action, not just as objects of analysis, but also in making myself understood. My experience of Pintupi culture, then, conforms to Wittgenstein's dictum not to ask what a thing means, but to look to its use.

The foundation of my analytic approach to sociocultural phenomena lies here. In this study, I start with the key symbols (Ortner 1973) of Pintupi daily life, and work out their "problematics"—that is, the relation between their meanings and the social contexts of their application. On the one hand, this procedure allows for some autonomy between the domain of cultural forms and the objective circumstances of their use. Certain cultural forms are employed in what, to me, seem differing domains. This perception is hardly my unique discovery and, like V. Turner (1975) and Silverstein (1976), I locate the meanings of symbolic forms in the intersection of form and function.

On the other hand, with this approach I have used the Pintupi understandings of their world to guide me in analyzing the structure of the system in which they act. It is by working through Pintupi notions that I have arrived, gradually, at an appreciation of the deeper cultural potentials that I discuss as broader and more abstract structural themes of autonomy, relatedness, and freedom.

I do not claim that Pintupi talk or think directly in these terms. It is fundamental to my argument, in fact, that they are not given to abstract formulations out of context. Often Pintupi informants have been unwilling to go much beyond discussing how one uses a concept, inevitably leaving a good deal of information incoherent to me. While this has left substantive gaps in my field notebooks, acceding to their practice has increased my empathy for the Pintupi ideas of what is important. I have taken their form of instruction to be itself informative about the individual's responsibility to formulate his own broader system of coherence.

For quite a long time in the field, I did not think I knew anything about the usual issues anthropologists discuss: descent groups, kinship roles, territory. Only gradually did I come to realize that I had been learning about what mattered to the Pintupi: the importance of "the other." For the Pintupi, contact with others and the necessity of response, of visibility and negotiability in all forms of action, yield little room for privacy. It struck me repeatedly that, despite the strain of limited resources and physical hardship, the Aboriginal people I lived with were much better at getting along with each other than most people I knew in my own country. The relations a Pintupi maintains with coresidents have a powerful impact on everything said and done.

This situation has both positive and negative consequences. Individuals enjoy a considerable degree of freedom and choice and a wide range of relatives to call on, but the emphasis on the individual's autonomy creates an objective reality of its own. Pintupi must confront this reality as a condition of their lives. Autonomy is not cheap coin here; there is, in Pintupi life, both violence and enormous concern for the welfare of others. I did not appreciate the importance of violence and conflict until I experienced the protective aura of a man willing to stand up and defend his kin against the

16   *Pintupi Country, Pintupi Self*

threat of others. Conversely, conflict and violence are avoided only through the action of individuals and their willingness to recognize the importance of their relationships to others.

The Pintupi are dominated by immediacy. Nothing seems settled unconditionally. Thus, a man who deeply desired that a particular girl be married to him could, through intimidation, force her relatives to break a promise of bestowal to another.

A similar context-dependence may underlie their relations with outsiders. This made me wary of the significance of agreements between myself and the Pintupi. Though a number of men, in private conversations, offered to tape songs or stories that were secret, I refused because I knew other individuals might oppose this action. Relatively isolated on the remote outstation, neither I nor my informants had special protection from the sanctions of Aboriginal Law. In time I had occasion to congratulate myself when I saw how agreements made in good faith, for the sale of paintings or performance in films, might be reinterpreted in light of a future change in context.

Much of my research involved quite technical traditional social organizational analysis: of land tenure, of travel histories, of kinship. I came to understand that *how* Pintupi did things was the most important element to study. Maintaining one's relationships with others seemed to be a primary goal in itself. I found that a good deal of politicking and negotiation surrounded almost every action, though Pintupi never discussed their actions in such terms. This was precisely the ethos of daily interaction that I was experiencing.

From this perspective, grounded in the level of individual action, I believe that the immediacy of *current* relations so dominates Pintupi social life that the production of an enduring structure that transcends the immediate and present is a cultural problem for the Pintupi and other Aboriginal people. In this phenomenological context, structure ought not to be taken for granted. The reification of Society, the existence of transcendental value itself, became for me a social process to be explained. I came to understand that hierarchy, positing an ontological order with a source outside human relations, provides a means of surmounting the constraints imposed by the need to sustain immediacy. This, I believe, is a problem of quite general order (cf. T. Turner 1984b), and one that continues for the Pintupi in the present as in the past.

Social Structure

Analyses of Aboriginal societies have frequently been mystified by turning the data of social action into reified systematic accounts of a social structure. This reification has been especially true of the group-oriented models of local organization (Birdsell 1970, Radcliffe-Brown 1930, Stanner 1965, Tindale 1974). Pintupi cultural constructs suggest, however, a different structure of organization in which social boundaries are not prominent. In their lives, group formations seem to have little significance. Pintupi life is highly personalized; for people to abstract from the intimate and familiar is unusual. They place emphasis on individuals, their autonomy, and their capacity to choose courses of action.

What is "structure," then, and where is it located? The problem is both empirical and theoretical. Many analysts of hunter-gatherer organization have ignored the process by which structures are created and reproduced through time. In their accounts, the informality and immediacy of daily life—the personal quality of events that typifies the activities in a small-scale society—are lost. Yet the most salient aspect of living in Pintupi communities is its affective basis, the reliance on emotional criteria rather than on rules as the framework of sociality. The individual is central to the structure of Pintupi sociality as the starting point of all my considerations.

To probe the relationship between cultural and social processes and experience, I have focused on the relationships between the individual and his or her society, emphasizing the processes unfolding over time. I gathered data on individual social and geographical mobility through detailed life histories.[1] Through these I came to understand the processes that have underlain Pintupi social life and how individuals make their choices within the contexts defined by such processes. The human life cycle provides the key to the temporal dimension of many small-scale social systems, where the development of social persons is the basic form of social production. Pintupi cultural constructs presuppose this structure. Conversely, starting with the individual and his or her development leads directly to a model of social reproduction—of society as embodying time. Because such a model is inherently nonpositivistic, it is capable of treating the social value of spatiality for people as problematic, rather than simply as an objective "ecological" given.

The significance of claim and negotiation in landownership has forced me to come to terms with the particular political economy of Pintupi life and the larger system (as perceived, in fact, by the Pintupi) of which local groups are a manifestation. What the Pintupi aim to achieve in politicking is not a universal content such as power. Rather, the logic of their particular system has made personal autonomy the goal of their lives. The contexts that give value to Pintupi spatiality are the politics of selfhood and personal autonomy.

To recognize some autonomy in Pintupi cultural constructs

leads to an understanding of Pintupi society as manifesting itself in space, but not as identical to "territorial organization." This view of structure has significant implications for the analysis of foraging societies, where the organization of people in space is a basic dimension of social structure. The importance given to "bands" in the study of hunter-gatherers reflects this problem. Most writers, like Radcliffe-Brown, have recognized a spatial component in social organization among hunter-gatherers. This spatial component is especially obvious among Australian Aborigines, whose social aggregates are often identified with place names. Yet the fact of this relationship between groups and places has resulted in differing interpretations.

One tradition of interpretation has identified certain units of social organization, called them bands, and asked how these units matched to land. Radcliffe-Brown (1913, 1930), for example, described the typical Australian society as made up of patrilineal, patrilocal bands ("hordes"). Having discovered the existence of patrilineal descent groups with a relationship to named places, he maintained that these local groups owned and defended their territory, living largely within their group boundaries and thus conserving resources for their own use. In this view, the correspondence between stable and enduring social groups and tracts of land was straightforward and one-dimensional. It is now clear, however, that confusion results from simply equating territorial organization with descent group organization (cf. Hiatt 1962), and that it is wrong to assume that local groups have constant, impermeable boundaries. In other words, this approach ignores the contexts in which organization takes place and fails to relate cultural concepts to the multiple dimensions of social reality.

A second tradition, reacting to the inadequacy of the first, has argued that permanent organizational units do not exist, and has maintained that analysis of hunter-gatherer territorial organization must start with resources. This approach treats adaptation to resources as the principal structural feature of foraging societies. The culmination of this analysis (Lee and Devore 1968; Lee 1976, 1979) emphasizes the flexibility of actual residential groups and the openness of access to resources, focusing on behavior (land and resource use) rather than on the ideology so important to earlier theorists. Indeed, the contrast between actual residence patterns and patrilineal ideology is a bulwark of this position. While correctly pointing out that people did not in fact live within exclusive, bounded, and defended patrilineal territories, and highlighting the importance of regional systems among foragers (Lee 1976), this ecological model has assumed that territorial organization is to be understood only in relationship to actual on-the-ground aggregates of people. It demonstrates no concern for the structures through time. Because it eschews ideology as epiphenomenal, this model fails to attend adequately to what a band is or to the connected question of how regional systems operate. Using the analysts' criteria for what the goals of social life are, such an approach misrepresents the nature of hunter-gatherer groups and their relationship to land by ignoring the dimension of temporality embedded in a people's own ideological constructs.

Both forms of analysis of spatial organization treat territory, in the form of "living space," as no more than a resource base among foraging people. Both also fail to situate localized groups within the larger structure of which they are but manifestations. Many Australianists have, to be sure, taken interest in social systems beyond the local level as well as in the actual composition of land-using groups (Hiatt 1965 and Meggitt 1962, for example). Indeed, in this regard, the ethnographic acuity of Hiatt's and Meggitt's studies has not been sufficiently appreciated. But while they show how local groups recruit residents from a wide category of people defined by broad principles of inclusion, and how bands vary regularly in composition, these studies do not explore the dialectical relationship between the organization of local groups and the larger structure of which they are part. In other words, they have accepted a view of territory not much different from those who ignored the larger structure altogether. They continue to view space as defined not by the totality of relations among people, but only by food-gathering activity.

It has been those anthropologists interested, following Lévi-Strauss (1949), in the constitutive social relations that might underlie localization in time and space, who have suggested that spatial organization may be motivated by relationships other than those of population to land. While Munn (1973) and van der Leeden (1975) have demonstrated that nonecological values may determine the definition of space, they have not linked their analysis to the practical relationships between land-using local groups and the larger social system.

To understand these small-scale societies in a way that makes them comparable with other forms of social life, one must reject the simplistic dichotomy between ideology and material/practical concerns. What human beings say and think about their social lives helps to reveal the structures that underlie organization, thus avoiding the *a priori* analytic assumptions of what constitutes the most "basic" level of a system. On the other hand, recognizing

Pintupi Country, Pintupi Self

Pintupi concepts as essential components of a structure of social life that is greater than the local group and reproduced through time does not mean we can ignore the consequences of material activity. My analysis suggests that the logic of practical activity is assimilated within the values that emerge from the internal structure of relations within Pintupi society.

As a regional system, the structure of this society materializes only over time. Because Pintupi culture incorporates this dimension, the indigenous models provide insight into the Pintupi system as a total structure. Here, the universe is not made up of "territory" or "land," nor society composed of "groups." Rather, the regional structure defines space in relation to its own temporal cycles.

Change and Temporality

Our data on Aboriginal social life are drawn from an ethnographic present that is not entirely the same life that people lived before contact with whites. But these data are no less meaningful for this. My return visits to the Pintupi represent the particular conditions of my learning; the importance of individual relationships and the historical changes I observed among the Pintupi themselves may well have made certain issues especially significant to me. This is not a source of falsity in my account, but rather a basis of what insight I have gained, teaching me to see what mattered to the Pintupi.

A particular set of historical circumstances also governed my encounter with the Pintupi. Shortly before my arrival in Australia, the Labour Government had inaugurated a policy of Aboriginal "self-determination." This policy set two processes in motion. With the withdrawal of government authority over settlements, local conceptions of land tenure and land rights began to reassert themselves. Since, at Yayayi, the Pintupi were residing in a region for which they had little traditional claim, the problem of their rights to be there remained always close to the surface. The second process was the organization of local politics in Aboriginal terms. The Pintupi were, of course, sedentary, but in contrast to the paternalistic settlements of the past, they were now living in an autonomous community without government supervision. Control of local institutions came largely into their hands.

My experience of Pintupi self-determination in this context made it possible to observe organization in their terms. This condition, as much as anything else, taught me about politics and negotiation as an irreducible quality of Pintupi sociality, about their sense of the community at Yayayi as just a manifestation of a desert-wide network that was "all family," and about the importance of the cultural terms in which social action was coordinated.

Permitted its own development, the temporal duration and structure of Pintupi sociality is a real, observable problem in contemporary life. The place where I began my research in 1973, Yayayi, exists no longer as a Pintupi community. Instead, I have encountered members of the Yayayi community at various stages of their poignant odyssey. At each location, similar scenarios of the process of aggregation and dispersal were acted out. No community represented, for any individual, the entirety of the social universe. Every individual stressed ties to other people in faraway places. They had gone out from the desert in all different directions, but their deepest aspiration was to somehow sustain these relations. Indeed, Yayayi itself lasted only a few years. A number of deaths, some of them violent, made the memory of the place sad. There have been new arrangements of people, changing communities, every time I have returned.

Though the Pintupi lived on other people's land, I learned at Yayayi that their hearts remained in the west, in their own country, and that they viewed their settlement in the east as temporary. Finally, they have moved back to their own country. The reinhabiting of the Western Desert began in 1981, with Pintupi living at Warlungurru (Kintore Range) for the first time in twenty years. And in October 1984, astonishingly, Pintupi who had moved still further west met nine relatives who had never had contact with whites at all.

Through all these changes—or, as I would prefer to say, manifest in these developments—the inner logic of Pintupi sociality persists, despite apparent transformations of societal form. The internal contradictions of this structure continue to set the limits of social life.

Three related patterns I witnessed in my experience of Pintupi life provide the underpinnings of this book's account. The first pattern is an emphasis on "relatedness," on extending one's ties with others outward, on being open to claims by others, on showing sympathy and a willingness to negotiate. This pattern involves the difficulty of sustaining an authoritative center that excludes others from consideration. The second pattern is a reluctance to permit others to impose their authority over oneself, an unwillingness to accept constraints on one's autonomy. These two patterns are countered, or resolved, by a third—the cultural representation of hierarchy as nurturance, as "looking after." This third pattern plays an essential role in placing certain principles beyond individual consideration, in constituting a transcendent realm of value. The three patterns relate in a way Bateson (1979) called "stochastic," limiting each other but having their own internal properties. Their relationship to each other gives these forms the meaning they have in my analysis.

The Plan of the Book

I have two broad goals in this book. On one hand, I aim to show that the salient characteristics of life in this "egalitarian" society make it sociologically necessary to emphasize the individual and the self. The high value placed on individual autonomy and the work and strategies required to achieve a polity when dominance must appear muted pose a problem for the society's participants, not one imported from outside. Collectivity *is* a problem for the Pintupi.

My second goal is to analyze this particular social order while retaining the ethnographic sense of active human participants working out the complexity of their social and political interactions with each other. By giving centrality to Aboriginal experience and practical understanding of what it is "really like" to be Pintupi, I show how one can combine the phenomenological attention to the "life world" of experience with an analytical grasp of the structures that underlie action. This study is intended as a contribution to our understanding of the emotions and the mind as reflexive products of social action, and to our comprehension of the logic and content of "politics" among hunter-gatherers as part of a larger totality of relations.

CHAPTER 1

Past into Present:
"We Are the People from the West"

They came in because they were hungry. They didn't know
they could not go back.

The recent history of the Pintupi Aborigines is one of dramatic outward changes. While they see these changes as an accommodation to pressing circumstances, their encounter with white civilization has the earmarks of a social drama: They have succeeded in conserving much that they value but, like other peoples, they have not been able to evade the ironies of history. As is often the case, this history exemplifies the essential themes of Pintupi social life. They have sought, in their movements, to extend their system of relatedness to include the new opportunities of contact with whites and at the same time to sustain their autonomy.

The Land

For the Pintupi, people and land are almost inseparable, and throughout much of their past the land was a critical element in their encounter with time. The Gibson Desert is a harsh environment, whose limited diversity imposes a pattern on any who would live there.

Most of this vast area is sandhill country, technically sand desert with parallel sand ridges that often stretch for miles. The characteristic vegetation on these east-west dunes and in the corridors of flat sand plain between them is the pale green spinifex grass (*Triodia* species). Areas of desert oak (*Casuarina decaisneana*) are also common in dune country. Although the sandhills predominate, the pattern is interrupted in some places by plains covered with a reddish, gravelly conglomerate that sometimes erodes into cliffs. Stands of mulga (*Acacia aneura*) may be associated with these

25

flats, usually in small patches near hills and between sand ridges. A few scattered hills, rising up to 300 feet above the plain, constitute a third habitat, important for resource items like hill kangaroos and seasonal water supplies in temporary rock catchments. In general, the country is flat and undulating. Numerous large and small dry lakebeds are scattered through the desert, the largest in the Pintupi area being Lakes Hopkins, Macdonald, and Mackay. Usually dry, after heavy rains these salt lakes hold water, but it is not drinkable. The availability of water has been an important determinant of group size and movement, setting much of the rhythm of Pintupi life. The country is extremely arid. Average annual rainfall may be less than twenty centimeters, though rain is unreliable and some years pass with little or none (Long 1971: 264). And when rain does occur, it does not always fall equally throughout the area. Local droughts are common. Following the monsoon activity in the Indian Ocean, heavy rains tend to fall in late summer (January–February) with lighter, drizzling rains drifting in from the Antarctic Ocean in the early winter months (May–June). One can expect extremely hot days (up to 120 degrees Fahrenheit) and warm nights in the summer; in winter, the days are usually mild but the cold of the night may leave frost.

For hunters and gatherers, the unreliability of water supplies poses the fundamental subsistence challenge. It is important to understand the nature of this resource. Although there are no permanent surface waters in the area, the Pintupi have found it possible to exploit other types of water supply. They have used large, shallow, and transient pools (*pinangu*) formed by heavy rain; claypans (*maluri*) and rock reservoirs (*walu*) in the hills that might be filled from lighter rainfalls; soakage wells (*tjurnu*) in sandy creek beds; and "wells" (*yinta*) in the sand or in the rock between the sand ridges (Long 1971: 266–67).

In both soakages and wells, water lies below the surface and one digs down to get it, but they differ in permanence. Soakages are accumulations of water that has seeped down from the surface after rain. Although they may be substantial in quantity, soakages are usually temporary and dependent on recent rainfall. True wells, on the other hand, result from pressurized outlets from underground storage and are far more reliable. Such wells have provided the Pintupi fallback source, since the first three are relatively imper-manent and incapable of sustaining people for lengthy periods of time. Nonetheless, some of the rock reservoirs are very large (over 100,000 gallons, for example) and in good years have supported large populations for months. Water is, then, a geographically specific resource, and Pintupi subsistence technology depends on knowledge of the location of water sources and the conditions under which they are likely to be usable as well as on movement to use them.

Over this land, Aboriginal people once moved in small semi-nomadic groups, without transport or substantial food storage. These bands numbered no more than twenty to thirty persons for much of the year. Few published accounts exist of such local groups, but we are fortunate in having the reports of Jeremy Long and other Australian patrol officers for the early contact period with the Pintupi. Long describes meeting groups in the late fifties that:

> ranged in size from two people (a man and a boy) to twenty-two, the term "group" being here used to mean a number of people camping overnight at a single waterhole. The group of twenty-two was found at a claypan west of Lake Mackay in 1957 shortly after heavy rain. It consisted of three men, their wives and children and three single women (widows), and a group of three single males was reported to be camped some kilometers away to the west. (Long 1971: 265)

He goes on to say, however, that generally:

> groups have consisted of one or two families, often with one or more adolescent males and/or elderly or widowed females. Such "family" groups ranged in size from three to twelve people . . . it is safe to assume that the people of this area lived in scattered groups of this size for most of the time. (ibid.)

The nature of Pintupi localization will be discussed in chapter 3 in detail.[1] Here I want to suggest that these bands were part of a larger regional system that accommodated the sparse population to the resources available. The geographical scope of this organization was immense, while the population was small—estimated to have been one person per 200 square kilometers (Long 1971: 264), approximately half the population density Meggitt (1962) reported for the neighboring Warlpiri. The comparatively poor rainfall did not support large populations.

Within this area, there were neither significant physiographic barriers to movement that might have restricted contact among populations, nor were there marked cultural discontinuities. Rather, the whole of the Western Desert population was a vast and interlocking network of persons who were themselves localized around a number of loosely defined areas. The unreliability of rainfall necessitated continual interdependence among people in a wide area for water and resources. Social isolation, in other words, was ecologically impossible.

Until quite recently, the harshness of this environment and its distance from white settlement protected the Western Desert people from massive incursions of outsiders. Neither pastoral settlement

nor mining ventures were feasible. Thus, unlike many other Aboriginal people, the Pintupi were not forced from their land. White
settlement on the fringes attracted them, however, and the aridity
that protected them eventually contributed, through prolonged
drought, to their movement off their homeland.

The People

The Pintupi people I came to study in 1973 lived far removed from
their traditional homeland in the Gibson Desert. At Yayayi, Papunya,
and Yuendumu in the Northern Territory dwelt various Western
Desert peoples who had been moving eastward to the fringes of
white settlement. They came from an area bounded by the Ehrenberg
Range on the east, the gravel plains west of Jupiter Well on the
west, Lake Mackay on the north, and the Walter James Range in
the south (see Map 1A). Starting in the late twenties, this movement
to missions, government settlements, cattle stations, and towns
ended when the last remaining families left the Western Desert in
1966.

The major Pintupi movements coincided with drought periods—
the late twenties, early forties, mid-fifties, and early sixties. From
their point of view, they had left their desert home because food
was easier to get elsewhere. They had not anticipated real change;
indeed, how could they have? The tragedy was that this movement
had unforeseen consequences quite different from anything in their
past experience. "They came," said one spokesman, "because they
were hungry. They didn't know they could not go back." In the
sedentary communities where they found themselves, much had
changed yet social relations retained a familiar form.

Even their name is an artifact imposed on them by changing
conditions. Though known in the area where they came to live as
"Pintupi," most say they never used this label to refer to themselves
before contact with whites. While they speak a common language,
with some dialectical differences, the people called the Pintupi do
not represent a single social entity, neither as a tribe nor as a
language group. Asked if a person is a Pintupi, they are likely to
respond that "he is from the west, indeed" (*yapurramalu kula*)! The
reply underscores a consistent view of social identity: that their
conceptual unity results from their migration eastward, a product
of time and place. Despite the reassuring presence of tribal groupings
on some ethnological maps such as Tindale's (1974), such overarching social identities hold little significance in this region and are
genuinely misleading. Names need not specify social boundaries.
Identity, as among many hunting-and-gathering peoples, is situa-

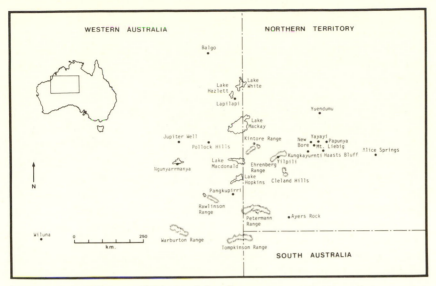

Map 1A. A History of Pintupi Settlement

"The people from the west" exist only in contrast to "the people from the east."

Those who have moved elsewhere are not identified with the same labels. Many people who had once inhabited the same traditional country as those at Papunya migrated to other settlements on the fringes of the desert, including Balgo Hills Mission in the north, Warburton Range Mission in the south, and Docker River Settlement, Wiluna Mission, and Jigalong Mission (see Map 1A). At these settlements the migrants adopted different tribal names. For example, one of Berndt's (1972) Gugadja-Mandjildjarra men at Balgo comes from the same place as those who, in southern settlements, are Pintupi. In parallel to the practice at Papunya but from a different geographical vantage point, those of desert origin at these northern settlements are known as "the people from the south." To argue about whether Berndt's informant is really Pintupi or really Gugadja is to misunderstand the relation between labels and social organization. The identity of being Pintupi—a product of recent developments—is not necessarily an enduring one. An observer must avoid granting more social significance to this identity than it has in practice. Indeed, in its shifting, impermanent, and political quality, the state of being Pintupi merely reflects various characteristic qualities of Western Desert Aboriginal society. Because the label embodies the existential situation of Western Desert people in a particular place and time, however, I continue to use it.[2]

For the Pintupi, the expansion of white civilization engendered a new reality with which they sought to accommodate themselves. The Pintupi attitude has been one of testing and uncertainty as they encounter the properties of a new order and attempt to sustain their values through its control. That their isolation and insulation has made knowledge of whites problematic is clear from their probings of the recent past.

The earliest known contacts between the Pintupi and the few white explorers who visited and crossed the Gibson Desert were insubstantial. These included Warburton in 1873, who traversed the northernmost area known to Pintupi; Giles in 1873–77, who visited the Petermann and Rawlinson Ranges; Forrest in 1874; Tietkens in 1889, who reached beyond the Kintore Range in the eastern Pintupi region; and Carnegie, who crossed the desert south to north in 1896 and back southward again in 1897. Carnegie encountered some fifty Aborigines in all. He captured a few of them and tried to make them lead him to water, securing them with ropes and later with makeshift chains (Carnegie 1898). No stories remain about these explorers, but the early experience of whites could hardly have been pleasant.

It was with the gold strike at Kalgoorlie, Western Australia, during the 1890s that depopulation of the fringes of Pintupi country began. Many whites came to this southern area of the desert, and the mining town they built attracted Aborigines from the desert. The process of outdrifting and depopulation that followed was gradual. As early as 1915, however, Aborigines from the Gibson Desert were reported to be living at Ooldea, far to the south of their traditional country (Bates 1966).

To the east, significant settlement in central Australia did not begin until the late nineteenth century, and its impact on the Pintupi was indirect. Alice Springs had been settled by whites in 1871 as a station on the Overland Telegraph line from Adelaide to Darwin. In the course of time, ever larger areas were taken over by whites running cattle stations, dispossessing the local Aborigines of their livelihood as foragers. Many of the dispossessed moved to the fringes of white settlements, to temporary employment on cattle stations, or to missions, but they were not the only Aborigines to move. As Elkin noted (1967: 56), white goods and settlement offered a positive attraction. Thus, the German Lutheran mission built at Hermannsburg in 1877 drew in first the surrounding Aranda people and later the Loritja people of the Western Macdonnell Range. The latter were the eastern neighbors of the Pintupi.

The movements increased, with or without appropriation of land. By 1937, T. G. H. Strehlow reported that the number of natives in the area from the Macdonnells to the Ehrenberg Range, uninhabited by whites, had greatly dwindled (Northern Territory Administration 1937: 25). What Strehlow describes as "the rapid and continuous drift of the natives from the Reserve within the last few years" (ibid.) was toward Alice Springs and any other small white outpost.

By virtue of their distance from the settlements, the Pintupi were affected less than their neighbors were, at least initially. As the country around them became rapidly depopulated, the Pintupi for the most part continued in their traditional ways. Those Pintupi who today remember that era speak about the large numbers of people they saw when they were children. Although their land was never appropriated by settlers, Pintupi people began to find their way into Hermannsburg by the early thirties. They came largely to trade dingo scalps for flour, jam, clothing, knives, and axes—a good index of what they desired from white civilization. These trips were infrequent and temporary, with only a few Pintupi staying on permanently.[3] The strains of living in larger sedentary communities with relative outsider status encouraged them to move back.

In 1932 the Adelaide University Anthropological Expedition, including H. K. Fry, T. G. H. Strehlow, N. B. Tindale, and cameraman E. O. Stocker, made contact with a group of Pintupi near Mount Liebig at the western edge of the Macdonnells. Much of this encounter was filmed, and genealogies were recorded. It was, retrospectively, a grand event, although in memory many Pintupi confuse it with a related encounter with missionaries from Hermannsburg (cf. Lohe, Albrecht, and Leske 1977: 48–53). Their perception is revealing. In both cases, what the Pintupi emphasize is getting flour and rice from whites and giving them Aboriginal foods in exchange. These events represented turning points, a period marked for them by the onset of social relations of equal exchange with whites. The stories of this period, wherever told, feature a similar motif.

Thus, a man who had been quite young at the time described to me how he and his relatives had heard reports of whites who had come to Yilpili soakage in the Ehrenberg Range, with food and matches. After trying some of the new food obtained by their kin, his family decided to go to Yilpili themselves. The whites, said to be Pastor Albrecht and Bob Buck, had left the water hole, but the traveling Aborigines came into contact with Rolf, a Native Evangelist from Hermannsburg. The evangelist conducted them to a base camp at Mount Liebig. Many whites and Aborigines, my informant remembered, were gathered there. When food was offered to his family, they feared being poisoned but others urged them to eat: "It's food; they are giving us what they have." He remembers that his relatives "gave spear-throwers, spears, and wooden dishes to the whites." Eventually, Strehlow took them eastward. They remained near Haasts Bluff for a time, but finally went to Hermannsburg.

Not surprisingly, Pintupi attitudes toward whites remained uncertain. Most stories about a white camel man, Kuunki, and his two helpers allege them to have enchained, killed, and eaten Aborigines, although some describe his friendliness to them. Finally, according to folklore, a missionary came and sent Kuunki away, calling him a "devil." Kuunki was puzzling to the Pintupi, but human. Most Pintupi had no contact with whites, but such stories contributed to the general apprehension of creatures called *warra-warra*, white people who were said to eat human flesh.

The situation in the thirties found the eastern Pintupi moving through now-empty Loritja country for brief times, seldom as far as Mount Liebig. The few who visited Hermannsburg[4] tended not to return as far west as their own country. They lived in Loritja country but followed largely a traditional style of band life, and visited the mission only occasionally. Increasingly large numbers of Pintupi and Warlpiri moved into this area, leading the Hermannsburg missionaries to establish Haasts Bluff as a ration depot (Northern Territory Administration 1961a). The people of this period probably regarded this arrangement as temporary, opportunistically taking advantage of abundant resources. In this sense, the migration eastward resembled population movements to richer areas in time of drought (Strehlow 1965).

Evolution of Government Policy

The impact of these movements was not felt immediately by the Pintupi, but the actions of the white intruders continued to define a new environment for them and other Aboriginal people. For white settlers, the Aboriginal migrations became a problem. While some whites hoped to reverse the ravages of contact, others found the ragged fringe dwellers to be a nuisance. Certain areas began to be set aside for Aboriginal habitation alone. As early as 1920, officials of the Northern Territory Administration had noted the advice of Sir Baldwin Spencer, a pioneering anthropologist who recommended establishing a reserve (Northern Territory Administration 1920: 19).

The two continuing concerns of the settler government were the preservation of the Aborigines (that is, that they should not die out), and their "betterment" and eventual assimilation into white

Australia. Consequently, Lake Amadeus Reserve, a huge area in the southwest of the Northern Territory, was designated in 1920 so that Aborigines there would not be dispossessed of their land and become dependent on charity.

In addition to insulating Aborigines from white civilization, this policy also served to keep Aborigines away from the towns where they had begun to gather as fringe dwellers. By 1934, attempts were made to persuade Aborigines from the Macdonnells and Petermanns area to leave Alice Springs and return home—reducing their debilitating contact with whites and returning them to an area of plentiful native food (Northern Territory Administration 1935: 8). At Hermannsburg, similarly, Aborigines were encouraged to remain out in the bush, coming in to the mission for short periods only. Christianized native evangelists were sent out to minister to the bush-dwellers (ibid.). For remote Aborigines, these policies sustained both the possibility of access to desirable white products and a continuing autonomy of movement in small groups. They did not diminish the attractiveness of the new and reliable resources that constituted the emerging basis of black-white relations.

If Aboriginal people saw this arrangement as a more or less satisfactory situation for the short term, Australian policy subscribed to another agenda: The dilemma of black-white relations could be resolved, it was believed, by the transformation of the Aborigines. By 1938, the reserves were "regarded as refuges or sanctuaries of a temporary nature. The Aboriginal may here continue his normal existence until the time is ripe for his *further development*" (Northern Territory Administration 1938: 22, italics mine). Thus, the Native Affairs Branch was launched by the government in 1939 to look after Aboriginal welfare. At the persistent urging of the Hermannsburg missionaries, the area of Aboriginal reserve was extended to inhibit white encroachment with the creation of Haasts Bluff Reserve in 1940. The following year, Haasts Bluff was taken over by Native Affairs as a ration depot, signaling the acceptance of a governmental responsibility to see that the Aborigines not go hungry (Northern Territory Administration 1945: 5). Other ration depots were instituted to this purpose as well as, in the case of Yuendumu, a Warlpiri settlement, to keep begging and stealing Aborigines away from road maintenance camps and station homesteads.

The initial Pintupi movement eastward to Haasts Bluff in the thirties occurred within this sort of climate, rather than with the open conflicts with settlers that had been experienced earlier by many of their neighbors. Rations were distributed to alleviate distress, and trading stores were established for the exchange of kangaroo skins, dingo scalps, and weapons for food and luxuries. This policy aimed to "encourage self dependence and industry" and to avoid "the necessity for natives to come to settled areas to dispose of such items" (Northern Territory Administration 1946: 28).

In the following years, the full flower of government policy was elucidated: Government stations would train Aborigines in crafts and industries, with the goal of enabling Aborigines to take part in the industrial life of the Northern Territory. Eventually the government was to assist them in developing the resources of their own reserves (Northern Territory Administration 1948: 19). With this view, 400 cattle were purchased for Haasts Bluff to train Aborigines in the cattle industry. The goals of this policy of development and assimilation, however, remained remote from the interests of the Aborigines. Pintupi accepted the theory of the government's responsibility toward them without perceiving it to diminish their own autonomy.

The Pintupi Experience

For the early Pintupi migrants at Haasts Bluff, settlement life constituted only a modification of their traditional patterns. They received some rations but continued to hunt for most of their meat. They lived in an encampment with other Pintupi, separate from the Warlpiri, Aranda, and Loritja. Many of the women married people of these other linguistic groups, presumably in an effort to cement ties between them.

Some of these early Pintupi migrants worked on building projects at Haasts Bluff and continue to feel a legitimate claim on the place as a result of their labors. For the most part, however, Pintupi resided only temporarily at Haasts Bluff, often camping for long "holiday" periods at nearby soakages or wells. Until the establishment of the cattle project, it seems improbable that they did much "work" or that the rhythms of their daily life underwent drastic change.

The Pintupi community at the settlement continued to grow. If for some, migration was motivated by Haasts Bluff's substantial stores of food, others left the bush to escape punishment or trouble. Among the early migrants were people fleeing revenge parties and others attempting to evade the repercussions of wife-stealing. The process continued inexorably, with those already in contact journeying back out west and persuading their relatives to come in for this new and abundant food.

Eventually, the increasing population in the vicinity of Haasts

Bluff began to place great pressure on food and water resources.[5] In the forties, a more sedentary community emerged. Mission records report "semi-permanent camps . . . in which women, children, and other dependents remained whilst their menfolk went out on hunting and ceremonial trips" (Northern Territory Administration 1961a). Sheer numbers alone would have dictated an increasing reliance on white foods and a decreasing emphasis on the nomadic life around the settlement. The onset of drought in the early forties undoubtedly helped to bring more Aborigines out of the bush in search of food and water. Dependence on government rations grew. The provision of rations constituted a signal to Aborigines of what sort of relationship whites were setting up and an expectation that the government should "look after" them.

More periodic droughts, along with knowledge that relief was possible, contributed heavily to the increasing migrations of the Pintupi. Waves of migration in 1953–56[6] and 1960–66 each occurred during extended droughts. By 1960 the remaining bush-dwellers were responding to the depopulation of the desert: They wanted to visit relatives long unseen. It was, apparently, no longer viable to continue traditional life with such dwindling numbers.

A recent account of Pintupi history (Nathan and Japanangka 1983) stresses the coercive nature of the contact between those remaining in the desert and the visits of patrol officers. Ultimately, it is true that expansion of the settler society created conditions that encouraged the Western Desert people to leave their homeland. Construction of portions of the Gunbarrel Highway through the Gibson Desert—part of a plan to establish a rocket range there—made for easier and more frequent contact by Welfare Branch patrol officers. The removal was not, however, a forcible one, nor was it the intention of the patrol officers to "bring people in." The history of the Pintupi migration was more ironic than that. When the Pintupi left, they did not foresee the destructive consequences of their move. According to their own accounts of contact with the Welfare Branch patrols, small bands of Pintupi made arrangements to wait at certain locations for Jeremy Long to return for them the following year. Some, in fact, grew impatient and simply walked in to Papunya in the winter of 1962, a journey of more than 150 miles. Participants in this migration remember, with typical Pintupi humor, that they "nearly perished" because they did not know where the water holes were along the way. Curiosity, drought, dwindling numbers, and the persuasion of relatives who accompanied the Welfare patrols—all contributed to the migrations.

Pintupi stories of early contact with whites lay heavy emphasis on the quantity of food they saw. When Pintupi men described meeting whites who worked on the roads built for the Woomera Rocket Range, they reported saying to their relatives, "Let's go and eat with them!" Clearly, one principal motivation for contact was an assured food supply.

Once people came to the settlements, however, they never fully returned to the traditional way of life.[7] Especially after 1956, the previous pattern of temporary congregation at the settlements and a largely continued reliance on hunting seems to have declined. For those who arrived in the last wave (1960–66), seminomadism seems to have been neither a possible nor desirable alternative. It was replaced by the goal of setting up a specifically Pintupi community, relying on supplies from the government.

By 1956, Haasts Bluff had a population of 477 Aborigines (Northern Territory Administration 1956: 85). They continued to live in traditional-style camps, often little more than windbreaks. The organization of the camps reflected the composite character of a community of diverse origins:

> . . . at times there were four distinct camp groups: to the east the more "Europeanized" families, long attached to the area; to the south a few Pitjantjaras . . . ; a large camp of Pintubi to the west; and a small camp of southern Walbiri to the north. More commonly there were three and sometimes only two camps with either or both Pitjantjara and Walbiri people moving in with their Pintubi relatives. (Northern Territory Administration 1961b: 10)

The Pintupi were considered ignorant bush natives ("Myalls") by many local people and in the local hierarchy were frequently treated as second-class citizens. By and large, they *were* unsophisticated in non-bush ways and presented, with more "new men" migrating in all the time, a continued image of the "naked native." It is likely that they received rather more than their share of blame for problems at the settlement, both from whites and other Aborigines. The newer migrants were described as "a source of disturbance and unrest to the settlement [Papunya] and to more sophisticated Aborigines there" (Northern Territory Administration 1969: 165). Disdain for the Pintupi was such that, for a long time (through to the late sixties), many people originally from the west maintained that they were Loritja and not Pintupi, to evade the derisory connotations of the latter label.

This negative reception may have helped inspire a Pintupi solidarity. There seems always to have been a separate Pintupi camp (or camps)—at Haasts Bluff, at Papunya, at Yayayi as a separate community from Papunya, and finally at Kintore.

Pintupi Country, Pintupi Self

Increased Government Role

The large-scale arrivals of the mid-fifties and the increasing pressure on Haasts Bluff's water resources, along with the dangerously high sulphate content of that water, caused the government to build a new settlement at Papunya, thirty miles away, in the late fifties. This development marked a transition in the amount of employment available; many Pintupi worked in the building of Papunya, and most moved there from Haasts Bluff in 1959–60. The final Pintupi arrivals from the west in the sixties all came to Papunya, which offered a much larger physical plant than Haasts Bluff's. Facilities included a school, carpentry shop, small retail store, numerous houses for the white staff, and a number of primitive "transition" houses for the Aborigines.

Papunya also featured a larger scale of government services than earlier Pintupi encampments, reflecting the government's more active policy of assimilation. A communal dining room with the intent of "educating both adults and children in acceptable eating habits" (Northern Territory Administration 1959: 42) was one example of this attempt to intervene in the adoption of Western values. For the most part, the Pintupi accepted the validity of such values for the settlement institutions—which they then regarded as "white-fellow business" and white-fellow responsibility.

The late arrivals to Papunya were known as the "new Pintupi," in contrast with the "old Pintupi" who had lived at Haasts Bluff and were relatively more acculturated. The groups differed not simply in degree of acculturation but perhaps more in terms of their experience of contact. The new Pintupi experienced contact with white culture in a far more developed environment then had their predecessors.

By 1960 there were 676 Aborigines living at Papunya. The employment of 174 of them reflected the new aim of the settlements, "to introduce the general concept of 'work' as a worthwhile aim in life" (Northern Territory Administration 1961c: 21). In this way the Aborigines were to be prepared for a future life in a wider community than the tribe. Ironically, at Papunya itself conflict between the new and the old continued, at least in the eyes of the Australian authorities, who noted approvingly that under the influence of those with longer contact, the newcomers (the Pintupi) were adapting well to the rules governing general conduct at the settlement (Northern Territory Administration 1961c: 29).

Soon after, authorities reported their satisfaction that attitudes to work were improving: "The knowledge that employment brings financial remuneration is now an accepted fact" (Northern Territory Administration 1962: 32). Wages remained low, however, to teach the Aborigines how to handle money and possibly to prevent them from visiting the towns. Food continued to be supplied by the government, and wages were directed toward the purchase of a few luxuries. At Papunya, people were fed in the communal kitchen, three meals a day, seven days a week. It was not until 1964 that the Aborigines paid for meals. According to that year's report, this innovation was readily accepted. "Some," it noted approvingly, "are now eating in family groups" (Northern Territory Administration 1964: 60). The Pintupi response, however, was to withdraw from the dining facilities altogether.

Although their good nature won them many friends, the Pintupi were not heartily welcomed into the Papunya community, either by other Aborigines or by whites, for whom their continued traditional behavior slowed the statistics of progress. One report makes this clear:

> The arrival of the new Pintupi put beyond doubt the question whether the Aboriginal people of Papunya had made any progress. The habits of the newcomers were strikingly different from those of the older residents and the latter took great pains to advise them on settlement behavior. This was particularly noticeable in the dining room. (Northern Territory Administration 1964: 61)

It is not difficult to guess how such "advice" was received among people who generally avoid outspoken criticism.

While the population of Papunya grew to 790 in the mid-sixties, the death rate also rose, especially among the Pintupi. Many of the Pintupi illnesses followed their sudden exposure to dense population and to the diseases introduced by white contact. The administration devoted much effort to persuading the Pintupi to accept white medical service. But the Pintupi interpreted the increase in deaths to sorcery by hostile strangers at Papunya. This conclusion contributed to hostility among the Aboriginal groups and fueled Pintupi desires to establish their own community.

The two salient historical trends are, on the one hand, increasingly overt intervention (for directed assimilation) by the government in establishing white authority and values and, on the other, a persisting Pintupi reluctance to relinquish autonomy. One report illustrates the overall picture:

> When ceremonies took place, Settlement life was forgotten. Little concern was shown at the loss of pay or the fact that certain routine jobs must be done each day to keep the Settlement functional. When efforts to train children in the European way of life conflicted with

Pintupi Country, Pintupi Self

tribal law, they were opposed by some of the more primitive parents. (Northern Territory Administration 1966: 113)

The Pintupi were prepared to accept the government's willingness to "look after" them—its food, clothing, and services—as long as it did not seriously abrogate their own values.

A *Pintupi Perspective*

Indeed, the view of many Pintupi reflects an underlying dissatisfaction with their attempt to maintain a relationship of fairness with whites. The following extended quotation summarizes one older man's assessment of the history of contact:

> Graham Swanton, the pastor (from Hermannsburg)—a white man— was at Mount Liebig. We Pintupi saw lots of camels and a lot of people lived with him. Many caravans and motorcars came here. He wired for them, called them, many white people. Important white men. There were no whites before him. Ted Strehlow came too. And said there was plenty of food at Hermannsburg. He had lots of camels. . . .
>
> Then was Paul Albrecht, number one [indicating approval]! All the Pintupi, we were all naked, climbed on the camels, and were taken to the mission [the informant was a boy in the early thirties]. He took us all to Hermannsburg, toward the food, for flour. We had not known about this food. He taught us about work. We cut firewood; we worked and we learned. We had all come naked from the bush. . . .
>
> Pastor Petering taught us about the Bible, made us Christians. We were put into clothes. Then we went back. [i.e., west] to Haasts Bluff, toward our *own* country. We showed the missionaries about bush tucker [wild foods], about *witjulyurru* [a species]. We built "houses" [buildings]; we worked like city fellows and made houses. . . .
>
> We were eating wheat, grinding it with stones and eating, making dampers. We were called back to the white-fellow, our pastor. Then Les Wilson called us again, back to Haasts Bluff. He came out with cattle, a lot of them. Les Wilson was a cattleman [manager of Haasts Bluff Cattle Project]. He—an important boss—called us. . . .
>
> We lived near him, doing a lot of work for him. We built stockyards and worked on the roads. We got grader drivers to dig a road out—like this one that goes [from Yayayi] to the west. This road goes a long way west. We learned. A big mob of us. We worked without money for a long time, only rations, a large group of Pintupi. We learned; we're not stupid.

We got angry about the money. Continually we talked about money. It's no good working without money. Les Wilson did the right thing [about money] when he was head stockman, but we did not get the right thing from Hermannsburg: no money. Jerry Long sent for Les Wilson and made him boss. Good fellow, Jerry Long. He put a price, and we worked for wages. Then Jerry Long came back and Les Wilson went to Darwin. We worked with Jerry Long for a long time. He gave us work and money. Then he thought that a sickness was from bad water. Maybe the water was bad? Many people died; we lost a lot of people at Haasts Bluff because the water was bad. Jerry Long called all the white people for work and they planned Papunya. The white people worked along with Aborigines. They worked for two white-fellows, Charley and Benny. They worked straight for the whites; they didn't cheat them. All the whites cheated money. It was big work. Other groups of Aborigines were afraid of that work; it was very hard. They worked for the whites the right way. They got only a little bit of money. Because it was big work. Maybe you [pointing to the anthropologist] will try to find their money for them.

Then we called them all [other Aborigines]. From Haasts Bluff they came to Papunya. A lot of Aborigines came. All the whites went back when they finished building. We Aborigines worked, we kept working at Papunya. There we lived, without rations or blankets. The head white-fellow stopped ours (rations). Then he gave us money, a little money he gave us, the one with the bad hand [ungenerous]. Like a white-fellow, he told us lies. We cut timber for the whites. The government made lots of promises. . . . They said, "You'll be like Europeans, with clothes and food." Nothing. We never saw that money. These two men never did the right thing. They said, "You will get no rations but will buy like Europeans." But we never saw that money. They lied to us. Citizens we are now. We can drink liquor. Only for this money we tried unsuccessfully. The white people tell us lies, a lot of promises, but never true. Like devils they deceive us: "It's fine, we will give you lots of money." Lies. The wind blew those words. . . . Later we got two other white bosses, still no good ones. . . .

Pintupi Separatism

This account does not really tell us what value money has for the Pintupi, a point well known but worth reiterating. Although money is an important article of value, the Pintupi have not accepted a commodity-based economy. They do not enter the larger Australian economy for work nor do they desire to do so. They want, as far as an outsider can see, primarily to remain in close proximity with their relatives. In this sense, they are inclined to use the value they gain through work or other payments for traditional ends like traveling and visiting. Many individuals work to earn enough money for particular capital items (a motorcar, a radio, fancy clothes) and then quit. A Pintupi man who was especially afflicted by the disparity between white and black culture described the contrast in these terms: "Money is the main thing for whites; they don't worry who will cry for them when they die."

Rather than integrating into a broader community, as the government hoped, the Pintupi continued to demonstrate a desire for separatism and a kind of isolation from the rest of the Papunya settlement. In a sense, the portability of a seminomadic life was maintained as they moved closer or further from the other groups while tensions rose or fell. At times, they withdrew to the western limits of Papunya, nearly a mile from the main settlement area (Northern Territory Administration 1972: 65). Here they lived with few facilities. Their participation in settlement affairs became minimal, consisting of buying food from the store, sporadic employment, collection of pensions, and medical treatment.

The increasing frequency of deaths, especially among the respected older people, contributed to a growing depression in the Pintupi population. They believed they were going to die out (Hansen, personal communication). In addition, the recent arrivals continued to experience great difficulty in adapting to the new circumstances.

As a result, several attempts were made to set up a separate Pintupi community. In 1968 200 Pintupi moved to live at a bore (a windmill-driven water pump) at Waruwiya, thirty-eight miles southwest of Papunya. Aided by the white staff in making the shift, this group consisted mostly of "new Pintupi" who were considered a source of disturbance. Less than a year later, however, the group returned to Papunya, unsettled by a spearing in an adultery case, a death in a car accident, and a frightening rise in infant sickness resulting from the poor quality of Waruwiya's water.

In 1970 the Pintupi moved again, this time to Alumbra Bore, not as far from Papunya. Their enthusiasm was reportedly great. Visiting officials noted it was the cleanest Aboriginal camp they had ever seen (Northern Territory Administration 1970: 22). Once the population reached 300, however, the enthusiasm waned and the community deteriorated. Pintupi accounts focus on increasing amounts of liquor consumption and fighting. In their view, the outstation ended with an assault on the Papunya superintendent and a policeman who, they felt, mishandled a youthful offender. Shortly after the incident, the Pintupi were moved back to Papunya. Their difficulties in organizing a group so much larger than any in their previous social experience had never been resolved.

Yayayi

From the collapse of Alumbra until the establishment of Yayayi as an outstation in 1973, the Pintupi continued to push for their own community. It was at this new community that I arrived in July 1973, while they were in the full flower of enthusiasm with a large government grant. The initial population was 300–350.

These Pintupi resided at Yayayi through the permission of its traditional owners, a few Loritja men. The place lies 181 miles west of Alice Springs and 26 miles west of Papunya, connected by a dirt-and-bitumen road to Alice Springs. Alice Springs serves as the source of all supplies in the area, which are shipped from Adelaide.

Yayayi was the site of my longest period of fieldwork with the Pintupi (1973–75). Other sites have differed in size and location, but the basic equipment has always been much the same. Goods (tinned food, clothing, bread, flour, and so on) were trucked in from outside for a period, but most of the time the Pintupi drove to Papunya to buy their supplies. More than half the food they consumed was purchased with money coming from training grants, pensions, child endowment payments, and paintings sold through the artists' cooperative (Papunya Tula Artists). After 1975 unemployment payments ("sitdown money") became the principal source of income.

The physical plant at Yayayi was minimal, consisting of one wind-driven water bore with a covered 15,000-gallon tank and two trucks. Most of the forty-six to fifty camps were provided with canvas tents for shelter. Initially, army surplus tents were purchased out of the government grant, and these were augmented by private purchases as new families moved in and some of those who left took their tents with them. All the conjugal families (married man plus wife/wives) had shelter of some kind, as did all the unmarried women's camps. The single men scrambled for whatever shelter they could find. At subsequent Pintupi settlements, corrugated iron has become the building material of choice. Both canvas and corrugated iron can keep out the rain and be taken apart and reconstructed elsewhere.

Pintupi camps typically array themselves around a bore, usually within a radius of 600 yards. The arrangement at Yayayi was not permanent, but one major consistency in aggregation was usually visible: the spatially distinct "old Pintupi" and "new Pintupi" camps. At Yayayi these aggregations changed in composition as social tensions arose among neighbors, rains forced people to move away from the rising creek, or deaths necessitated relocation.

However, the outlines of this social division always remained visible. They reflected a social boundary in that the "old Pintupi" interacted with one another more often than with the newcomers and in that the groups had differing traditional geographical origins. The eastern "old Pintupi," closest to Haasts Bluff, were the first arrivals. The "new Pintupi," from further west in the Gibson Desert, arrived later. They were, nevertheless, closely related.

For most of my stay, the average population of Yayayi was 200–220. Except for the large number of people, domestic arrangements in Yayayi differed little from those of seminomadic camps. Many people spent varying lengths of time at Papunya or visited other settlements, some for as long as a month. Visiting relatives in other locations is highly valued, so the actual population of an outstation changes considerably through time. However, the same people tend to return to a place they consider home. The Pintupi communities are not anything like a clan or even a series of clans. They are much more an aggregation of individuals based on complex, bilateral ties. Most people in these settlements have relatives, often their closest kin, living at other quite distant settlements.

Three kinds of living units are common to Pintupi residential arrangements. While they vary in size, family camps of married people and small children, camps of unmarried women and children (*yalukuru*), and camps of older boys and young men (*tawarra*) all average between four and eight residents.[8] Family camps and the women's camps serve as effective households, while the young men camp rather haphazardly. Except for meat brought in from the hunt, most food is prepared by women. Unmarried men therefore usually go to the camp of a mother, sister, or father's sister for tea and damper. In turn, they give money to those with whom they eat— to help pay for the food. If they are successful in the hunt, the proceeds are distributed among those who feed them regularly.

In theory, a person could ask anyone in the entire community for food. In fact, however, such food-exchange relationships are circumscribed. When food is plentiful, one eats with one's closest relatives, especially at one's own camp if married, or one's father's or mother's camp if unmarried. Young men and women whose mothers are widows or elderly and living in a women's camp go to the mother's camp for food.

Where people camp often reflects their current choice of inter-domestic cooperation. As Shapiro (1979) argues for Northeast Arnhem Land and Lee (1979) for Kalahari San, Pintupi residential aggregations are not predominantly organized by patrilocal ties but by a variety of affinal and kinship connections. At Yayayi the most prominent forms of residential association involved close proximity between camps of brothers-in-law, married couples living near a wife's parents, and married couples living near a husband's parents.[9] Other associations also exist, based on ties of friendship or kinship, but they are less prominent as patterns.

The spatial organization of camps offers a useful guide to social ties, but the actual location of a camp may not indicate all of the inhabitants' residential considerations. People may face conflicting alternatives, such as whether to live near a husband's mother or a wife's mother. While some men lived at Yayayi to be near their wife's parents, for example, they did not live in an adjacent camp. Thus, the obvious spatial connections between camps may not accurately represent how significant these relationships are in determining residence. The more revealing index is the decision to live within the community at all.

Despite the divisions between old and new Pintupi, most members of the community considered Yayayi to be "one family," "all kin," or "whole lot Pintupi." This criterion prescribed sharing and cooperation with a give-and-take, long-term reciprocity in mind. These links are essentially moral. Living in small, face-to-face communities, the Pintupi are motivated by affective concerns like "compassion" and "grief." The great degree of sharing that took place attested to the importance of this consideration for people, far more noticeable than in the more disparate Papunya community. Yet during the period I lived at Yayayi, the Pintupi's sense of *communitas* as a group of kin declined as the initial enthusiasm was eroded by tensions within the group. In this dynamic, to some extent, Yayayi continued to be the equivalent of traditional local groups.

Smaller and Smaller

The Pintupi do not regard settlement as a permanent condition. Even at Yayayi, the Pintupi remained part of a wide contact society that circles the Western Desert in a series of settlements. They visit relatives at Yuendumu and as far away as Jigalong, Wiluna, Balgo, and even Broome. More frequently, they travel to closer places such as Alice Springs—where alcohol, clothing, and automobiles are easily available and a great many non-Pintupi are encountered. Although traveling remains highly desirable in itself, most Pintupi do not like to stay long, and they worry about the intentions of people from "far away," fearing sorcery.

Contact with distant communities continues to be structured

largely through ceremonial gatherings, such as initiations, that require large numbers of men. In recent years, initiatory contact has involved people from Yuendumu, Amata, Jigalong, Warburton Range, and Balgo; the distances they have traveled are impressive, often 500 miles or more. Through this means a pan-Aboriginal community is being established.

The tendency of Pintupi settlement in the last decade has been centrifugal. A greater availability of motor transport, through private purchase or government grant, underlies this development, as people have been able to move to smaller and more remote communities while still staying in touch with the resources of larger settlements. Even while I was living at Yayayi, by mid-1974 another Pintupi outstation had been created at Kungkayurnti (cf. Morice 1976, Moyle 1979), its population varying from as few as twenty-one to as many as a hundred.

When I returned to visit the Pintupi in 1979, outstation communities had proliferated in the Papunya area. These communities were quite small. Pintupi lived at Yinyilingki (thirty-seven persons in nine camps), Yayayi (fifteen persons in three camps), and in similar numbers at Kungkayurnti and Mount Liebig. Still other members of the original Yayayi community had moved to Balgo Mission in Western Australia or to Docker River, and some had returned to Papunya.

Such communities remained extremely fluid, aggregating and dispersing according to need and desire. Thus, in December 1980, more than ninety people were living at an outstation near Mount Liebig known as New Bore. The core of the residents here—the previous settlers of Yinyilingki fifteen miles away—numbered only between twenty and thirty. For the summer, however, people from Kungkayurnti and Alumbra joined them because transportation was scarce and centralization necessary to distribute store food. Others moved to New Bore because a death in their own community required their temporary relocation. And still others joined this larger group for the pleasure of a temporary sociality while they prepared to move yet again, en masse, to Papunya for an initiation.

A smaller population better distributed over the landscape makes hunting and collecting in the vicinity of these communities more productive than it is near larger groups. Residents of outstations enjoy a much higher proportion of wild foods, both meat and vegetable, in their diets than do the people in the larger settlements. This is one reason many prefer to live in such conditions. Indeed, foraging—whether aided by automobile transportation or not—constitutes one of the chief activities of outstation life.

The Last Step?

Movement did not stop with the outstations. In mid-1981, the Pintupi moved back to a site near the Kintore Range, known to them as Warlungurru. This area was, for the first time in twenty years, their own country—located 150 miles west of Papunya. The older Pintupi saw the creation of this settlement as a step toward autonomy and a reassertion of control over destructive outside influences. Nonetheless, the actual move to Kintore depended on the grudging willingness of the government to support the new community and the provision of a white administrator to handle the business with Alice Springs. As the Pintupi had hoped, however, the distance has made alcohol difficult to obtain, and they have prohibited its use in Kintore.

Those who moved from Papunya have been joined at Kintore by relatives who had once left the desert for Balgo, Warburton Range, or Jigalong. And the thrust of recent developments is an increasing ritual and pragmatic communication among Western Desert communities that had previously been individually isolated on the fringes of the Gibson Desert. Even so, access to the more remote parts of the desert remains difficult. The limited water and transportation resources in the Western Desert initially restricted the population of 300–350 Pintupi to living in one settlement at Kintore. But their plan, since the move, has always been to create a number of small outstations in the Gibson Desert. The drilling of new bores is now making this last movement possible, with fifty Pintupi living still further west at Kiwirrkura and other outstations. This development promises, one hopes, an eventual end to their odyssey.

CHAPTER 2

The Dreaming: Time and Space

It's not our idea, it's a big law.
We have to sit down alongside of that Law like all
the dead people who went before us.

Throughout Australia, the Aboriginal outlook on human life and the universe is shaped by a distinctive and subtle conception that they refer to in English as The Dreaming. A series of celebrated anthropologists from Spencer and Gillen (1899), Roheim (1945), and Strehlow (1947), to Stanner (1956, 1966), Meggitt (1972), and Munn (1970) have grappled with the significance of The Dreaming, each arriving at fruitful interpretations. Taken together with the theoretical extrapolations of scholars such as Durkheim (1912) and Lévi-Strauss (1966), these accounts provide illuminating analyses of this distinctly Aboriginal cultural construction. Pointedly, they all agree on the importance of The Dreaming in Aboriginal social life and its central place in constituting their lived world.

Yet for all that has been written, the relationship between this cultural construction of time, space, and personhood and the particular varieties of social life remains problematic. It is with this in view that I address again the problem of The Dreaming among the Pintupi.

Initially, the constitution of the world by The Dreaming must be treated phenomenologically as a given condition of "what there is," an endowment of being and potential that defines for Pintupi the framework of human action. Like all symbolic constructions, however, its meaning requires further interpretation (Geertz 1973, Ricoeur 1970, Rosaldo 1980). Because it touches so many dimensions of Pintupi life, The Dreaming (*tjukurrpa*) possesses no single or finite significance. It represents, instead, a projection into symbolic space of various social processes. We understand the social meaning of such a construct only when we are able to relate it to the particular circumstances of those who use it.

47

For the Pintupi, at least, particular attention should be paid to the precarious achievement of Society within the constraints of life in dispersed local groups as a construction that transcends the present and immediate. Essentially, the form taken by The Dreaming among the Pintupi represents this dilemma. Its structure is a product of the way Pintupi society reproduces itself in space and time. Indeed, the distinction that the concept of The Dreaming establishes between two levels of being reflects the structuring of Pintupi space. Such a view sustains the intuition that two other constructs of major importance in Pintupi social life—*ngurra*, meaning "camp," "country," or "place," and *walytja*, referring to "family," "relatives," or "kin"—are fundamentally linked to the concept of The Dreaming. It is in relation to this practical logic that space and time, defined by The Dreaming, acquire their value.

The Dreaming: Tjukurrpa as Ontology

Far more than a set of just-so stories, the concept of The Dreaming is basic to the Pintupi view of reality. The distinction between The Dreaming and all else underlies every feature of their universe. Both the country (the landscape and its form) and the people are thought to be "from The Dreaming" (*tjukurrtjanu*), the ground of being. Pintupi describe a large hill in the Kintore Range, for example, as the body of a monitor lizard, *Ngintaka*, who traveled from the west. At Kintore, the monitor lizard came upon a group of women and children dancing. He killed them with his tail and, raising his head up in a position that is represented in the shape of the landform, turned to stone (*purlirringu*). The hill that arose is known as *Yunytjunya*, in reference to the exposure of the lizard's throat (*yunytju*).

As Pintupi use the term, "Dreaming" may refer both to the specific stories and to the whole creative epoch of which the stories are part. A narrative of the traveling ancestor who killed the dancing women becomes, then, Monitor Lizard Dreaming.

An important semantic opposition reveals the consistent ontology underlying the Pintupi conceptualization of The Dreaming. When they describe events, Pintupi contrast The Dreaming (*tjukurrpa*) with those events or stories that are said to be *yuti*. The word *yuti* signifies visibility or some other form of sensory presentation to a subject. A person might be directed to an ax he wants to borrow by the phrase, "There it is over there, visible" (*yuti*). A kangaroo emerging from behind a bush has, to the Pintupi, "become visible" (*yutirringu*). But other senses equally convey the information that makes an object *yuti*. For example, a native curer once told me he was certain that a car was on the way to our camp. After waiting and listening for several minutes, he turned to me triumphantly and said, "Listen, the motor sound has become *yuti*." Whether or not something is *yuti* is very important to Pintupi, who place great emphasis on personal experience and distinguish between what is witnessed and what is reported at secondhand. The contrast between *yuti* and *tjukurrpa*, however, does not depend on a person's actually having seen an event. As long as somebody *could* see an event, it may be described as *yuti*. What is critical ontologically is not whether a particular person witnessed the event, but whether it is in principle witnessable.

A late arrival to a conversation often asks a storyteller about the status of the narrative: "Are you talking about The Dreaming?" "No," he may answer, "not Dreaming; I'm talking about the visible" (*yuti*), or "not Dreaming; I'm talking about what really happened" (*mularrpa*). Since the word *mularrpa* usually means "real," "true," or "actual" as opposed to "untrue," "fictitious," or "lie," its contrast with the concept of The Dreaming may seem puzzling. However, The Dreaming is not viewed either as a fiction or a lie. In fact, there is no category of fictional narrative in Pintupi. A story either happened or it did not; if it did not occur, the story is a "lie."

The relationship between these two realms of the universe (*tjukurrpa* and *mularrpa*) is not, therefore, one of simple logical opposition. Rather, The Dreaming constitutes the ground or foundation of the visible, present-day world. What speakers define by choosing between these words is whether an occurrence is in the phenomenal (*mularrpa*) realm or in the noumenal, whether it is witnessable. For the Pintupi, the veracity of The Dreaming is assured, no matter how imperfectly it may be known by humans who did not witness it. These stories, they insist, are not "made up just for fun" (*ngunytji*); they really happened. The existence of the lizard's hill is proof enough that the event occurred as postulated.[1] Thus, informants assured me of a Dreaming story's truth by insisting they had seen the place where it happened.

Pintupi apply this theory of existence to everything in their world. Persons, customs, geographical features, all are said to have originated in The Dreaming. The phrase they use—"from The Dreaming, it becomes real" (*tjukurrtjanu, mularrarringu*)—represents a passage between two planes of being.

If The Dreaming can be said to transcend the present in this fashion, the fact that the landscape is a series of stories allows it, also, to transcend the immediate. Frequently known as totemic ancestors in anthropological literature, the mythological personages of The Dreaming traveled from place to place, hunted, performed ceremonies, fought, and finally turned to stone or "went into the ground," where they remain. The actions of these powerful beings—animal, human, and monster[2]—created the world as it now exists. They gave it outward form, identity (a name), and internal structure. The desert is crisscrossed with their lines of travel and, just as an animal's tracks leave a record of what happened, the geography and special features of the land—hills, creeks, salt lakes, trees—are marks of the ancestors' activities. Places where exceptionally significant events took place, where power was left behind, or where the ancestors went into the ground and still remain are special sacred sites (*yarta yarta*) because ancestral potency is near. For almost all the landscape (hills, water holes, and so on), the country (*ngurra*) takes its name from The Dreaming, either from the event or from the associated rituals and songs. Finally, while Dreamtime action gives name and identity to each location, the connections a story may make between places also links them into a larger country whose parts share identity.

Other aspects of Pintupi life derive from this epoch as well. One hears repeatedly about customs and of human beings that "from The Dreaming, [they] became real." Nothing is created by human beings; it was all there "from the start." Pintupi believe that The Dreaming left behind at various places the creative potency—or spiritual essence—of all the natural species and of human beings. They speak of conception and birth as the emergence of an individual from the plane of The Dreaming onto the physical, phenomenal plane of existence. Logically, then, conception in the Pintupi sense refers to the quickening of the fetus, when the mother first notices physically that she is pregnant. An individual is said to have been "sitting as a Dreamtime being" (*nyinama tjukurrpa*) and then to have become visible (*yutirringu*). Alternately, the transformation may be characterized as "becoming body" or "becoming a human being" (*yarnangurringu*). Individuals are thought of as being "left behind" (*wantingu*) by The Dreaming and subsequently to emerge into the present-day world. Birth thus represents a movement from the significant, invisible, temporally prior situation to the present, visible one; and quite unambiguously, the spirit of an individual preexists, autonomously, apart from parental contribution.

The Dreaming also links people and place. The place from which a person's spirit comes is his or her Dreaming-place, and the person is an incarnation of the ancestor who made the place. A person's Dreaming provides the basic source of his or her identity, an identity that preexists. It is not unusual, therefore, to hear people describe actions of The Dreaming in the first person. For the Pintupi,

Pintupi Country, Pintupi Self

individuals come from the country, and this relationship provides a primary basis for owning a sacred site and for living in the area. In such ways, present-day arrangements are prefigured by The Dreaming, although the Pintupi see themselves as following The Dreaming. As the invisible framework of this world, The Dreaming is its cosmic prototype.[3]

Dreams

Although Pintupi make a sharp conceptual distinction between "dreams" and "The Dreaming," certain cultural understandings underlie both. Therefore, the word *tjukurrpa* is also used to signify actual dreams. Sometimes, Pintupi will describe the act of dreaming as "seeing Dreaming" (*tjukurrpa nyanginpa*) or just as "dreaming" by adding a suffix to the root to create a verb (*tjukurrmaninpa*). In this way, the experience of dreams is contrasted with the visible, but The Dreaming remains a different order of reality. Conventional dreams are usually considered matters of "little import" (*ngunytji*). To sustain the distinction when necessary, the word *kapukurri* unambiguously refers to actual dreams and is never equivalent with the concept of The Dreaming as the mythological past. The relationship between the two derives, presumably, from their joint reference to situations of nonordinary reality, but the connection between them is culturally problematic.

The common Pintupi view of what happens in dreams is that one's "spirit" (*kurrunpa*) travels apart from the body and observes things not ordinarily within the field of sensory presentation. These observed events may be distant in time or space but, significantly, others cannot witness them. Sometimes individuals are believed to come into contact with the ancestral figures of The Dreaming, who may give them special knowledge, usually of songs and ceremonies. These experiences are considered to be revelations of matters people did not know of before. What one sees is believed to have always existed. As other observers have pointed out (cf. Stanner 1956), the experience of dreams—as a dimension of existence that is parallel to everyday life but invisible to it—makes them a good metaphor for The Dreaming. Like the latter, dreams also are said to be "not real" (*mularrpa wiya*). The relationship is more than metaphorical and, consequently, more complex.

The major question of all such experiences is whether or not they are "true." Though usually considered insignificant, their value is negotiable, as the tentative ambiguity of the commonly used phrase "I saw something" suggests. When people wake up in the morning, it is not uncommon for them to mention a dream. They may wonder about what they saw, what it means, and whether it is an omen, but a dream's potential portent seems prominent only in situations of uncertainty and danger. Although a dream of violence that a man interprets as a killing at a distant settlement may arouse anxiety if relations are strained between groups, it will be forgotten if nothing transpires. Or such a dream may gain importance in retrospect, if the appearance of an event confirms an interpretation of it.

The significance of dreams, then, becomes a product of negotiation and not a given. Even if one believes one has come into contact with ancestral beings, to validate this publicly one must be able to persuade others to accept the claim. Most often, people express a puzzled curiosity rather than an insistence on any value as omen. In this way, the mystery of dreams parallels that of The Dreaming. While they offer a certain amount of information, one cannot be sure about their meaning and no one else will have witnessed them. That they lie outside of human control—unwitnessable—gives dreams much potency: They remain open to enormous interpretive possibilities, while individuals need not commit themselves to a particular meaning. Social construction can take place around them without attributing creativity to individuals.

Time as Continuity

What is critical about the concept of The Dreaming is that it denies creative significance to history and human action, just as it denies the erosions of time. It represents all that exists as deriving from a single, unchanging, timeless source. All things have always been the same, forever deriving from the same basic pattern. The Dreaming, which cannot be altered by human action, is the very image of self-direction and the source of a given autonomy in human life.

In the Pintupi view, things as they are—the familiar customs of male initiation, death, cross-cousin marriage, sorcery, and burial, for example—were instituted once-and-for-all in The Dreaming. Human beings neither made it so nor invented these practices. Like everything else of the cosmos, people and their practices are simply part of a single, monistic order of existents established long ago. The vital essence of men and women appeared as spirits (*kurrunpa*) from The Dreaming. The Pintupi ontology thus emphasizes the relatedness of the cosmos, rather than the opposition of spirit and matter, natural and supernatural, or good and evil.

It is also a world view that implies continuity and permanence. The historicity of hills unchanged through time proclaims that the cosmos has always been as it is and that, indeed, it cannot be different. The Pintupi, like other Western Desert Aborigines, some-times mark this quality of "life as a one-possibility thing" (Stanner 1966) when they describe The Dreaming as "the Law." In doing so, they emphasize not only the norms or precedents established in The Dreaming, but also the sense of moral imperative it embodies. People must continue The Dreaming and preserve it, making first things continuous with last, by "holding the Law" for coming generations. Thus, human beings play a role in the maintenance of the instituted order. Pintupi explain about The Dreaming that it is not a product of human subjectivity or will. It is, rather, an order to which all are subordinated: "It's not our idea," men told me. "It's a big Law. We have to sit down alongside of that Law like all the dead people who went before us." Indeed, not only do the Dreaming narratives tell how the world came to be, but the raw material of the stories, the symbols themselves in the form of the landscape, signify the same concern on another level. Human life and being, they imply, are as permanent, enduring, and unchanging as the land itself.

These concepts are subtle and complex. In Western historical terms, changes have always taken place. The evidence of new customs and new cults is unassailable; life is not static. The Pintupi understandings of the historical process are not totally static either, but the concept of the The Dreaming organizes experience so that it *appears* to be continuous and permanent. For the Pintupi, the dynamic, processual aspect of history seems to exist as one of dis-covering, uncovering, or even reenacting elements of The Dreaming.[4]

The basis for the present-day association of people, in the Pintupi view, is that they come from one Dreaming, that is, a single geographical track of a story. Since the forties, Western Desert Aborigines have been moving out of the deepest desert areas and congregating around government settlements and mission stations. This process has brought together people who previously had had little contact with each other. Some Pintupi wound up hundreds of miles to the north, at Balgo Mission. Until 1975 I had been told that one of the main Pintupi Dreaming tracks ended at a place called Pinari near Lake Mackay. However, after Pintupi from my community visited their long-separated relatives at Balgo, they returned to tell me that "we thought that story ended, went into the ground, at Pinari. But we found that it goes underground all the way to Balgo." Apparently, this revelation was discovered in a vision by a man from Balgo. The example shows that historical change can be integrated, but that it is assimilated to the preexisting forms: The foundation had always been there, but people had not known it before.

What appear to be changes do not challenge the fundamental ontology of all things ordained once-and-for-all. New rituals, songs, or designs—for Westerners the products of human creation—are for the Pintupi clearer sights of what was always there. This construction denies the impact of human actions by asserting that the events and existents of the visible world remain reflections of an ontologically prior set of events. Though we might see in The Dreaming merely the "moving shadow of the present" (as Stanner once described it), its participants see sustained correspondence. Time—in this sense as an abstract dimension detached from subjectivity—is captive to the cultural constructions of continuity. A similar structure underlies the Pintupi ordering of space.

Ngurra: Extension in Space

Orientation in space is a prime concern for the Pintupi. Even their dreams are cast in a framework of spatial coordinates. It is impossible to listen to any narrative, whether it be historical, mythological, or contemporary, without constant reference to where events happened. In this sense, place provides the framework around which events coalesce, and places serve as mnemonics for significant events. Travel through the country evokes memories about a fight that occurred at a nearby water hole or a death in the hills beyond. Not temporal relation but geography is the great punctuator of Pintupi storytelling. Upon close examination, it is activity that creates places, giving significance to impervious matter.

Thus the world is socialized by the Pintupi, although they do not build a spatially centered cosmos of domesticated culture and wild nature as many more settled people have done. A social life with so much movement seems to preclude such a construction. Instead, they seem truly at home as they walk through the bush, full of confidence. A camp can be made almost anywhere within a few minutes—a windbreak set up, fires built, and perhaps a billycan of tea prepared. Unmarked and wild country becomes a "camp" (ngurra) with the comfort of home. The way of thinking that enables a people to make a camp almost anywhere they happen to be, with little sense of dislocation, is a way of thinking that creates a universe of meanings around the mythologized country. These people who move and shift so regularly from place to place have truly culturalized space and made out of impersonal geography a home, a ngurra. The threat to this construction is not the overgrowth of wild nature but the ravages of time.

As the Pintupi portray it, this universe of meaning is not restricted to their own creations or those of their forebears. The world as it now exists, in their conception, is the product of powerful mythological beings and the formative events in which they took part. Evidence of this enduring reality is all about them, in every formation of the landscape. To travel across the land with them is to learn that at this hill or in that creek something happened "in The Dreaming."

There is a consistency in these structurings, embodied in the dual meaning of *ngurra*. This word has two distinct references to socialized space, in referring both to a temporary camp in which people live and also to an enduring "country" or named place. *Ngurra* is not only the human creation of "camp" but also the Dreaming creation of "country." Thus, as the concept by which the Pintupi most frequently appropriate space, *ngurra* always relates demarcated places to activity that gives them meaning. As with the Nuer use of *cieng* (Evans-Pritchard 1940), it is through this concept of spatial order that the Pintupi articulate their own social organization. The idea of a camp combines people who live together with a site at which they are localized; it is the fact of people living there that makes a space a camp.

Although the identification it formulates is more complex, the usage of *ngurra* as country or place similarly does not refer to an objective, physical space. Because named places acquire their identity through the activities of mythological personages in The Dreaming, *ngurra* continues to be based on a social reference. Neither "camp" nor "country" exist apart from the significance created by action or event, but "country" retains an identity enduring through time as something beyond human choice. Human and Dreaming action each contribute to the definition of landscape, although their constructions have differing properties. In relation to human action, one is historical while the other might be termed transhistorical.

The realm of human action is surely primary in its meaning, and at its simplest, *ngurra* is the place where one belongs or where one sleeps. It is common for Pintupi to classify a water hole and its environs as a *ngurra*. But when describing a particular site, they clearly distinguish between the place where one camps, sleeps, and prepares food (the camp), and the water hole nearby (*kapi*). In this sense, a *ngurra* may be anywhere that people decide to sleep.

Just as a bird's nest is its *ngurra* and a kangaroo's home is the plain, one's *ngurra* is the place where one belongs. Within the daily routine of leaving a camp in the morning and returning, perhaps after a day's hunt, in the afternoon, the *ngurra* is the place to which one returns. Here, food is likely to be shared and resources pooled. Through this association, the concept of *ngurra* involves the idea of "relatives" (*walytja*) or "family group," in the sense of people whose daily lives are tied together. In Pintupi thinking, therefore, *ngurra* is the embodiment and image of sociality, the physical expression of a basic social unit, the conjugal family. Just as proximity implies cooperation, so does social distance lead to spatial separation: When the social ties between people weaken, they move apart. Because it embodies sociality at a primary level, the concept of *ngurra* is used by the Pintupi as an idiom of social classification.

It is characteristic of folk terms like *ngurra* that, unlike analytic concepts, they may be used at quite distinctive levels of organization. Conflating these has often led observers to treat the organization of small-scale societies as less complex and more rigid than it is. What Pintupi mean when they talk of *ngurra* can be sorted into several distinct contexts.

When speakers refer to the camp of an individual man and his spouse, as opposed to the nearby camps of coresidents in a local group, the term *ngurra* delineates social boundaries of privacy that, ordinarily, people should respect. Further, a married man who lives with his wife and young children is said to be "with camp" (*ngurratjarra*) and differentiated thereby from unmarried men and boys who are described as "from the single men's camp" (*tawarrangkatja*).

At a broader level, the word *ngurra* may be used to distinguish a set of camps (individual units), whose members consider themselves to be a group—that is, spatially separated from the camps of others who may be living nearby. Those of the same *ngurra*, in this sense, cooperate more closely within the designated cluster than between them, and people will speak of "our camp" as opposed to "their camp." Such classification is quite noticeable in settlement life, especially in the continuing separation of the "old Pintupi" and the "new Pintupi."

The difference between *ngurra* as "country" and as "camp" is especially significant. Among people who move so frequently, camps are physically impermanent, and their membership changes through time. The idea of *ngurra* as "country," on the other hand, is enduring. In this sense, the two forms of appropriating space (*ngurra* as camp and as country) imply different temporal dimensions. A camp, as a human creation, never loses its identification with those who made it or lived there. Not only do the Pintupi move away from camps associated with someone who has died, but they avoid the places for years, as they avoid all other extensions of the deceased such as name or property. Places, they say, remind them of the dead person and make them sad. People also avoid setting up camp in the precise spots where others have camped. But despite these identifications

Pintupi Country, Pintupi Self

with people who lived there, camps are impermanent. Eventually they are overgrown and their associations forgotten, while significant new spaces are constantly being established.

Ngurra as "country" represents a more inclusive level of the social system: These named places are the camps of The Dreaming. In this way, as several theorists have suggested (cf. Leach 1958, Turner 1979a), the higher level of organization is constructed through a recursive transformation of the lower-level unit. *Ngurra* as country employs a relation of people to each other through place modeled on the camp, but it becomes a different sort of social object. Whereas camps come into and pass out of existence, country endures as a reality which people cannot, in theory, alter. Country is collectivized or turned into a socially enduring object because its creators are outside the immediate social world. Though it is modeled on the camp, it exists through time, providing a social framework that appears to have objective status to humans. Further, if *ngurra* as camp represents social ties that exist at the moment— relatives organized around a camp—those sharing a country are identified as a fundamental, enduring corporation. That The Dreaming is invisible and, in a sense, not knowable with finality makes it possible to turn the lower-level realities into social ties of more permanent status.

Place and Place-Names

To the Pintupi, then, the landscape in which they move is a life-world of constituted meanings. Though it is not possible to ignore the social concomitant of places, the rest of this chapter will outline the significant features of "country" as a frame for action. We will consider country as if it were simply culturalized space, noting as others have before (Gould 1969a, Tonkinson 1978) that the Western Desert is dotted with places named and known by its Aboriginal inhabitants.

Almost invariably, Pintupi discussions of country are punctuated by descriptions of what happened in The Dreaming. Every significant feature is held to result from Dreaming events. Yumarinya, for example, means "wife's mother-place." The *yumari* of this case is the mother-in-law of a mythological man, who copulated with her at this place. Rock outcroppings, a rock hole, and various markings within a few hundred yards are interpreted as the result of the abhorrent actions of the mythological beings. The name signifies a specific feature of the event.

Two places have the name Kurtitji-nya, "shield-place." In one case the name refers to a shield made in The Dreaming. The other refers to a ritual performed in a boy's initiation in which men beat a shield with a boomerang and sing while the women dance. In the second case, the site was said to have been a result of the ritual being performed there in The Dreaming.

Not all names are Dreaming-derived. Wanaritjarra-nya, "mulga tree-having-place," refers to the physical attributes of the area around a water hole surrounded by mulga trees. Names such as this seem to resemble descriptive labels rather than proper names. If the word *wanari* became taboo, owing to the death of someone with a similar name, the place would be referred to as Kunmarnutjarranya, meaning "with name avoided."

An increase center for wild black currants, whose essence was left there by a group of men in The Dreaming, is known as Yawalyurru-nya, "black currant-place," or as Tjartupirrnga, a synonym. It is also known, and preferably so, as Tjukulanya, describing its feature of a large sinkhole in the ground. This last name is used as a matter of etiquette and respect by those who feel a close identification with the site. Some substitutions of this sort are meant to deceive or to focus on nonritual or nonsacred associations in the presence of uninitiated persons.

At the level of "country," the world *ngurra* may apply to any named place. Pintupi refer to Yumarinya as a *ngurra*. All its features hold mythological significance. When people say they went to Yumarinya, they refer to the whole clustering, a single name referring to several features. Although included in the one name, particular aspects of a site may be designated by context or by further linguistic additions.[5] For example, a speaker might distinguish between Yumarinya the water hole (*tjiwiri*) and Yumarinya the sacred part (*yarta yarta*).

Likewise, a single name may be used to refer to a number of individually named places that are geographically clustered. Thus, a trip to the Pollock Hills in Western Australia was described as a trip to Yunarlanya. We camped on a creek with that name, taken from the tuber plant growing beside the water. Pointing to the hill beside us, men named three distinctive places on it: Tjikarrnga, Pantukurunya, and Yunarlanya. In ordinary conversation, particularly when the place is remote, speakers would refer to the whole area as Yunarlanya; knowledgeable listeners understand that the other features are nearby. As other cases could further illustrate, Yunarlanya is not a more general and logically inclusive term for the whole area or hill, as Pennsylvania is for Philadelphia and Pittsburgh. It is merely one of the several named places in the cluster. Another site name could be similarly used to refer to them all.

The names of *ngurra*, in other words, refer to specific features rather than to an area enclosed within spatial boundaries. In addition, the names are not organized in an ascending series of mutually exclusive units, as with cities and states. One name may be used to designate collectively a series of place that are considered to be unified or defined by some set of activities as a single living area.[6]

The Pintupi names of places should not be understood as proper names. Alternative names or references are frequently employed, such as words from a song or some other referential system. A large salt lake in the west is variously known as Ngunarrmanya, Pinarinya, or Nyaru. The last term refers to the fact that the Dreaming event there was a fire that left a huge burned-out area (or *nyaru*). The second name and probably the first derive from the words of associated songs, although they have a meaning in themselves. To the Pintupi, then, a place itself with its multiple features is logically prior or central; its names are simply standardized forms of reference or description. This view of naming parallels a Pintupi tendency to circumlocution in talking about individual persons and a zest for oblique but descriptive reference.

The Country as Story

One cannot speak of places, as the Pintupi view them, without considering their mythological associations. For two reasons, at least, the metaphor of country as story is particularly appropriate.

First, in discussing an individual's ownership of a place, Pintupi men frequently use the English equivalent, "That's his story." This phrase focuses on what is significant about a place for ownership—the ritual or sacred associations that Stanner (1965) called the country as an "estate." The usual word for sacred object, *turlku*, means variously "song," "sacred board," "ritual object," "ceremony," or "story." It is significant that all these referents are classified by the single term, as Strehlow (1947) noted for the Aranda concept of *tjurunga*. Within the category delineated by *turlku* there are, of course, more precise words for different kinds of objects, but Pintupi usage emphasizes the underlying commonality of the referents as manifestations of a story, The Dreaming. This view expresses a fundamental feature of Western Desert thought, as Munn (1970) observed: Sacred objects, country, or songs become the embodiment of events, of activity that has, in a sense, turned into these objects.

Second, Pintupi mythology consists mainly of narratives of beings traveling from place to place. Consequently, all the places visited may be part of one larger story or myth. Each place is discrete and separate, but also is part of a continuous series of places linked by the one story. As a way of classifying places into potentially larger systems, this tradition of geographically based narrative is extremely important both here and elsewhere in Aboriginal Australia.[7] Principally it establishes a framework for the theory and politics of "ownership," in which claims about rights may be based on the geographical continuity of a single Dreaming. The system is not, despite appearances, a closed one. Reworked and recreated even now, systems of stories constitute a changing political charter of who and what are identified at various levels. With the "discovery" that the *Tingarri* Dreaming traveled underground northward to Balgo Hills Mission, for example, the Pintupi found themselves able, in certain contexts, to describe the people of Balgo as "from one country, from one Dreaming."

Country as a Continuous Entity

It is as a manifestation of an underlying story that the Pintupi perceive of country as, essentially, a continuous entity. This structure accounts for some initially puzzling features of Pintupi attitudes toward their homeland. Sociocentric boundaries are difficult to draw; one cannot say that an area X, made up of such-and-such places, constitutes a "country." When individuals describe their "own country," their lists of places are likely to overlap without being identical. Indeed, no separate technical term exists for a larger unit of space composed of a number of named places. What Pintupi emphasized, instead, was that there was one country for everybody, that they were all one family. As one patient older man said, Pintupi country was not like a paddock that is fenced off; if he saw smoke from a fire, he would be happy to go to see who was there.

Pintupi frequently claim that theirs is "one country," nonsegmentary and belonging to everybody. Like so many sweeping ideological assertions, this is both true in one way and not true at another level. Such claims represent, certainly, an assertion of the unity and identity of the people who had come to live together in settlements to the east, using their traditional country as an ideological basis for current relations. Far from being an exception, this assertion represents a major consideration in the cultural organization of space. Thus, one reason given for considering the Pintupi as one group, one "family," is that they are all from the *Tingarri*, one long and interconnected Dreaming story.

They do not mean, of course, that all Pintupi are incarnations of the same Dreaming, *Tingarri*. As everyone knows, there are people of all different mythological origins. A clue to the meaning of the claim is a contrast related to me. The Pitjantjatjarra ceremony

Pintupi Country, Pintupi Self

was the Kangaroo Dreaming, according to a thoughtful informant. The Warlpiri was Shield (*Kurtitji*) Dreaming, and the Pintupi had *Tingarri.*

While considerable complexities surround the meaning of *Tingarri,*[8] in the context of Pintupi claims about their country the word refers to mythological traveling groups of men and ceremonial novices. Pintupi glossed it regularly as "all the men" or "many novices." Three major geographical lines of named places are described as *Tingarri,* visited and created in The Dreaming by three groups of traveling people. These groups were made up of novices who had already undergone circumcision (*punyunyu*) and who traveled under the guidance and discipline of powerful, authoritative "bosses." Secluded from women and the uninitiated, such groups performed and witnessed ceremonies of revelation, as well as hunted, argued, and fought, just as present-day Aboriginal people do. Action in the myths themselves interrelates the three groups, and consequently some basis exists in Pintupi thought for considering *Tingarri* to be a proper name for the interrelated complex. It is worth examining a small portion of this myth system to illustrate how places are linked in The Dreaming and how country operates as a continuous entity.

Tingarri and Pintupi Country:
The Native Cat Story

Though most of Pintupi country (and even territory beyond that) is linked by the *Tingarri* complex, a portion suffices to show how Dreaming and country relate. Referring to the northern, middle, and southern routes of *Tingarri* groups as A, B, C respectively (see Map 2A), I take up the story of *Tingarri* group B.[9] This particular segment of the larger complex links people from the Tikartika region in the east with Lake Macdonald and Yawalyurru in the west. The story is punctuated by place—emphasizing localities (named places), relations in space, and evocation of specific kinds of place (sandhills, water holes, and so on).

This particular narrative will provide background for many additional issues discussed in later chapters. (The extended case of claims to the sacred site of Yawalyurru, for example, is an important part of the discussion of the politics of landownership in chapter 5.) As a product of the mythological imagination, this narrative emphasizes the motivations and appropriate relations among people "from one country" (sharing), the geographical expanse of such relations, and the violent consequences of failing to respect the rights of others.

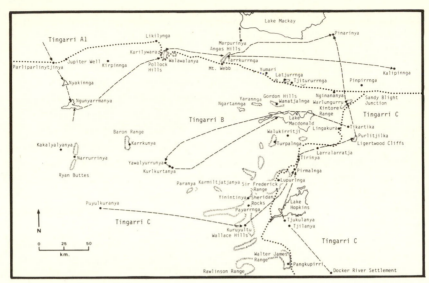

Map 2A. Tingarri Routes

The underlying motif of this story is the Native Cat's (*kuninka, marsupial cat*) desire for revenge against the *Tingarri* men from Yawalyurrunya.

> Native Cat's home country, men say, is Lake Macdonald (Karrkurutintjinya). While walking near here one day, he came upon a piece of emu fat and saw the tracks of men who had dropped it. He realized that the *Tingarri* men had speared an emu east of the lake and cooked it at Tikartikanya. Native Cat became angry (*mirrpanpa,* "no compassion") because the men had sneaked into his country unannounced and not shared the meat with him. He told his two sons at the lake to prepare themselves, for he was going to bring back these people. He started westward then, following the *Tingarri* men's tracks. These latter had transformed themselves into wild dogs for their return. Heading west at night, he passed the Possum people among the claypans of Yiitjurunya, the most eastward of a north-south line of fairly permanent waters in the sandhill country south of the Pollock Hills.
>
> The possums were a revenge party chasing a man who had eloped with his mother-in-law and fled south from Warlpiri country. Gathered for a ceremony when Native Cat burst into view, they were frightened by his demeanor as he ran up a sandhill and ululated (*tjamarlangarangu,* a signal from elder men that indicates a ceremony is about to begin). Native Cat ran down the other side of the sandhill, racing across the claypans in the high-stepping action which men use in ceremonial performances and in displaying anger.

Pintupi Country, Pintupi Self

He did not speak to the possums as he decorated himself with vegetable fluff[10] in the design used now in ritual to represent him. At this place, a large bloodwood tree arose, marking the spot. Then, Native Cat raced up another sandhill and ululated, holding a large ritual object in his hand. To this terrifying and dangerous sight, the possum men sang a verse which is included in the *Tingarri* song cycles now performed.

Then he headed further westward, finally sleeping near Mintjirnga. In the morning he approached Yintjintjinya, where the women of the *Tingarri* men were camped. He climbed a sandhill and sent up a smoke. The women saw it and tossed dirt into the air, as people do to ward off a dangerous spirit (*mamu*). Frightened, the women did not speak to him as he turned south for the men at Yawalyurrunya. He approached from the north as he saw smoke rising from a small hole in the ground. The *Tingarri* men were underground, "inside." From the desert oak on the north side of the site, he called to them. He "questioned" them in the ritual manner used by older men toward secluded novices. There was no answer, so he hurled a throwing stick at them, but it bounced away. He stepped back then and circled to the south side of the site. He drew on his hairstring belt, grasped another throwing stick and thrust it vertically down into the ground, twisting it back and forth, opening up a huge hole (which is now Yawalyurrunya) "like dynamite."

The first men to see him as they climbed up were those on the north side. They looked around expecting, because of the power displayed, to see many men, but there was only Native Cat. He was sitting on the edge of the sandhill to the south of the hole, crying because he was "sorry" (*yalurrpa*) for these novices whom he had blasted. Where he sat with an arm covering his face, a gnarled tree now represents him. The *Tingarri* men climbed up his throwing stick, just as contemporary men who care for the north side of the site climb a ladder (*tjukalpa*) to prepare the increase center. From the black currants (*yawalyurru*) the *Tingarri* men had with them inside the ground, it is said, come the black drippings on the walls of the sinkhole. When all the men had climbed out of the hole, they decorated themselves with ceremonial down, the process leaving loose reddish stones on the southern edge. Native Cat told them to leave the black currants behind and go to Kurlkurtanya, to wait for him in the sandstone hills to the east. He sent them away "just like children." Because they left the black currants behind, their essence from The Dreaming is still at the place which men visit to make the fruit grow throughout the country.[11]

After he sent them away, Native Cat flew westward to Puyulkuranya to direct another Tingarri group [C] eastward toward Docker River (Wintalkanya) and then to Tjukulanya, Mitukatjirrinya, and Pinarinya [see Map 2A]. Native Cat returned from Puyulkuranya to Kurlkurtanya and took the *Tingarri* men and women to Lake Macdonald, hunting and performing ceremonies along the way. Their actions gave rise to the features of this landscape. At Lake Macdonald, finally, the *Tingarri* people were killed with hail and lightning by Native Cat's two sons. Exhausted by this exercise of their powers, however, the sons died and turned into snakes at the salt lake. Stricken with grief (*yalurrpa*) at the sight of his dead sons, Native Cat bashed himself in the forehead with a stone axe. Where he died, his body became a stone formation still visible out in the lake.

As this brief narrative shows, Dreaming stories may be both extensive, in linking up many geographically distant places, and intensive, in organizing myriad details of a single place. The stories account for far more precise and intricate detail than I have given here, but in most cases the information is considered to be secret and sacred. Because such detail is intimately related to men's and women's ritual, access to the information is restricted. Thus, frequently, only initiated men are permitted to visit sacred sites, and women and children are excluded.[12]

Transforming Landscape into Narrative

The process through which landscape is assimilated to narrative structure is still active. I had the opportunity to see it take place on one occasion at Yayayi in 1974.

One morning a group of men gathered near a white gum tree on the creek bank where they waited for two older men. A younger man had, as they put it ambiguously, "found something." But they did not know what it was. Because they had close relationships with the traditional owners of this area, the two elders were presumed to have special knowledge of local myth. On the one hand, the men were fearful about the consequences of the discovery, lest the owners of the country attack them with sorcery for disturbing a secret site. On the other hand, they wondered if the discovery were "gold" or "opal," value for which the owners might pay them.

When the older men arrived, the group went down to the creek and examined the discovery, an outcrop of some sedimentary crusty rock that had been exposed by erosion. The men chipped off a bit and examined the colors, then dug around the area to expose more of the rock. Although one man expressed his fear of sorcery for having desecrated a sacred site belonging to others, the enterprise continued. One of the two elders speculated confidently that this rock must be from the Kangaroo Dreaming with which the creek is associated. Knowing that two men in The Dreaming had speared a kangaroo at a point five miles east, he deduced that they must

This view of Yunytjunya, in the Kintore Range, from the southeast
shows the outstretched neck (at the right) of the Dreamtime Ngintaka,
the Monitor Lizard, as it turned to stone. (1974)

Yanyatjarri Tjakamarra's unusual figurative painting (acrylics on
canvas) of Yunytjunya represents the hill as the Dreamtime Ngintaka
who turned into stone there. (Yayayi, 1974)

have gutted it here on the way back. No one had ever told him this, however. The Papunya people were ignorant of this fact, he said.

This Kangaroo Dreaming, the men maintained, is important because it is associated with ceremonies in which men "show special designs (*wamulu*) and make women and children go under a blanket." As the men continued digging, three of them looked to see if there was gold in the composite; for others, "gold" was simply a metaphorical equivalent to the traditional value of sacred sites. Throughout the inquiry, the participants oscillated between assuring themselves that the owners of the country had told them not to be afraid if they found anything hereabouts and a hopefulness that they would be paid for "finding" this thing.

Finally, examining the uneven distribution of colors in the composite, they decided it was the sloppy stomach contents of the gutted Dreaming kangaroo. The red elements in it, one man suggested, must be the vegetable fluff that had been colored with red ochre and stuck to the two men's bodies, since traveling with body decoration was common for many mythological figures.

All in all, the men's behavior showed cautious concern, meant to avoid punishment for desecration. They justified their digging up of the composite and chipping of it by saying it was necessary so that the owners would not think they were lying when they went to tell them they had found "gold." Eventually the spot was covered with leaves and the old men told the women camped nearby that no one was to go near the area. Subsequently, little was made of the event, at least to my knowledge, but one man continued to talk of the find. He was concerned, he said, because his son was "from this Dreaming," that is, conceived nearby. By now, everyone was satisfied that the rock was the stomach contents of the gutted kangaroo who had been speared and must have been crawling along the creek trying to return to his *ngurra* near Yayayi soakage.

Geography as Code

We can see in this episode not only how previously unknown local detail can be incorporated into an already known myth by a deductive process, but also the concern that the Pintupi have for "explaining" the existence of strange geological formations and shapes—or more generally why there is something at a place at all. People who go out hunting sometimes return with a pocketful of strangely shaped or colored rocks, pointing out that they are, unexpectedly, "different." They seem to ponder these occurrences as *possible* new information, but they do not produce theoretical explanations easily.

The unusual is valuable in itself. Within the contemporary cash economy, the finder may suspect that the unusual is "gold" and hope to exchange it for money. For most, the worth of gold is a metaphorical equivalent for the value they already attribute to things that are "different." Most sacred sites are said, therefore, to be "gold."

The process by which space becomes "country," by which a story gets attached to an object, is part of the Pintupi habit of mind that looks behind objects to events and sees in objects a sign of something else. To the hunter's mind, anything other than the ordinary on the ground can be a sign that something has happened. The landscape itself offers clues about what may have happened. Not only does it reveal something about the invisible, but it offers a link to the invisible forces that created it and whose essence is embodied in it. As with a code, "country" signifies the whole event of which it was a part, carrying "a meaning which refers to the missing parts and is information about those parts" (Bateson 1972: 414).

The concern of the Pintupi is to gain knowledge about that which is invisible, which is important and powerful. Conversely, they are uncomfortable about that which is hidden (*yarrka*). Dreams may be seen as signs, as potential sources of information about what will happen, or as revelations of The Dreaming, but it is hard to be certain about such information. What the Pintupi must rely on is the knowledge that is handed down socially. The designs and stories they paint on novices, Pintupi emphasize, are not made up. One's predecessors, "those who are dead," had known these stories before; they are from The Dreaming. The value of ceremonies, designs, and objects, as the Pintupi formulate explicitly, is that they are true, their veracity guaranteed indexically by their actual connection to "first things."[13] These properties enter into the social processes of Pintupi life in several ways.

The Pintupi use the visible evidence of the world as a sign to interpret that which happened and is invisible. Country is valuable both for its iconic relationship to The Dreaming (telling a story) and also for the indexical relationship between places and the ancestral power left behind in them. However, the information visible in the landscape is not sufficient in itself to illuminate the underlying reality. Nor is knowledge of "what happened" in detail freely available. The necessary keys are the highly valued ("dear") ceremonies, which reenact The Dreaming's events at particular places. Custodianship of these rituals and the associated sites is a zealously guarded prerogative. Indeed, knowledge of this sort is controlled by older people, and each site is identified with a group of "owners."

Those who "own" a ritual and a place, the joint entity called an "estate" by Stanner (1965), assume responsibility for their care and preservation: They must "hold on to The Dreaming." They must also pass it on to the future. Through initiation and a long process of epiphany in revelatory ceremonies, younger men and women gradually are taught how to interpret and act toward the invisible world that underlies their immediate physical and social world. Pintupi describe the process as giving (*yunginpa*) knowledge to young people, as revealing (*yutininpa*) it, or as teaching it (*nintininpa*). In this regard, the visibility/invisibility contrast reproduces the temporal process of generational succession in Pintupi social life.

However, given the nature of The Dreaming, this knowledge remains particulate and localized. If the imprint of Dreaming events on the country embodies a temporal process, the fact that Pintupi country is continuous—a set of interconnected Dreaming tracks— is equally significant. This property of the country is a concomitant of the continuity of social networks, ultimately deriving from the sharing of knowledge of places among people who are geographically disparate.

From one point of view, named places are signs from which Pintupi can interpret events in The Dreaming. From another perspective, it is also true that places can code or punctuate events in the phenomenal world. For Maantja tjungurrayi, the place Walukirritjinya is where his father was killed and buried; Tjulyurunya is the place he himself was conceived; at another place he was initiated; his mother died at Tjitururrnga; and so on. For each individual, the landscape becomes a history of significant social events. Geography serves, it would seem, as a signifier of experiences; previous events become attached to places and are recited as one moves across the country.

History, then, is incorporated into the unchanging, ever-present features of the physical landscape. The question is really to what extent this incorporation of history occurs: What endures and what is erased? The concept of *ngurra* offers considerable flexibility for expressing different kinds of relationships between persons and between persons and space, but it also elides their differences. The Pintupi inclusion of two levels of organization, "camp" and "country," in a single term reflects this possibility of reification, of action being converted to a structure that becomes the foundation for further action.

What leads a people to emphasize a changeless, timeless permanence? I am not, of course, describing a "philosophy" in any formal sense, but rather a construction of reality to which people subscribe in less self-conscious ways. The principle embodied in The Dreaming is nothing less than the principle by which parts of Pintupi social structure are ranked in relation to each other, the relation of part to whole that Dumont (1980) calls "hierarchy." Ultimately (and I explore this in detail in succeeding chapters), the structure of Pintupi society defines the meaning of "the world."

To be sure, the erasure of the historical is not confined to The Dreaming. Taboos on mentioning the names of the dead, shallow genealogies, and the lack of a written record also serve in this regard (cf. Sansom 1980). The Dreaming—"the Law"—provides a moral authority lying outside the individual and outside human creation. It is not his idea or his will. Thus, although The Dreaming as an ordering of the cosmos is presumably a product of historical events, such an origin is denied. These human creations are objectified— thrust out—into principles or precedents for the immediate world. As in Plato's Cave, the Ideal comes first. The principles to which the Pintupi look for guidance and which they manipulate in daily life are not seen as the creations of contemporary men and women. Consequently, current action is not understood as the result of human alliances, creations, and choices, but is seen as imposed by an embracing, cosmic order. This construction of temporality is intricately tied to Pintupi politics, Pintupi ideas of what a person is, and theories of action.

The Dreaming, then, can be reduced to its significant features, which constitute it as transcending the immediate and present. The concept dichotomizes the world into that which is *yuti* ("visible") and that which is *tjukurrpa*, where the latter lies outside human affairs and constitutes an enduring, primary reality. This construction occurs in space, on the landscape, where it creates places with enduring identity and relationship to other sites. Finally, The Dreaming provides the source of both humanity and the landscape. As we shall see, this construction reflects the reproduction of Pintupi social life through time, organizing a basic and given autonomy into a larger system.

While the two critical qualities of The Dreaming, timelessness and segmented extension in space, correspond to Lévi-Strauss's theory of "totemic structures" as synthesizing constructs (Lévi-Strauss 1962, 1966), their meaning for the Pintupi should be sought within a particular form of social life rather than in ahistorical philosophical concerns. Through their inclusion in The Dreaming, the principles employed by people in the negotiations of daily life have a claim to being outside the creation of the manipulators; they are instead timeless truths. Erasing the specific past, The Dreaming pursues continuities between current human action and a realm of order transcending human affairs.

The Pintupi appropriation of temporality is guided, I will show, by the two basic problems of Pintupi social life, the tension between relatedness and differentiation and that between hierarchy and equality. As an order outside of human subjectivity which is morally imperative, The Dreaming can also be understood in relationship to the problem of hierarchy in a small-scale society where egalitarian relations are valued, and to the organization of a regional system of sociality. It is not accidental that the sources of what Westerners would think of as autonomy and authority are considered by the Pintupi to exist "outside" the self, projected outward into The Dreaming and onto the landscape where they are available as social artifacts. This projection of a domain "outside" society answers two constraints that impede certain kinds of coordinated social action: (1) the web of mutual obligation and relatedness between people in this society of former hunter-gatherers, based on their need for help from each other, and (2) the value placed on equality or personal autonomy, such that no one is prepared to be told by others what to do.

CHAPTER 3

Individuals and Bands

*My country is the place where I can cut a spear or make a
spear-thrower without asking anyone.*
(Western Desert man, quoted in Tindale 1974: 18)

Problem?

This chapter takes up one dimension of Pintupi organization in
space: the problem of "bands." The variability of these formations is of central importance. Pintupi people did not always live
with the same coresidential group or even within a single territory.
I do not treat this variability, however, as just one more example
of the "flexibility" of hunting-and-gathering social systems (Lee and
DeVore 1968). In the Pintupi case, the mobility of individuals is a
primary feature of the social structure. As such, it encourages a
significant revision of our thinking about bands.

To do so suggests that we should recognize the spatial component
of production in hunting-and-gathering societies, rather than envi-
sioning the organization of productive roles as reflecting only the
division of labor by sex. Among the Pintupi, the relationships of
individuals to land enter into their social identities in a direct and
immediate fashion. Pintupi insist, for example, that individuals
who can marry must be from different localities. Locality is not
something merely added on, so that productive units can be situated
in space. Marriage establishes not only the immediate relations of
production but also, by creating ties between distant people, establishes relations of production and access to land within a larger
ecological region.

Bands, Land, and People

The prolonged debate about the kind of groups in which Aborigines
live (Radcliffe-Brown 1930, Hiatt 1962, Meggitt 1962, Stanner 1965,
Birdsell 1970, Tindale 1974, Peterson 1975, Myers 1982) has focused
largely on the relationship between residential groups and ownership

of land. These arguments reflect theoretical assumptions about social structure that give priority to actual groups.

Indeed, when Radcliffe-Brown (1930) conceptualized the problem of organization, he treated groups as given and basic units. In his formulation, the basic elements of social structure in Australia were the family and the "horde." The horde, "a small group owning and occupying a definite territory or hunting ground" (Radcliffe-Brown 1930: 321), was the most important local group throughout the continent, an independent and autonomous unit that acted as a unit in relations with other hordes. Others followed him in this view of a system of bounded, patrilineal, and patrilocal groups (Steward 1955, Service 1962, Birdsell 1970), identifying landowning descent groups with residential groups.

Such a nondialectical view of descent and groups has not only been questioned on general grounds (Barnes 1962, Scheffler 1966). As a form of territorial organization among hunters and gatherers in an inhospitable environment, the closure of such formations is empirically improbable (cf. Lee 1968, 1976, 1979 for the !Kung San). Although descent theorists' concern for what endures through time is not entirely mistaken, it is cast at the wrong level.

Pintupi territorial organization diverges markedly from such models of group closure. Their mobility makes it inappropriate to assume the existence of enduring, physically corporate or coresiding social groups. Doubtless, structures emphasizing more bounded groups have existed elsewhere in Australia. Understanding Pintupi conceptions of spatial organization, however, implicitly challenges the positivist bias of treating bands as a given; the formation of a group should be seen as a social accomplishment, and not simply taken for granted. Furthermore, the significance of individual mobility in Pintupi social life does not mean that all enduring structures are lacking. The ego-centered qualities of Pintupi society are themselves social facts, the products of a larger system. To grasp these dialetical relations, one must start with individual action, as the Pintupi do.

Pintupi data make it necessary to differentiate between two levels of spatial organization that have been called, often ambiguously, bands: on-the-ground residential groupings and more enduring social formations (landowning groups) related to place. Because this distinction frequently becomes a matter of some confusion among those who write about hunting-and-gathering peoples, and especially so in the secondary literature, my discussion will be as concrete as possible.

Generally, in Australia, the term "band" has been used to refer to on-the-ground residential aggregations of persons for economic,

Pintupi Country, Pintupi Self

land-exploiting purposes. These groups have been analytically distinguished from "clans" or "descent groups" of persons who own or control land as ritual property, what Stanner (1965) called an "estate." It is land as ritual property, essentially, that constitutes the object of ownership.[1] More narrowly economic aspects of the land have been defined, contrastingly, as "range" (Stanner 1965: 1–2), that is, the area in which a group normally travels in pursuit of routine economic activities. In the face of these potentially different domains of organization, informant statements about space, group life, relatedness, and living arrangements ought to be interpreted as complex statements relating to multiple areas of social reality.

The native model of local organization differs in important respects from most theoretical accounts of hunter-gatherer organization. Not only is it essentially individual-centered, but the Pintupi concept of "one countryman" incorporates a temporal perspective: It focuses on the set of social relations (of coresidence and economic cooperation) with numerous others that an individual can expect to exercise over a long period. Thus, at both levels of territorial organization, residence and landownership, groups are the outcome of processes of individual choice and negotiation, influenced by demography and environmental pressures.

In my analysis neither actual bands (as units) nor cultural rules (as principles of recruitment) are basic. For the Pintupi, the basic organizational category ("one countryman") instead represents the social relations of production within a region. The productive dimension can be realized, however, only in temporary and changing band formations. This condition makes the actual properties of band life extremely important. The lack of closure and the emphasis on negotiability in membership—as well as the dispersive tendencies of bands—are dialectically related to the organization of the larger regional system. Rather than postulating concrete local groups as basic units of a larger system, the indigenous model of relatedness among individuals reveals how mobility and flexible boundaries for land use are organized into a larger structure of regional organization.

The details about the organization of Pintupi individuals and groups presented in this chapter are derived from life history material; they are, therefore, largely reconstructions of past movements and subsistence. For this reason, I use the past tense to describe events and practices as they occurred prior to contact with whites. Where these activities continue in the present, I use the present tense. While admittedly awkward in places, this choice makes clear the necessary distinction between a theoretical "ethnographic present" and the true present.

Local groupings reflected the necessities of making a living in the Western Desert, although they were not simply production units. Band life provided both an emphasis on relationship with others and a basis for autonomy, not only in terms of immediate production but over the longer-term cycles that brought people into contact with varying others.

In the traditional subsistence pattern, an ideal division of labor by sex is symbolized by the contrast in men's and women's tools (cf. C. Berndt 1974, Hamilton 1980). This division of labor is critical in defining gender identity, with males often specified in ordinary conversation as "those with spear-throwers" (*lankurrutjarra*) and females as "those with digging sticks" (*wanatjarra*). Characteristically, Pintupi men used the spear-thrower, spear, throwing stick, boomerang, and shield. Women, on the other hand, used digging sticks, carrying dishes, and grinding stones. The maintenance tools for this set, such as the stone ax and adze, belonged to men and were usually used by them, although women were able to use them to make tools. It was most often men, however, who made implements for women.

In subsistence, women gathered relatively immobile foods, including plant foods (*mayi*), honey ants, wood-boring grubs (*maku*), small lizards, and feral cats. They ground grass seeds of many varieties into cakes to be cooked or into a wet paste. Fruits were usually eaten right away but could be pulverized into storable balls.[2]

Men hunted, when possible, large meat animals such as kangaroos (*marlu*), other large marsupials (hare wallabies [*mala*], for example), or emus (*tjakipirri*). When these were unavailable, as was frequently the case, men collected lizards or hunted feral cats, small marsupials, and rabbits. Throughout the year, lizards of many varieties provided the bulk of protein for the desert-dwelling Pintupi, and were collected by both sexes (Gould 1969b, Long 1971: 268, Thomson 1964: 202). Though men also collected fruits and grubs when they came of season in large quantity, they did so largely for their own use. Lacking carrying implements like the women's dishes, they did not collect and bring these items back to camp for sharing.

Despite the importance of small reptiles, for much of the time the Pintupi remained dependent on vegetable foods. Women were the primary collectors and preparers of this staple, estimated to provide between 60 and 80 percent of the diet in desert areas (Gould 1969b: 258, Meggitt 1964). Thus, women were able to provide for the regular day-to-day food supplies, and men were able, as Peterson remarked more generally, to "leave their families for weeks at a time to go to a ceremony or visit another band" (1974: 22). This organization of production allowed considerable economic autonomy. Both adult men and women were able to maintain themselves independently of the opposite sex (C. Berndt 1974: 80). The complementarity of men's and women's activities made conjugal families reasonably independent in production, though a family would rarely live alone.

Frequent movement to different localities was necessary, but the usual pattern of subsistence was to exploit the resources around a base camp near a water hole. Foragers would move from this base during the day and return to it in the evening. According to Gould (1969b), when the supply of vegetable food within five miles of the water hole diminished, the camp would move to another source of water. Likewise, if the water ran out, they moved.

This combination of resources (disparate patches of vegetable foods, scattered water supplies, and nongregarious meat animals) and technology (tools requiring the operation of one person) made cooperation in production itself unnecessary, though often beneficial. Men occasionally engaged in cooperative drives of hill kangaroos or of hare wallabies (Finlayson 1935: 46, 61), but more commonly they went hunting alone or in small groups. When men were successful in hunting large game, the food was distributed inter-domestically, to those others throughout the residential group who shared their production with the hunter(s). Gifts of meat could satisfy other obligations (for example, to one's in-laws or parents) as well. The greater bulk of a fifty- to sixty-pound kangaroo would make such distribution economically practical: Without methods of preservation, a large supply of meat spoils in the time it takes for a few people to eat it. Distribution, on the other hand, leads to a future return in kind.

In any case, the preparation of large game treats it as a social product. According to custom, a hunter gives the kangaroo he kills to others for preparation. For his services, the cook gets the tail, prized for its fat, but the hunter tells the cook how to distribute the parts of the cooked animal (Gould 1969a: 17) and keeps the head for himself. A hunter who is married and has a family may keep several other parts as well. Thus, a man's kill would be distributed in cooked form beyond the conjugal family, and the meat would be eaten at other camps. While men and women may distribute small game such as lizards, it is not mediated by another person's preparation. The hunter either cooks the lizards and gives them to people or distributes them in raw form.

Though women, often with their children, foraged in small

groups for protection, the actual collection and preparation was performed singly. Much of women's production was brought back to the residential camp for final preparation and consumption. Women usually prepared what they collected themselves. In camp, the food was shared with the immediate family, often given in exchange for child-care services while a mother was foraging (B. Clark, personal communication), and distributed to coresidents who had not fared well. In addition women commonly provided vegetable food, as "sisters," "mothers," or "father's sisters," for unmarried male relatives. The exchange of women's products was, like men's, interdomestic although more informal and confined to close kin.

An observer sees such products move rather freely throughout a residential group. Generally, coresidents are expected to share with each other. That frequently this sharing takes place only on request of the needy lends the distribution of production more of the character of "mutual taking" than of some idealized primitive communism.

Production could be accomplished by a single individual or by a single nuclear family, but there were some economic advantages to living with others. One advantage was to reduce the burden of supporting the very old and very young by sharing it among a larger group of active producers (Peterson 1974). Another advantage of coresidence was contingent on the regular distribution of large game throughout the camp: The overall chance that someone in the group might bring back a game animal would improve with a larger number of hunters, because they could cover more area. Having several hunters in a band also meant that a fairly constant supply of meat could be maintained without the same individuals going out every day. A similar advantage is implied in the women's exchange of services. One woman could stay in camp looking after children and old people, while another went out to forage and then shared the return. A final value in aggregation, however, cannot be construed in production terms: that is the protection from attack.

The advantages to gathering in a band would not have accrued ordinarily to a very large group. Water supplies did not, in any case, permit continuous large aggregations, but other resources remained fairly sparse as well. If population in an area were increased dramatically, the returns from hunting would decline. Further, distribution of foraging production in a large group creates pressures and conflicts. Judging from current patterns, these conflicts were frequently concerned with sharing and allocating products and services among a large group of coresident "kin." Since all coresidents had some claims on each other, large groups placed a considerable strain on individuals, producing conflicts of loyalty as well

Pintupi Country, Pintupi Self

as continuous impositions on one's generosity. Indeed, the pressure to share one's products with coresidents may not only have diminished people's incentives to hunt and collect more than they absolutely needed, as Peterson (personal communication) suggests,[3] but also have led gatherings to disperse.

On the other hand, a good deal of individual autonomy is sustained within this system of production. Though cooperation with others in a band may have utility, it is possible for people to live on their own, or to leave a band and join another. Unlike Eskimos on the winter ice, for example (Balikci 1970), Pintupi could leave a group, and unlike Pygmies (Turnbull 1961), they could forage without benefit of cooperative labor.

Movement

Since resources in any one area were quickly exhausted, the daily rhythm of Pintupi life around a camp was part of the larger nomadic pattern of movement from water hole to water hole. The likely range of a year's movement for a nuclear family was within an area of 3,000 square miles. These movements and the aggregation and dispersal of people into larger and smaller groups depended on seasonal changes.

In the hot, dry summer months, people congregated around a few permanent, well-known, and reliable water sources—usually wells. One much-used line of wells, for example, is known as *yintawara* ("line of big waters") and runs from Jupiter Well south toward the Baron Range. Although requiring some aggregation of population, these gatherings rarely exceeded fifty persons (Long 1971: 266). The great distance between waters made movement between places difficult, so people remained somewhat confined during summer. When a water supply did diminish, travel by night to another "permanent" water source was a common way to avoid the day's heat.

With the onset of heavy summer rains, the congregations split up into smaller groups, moving out to exploit the smaller temporary surface waters (*pinangu*)—claypans or rock holes—and the game there. In areas with large claypans, great supplies of the seed plant *mungilpa* attracted significant gatherings of people.

In the cold winter months, lizards (especially goannas) were hunted in their burrows by firing off the grass cover. This period was described as one of little vegetable food and great reliance on meat, necessitating short stays in each camp site and frequent moves. Judging from the few observations on record, winter groups rarely exceeded twenty persons (Long 1971). The Pintupi took advantage of the necessity for frequent movement by making this period one of visiting kinfolk who lived far away. At large water holes, groups could gather for a time to perform religious ceremonies and general camp singing, learning new song cycles from their distant relatives. As the season turned again toward the hot time, when the goannas emerge from their burrows for mating (spring [*tuulparra*]), people began to return to their own permanent waters for another summer.

If the locale provided sufficient abundance at any time during the year, messengers might be sent to invite neighbors for a large ceremonial gathering. Desert rainfall is unpredictable, but winter seems to have been a common time for such events. One of the chief reasons for large ceremonial gatherings was the initiation of young men. When a boy was seized for initiation by members of his local group, he and ritual guardians would be dispatched to locate distant groups that would send men and women to his initiation (see chapter 8). During his journey as a "pre-initiate" (*yulpuru* or *malulu*), his own host group moved along a preplanned travel route and the visitors accompanied the boy on his return. The congregation for an initiation would be temporary, perhaps one week, followed by the visitors' return to their own countries. Some individuals frequently stayed on longer. Most men attended such an event every year.

Gatherings for other male rituals seem to have followed a similar pattern of sending out messengers to bring back participants. Significant among these was the *Tingarri* ritual cycle, performed for groups of secluded postinitiation novices by senior men. Those who came either participated as novices or "showed" the revelatory ceremonies of which they were the custodians. On occasions such as these, men often left their wives behind and traveled with a group of men. Young unmarried men traveled long distances to take part in such ceremonial cycles. On other occasions, groups came together so that a large number of men could visit a sacred site and perform a ritual there.[4] According to the Pintupi, one must not visit a sacred site without a large group of men. Those who had not previously visited the place were instructed in its mythological associations.

Consequently, in the course of their lifetimes, Pintupi individuals traveled far outside of their traditional country. My estimate is that people were well-acquainted with an area no less than 200 miles in every direction from their main water hole. The families encountered by Thomson (1975) and Long (1971) in 1957, for example, had been living 100 to 160 miles from their country. Beyond such limits, it seems, the country was inhabited by those whom people did not know well. There they felt insecure. Distance, we shall see, imposed itself as a constraint on the Pintupi organizational structure.

A Glimpse at the Social Reality of Band Life

It is necessary to conceptualize Pintupi social life at the residential level through individuals. Pintupi maintain that society, as they see it, is potentially boundary-less, that individual networks and ritual links extend beyond any definable group. No one, they say, lived entirely in one place, with a single set of people, at one water hole, as if in "a paddock."

I recorded several life histories of men, and one of a woman, who had lived as hunter-gatherers relatively uninfluenced by the presence of white Australians. Their narratives indicate that Pintupi moved around, changed residential groups, visited, and regularly encountered new persons and places. Consideration of one of these life histories will help to relate statements about group life, group membership, relatedness, and living arrangements to the complex and multiple domains of social reality as experienced by the Pintupi.

The particular narrative discussed here was gathered during 1974 from Maantja tjungurrayi, a man from the Lake Macdonald region who was then about sixty-five years old.[5] Only a few excerpts will be offered to illustrate characteristic patterns, as well as to indicate the highly personal nature of local organization. (Those who wish to pursue the life history in detail will find more extensive portions in Myers 1976: 234–308.) For convenience, I have segmented the narrative into meaningful chunks, for which I provide some comment and cross-references to several maps.

The account begins with Maantja's childhood:

Maantja remembers playing as a child in the sandhills around Wartangkatjanya while his father had gone hunting. Two men approached the camp; they had seen the smoke of Maantja's family's fire. They were Putarru tjakamarra and Tjuntalnga tjupurrula, "one countrymen" of Maantja. Putarru asked where Maantja's father was, and referred to Maantja's mother, Manngawa nakamarra, as "sister." When Maantja's father returned, tjakamarra told him they had left a group of people behind and invited Maantja's group to accompany them to Wantaritjanya. Here, women welcomed his father, whom they knew, but although Maantja saw children playing he was too shy to join them because he did not know them. The combined group now went on to Minyuratjanya. They were traveling along small water holes because it was spring (*tuulparra*). After Tjuntalnga speared a kangaroo and a second was killed by a hunting dog, women collected firewood and the meat was cooked in the camp. During the

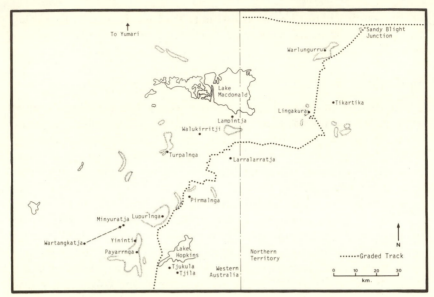

Map 3A. Maantja's Travels

days, children played around camp until the adults called to them to
go to sleep. At this place, they ate a lot of *pura*, a wild tomato
(*Solaneum* species), as well as meat, women returning in the
afternoon with food. While his mother was foraging, other "mothers"
or "father's sisters" would look after him, feeding him and then
sending him back to his own camp to wait. When his mother came
back, he would go and get a goanna from her. Later he might see his
father return and excitedly observe, "Oh, he has a cat." (Map 3A)

Maantja describes the group as including his parents, his "mother's brother" (Putarru), and Tjuntalnga. Putarru's own country,
however, was northeast of Lake Macdonald, about sixty-five miles
from Minyuratjanya. Though Maantja describes some people who
regularly coresided with him as Tjuntalnga's "close brothers,"
Tjuntalnga was born at Warlungurru (Kintore Range) and was of the
same country as Putarru. Tjuntalnga's sister was married to an older
man of Maantja's country, Niwilnga.

Next the group traveled to Tjunukutjarranya. They noticed the
smoke from a fire in the south, at Tjalirangaranya. Two men came
and informed them that a large group of people were gathered there.
The gathering included those on their way from cutting *mulyarti*
(one variety of acacia tree, ideal for spears, that grows in restricted
areas of western Pintupi country) as well as some Pitjantjatjarra
people from the south. Maantja's group joined the others, who

Pintupi Country, Pintupi Self

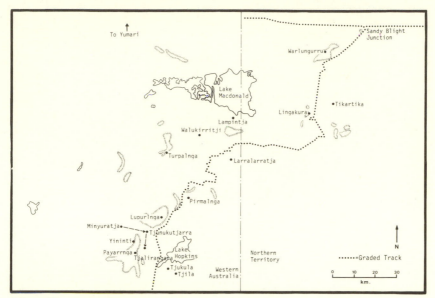

Map 3B. Maantja's Travels

included the father of Karawa tjapangarti—a close countryman of Maantja. A fight broke out when a man discovered someone had "stolen" one of his wives. The combatants shed blood copiously from spear wounds in the thighs, and the children cried at the sight. The two co-wives fought as well. Finally, the fight ended with injury to all. The aggrieved man told his rival, "Okay, you keep her," and the two wounded men slept by the same fire. (Map 3B)

These groups came together, having sighted each other's fires. The Pitjantjatjarra were traveling with Karawa's father to obtain special spear wood, since the latter could visit the western spear-wood country as a relative of its residents. He was also considered a close countryman of Maantja. Maantja himself frequently lived with Pitjantjatjarra people, whose own country was immediately to the south of his. The fight, a typical one between two classificatory brothers over women, resulted in the husband spearing the amorous suitor of one of his wives and then, his rights satisfied, relinquishing his claim.

From Tjalirangaranya, the group split up. Some went to Ngitjitju-turunya, while Maantja's group went to Mipantjarranya, his "father's country." They saw a fire from the direction of Tjitururrnga (Buck Hills) in the north, and then they awaited the arrival of Katji tjapangarti, whom Maantja called "my daddy."[6] Katji, an unmarried man, said he had recently left Yumarinya. He joined their group, and

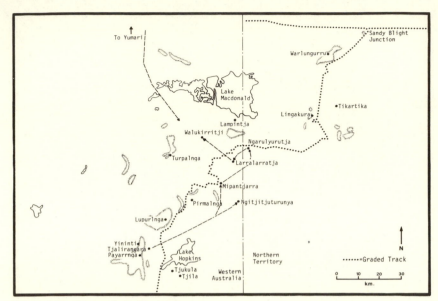

Map 3C. Maantja's Travels

all went to Ngarulyurrutjanya, where they camped. Then they went to Larralarratjanya and on to Walukirritjinya, a large permanent water source in the Turner Hills. Here they were joined by a large group of people who came from Yumarinya and Tjitururrnga, of which Katji had been the advance party. There were a lot of people and, again, Maantja was "shy." They danced and sang a *tjulpurrpa* (a ceremony in which men, women, and children sing, but only men dance). The northerners knew it and taught it to Maantja's group. (Map 3C)

Katji was a good friend of Maantja's father and they often traveled together. Katji's country was said to be the Gordon Hills area and north of it, thirty-five miles north of Maantja's father's main water source in the Turner Hills; these were adjacent local areas and visiting common. Shortly after his arrival, more of Katji's countrymen from the north joined the group, and all went to the larger water hole at Walukirritjinya. Indeed, subsequent interviews showed that Maantja remained in close relationship with Katji. It is important to notice that Putarru, Tjuntalnga, and Katji were all visiting temporarily with Maantja's group at the same time. Such common experiences of coresidence appear to have considerable consequences through time: Many years later, Putarru's son and daughter married Katji's daughter and son. Similarly, Tjuntalnga's sister's son (Bobby, Genealogy 6B), though a countryman of Maantja,

Pintupi Country, Pintupi Self

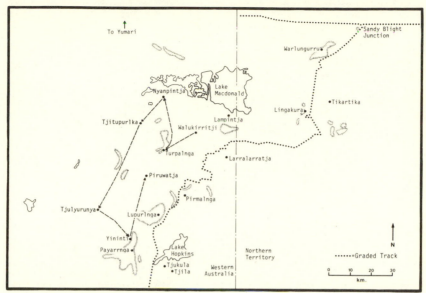

Map 3D. Maantja's Travels

continues to maintain important relationships with the people of Warlungurrunya. These connections are indicative of how residential associations are reflected and reproduced through time by means of marriage.

> From Walukirritjinya, the group traveled to Turpalnga, a large water source nearby, where the men hunted locally abundant euros, a hill-dwelling variety of kangaroo. Then they went to Nyanpintjanya and subsequently to Nyuntinkutjarranya (a soakage), to Tjitupulkanya, and to Warrpungunya. They were heading around to meet "Tupa's mob," who were south of here. (Tupa tjangala was a boy then, a contemporary of Maantja and still a close associate.) So they went on to Tjulyurunya and then to Yinintinya where they came together, "all family." Then they went to Yarnangkatjanya and to Piruwatjanya. (Map 3D)

It is difficult to say precisely who was included in Tupa's group at this time. Since he was a boy, he was probably with his father. One of his father's wives was the daughter of Niwilnga and the sister's daughter of Tjuntalnga. Despite their close relationship, the residential paths of Tupa and Maantja have intersected only at times. Their families have different kinship and affinal orientations.

> At Piruwatjanya, they encountered three Pitjantjatjarra men from the south who had seen their fires. These men had gone west for

Individuals and Bands   83

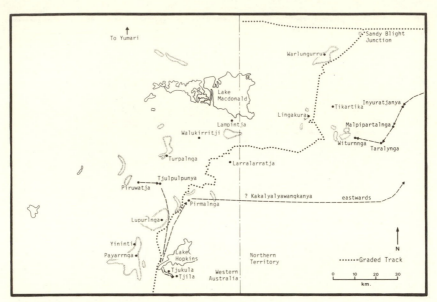

Map 3E. Maantja's Travels

mulyarti wood and were returning. From Piruwatjanya, Maantja's group went to Tjulpulpunya. It was summertime (*yupuntju*), the period of extreme heat when the small waters are dry and only the large semipermanent waters (*yinta*) can sustain people. They went to Tjilanya, a large water source near Lake Hopkins, and then to Pirmalnga, a major water supply. They stayed here until it rained (heavy rains often fall in midsummer). During the rain, they went to the caves at Kakalyalyawangkanya for shelter. From here they went to Ilpilinya, a large claypan that fills up with surface water after rain. They camped here and subsequently journeyed to Pukaratjanya. It was *pinangu* time, when surface water lies on the ground in puddles and the small waters are replenished; travel is then easy, and people leave the main waters where food has grown scarce. They saw fires in the east, burning near Yilpilinya (referring here to the Ehrenberg Range). Tukinnga tjungurrayi, a Mayutjarra man, came to meet them. He said that a group of people was gathered to the east, at Mount Liebig and Wilpiyanya, so Maantja's group accompanied him eastward to Inyuratjanya, Malpipartalnga, and then to Taralynga, from which they could see a lot of fires. They continued eastward to Ngarrkalirrinya, nearing the smokes, and at Witurnnga they met the large group. Maantja remembers seeing a large number of people and a fight over an old grievance between Tukinnga and a classificatory brother. (Map 3E)

This encounter seems to have been with a group of Mayutjarra

Pintupi Country, Pintupi Self

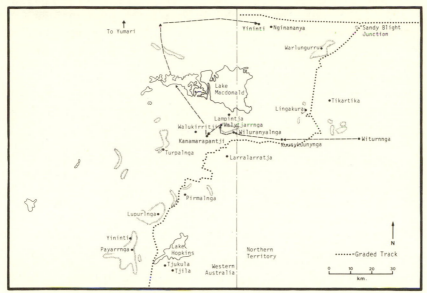

Map 3F. Maantja's Travels

(often called Loritja) who lived east of Maantja's country and south of Mount Liebig. The messenger who conducted them is mentioned several times in Maantja's accounts: he is a regular acquaintance. (Incidentally, Tukinnga's son regards Maantja as his "father," insisting they are "from one country.") This meeting lasted only a few days.

> After a few days, everyone went west: to Tjalpiyatjanunya, Tjutirangutjanya, Kuunykuunynga, and Wiluranyalnga. They saw a smoke and headed toward the rock hole at Walytjarnga. From here they traveled to Wakalpukatjanya, to Lurngunya, and then to Kanamarapantjinya. Maantja saw the people at Yinintinya and they all went to Nginananya (east of Muwinynga); these people were those associated with the Kintore Range. They went to Yultutjarranya, and Maantja remembers asking about white people; they had heard of them but never seen any. At Yultutjarranya, men, women, and children sang *pulapa* ceremonies. People from Marpurinya, Pinarinya (to the north and northwest), and Ngalia (Warlpiri) from the northeast all danced. They knew the songs, but Maantja's group did not. During the day, women and children went for food, while men performed secret aspects of the ritual. Women told the children to stay away from the men. In the afternoon, the old men came up, informing everyone to come to the public performance: "We're ready now." Maantja remembers seeing people whose country was far to the west. (Map 3F)

NoMADS

Obviously, this large gathering just after summer was for ceremonial purposes. It is impossible to determine how many people were present, although it is clear that those present included people from several local areas. That some were from as far away as the Pollock Hills, 100 miles to the west, indicates the range of Maantja's own orbit of acquaintances. He encountered many of these people again later in life, when he married a woman from the area.

Finally, the ceremony finished and everyone returned to their own countries. The Mayutjarra people went to Yilpilinya in the Ehrenberg Range. Maantja and his group traveled to Tjitururrnga, and the western people ("those from *mulyarti* country") turned homeward. Maantja's group next went to Tjinaltjanya (south of Karlutjarranya), to Palkartinya (an Emu Dreaming place), to Ngukarnunya and Tampirrpungkunya (both Emu Dreaming places), and to Yarannga. They camped there and then went to Piripirinya and to Ngartannga, which he identified with Tjiwa Tjiwa tjangala. From here they went to Kukakutjarranya: they were "returning" to Walukirritjinya, which was "close now." In the sky, they saw the smokes of fires lit in the hunt for meat. They went south to Kuunykuunynga, Putantatjanya, Kakalyalyawangkanya, Piltjatjanya, Nyuuntjarranya, Papunynga, Miturmalunya, and Nyiinkuwakalnga. On the way, he remembers, the heat of the ground burned his feet. They turned east toward Yarnangkatjanya. Here the group split up and one large part went to Mulpunya. It was "green" (*yukiripiri*) time, after the summer rains. Maantja's group went to Piruwatjanya, to Warlilinya, and finally to Kartjilnga in the Sir Frederick Range. From here they went to Yalkarnintjanya and then east to Tjukulanya (south of Lake Hopkins). They met Pitjantjatjarra people there, where he remembers seeing Nami napanangka, who later married Tupa. Then they went east to Tjarlpalynga and to Nyuunkunynga, where two men fought about a dog that had eaten kangaroo meat stored in a tree. Piyapa tjakamarra, a countryman and father of Maantja's close friend Mulpu, speared the dog and was, in turn, speared by its owner. They traveled to Parurrunya and then to Tjulyurunya, a place in Pitjantjatjarra country north of Docker River. From here they journeyed to Tjaninya and to Tjukulayarnnganya and then "started back." They went to Yiltitjarranya and Pirrupirrutjanya, where Maantja fell out of a tree and was rather scraped up. Then they went to Rilynga and to Tjunukutjarranya, "around our own country at last." Piyapa's group was living at Kuruyultunya in the Wallace Hills. (Map 3G)

In this series of movements, the residential group includes at least three conjugal families. More important is the indicated joint residence of Pintupi and Pitjantjatjarra at Tjukulanya, a place said to be owned by people of both languages. After the fight, Piyapa seems to have left the group, heading west, while Maantja and family continued south with their Pitjantjatjarra relatives. Piyapa

Pintupi Country, Pintupi Self

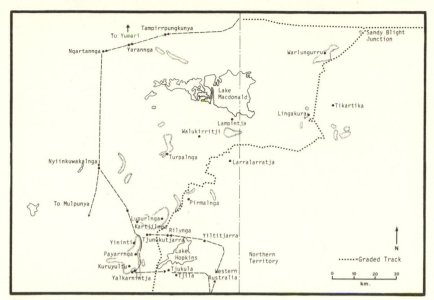

Map 3G. Maantja's Travels

and Mulpu, his son, were usually described as being "from Pay-arrnga," about thirty-five miles from Tjukulanya. They were always said to be countrymen of Maantja, his frequent coresidents.

> Maantja's group next headed to Pirmalnga, then to Lupurlnga, and to Pakirritanya, Tjanpimarrarrunya, Minyurratjanya, Warnkarnkinya, Pulpurtatjanya, Tjinangkatjanya, and to Karlututjarranya. Here, a Tjungurrayi man followed a girl who went gathering *pura*. He was already married. When he returned, the girl's father speared him, while the girl fought with the man's jealous wife. He was trying to get two wives. Her father speared him "a little bit" because she was not married. Then the group headed towards Turpalnga, stopping at Marlapilintjinya (a soakage). It was "cold time" (*yaltangka*) now, winter. (Map 3H)

This group coresided during winter time, after Maantja's family returned north from Pitjantjatjarrra country. Maantja reiterated that one goes to big waters in the hot time. At such times, one would find Tupa at Walukirritjinya. He stayed close to his own country because his father was very old, balding even. Maantja's father, on the other hand, was a young man who took him on long travels.

Life History

The physical details of Maantja's account are clear. They indicate that persons traveled widely, not confining themselves to a "band

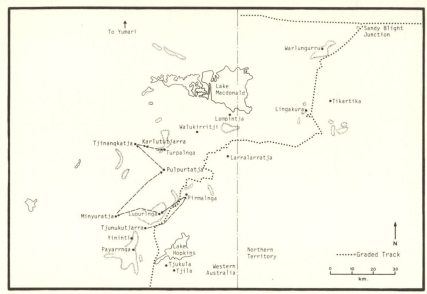

Map 3H. Maantja's Travels

area" in the sense that most sociocentric analyses of band territories imply. His journey regularly took him through areas that he ascribes to several different named groups of people. Among others, he refers to the Mayutjarra people, the Warlpiri, the Pitjantjatjarra, the Yumari mob, and those from *mulyarti* country. In Maantja's life history, as well as the others collected, the composition of coresident camps (*ngurra*) was highly variable and fluctuating. Maantja lived sometimes with various individuals and their families and at other times with people unrelated to the former. He considered all these people to be, nonetheless, his "one countrymen."

The account shows regular exploitation of certain seasonal items. These include, especially, *mungilpa* (a seed-bearing plant that grows bountifully in claypans) near Lake Macdonald, the euros at Turpalnga in the hills south of that lake, and seasonal water supplies. These were constraints on the movements of individuals and groups, but it is clear that there was no band of unvarying individuals traveling constantly between points. Individuals or small aggregates of families moved through the landscape for purposes of their own, seeing evidence of other people nearby, going to visit them, traveling with them for a time, and then returning to their own more typical grounds.

In the hot time, from November to February, people gathered at the large permanent water holes to wait for rain that would bring

They could never have a single leader b/c of their nomadic lives. *Pintupi Country, Pintupi Self* water to the smaller and temporarily dry water holes. Maantja's account indicates a general pattern of spending the hot time at one of the main waters in his "own country" as the latter was most narrowly conceived: the water holes of Walukirritjinya, Turpalnga, and Pirmalnga. When the rains came, he moved out of these to travel northward or southward, sometimes east with a small group drinking at various temporary water sources and foraging for small animals since vegetable foods were not yet ripe. The availability of these small, temporary sources of food and water allowed people to travel freely across the country, and it was during these seasons that Pintupi journeyed to distant places to visit affines and other relatives. Maantja often traveled considerable distances before turning back; usually he returned to his own large waters for the summer. Later in his life, when he was married with two wives from the north, he stayed longer there. In some years, he did not return to his "own country" at all, remaining instead with these northern affines as well as with his elderly and remarried mother. Thus, we find him frequently around the Buck Hills (Tjitururrnga). Maantja's children were all conceived in the north, which suggests that typically he resided there for some time.

These narratives document wide-ranging movement and temporary coresidence with people of various locales. There was neither expectation of nor reality to the idea of people hunting and gathering within a single "band area" with occasional visits to other bands. Maantja's commitments and obligations to a variety of individuals who were spatially separated illustrates a pattern common to all the narratives collected. Similar shifting residence patterns exist today, and even now for the Pintupi the local group does not constitute the boundaries of society or of kindred. This reality relates directly to the way Pintupi conceptualize the ties among people.

Life Cycle

A process-oriented view of Pintupi life is necessary, not only to understand residential groups and their formation, but also to realize the significance of individuals' life cycles. Indeed, Pintupi expectations recognize this. Young men described themselves as "traveling men," unable to settle down because they were too restless. Several men told me that they were always fighting when they were young, or that they used to do other dangerous things such as stealing from whites. As one man put it, "I was a young fellow then, but I'm married now." The widest range of travel that men described occurred during their young adult years, when they were too young to marry and when they sought to make connections and acquire ritual knowledge vital for maturity and political success. The onset of marriage usually brings on commitments to future affines. Young men begin to travel with those they hope will become in-laws, providing them with meat and helping them in expectation of receiving a wife. After marriage, they tend to remain with their wife's kin, or to move between their own country and that of affines.

Like their male counterparts, women at this age are not yet considered responsible. Thus, a young married woman remains with her parents, her mother does much of the cooking and looks after the children, and her kinswomen can help in the birth of children. As she grows into adult responsibilities, the couple makes a camp more distinctly their own.

Ultimately, as a couple becomes older, the man stays more consistently in his "own country" or the country to which he has become attached. Maantja described a number of such old men in his life history and characterized them as being highly localized, residing close to their more important sacred sites. Data from the other life histories support this contrast between the movement of young and old men, indicating a life-cycle pattern. Thus, the composition of bands reflects various developmental processes in Pintupi social life as well as the constraints of resource availability (cf. Peterson 1972, 1974).

One Countrymen

Pintupi articulate a view of their social reality in the concepts they translate as "country" (ngurra) and "one countryman" (ngurra kutjungurrara). Proper understanding of these concepts brings us closer to comprehending the content, quality, and processes of Pintupi social life.

The concept of "one countryman" does not necessarily refer to people who live in one territory together, nor to any sociocentrically defined group.[7] This is reflected in the discrepancies between people's view of who their countrymen are. If the groups were sociocentric, individual members of a group would each name a similar set of people as their countrymen, but they do not. Instead, the concept is ego-centered: each person has his or her own set of "one countrymen." These are the people with whom one is likely to camp. The term indicates the social reality experienced by individuals who do not always live with the same residential group or even within the same range (exploitative) area. One informant explained that he considered various people to be his "one countrymen" because they "used to travel together," even though their homelands were separate.

People, however, are also organized around ritual ties to the land—to *ngurra* as named places or "country"—as "estate." Those who share ownership of a country as an estate can also call each other "one countryman." We have noted that ownership of named places consists of rights to the ritual, sacred objects, and stories associated with these Dreaming-places. What is relevant here (and will be further explored in chapter 5) is that these country-owning groups overlap, and that individuals are able to affiliate with more than one group, each defined by ownership of a common place. The fact that people are also organized around ritual ties to the land should be treated at another analytical level, that of groups of persons defined by identification with immovable places (*ngurra*). Although ritual groups and local groups are not coextensive, the distinction is often blurred without the evidence of context and purpose. Pintupi conceptions of local organization are two-tiered, and this complexity is contained in the polysemy of *ngurra* as "named place" and as "camp." The classification of people as "from one *ngurra*" can refer either to ritual groups or to ego-centered social networks.

The concept of "one countryman" as delineating a widely extended set of persons with whom one might reside and cooperate helps us to understand the link between social relationships and space: the flexibility of both territorial boundaries and groups. While who may be a countryman is open to negotiation, what seems important is that people from one country should help each other and that claims to be "countrymen" thereby open up access to resources and labor. Because people who live together cooperate in the food quest and share resources, the egocentric concept of "one countryman" defines the set of productive relations necessary and appropriate for the conditions of Pintupi life, where one expects to live temporarily and cooperate with a variety of persons and groups.

Ngurra and People: Semiotic Links

Statements about people being "from one *ngurra*" presuppose a linkage between people and place, but not in the sense of a group living together in a single territory. Thus, Jerry tjakamarra explained to me why Simon tjupurrula, who was not his real son, ate at Jerry's camp rather than at the camp of his actual parents. According to Jerry, Simon was a "countryman" of his wife Nyinti, because Simon's mother, Mamiya, was a "sister" of Nyinti. The women were real sisters in his view because they were "from one country." Since Nyinti's father was supposed to be from Walukirritjinya in the south and Mamiya from the Yumari area in the north, this statement surprised me. Jerry explained that Nyinti had grown up in the north, along with Mamiya: extended residence and shared experience had made them "countrymen." The underlying idea is that coresidence in a camp is the spatial expression of a group of kin; shared activity constitutes people as related. There was another possible explanation, simultaneously true, and it fleshes out the significance of *ngurra* as a code for relationship. Other informants explained that Nyinti's mother, Kanawa, was from the western area around Pollock Hills. Because Kanawa and her own mother were "countrymen" and therefore close sisters, Mamiya and Nyinti were sisters, each regarding the other's mother as her own.

The idea of those who are "from one *ngurra*" refers to people who camp together, to be sure, but the relationships established through shared residence have a temporal dimension, an identity that endures. Such coresidence constitutes the substance of kinship in the Pintupi view of "relatives" (*walytja*).

The concept of *ngurra* works in two directions. Maantja considered the Buck Hills to be his *ngurra*, through his mother: she lived there for a long time and, more importantly, died there. Therefore, other people from the Buck Hills were Maantja's "countrymen." They were also his "countrymen" in another sense, because they used to camp together. In effect, the concept presents place (or localization) as the embodiment of relationships among people. Without broaching here the more complex problems of kinship reckoning per se (see chapter 7), it seems clear that a *ngurra* can serve as a code for a set of people related to it. Places are imbued with the identity of those who live there. In other words, the Pintupi can discuss a country and thereby also refer to the people associated with it, who typically camp there. One is talking of a "named place" but treating it as the site of a "camp." It makes no difference, in Pintupi thought, because what they continually stress is that sharing a *ngurra* is an expression of relatedness. To hear mention of a place is, for the Pintupi, to identify the persons associated with it, and to hear of people is to think of their places.

There are considerable parallels in Pintupi thought between country (*ngurra*) and kin (*walytja*) as interchangeable indices of a single experienced reality. The area a Pintupi considers his or her country represents the projection into space of his or her social relations with kin. Maantja's participation in a revenge expedition (*warrmala*) against a Warlpiri man who had killed a relative is illustrative: He described leaving the women behind and traveling

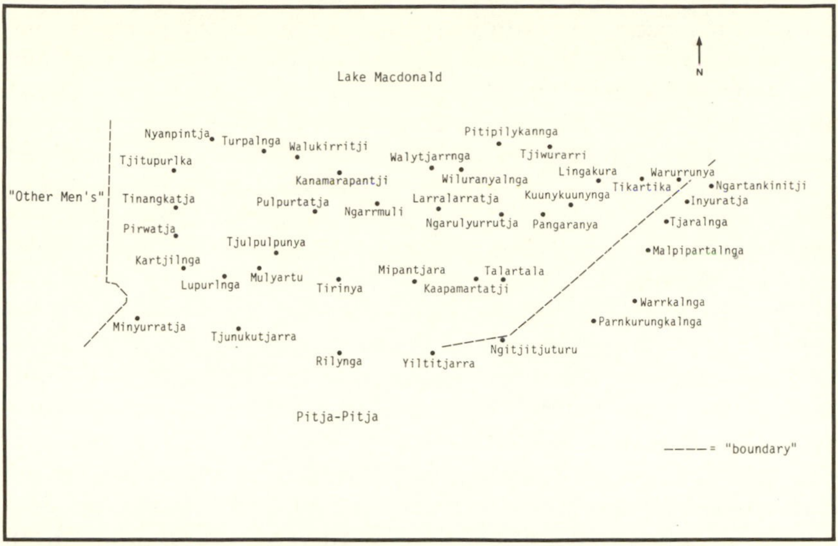

Map 3I. Maantja's "Country"

far to the north toward Mount Doreen, where they believed the man to be. Although they actually came in sight of Mount Doreen, they "got homesick" and turned back to return to the places with which they were familiar and comfortable. For the Pintupi, in most ways, relatives and country are the same thing. Thus, when Maantja told me, "We were homesick because it was a different country," he was not simply expressing his fear of unknown territory. In far less ambiguous circumstances of travel, he described to me how his wives would get "homesick" for their country. They would, then, abandon the journey and return. And when the revenge expedition turned back, the men rejoined their women and journeyed southeast toward Kalipinnga, "around our own country at last" (ngurra walytjawanalpi). It is in this context that statements about being "from one country" must be interpreted, images of persons and country as mutually embedded.

Boundaries and Relation

This inseparability of people and place makes territorial boundaries highly flexible if not insignificant. From another perspective, we would say that Pintupi statements about country require contextualization.

The accompanying map (Map 3I), for example, represents Maantja's sketch of the most limited version of his country. He described this area as "my camp, my family all around," including in this explanation the experience that underlies Pintupi ideas about localization. People from the north, south, east, and west came in and out of this country, visiting, he said, "like white people going to different houses." Repeatedly he insisted on the insignificance of boundaries and the importance of kinship. The area was not fenced in; if they saw a smoke, they would go to meet the people, happy because they were family. Other countries were, after all, within easy walking distance, "not far."

In widest application, Maantja described the whole area from Pirmalnga to Tjikarrinya (far to the north) and west to Yumarinya as "one country." Between Tjikarrinya and Pirmalnga is Tjitururrnga. They are "a line." If he saw a smoke in the next country, he might go and visit, and so travel on to Tjikarrinya or to Yumarinya. The people associated with these places are "one countrymen" because they always travel that way. He excluded from this category the people from the Pollock Hills and Mulyarti country, those from the far west. The other places were "level" (*yitingka*) or close together and easy to reach. These considerations often affected Maantja's decision about who was "from one country" with him. If I asked whether specific people were his "countrymen," his explanation would inevitably move to discussion of residence and travel. Quite clearly, the category did not constitute a discrete set of persons equivalent to any corporate group, either band or descent group.

At his most expansive, Maantja confirmed that Pintupi people traveled all over, visited other distant waters, and joined up with or met other persons. They were all "family" (that is, relatives). He added that it is really all one country, with the Gunbarrel Highway going through it all and joining it together. Drawing diagrams of places, Maantja indicated people moving about: "everybody, everywhere." People travel, meet others at a water, accompany them for a while, then split off and travel on.

Country is thus not an unambiguous index of social identity, separable from relational networks. In fact, not only assertions concerning "one countrymen," but also the use of country names as identity markers are merely expressions of actual, concrete residential and economic relations reflected in spatial array. Tjiwa Tjiwa tjangala, for example, described his country as being bounded on the north by Lake Mackay (Wilkinkarranya), on the east by the Northern Territory border (Muwinynga), on the south by the Gordon Hills (Yarannga), and on the west by Kurrilynga (see Map 1A). It was, he said, "one country, one family." Frequently, he and others referred to "Tjiwa Tjiwa's mob" or the "Yumari mob" (people from Yumari). When I asked him who was from the "one country," he enumerated several men. Yet one of them was Wally tjapanangka, a man described more often as "from Yarannga" than as "from Yumari." Two others from Tjiwa Tjiwa's list were primarily identified as "from Tarkurrnga" (Angas Hills), and another still was "from Marpuri." Nonetheless, when I asked these men if they were "from Yumari" and if Tjiwa Tjiwa were a "one countryman," they said it was so. They all traveled together frequently and spent much time at Yumari.

There is more to the story, however. Out of the seventeen people Tjiwa Tjiwa listed as "one countrymen" (Myers 1976: 330), two men were also listed by a man from further west, Johnny tjakamarra, as *his* "countrymen." Further, Johnny described his "countrymen" as "from Tarkurrnga," a place Tjiwa Tjiwa had included in his own country. In explaining, Johnny said that he used to live at three main waters: Tarkurrnga, Wirwilynga, and Marpurinya. These were close together; one could travel from Marpurinya to Tarkurrnga in one day and, similarly, from Tarkurrnga to Yumarinya in a day. Although one of his countrymen was "from Walawalanya" (Pollock Hills), that was said to be a bit far off. Johnny often went there after the rains had come: "all the family used to come together at Walawalanya." He described Walawalanya as being "one country" with Tarkurrnga and Marpurinya because the same Dreaming, *Tingarri*, came through them.

Resource Use and Defined Areas

Despite individual variations in movements and rights of exploitation, there also seem to be definable resource nexuses of the sort once simplistically described as "band territories." These create repeated patterns of movement throughout the year, a sort of basic schedule of resource use. The significance of these defined areas—particularly their relationship to social units—requires analysis.

No set of individuals lives entirely, for even a single year, within the boundaries of a single local area. In fact, Pintupi social groups are characterized by considerable permeability in regard to rights in using the resources of such "ranges." Exploiting camps are bilateral, with their composition actualized from numerous organizational categories, including kinsmen, affines, and ritual partners.[8] Pintupi individuals have highly variable ranges, depending on their particular social relations, which are not limited, as we have seen, to a particular band or its territory. Use rights to land are multiple and easily gained, limited only by initiative, and acquired through "ownership" or social relations to "owners" (see chapter 5).

Such openness of access for individuals does not mean there are no "objective structures" (Bourdieu 1976) defining the limits and patterns of associations. Sharp, for example, described patterns of land use in another part of Australia (Cape York Peninsula) similar to those of the Pintupi:

> People gather and hunt, ordinarily, in whatever country they will.
> Thus there is practically a standing permission which opens a clan's countries to all. . . . (Sharp 1934: 23)

He also pointed out, however, that ". . . this permission may be withdrawn by the clan for those who are *persona non grata.*" Sharp maintains that "owners" (in his case, a patrilineal clan) hold the right to exclude people but that such a right is exercised only in exceptional cases.

There are defined resource areas (sociocentric ranges) in Pintupi territorial organization. They are defined primarily around the permanent or semipermanent water holes to which people return during the dry summer. In other seasons, these people may disperse and use small water holes to visit relatives in other ranges, as already described. There, rights to forage are acquired as part of residence, as a "one countryman." In every range, known resource points exist at which people gather at times of the year when they know food is available. One example is the *mungilpa* seed plant in Maantja's country; people came in large numbers from far away to collect these seeds. The Buck Hills similarly offered wild yams *(pitjara).* Clearly, visiting and congregating at periods and places of temporary abundance was common.

Such periodically abundant resources offer no adaptive advantage for rationing by one group (cf. Dyson-Hudson and Smith 1978), and Pintupi informants insisted that they would never send someone away from their country unless he or she committed some wrong. The value placed on "compassion" (see chapter 4), as well as the opportunity to be reciprocated at some future time, inclines people to share resources. Thus, a person extends rights to use resources in his country to all his "countrymen," with the expectation of reciprocal privilege. To view local groups as basic units and local scarcity as compelling reciprocity is to miss the point of this arrangement. Aborigines themselves emphasize instead the positive qualities of exchange, of increasing societal intensity by taking turns hosting larger groups, and of enabling greater overall efficiency of resource use.[9]

The consistency and recurrences in the travel histories of individuals provide some idea of the pattern of movements by which Aborigines took advantage of the seasonal appearance of food and water. Variation among persons from a single range shows that individual movements were also scheduled to pursue other possibilities, such as visiting certain people and seeing particular sacred sites. This process, of course, reproduced those social relations ("one countrymen"), which must be seen therefore as significant regional-systemic relations of production.

It seems sensible to characterize Pintupi bands as hypothetical entities moving through an optimal pattern of resource-scheduling, with different individuals affiliating themselves to these groups as they move from place to place, traveling with them for a while and then moving on. The size of this abstract band may remain relatively constant while the actual composition may vary greatly. The important requirement is that individuals must affiliate with the residential group to use the land.

The state of resources determines where people may be, but not necessarily where they actually are, or precisely who is where; and this is what an accurate model of Pintupi territorial organization must reflect. The Pintupi concept of "one countryman" seems to argue that bands are largely the outcome of individual decisions, and their actual composition can be explained only through the history and processes of individual affiliation.

One therefore should not construe assertions—such as the Pintupi frequently make—that an individual is "from" a particular country as necessarily referring to "range." To say that Maantja is "from Walukirritjinya" is not to make a simple statement; its interpretation requires placing it within a universe of nomadic practices. Pintupi statements of this sort are largely predictive, reflecting the social reality that people are likely to return to their home area, especially in the summer. While returning to home waters has the effect of controlling the number of people at any water hole at a time of year when resource capacity is most diminished, *how* this occurs is also significant. "Regulation" does not depend on defense of territory.

Because permanent water is scarce, seasonal congregations at sites of abundant water are relatively large. And because in summer there are no intermediate waters, individuals do not really have the usual option of moving away should conflicts or disputes arise. As previously mentioned, considerable strain occurs in such large groups.[10] Thus, according to the life histories, by the end of summer people were eager to move away into different and smaller groups.[11] To be among more distant "kin" in the summer presented the

Purungu Napangarti and Ronnie Tjampitjinpa, wife and husband, enjoy the result of recent hunting, after distributing the rest to kin. (Yayayi, 1979)

disadvantage that while disputes were likely to be more frequent, one's support would be weaker. Nonetheless, it supports this view of the processes by which adaptation occurs that every individual I questioned had spent some summers away from the country with which he or she was most closely identified.

The content of Pintupi territorial organization is neither the exclusion of others from access to resources nor the division of people into discrete, mobile, but permanent bands. In this sense, the importance of defined "ranges" has too often been misconstrued as implying territorial defense. What seems more vital to a foraging adaptation is sensitivity to the relationship between population and resources (Peterson 1975: 59)—knowledge of resources available and location of people. The short-term processes by which such adaptation is accomplished depend on the meaning of "ownership" as Pintupi construe it.

Always Ask

Denial of access to resources is infrequent. In the Pintupi view, the utility of resources does not constitute a reason to maintain exclusive access to them. Access is freely granted, but people still must know how many persons are exploiting an area and where they are to plan suitable strategies of exploitation.

Tindale summarizes the major focus of Western Desert concepts of "ownership" when he writes that a man told him, "My country is the place where I do not have to ask anyone to cut wood for a spear-thrower" (Tindale 1974: 18). The content of "ownership," in other words, is the right to be asked. In this sense, what a Yankuntjatjarra man once defined as "the first law of Aboriginal morality: Always ask!" (Derek Freeman, personal communication) provides a key for resolving much of the ethnographic confusion about local organization.

Pintupi are very concerned that they be consulted over matters in which they have rights, particularly in matters concerning land. When a group of men visited an ochre mine in the Gibson Desert, for example, a few chipped off some of the material for later use. Subsequently, at a meeting in Docker River Settlement, the primary custodian of the place threatened to spear them and made a great show of anger. His rights had been violated because they had not asked him before digging up the ochre. This notion continues in relations with whites. Over the years, men have grumbled about white people driving out to Pintupi country without seeking any- one's prior permission. In my experience, the Pintupi have never refused anyone permission, but they felt their rights were being violated if they were not asked.

For the Pintupi, to own something is to have the right to be asked about it.[12] The norms of kinship and compassion force one to grant the request, but one should be asked. Given the political economy of Pintupi social life, what do the Pintupi seek to gain as value here, and what do they lose? In a sense, what they seek is prestige, the chance to be first among equals (Fried 1967), or more properly, I think, to maintain personal autonomy. All this is satisfied when others recognize one's rights; recognition achieved, what else is to be gained by forbidding access? Consequently, it is important for outsiders to understand that while use rights to land are freely granted, one must ask in order to obtain them.

Pintupi acquire rights to use land by joining a residential group already exploiting it. As Peterson (1975) points out, the boundaries to such groups are "defended" with rites of entry. People who want to join a group do not simply walk into its camp, no matter how close their relationship. They announce their presence by lighting a fire at some distance from the camp and then waiting there for members of the camp to identify them and bring them into the camp. They must "ask," and "one-countryman" links make it possible to do so.

This process constitutes an etiquette of "asking" to be admitted to the group and to its rights of resource use. The Pintupi maintain that they would not send anyone away, a statement that conforms to other data I have. Maantja, for example, described Pitjantjatjarra men traversing his country to go west for special *mulyarti* wood for spears; but the narrative implies that they had established this right with residents beforehand. Indeed, what makes people angry is unannounced travel, going in a secretive (*yarrka*) fashion. When moving into another's range, therefore, one should ask or somehow announce one's presence as a form of deference. Usually it is sufficient to send up a smoke.

Such "announcing" behavior provides the information for which Pintupi are so eager. Knowledge of resources, people, and their whereabouts provides the basis of local organization, suggesting where groups can go next and allowing them to assess the current relation between population and resources. Are poor returns on foraging a result of personal inefficiency, of chance, or of overpopulation (Peterson 1975: 59)? Information enables people to decide on their travels and to avoid coming upon a string of areas that have already been exploited. Equally, it is important for assessing the intentions of visitors. Who are they, and are they friendly?

Even now, when people visit Pintupi communities from other settlements, it is clear that their behavior remains somewhat restrained, that they exhibit "embarrassment," "shame," or "deference" (*kunta*) at seeming to assume too much. Visitors are tentative in announcing their intentions and take few rights to be theirs automatically. In this way, visitors are always "asking," making sure it is acceptable to act as they intend.

This is the context, then, in which Pintupi statements about their travels are interpreted. Smokes from certain directions were known to be from "that Yumari mob," or "that Warlungurru mob," indicating that groups were residing in a location that a knowledgeable person could determine, given the time of year and location of the smoke. If they were on good terms with those people and if resources allowed, those nearby might go to visit. Maantja told me that in such cases one did not have to ask formally because everyone was "family," a term he used for frequent coresidents. For these people there would be a minimum of formality in incorporation into the exploiting group.

If we follow Maantja still farther from his country, we find him reporting that other people are "guiding him" (*kati yaninpa*) through their country. This more formal arrangement allows for someone to vouch for him as he travels farther from familiar places, to give information about him, to guarantee his good intentions to residents. Though wide-ranging, individuals' travels are not unrestricted in extent. At greater distances, travel is less frequent. Because people are not well known, it is more dangerous. Strangers (*munuwati*, "not human" or "different men") are suspected of evil intentions, of being dangerous because one does not know how to predict their behavior. This suspicion ultimately restricts population movement, confining people to some extent.

After traveling in the cool part of the year, people regularly return to their own major waters. The reason for such return seems always to be sentimental rather than "jural," at least in the Pintupi formulation. As they traveled farther and farther, people recount, "We got homesick and turned back to our own country." When Maantja continued his narrative, he described his movements homeward and then mentioned sighting a familiar place with emotion: "My own country at last."

If this were the whole story, of people moving to and fro with ease, we might well wonder how the system works through time. The question of what maintains the array of people in space can only be addressed at a higher level of this system, through analysis of the politics of landownership. There we will see that rather than territorial organization being maintained through defense of resource, it is structured by the pursuit of another value—autonomy.

Conclusion

Pintupi residential groups can best be understood through the concept of "one countrymen" as those who potentially share a camp and cooperate in the food quest. The concept is an egocentric one whose boundaries are expandable and relatively undefined. Through actualizing this potential social relation, individuals acquire rights to forage in a number of ranges. Therefore, rights to use the resources of a range are relatively permeable to access by others, although there seems to be considerable variation in actual boundaries around different resources (Dyson-Hudson and Smith 1978).[13]

In a sense, this system is what one would expect among hunter-gatherers in an environment with unpredictable rainfall. One might even conclude that such flexibility is determined by the productive system. The Pintupi social system does not just happen, however. Indeed, despite the need people have of each other in the long term, considerable evidence suggests that the expansiveness of this system of relatedness is endangered by conflict and by fear of those who are not in regular association. The tendencies to differentiation are endemic, partly a product of the egocentered category of "countryman" as the basis for relatedness among people within a region. This very expansiveness, vital to relations of use and residence, makes it difficult to sustain any particular set of "countrymen." In allocating one's attention and services, a person inevitably must decide who among his or her "countrymen" are most important. Choice of some entails a neglect of others.

Viewed in this light, the fact that band aggregations are both shifting and a matter of choice has significant consequences for the Pintupi. Relatedness exists in tension with the tendencies toward conflict. It must be produced and reproduced, in the form of relationships of identity, in the face of differentiation.

CHAPTER 4

Being a Countryman:
Emotions and the Cultural Subject

My uncle, do you have anything for me?

Be compassionate, give it to him!

*I*t is common for descriptions of Aboriginal societies to treat the
organization of behavior as defined by the rights and duties of
"kinship." Among the Pintupi, the concept of *walytja*, meaning
kinship or relatedness, is indeed critical to understanding social
life, but their own emphasis is on the affective relationships among
those who are relatives.

Traditional Pintupi society has neither centralization nor formal
political structure. What order and cooperation existed in these low-
population-density groups depended largely on the ties of recognized
relatedness and their emotional considerations. The discourse of
daily life is heavily nuanced with expressions and demonstrations
of such emotions as "compassion," "melancholy," "grief," "happiness," and "shame." In this respect, the Pintupi resemble other
hunter-gatherer groups that seem to have similar ideas about
emotions, especially those of embarrassment when acting in the
public domain. These attitudes are correlative of the general restraint
and unassertiveness of individuals over their comrades. Marshall
describes how the !Kung fear the embarrassment of wrong, foolish,
or outlandish behavior:

> Their desire to avoid both hostility and rejection leads them to
> conform in high degree to the unspoken social law. If they do deviate
> they usually yield readily to expressed group opinion and reform
> their ways. I think that most !Kung cannot bear the sense of
> rejection which even mild disapproval makes them feel. (Marshall
> 1961: 235)

103

Such constraints are equally important in Pintupi life. The emotions, as culturally defined, are an important medium of interpersonal activity. When one Pintupi calls another "kin," a system of appropriate emotional responses is called up: One should be "compassionate" to the other and should help him. Kin status is largely a matter of feeling, and if a person feels unkindly treated, he may complain that the other does not "like" him or her and thus is not really *walytja*. The negotiation of such relationships is of critical concern to Pintupi, and the intent of this sort of complaint is to get the other to reflect on how he or she *should* feel. One might reflect whether this person, for example, is "close."

The fragile associations of residence involve complementary organizations of feeling. Thus, a full understanding of the Pintupi experience of life must grasp the cultural meaning of these emotions. My argument is that by defining shared identity with others as a primary feature of selfhood, the Pintupi formulation of the emotions establishes the moral order of kinship in subjective terms. Their concept of shared identity represents a cultural appropriation of the significant relations of cooperation and exchange that lie at the heart of Pintupi social life: the sharing of food and labor within residential groups, and the openness of access to resources. Because the formulation of the emotions is also symbolically transformed into larger and more encompassing structures, the extended system of regional relations depends upon the organization of what I call the "cultural subject" (cf. Turner 1980b: 137).

Subjectivity

I use the notion of the "cultural subject" to distinguish my cultural analysis of the emotions from any psychological constructions. Anthropologists have often employed the constructs of "self" or "person" to consider the problem of subjectivity (cf. Geertz 1973, 1975; Hallowell 1955; Panoff 1968; Shore 1982). The psychological implications of "self" make it problematic, however, as a comparative construct for the sort of analysis I am doing. When Hallowell (1955) writes of "conceptions of the self" as having fundamental priority in the organization of social life, he means models for the articulation of personal experience into a coherent pattern. Basically, this view of the self is another version of the Freudian "ego," the structure of meaning an individual uses to organize his or her own experience (Fingarette 1964).

Because cultural models are not necessarily psychological reality, I prefer to restrict the concept of "self" to the actual constructions that individuals produce of themselves. Although "self" and "subject" are related, the distinction leaves open the relationship between cultural models and psychological organization. At the sociological level, too, we should be careful about imposing on other cultures a Western concern about "self" and "selfhood," with its belief in the irreducible reality of the individual (Dumont 1965). Even within our own tradition, some have argued, the obsession with the integration of personal experience is a historical product. In his analysis of the bourgeois novel's focus on inner space, Lukács (1973) suggests that the existential problem of giving meaning to one's action and place in the world is not universal.

The idea of the "person," in contrast, ordinarily refers to cultural beliefs about the nature of people. Theories of substance in which a person is made up of maternal blood and paternal bone, for instance, exemplify this sort of idea. Again, although they may be related to how an individual thinks about himself, such constructs primarily represent the individual as appropriated from outside.

The concept of cultural subjectivity derives from the view that human subjects know themselves not as they are in all their human potential, but in determined forms of "social being" (Marx and Engels 1947). [1] They come to know themselves only through practical activity. Whatever the objective dimensions of social life, actors engage the world from a particular point of view. They coordinate the reality of social life as a field of action *for themselves*. If the structures of subjectivity that result are a product of human action, they reflect the conditions of that action as much as individual intention. The properties human beings possess as actors are given value and meaning within a specific set of social relations. Thus, to discuss a "cultural subject" is to distinguish between an individual and his or her contingent subjectivity.

Subjectivity is a representation of the social system from the point of view of an individual agent, but it is also the condition of that system. The two structures are dialectically defined, each "assuming" the other. Bateson's (1972: 134) example of the shark's shape as a form of "knowledge" of the laws of hydrodynamics presents one side of the dialectic. The ocean's structure, responding (albeit minutely) to the shark's shape and activities, is the other side. Similarly, although Pintupi subjectivity is determined by band life, the larger system of territorial relations is also influenced by this emergent form.

Emotions

In this view, emotions represent forms of judgment: means of evaluating the relationship between an individual and his or her circumstances. I would explicitly contrast this approach with theories of the emotions that identify them with sensations or feeling (cf. James 1884). [2] The Jamesian view gives priority to bodily symptoms, treating emotions as simply the names given to various states of central nervous system arousal. What I call the "cultural view" of emotions maintains that people find out what emotion they are experiencing for themselves in the same way as they do for others: by observing the associated circumstances and behavior. Does one, after all, know one is ashamed merely through the perception of a sensation in the ears or a redness in the face? Instead, the emotions can be better understood as cultural constructions, making intelligible the relationship between circumstances and behavior.

Emotions are not simply reactions to what happens, but interpretations of an event, judgments "about my situation and about myself and/or about all other people" (Solomon 1977: 186). Suppose, for example, I am angry because I realize someone has cheated me. This is not merely a product of interpreting an event as cheating. It is also an evaluation of cheating in relation to myself. Whether cheating is evaluated as a hostile act against me or as an action morally reprehensible in abstract terms, my anger defines me in relation to something valued. In this way, the emotions are constitutive both of the world and of the subject.

The emotions, then, can be considered truly cultural phenomena. The emotion of anger should not be identified with a physical feeling—whatever that is, perhaps a constriction of the throat. [3] When I obtain revenge ten days later, my throat may not be constricted; does this mean I am not angry? Anger represents an interpretation of my relationship to a set of circumstances. Indeed, it is not only common for people to deceive themselves about their feelings, but as Ryle suggests, individuals must learn how to apply culturally given constructs to their own situation and experience. "A child," he writes, "does not know whether the lump he feels in his throat is a sign of misery, or a sign that he is sickening for something" (Ryle 1949: 101).

One learns how to apply these judgments to events, but as cultural concepts the emotions do not necessarily represent the inner states of participants in social life. People may consciously interpret their acts and feelings as "compassionate," while the truer motivation may be egotism or something else. Consciousness-raising may suggest that a divorced woman's "depression" is really "anger" (Scheman 1980).

My interest here, however, lies not so much in this reinterpretive capacity of emotional constructs as in their place within a larger cultural system of meanings. If the emotions are relational, the relationships they constitute are given meaning and value by the social processes in which they are embedded. The values in relation to which emotions define a "cultural subject" are socioculturally variable. Thus, processes such as the exchange of food among coresidents of a band imbue "compassion" with a special value in Pintupi social life.

The Pintupi concepts of the emotions exhibit a consistent logic that derives from the social value placed on relatedness with others. Defining the subject as substantially identified with others and evaluating action in terms of the postulated shared identity, this formulation is grounded in the practical activities of band life. Finally, the Pintupi cultural emphasis on emotions as the basis for action is itself a consequence of the relative nondifferentiation among "kin," intensifying the view of kinship as identity with others as part of the self. For the Pintupi, being a relative is more important than defining what sort of kin one is.

Learning How

The cultural selection and communication of appropriate emotional states plays a vital role in the socialization of children into adults. Essentially, such maturation depends upon the ability to recognize one's relatedness to others, and to subdue one's will in order to sustain relatedness. In Pintupi theory, this development is perceived as an increasing ability to "understand." Young children are said to be "unaware," "oblivious," or "deaf" (*patjarru* or *ramarama*) and therefore not responsible for their actions. Children do not *know*; they understand neither events nor when to be ashamed. Small children are "unheeding" (*ramarama*) in that they do not comprehend the importance of social events; rather, they throw tantrums, do not listen to or respond to parents, sit too close to an affine, play with fire, and so on.

However deficient in understanding, children are not lacking in will. Adults recognize and respect the willfulness of children, who are seen, even at an early age, to direct their activities by their "own idea" (B. Clark, personal communication). Unlike comprehension, personal autonomy seems to be a given in human life, as reflected in the origin of the spirit outside of society, in The Dreaming.

What children acquire socially is awareness of others. In the Pintupi view, the concepts "thinking," "understanding," and "hearing" are expressed by a single term, *kulininpa*, which means literally "to hear." The organ of thought is the ear, but emotions take place in the stomach where the spirit is located. To be unaware (*patjarru* or *ramarama*), constrastingly, is to have one's "ears closed." Young children do not process the available information about who is present and what is happening. Those who do are said to "know" (*ninti*) or "to understand"—implying that one learns what responses are held to be appropriate for various situations. What children learn, then, are what Hallowell (1955: 89–109) calls the "basic orientations for the self provided by a culture"—a folk theory of motivation (how to understand others) and morality (how to place oneself in relation to these expectations). An adult Pintupi should be aware of what is happening and who is present. There is constant evaluation of the state of the social and physical world.

Pintupi apply the term *ramarama* ("deaf," "oblivious") to those whom they consider insane and to drunks. Such an individual does not hear or take note of relatives, possibly injuring close kin or failing to recognize them. In other words, such a person is not in touch with the reality upon which everyone else agrees. One who is unable to "think" in this way is, like a child, not held accountable for his or her actions.

Understanding thus constitutes the precondition for social maturity. The development of that maturity, however, results from an increasing elaboration of ties of shared identity with others. At first children tend to be shy or ashamed in the presence of all new "strangers" from outside their camp; gradually, they learn to recognize those with whom they are related, and to modulate their shyness according to the degree of identity they recognize. The Pintupi moral order is based on a specific view of the self: Individuals see, understand, or feel themselves to be related and identified with close kin. Pintupi ethnopsychology seems to view an individual's internal states as extensively connected with a web of significant others or with "objects" that Western observers would describe as external to the self. The special identification of persons with place in Pintupi thought should be considered part of this web.

Róheim, who studied the Pintupi and their neighbors fifty years ago, grasped the importance of this particular view of the self, although his polemical style tended to obscure his acute ethnographic observations. He argued that the landscape has an important psychological relationship to central Australian Aborigines. "Both myth and ritual," he concluded, "are an attempt to cathect environment with libido" (Róheim 1945: 214). Munn (1970) has also explored how among other central Australian Aborigines important external objects—parts of the material world like the "country"— come to provide individuals with images or "fragments" of themselves. As she points out, "In the normal personality, these 'images' are recognized as being outside the person and separate from him, and yet are experiences *inextricably* bound up with him" (Munn 1970: 158). In other words, individuals come to identify places and ancestors as parts of themselves, referring to them in the first person.[4]

The Moral Order of Walytja

Róheim and Munn stress the identification of the self with parts of the physical environment, but the Pintupi notion of this relationship encompasses a much wider rubric of identification. In this respect, the key symbol for the Pintupi social order is the concept of *walytja*, which recognizes the relationship of the self to various others. Given the emphasis in Western cultures on a bounded, integrated self (Geertz 1975), psychoanalysis has made much of the way in which "cathected objects" or others external to the physical individual become part of an individual's self-orientation. The Pintupi, however, have based their culture on the concept of *walytja* as the dominant symbol of shared identity and mutual support. Official representations of Pintupi social life stress that they are "one family" or "all related" (*walytja tjurta*). For any individual, the social universe is divided into two categories: those who are "kin," "relations," or "family" (*walytja*), and those who are not kin, who are often described as "not men" or "different men" (*munuwati*).

The term *walytja* specifies a sense of belonging together or shared identity. It is used to refer to (1) possessions, (2) "kin," (3) "one's own" (my own), (4) a wider sense of belonging, and (5) "oneself," as in the phrases "he did it himself" or "she is sitting by herself." This reflexive use of *walytja* as "self" suggests that the critical notion of relatedness is rooted in the givenness of the individual, extending outward from a spirit whose identity derives from The Dreaming. The concept asserts a relationship between oneself and persons, objects, or places; it recognizes as fundamental in Pintupi life the identity extended to persons and things beyond the physical individual.

In contrast, those who are not truly *walytja* are described as "nothing to do" (*mungutja*), as "other" (*munuka*), as "not the same," or—with a metaphor of spatial separateness—as "outside." All such explanations imply that nonrelations are those with whom one experiences little or no interaction. The term has expanding application in relation to social space, depending on whom the speaker is viewing in contrast with "relations."

As with the more specific category of "one countrymen," one's *walytja* are not necessarily actual consanguines. They include those with whom one grows up, those with whom one is familiar, those who have fed and cared for one, and those with whom one camps frequently. Strangers, people who are unknown, are likely to be feared or suspected dangerous.

The moral category is grounded in the most intimate and basic experiences of social life, those of nurturance, sharing of food, labor, and concern. The usual domestic unit of a "camp" including husband, wife or wives, and small children defines the closest group of *walytja* and the primary food-sharing unit. Beyond this unit are other family camps that may frequently coreside or reside as parts of the same band. The members of different camps may spend considerable time with each other, sharing meat, looking after small children, feeding them, and lavishing attention on them. During the day, infants may be handled by a variety of women and girls, and men will play with or feed a child, although it will rarely be permitted out of the mother's sight. These people, who cooperate in economic life as well as in recreation, are also seen as relatives.

Some attitudes concerning *walytja*—expectations of unqualified support and acceptance—are highly reminiscent of childhood experience. Among the Pintupi, small children are rarely denied their desires, and any discomfort perceived is met with attempts to relieve it. Mothers almost never refuse the breast, for instance, and children are encouraged to respond favorably to those who play with them, as these are seen as a child's *walytja*.

These observations should not imply that Pintupi children are entirely subsumed by their relations to others. Autonomy is basic, realizing itself through relations. The parental concern for a child's well-being does not restrict its independence for its own welfare. Children are granted an autonomy of desire: If a child does not want to eat, that is regarded as "his business" (Clark, personal communication). Indeed, children are expected to assert themselves to gain satisfaction for their desires. They make their hunger known by crying or by demanding food. Related others become for them a necessary part of achieving their own desires, and those who help are considered *walytja*.

Although Róheim (1945) grounded his explanation in a Freudian framework of "separation anxiety" from the mother, he recognized the fundamentality of the Aboriginal need for the other, the desire to complete oneself in "dual unity." The paired heroes of male mythology, he argued, were invariably representations of dual unity, as was the combination of circular symbols on phallic sacred objects. Whatever the psychological motivation, the cultural formulation maintains that one becomes complete and autonomous only through sustaining relations with others.

The qualities that feature so strongly in the Pintupi child's world—support, generosity, familiarity, and warmth—become precisely the qualities that ideally characterize relations among adult *walytja*. They should help each other, should not frustrate each other's wishes, and should share food. In moments of tranquillity, one is likely to hear Pintupi talk of themselves as "all one family." On occasions of dispute, the others are *not* kin. Of course jealousy, envy, dislike, and greed are enduring parts of Pintupi life, but the official representation of themselves is as "family." Acts that indicate feelings to the contrary are not usually displayed openly.

The cultural expectation of *walytja* as shared identity provides the framework against which the emotions, as judgments, evaluate relations between "self" and "other." The concept of *walytja* can be said to define the moral order of Pintupi society as "family," in contrast to relations with strangers, which are full of fear, hostility, and suspicion. This view portrays the larger Pintupi society as a group of closely cooperating kin, each no better than the rest, with all sharing some kind of identification, and mutual concern. The Pintupi view of the self and the other, therefore, receives validation from the experience of social life in which kin throughout a region should and do help each other.

"Happiness"

The central themes of the Pintupi moral order revolve around the ideal of closely cooperating kin, and it is in terms of this understanding that Pintupi attempt to define when and how one should be "happy" (*pukurlpa*). Pintupi find it unusual that one could be happy sitting alone. To be among kin, to be shown affection and concern, and to show it: these are what should make one happy. Those who travel alone, for example, are suspect, and those who wish to be alone usually offer other reasons. While feeling "happy" is an endopsychic matter—described as a "rising of the spirit"— Pintupi seem to think that an individual experiences such states largely as the result of smoothly running relations between the individual and those he or she considers *walytja*.[5] One rejoices when one sees relatives coming to visit. These relations are to be valued much more highly than ordinary possessions, and one who fails to do so is considered "selfish" or "greedy." A man who is unwilling to let relatives borrow his vehicle is deprecated as "hungry for that motorcar." As among other ethnographically known people, satisfactory relations are achieved through activity, through exchange of food, labor, women, sacred objects, and so on. Exchanges demonstrate that one cares for and trusts the other. These days, kin who are separated by distance often send money through intermediaries to show that they are thinking of each other.

The structuring of subjectivity is predicated on this positive value of satisfactory relations. Being unhappy is conceived of in terms of other specific states: "lonely," "sorry," "frightened," "angry," or "ashamed." These concepts represent different, unsatisfactory sorts of relationships with *walytja* and with the world.

The cultural meaning Pintupi attribute to "happiness" is clear in the following example. Informants frequently told me that the settlement where they lived was "not a happy place." There were fights all the time because there were "no ceremonies." There should be, they said, "ceremonies all the time." Indeed, on a day in which numerous fights and arguments were occurring, several men suggested that a ceremony be organized to stop the fighting. This would, it was thought, make everyone happy.[6]

There is a reality to this expectation. Singing functions as a "ritual process" (V. Turner 1969b) that reduces discord, and it also presents participants with a lesson about what it means to be among *walytja*. Typically, when ceremonies take place among people who do not usually camp together, they are organized to reflect cooperation and complementarity (through exchange of functions and meat), drawing symbolically on the model of the individual camp. Ceremony presents intergroup relations as involving the same mutuality and sharing as other relations of *walytja*. Indeed, those with whom one takes part in a ceremony become *walytja* to a degree.

To the Pintupi, singing provides a salient image of sociability. Whenever large groups came together in traditional times, they would sing together at night. Ceremony—song and dance—was the real content of most intergroup relations. The initial approach of a visiting group was (and is) fraught with tension and excitement, and is highly ritualized. Visitors' intentions are uncertain, undetermined. On important occasions, grievances and long-standing grudges are settled before singing begins. As Maantja described such encounters in his life history, men who met after long separations were likely to fight because of old, outstanding grievances, and then to sit down at the same fire and sing all night.

Singing is viewed as a public, community entertainment, in contrast with the private pleasure of sex, which occurs in a camp; men are supposed to give priority to the first. Those who prefer to remain in their camps or otherwise pursue private pleasures are teased and shamed. Ideally, in fact, Pintupi males should not be able to enjoy the private pleasures of sex until they have been initiated as men: This orientation to the public pleasures of cere- mony and singing, to activity with other men, should precede the individual enjoyment of sexuality. Indeed, the replacement of "pri- vate" with "public" constitutes a recurring theme in Pintupi culture.

The Pintupi recognize, of course, that happiness may be achieved in many ways. They understand that fighting makes some individ- uals happy, as does sex or gifts. Nevertheless, to be happy at a death, at another's suffering, or at one's own success compared to another's failure, would be bad. One might hear such expressions from children, but the transition from childhood to adult is marked by the attempt to substitute public values for the private. The impor- tance of these notions of "public" and "private" (terms that I apply to implicit Pintupi notions) lies in their capacity to maintain the official representation of coresidents as "one family," as all *walytja*.

Fragments of the Self

Another set of concepts possess what Wittgenstein (1958: 32) called "a family resemblance," which the Pintupi themselves recognize in using the term *ngaltutjarra* as the conventionalized expression for any of these feelings. In reference, however, each may be distinguished from the others. Both "compassion" (*ngaltu*) and "grief" or "sorrow" (*yalurrpa*) refer to a judgment of sorrow or concern for another, a kind of compassionate empathy, although "grief" represents the more extreme emotionality. The concept of "melancholy" (*watjilpa*, also "lonely" or "pining") seems to convey a similar state of spirit, but one whose original source is oneself. Thus, a man might say, "*Ngaltutjarra. Ngayuku ngurra,*" meaning something like "poor me, my own country." He points to himself, his feelings of melancholy, as one who should be pitied.

Underlying the concept of compassion is a recognition of "relatedness"—a recognition of shared identity or empathy between the person who is compassionate and another. This identity is the source of the other's legitimate claim on one's compassion. Not to have compassion or not to display it is interpreted as "not liking" the other person—that is, not recognizing the link. And this "liking" is a matter of great concern to Pintupi.

As one might expect, to be a compassionate person (and knowing when to be such) is the goal of considerable childhood training. Typically, young children in possession of something desired by another are told to "be compassionate, give it to him" (*ngaltutjarra, yuwara*). Adults play at this with children, pleading for an item,

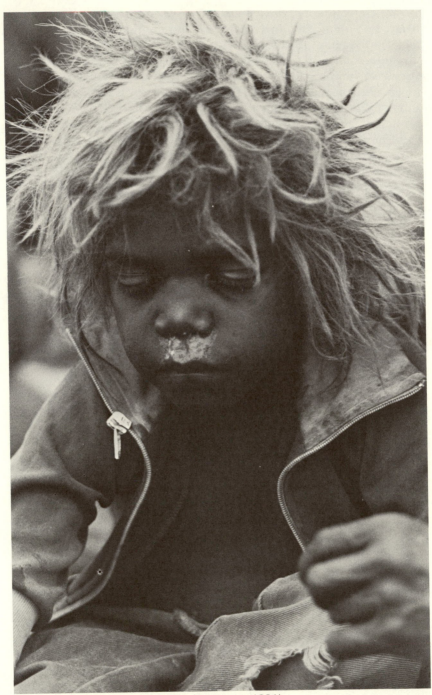

Ray Tjapaltjarri, age six years. (Papunya, 1981)

and even the very young become accustomed to sharing. Similarly, on hearing of some misfortune that befell another, Pintupi bespeak their compassion, "Oh, the poor fellow" (*ngaltutjarra*).

The Pintupi live up to these ideals often enough. They are moved to help by the sight of another's pitiful condition. Food is never denied to the hungry (although individuals may hide food so as not to be asked for it). Nor, for similar reasons, should one threaten the weak and infirm. "Poor thing, she is harmless," they may say of a woman whose husband had beaten her viciously.

On this basis, relatives bring pressure on those who are better off. Among kinfolk, after all, the considerations of shared identity are most important: One who has something should share with the less fortunate. Since a relative cannot share with everyone, whether he does share or not is considered to be a manifestation of affect: It shows whether or not he considers the relationship to be important. Conversely, one who is not given food may complain that the other "does not like me." Those who do not demonstrate feelings of relatedness with generosity are believed to be "hard" or, as the Pintupi sometimes put it, "like rocks." Like rocks, they are without emotion, without recognition of shared identity, and perhaps not quite human.

I have heard Pintupi threaten those whom they considered to have responded too often in less than human fashion. To deny relatedness invites physical retribution. Those who are rejected protest the lack of concern by drawing attention to the bases of shared identity, to their past concern for the other, and to their own humanity. Thus, they exclaim, "I'm not a bullock!" Or, perhaps, they remind the other of what they have previously given and the need for reciprocity: "I gave you a lot of meat!" (On the other hand, gifts and regular exchanges are greeted with satisfaction, as proof that shared identity is recognized.) It is difficult to demonstrate one's sympathy for everyone all the time, of course. A continual failure to do so, however, results inevitably in conflict or changes in residence. If coresidents refuse to share, people are likely to join another group.

The Pintupi concept of compassion can be best understood as the possibility of being moved by another's wishes or condition. In daily life, this "compassion" is both a characteristic quality of social relations and a commonly alluded-to concept. It has significant implications for decision-making and consensus. No matter how well-intentioned, most threats of sending away wrongdoers or removing individuals from their jobs are rescinded subsequently with the decision to "give them one more chance." The wrongdoers often prompt this result by referring explicitly to kinship links—

for example, "I have a lot of fathers here"—or implicitly doing so by asking, "Don't you trust me?" These actions rarely fail to evoke "compassion," as the initial plaintiffs reflect on their relationship to the culprit. At the same time, this strategy enables plaintiffs to display publicly the moral quality of compassion for *walytja*. These constructions retain an important public and ideological quality: Despite their show of "compassion" in such circumstances, plaintiffs do not seem to forget or truly forgive an offense, as private comments after such occasions sometimes reveal. Strangers are less likely to receive much concern, although the Pintupi are certainly capable of extending their "compassion" to anyone with a good case.

As values held among people whose resources are unreliable and who have need of each other through the long term, "compassion" and "pity" are highly adaptive qualities. It is not surprising that men claim they would be unable to send visitors away from their own water holes in time of drought. At another level, however, the moral valuation of empathy defines the limitations on an individual's autonomy and imposes on decisions the constantly shifting push-and-pull of consensus. The possibility always exists of moving another's actions toward one's desired end, because he or she will be "compassionate" or because one makes him think he should feel it.

The value of "compassion" does not mean that Pintupi are never selfish. People sometimes hide possessions to avoid sharing, and giving is often prompted as much by veiled threats as by spontaneous generosity. With possessions carefully hidden—be they meat, cigarettes, or extra clothing—one may express "compassion" without having to give up anything. This withholding may be later rationalized by commenting that the other is "not really *walytja*." On the other hand, some individuals exhibit generosity as a means of building a network of followers. Such an informal leader acquires only limited power, since his position depends upon his giving and his continued openness to the claims of compassion. He cannot impose hard decisions. Rather, he must be "compassionate" with people or lose his following. To stick to his decisions, he needs a basis of support outside the community to which he can defer.

To show "compassion," then, is a social requisite, and not necessarily the expression of an internal state. In this sense, the expression of such emotions is genuinely a "compromise formation" (LeVine 1973: 132), adopted as a means to other ends. Perhaps even fear of retaliation by the offended party can be its motivation. Only thorough knowledge of an individual's history and her or his disposition or personality would enable outsiders to interpret the motivational basis for her or his acts. By displaying "compassion," whatever the motivations, one's act is presented in a favorable light for oneself and for others.

All social activity takes place within this rubric of relatedness. Insofar as being *walytja* is the necessary condition for all meaningful interaction, compassion should characterize the relations among people. Consequently, this emotion amounts to a moral ideal, an emotion Pintupi expect people to have, similar to expectations in American culture that one should love one's spouse and children. The cultural value placed on such emotions inclines individuals to elaborate and emphasize them in accounting for behavior, both in understanding themselves and in comprehending others. This folk theory of motivation as a means of apprehending subjectivity has a social basis, judging individual action in relation to shared identity.

In Pintupi theory, "grief" or "sorrow" (*yalurrpa*) is equally rooted in social relations, generated by loss or threat of loss of some related other and represented as a loss of part of oneself. Such "grief" is expressed by wailing at the news of a death as well as through a set of expected self-inflicted injuries, such as gashing the head or stabbing the thigh. These injuries and the marks they leave, appropriate to the kinship relationship one has to the dead, represent the inscribing of the body social onto the individual. People like to recount the origin of each mark.

"Grief" is a powerful emotion, a real shaking of the foundations, leading to self-punishment as often as to anger and revenge against the cause. As seen by the Pintupi, sorrow is a particularly important human trait, attaching to many situations surrounding death and loss. For years after a death, one should not mention the names of the deceased because relatives will be too "sorry." They may even assault the disrespectful. Some women wail long after a son's death, a disconsolate keening they send out into the night when thoughts of their loss are no longer distracted. Pintupi explain that the woman is "thinking about her son," and wailing establishes her identity for others as "one who has lost a child" (*yurltu*, "empty"), or "one who has lost a husband" (*pinka*), and so on.

Because people are "too sorry," one avoids the place where kin have died until the memory has faded in intensity. For others to approach such a site would bring anger from the deceased relatives, implying disrespect. Abandonment of a place in which death occurs is thus a cultural convention. As with other actions, it need not derive spontaneously from "authentic" feelings of grief, but the display is clearly needed as an expression of one's relatedness to the dead.

Not only does the significance of place in Pintupi thought derive some emotional force from the displacement of emotional ties with the dead to places associated with them, but the value of the sacred owes much to the accretion of "sorrow" for the dead. On sight of ritual paraphernalia and the sacred places of The Dreaming, older men often begin to wail because they are "sorry." One man explained this with reference to the designs incised on his spear-thrower:

> Dead men schooled me, gave this to me. When people see it, they get sorry. Give one like this to a man, and people will see it and give you a woman. Too much crying [from sorrow] for this one.

Ritual and sacred things are associated with the memory of people who previously handled them and passed them on. This heritage provides the source, in part, of their emotional value. Charged with reminders of the dead, they may make one cry with "sorrow," remembering that which binds them to this object.

The Pintupi make this meaning explicit in revealing rituals to young men. "This belonged to dead men," elders emphasize; "you have to hold it and pass it on." Thus, ritual draws upon the strongest elements of relatedness and continuity, juxtaposed with mortality, to imbue that which is of universal and transcendent value—The Dreaming—with the most powerful sentiments of identity available. In the deepest sense, the Pintupi world is a personal one, and its greater, more enduring structures are built on the foundation of the most intimate relations, as objectifications of subjective identity.

The significance of this binding or "cathecting" of initiates to the transcendent also reflects the other fundamental social implication of "sorrow": the openness to recognizing the other. Many revenge expeditions were reported to have turned back because of "sorrow" or "compassion." If they had sufficient time to think about the identity of the one they intended to kill, Pintupi men often became "sorry." In several reported cases, revenge parties threw spears at a guilty man, which he repeatedly and successfully dodged. Finally, recognizing their shared identity, they became sorry for him and let him go.

Paradoxically, the explanation for expeditions of punishment is often "sorrow," a social sentiment representing the loss of one who was related. Pintupi explain that such a loss must be reciprocated, "square and square," by killing the person responsible for the death. The particular motivations to enact one's "sorrow" may be vastly more complex, of course. One may participate out of duty, honor, love, hate, or even self-hatred.

While "compassion" may lead men to abandon revenge, it is often the case that a man who committed a grievous ceremonial offense is killed "without sorrow." The emphasis Pintupi place on this formulation identifies a clear problem for those who want to bring sanctions to bear on offenders against moral law: How does one overcome the "sorrow" or "compassion" for relations that might prevent the carrying out of punishment? When close relatives might be "too sorry" to take part in punishment, the dilemma of relatedness can be circumvented by asking outsiders to impose sanctions on relatives who violated Dreaming prescriptions.

When they discuss punishments that have been carried out (such as past executions of wrongdoers), the Pintupi often mention that there was "no sorrow." The Pitjantjatjarra, they said, would kill *anyone* who crossed the path of their traveling secret ceremonies—women, children, or whites; they were not moved by "sorrow." Great anger, as at the sight of a heinous moral crime, could move men to "spear anyway" (*waparltu wakala*), that is, without recognition of the other. Similarly, drunkenness may provide the same excuse for violence: ignorance of the identity of the other. Given this view of accountability, one can understand the threats to get revenge "any time, when I am drunk."

What sustains the social objectivity of norms that transcend immediate relations? One might argue that the importance of male initiation and male cult provides a way in which a man is reoriented to a greater value than his relatedness to kin—to The Dreaming. Those who violate The Dreaming's Law, say the Pintupi, will be killed "without sorrow." Male initiation provides a mechanism for reorienting subjectivity, for assuring conformity to things of transcendental value, for ensuring that concerns beyond the immediate feelings of relatedness will prevail when vital moral issues are at stake. The description of sacred objects, songs, and the like as "Law" emphasizes their obligatory power. In Pintupi theory, it appears, the binding power of Law over compassion comes from "sorrow"—itself the very expression of relatedness to others, just as in Freudian theory the superego derives from the id in order to oppose it. How else could Pintupi overcome the tendency to "compassion"? Men are bound to the higher Law through the same considerations of relatedness and "sorrow" for the dead, and they deny "compassion" as agents of a higher authority and not of their own will. It is not an egotistic denial of relatedness but an acceding to the authority of the framework on which Pintupi society is based. Thus, they are not responsible personally: The Dreaming is something outside of them to which they must conform.

I will mention only briefly the third concept of this family, *watjilpa*. This term is often rendered as "homesick," "pining," "lonely," "worry," or "melancholy." At its core it refers to separation from objects or persons of security and familiarity—places and people among which and with whom one grew up and where one feels safe and comfortable. Separation from these provides the source of "worrying." People are anxious for news of sons, husbands, or daughters who are separated from them: They "pine" for them. One of the later migrants eastward to Papunya from traditional Pintupi territory explained his reluctance to go to Papunya because of "worry" (watjilpa) for his country. This sentiment plays an important role in local organization. Time and again, Pintupi talk of their travels and the "homesickness" (watjilpa or yirraru) that lead them to return to their own country. One friend, who had not seen his country for a long time, explained to me:

> I close my eyes and I can see that place. It's very green. There's a rock hole and a hill where I used to play. My brother pushed me down. . . . It makes me homesick.

When men sing the songs of their own Dreaming, they may describe themselves as watjilpa, nostalgic at the separation. Similar aspects of this kind of sadness are stressed when the Pintupi describe a sulky person as "lonely" (watjilpa), emphasizing that the sulkiness is due to "missing" something desired. A young married man whose wife preferred her mother's company spent long days in his own camp, waiting dejectedly for food. He was, I was told, "lonely."

"Shame"

Finally, let us consider the concept of "shame" (kunta), an emotion anthropologists have frequently analyzed as a mechanism of social control. The Pintupi concept of kunta includes within its range the English concepts of "shame," "embarrassment," "shyness," and "respect." "Shame" is usually associated with the discomfort of being observed by others in the public domain, especially at being seen to do something that is poor etiquette, ill-mannered, or wrong. It is therefore explained by Pintupi as an important consideration in conduct. Small children often "become shy" (kuntarrinpa) when strangers approach: running behind their mothers and holding on to them, they peek out fearfully.

Kunta also involves awareness of others and a notion of hiding negatively valued qualities of the self. In a sense, "shame" is a metasentiment, defined only in relation to other emotions and evaluating the self as a totality with respect to positively valued qualities. It coordinates the demands of relatedness with those of personal autonomy. As a representation of the relationship between a subject and the other, "shame" helps separate what is defined as "public" from the "private."

If the emotion of "shame" constitutes the difference between "public" and "private" it is, correspondingly, peer group pressure, from those roughly one's equals, that effectively socializes the Pintupi young in toilet training and other matters through ridicule and shaming. In its developed sense, "shame" is a quality of the socialized person, involving a growing awareness of standards and propriety. The give-and-take of daily life, the intimate and informal association of people, depends on activating considerations of "respect" or "shame" that make individuals reluctant to impose themselves or their wishes overtly on others.

The concept of "shame," therefore, is most applicable to formal or ceremonious occasions, to the etiquette of confronting elders, to the subject of sexual relations, to meeting strangers, and to highly structured social relationships. Conversely, it is far less relevant to relations among intimates. Without putting too much emphasis on the content of the categories at this point, I would argue that "shame" distinguishes between the public and private as social and infrasocial. Geertz (1973: 399) has related the Balinese concept of shame (which he prefers to call "stage fright") to "the cultural attempt to block the more creatural aspects of the human condition from sight." In Bali, he argues, shame is attendant upon the lack of control or skill that destroys the illusion of a "play" and allows the actor to show through his or her part. The Pintupi concept of *kunta* maintains a public presentation of self that is largely devoid of egotism, selfishness, individuality, or "animality." It should be understood in relationship to the ideology of relatedness (*walytja*), which emphasizes the shared goals of egalitarian, closely cooperating kin and suggests that autonomy must be expressed through sustaining relatedness to others. By rejecting "vulgar" or "unrefined" private feelings, desires, and behavior as inappropriate for the public domain, the ideology is experienced as a true representation of social relations and of human nature.

"Embarrassment" often accompanies public occasions of speaking, as a means of avoiding the appearance of egotism, self-assertion, or private willfulness, and accepts identity with others as part of the self. Young men rarely speak on these occasions, fearing the embarrassment of appearing to make too much of themselves or their knowledge. Older men habitually begin their speeches with forms by downplaying their contribution. "I am," they regularly begin, "just telling you a little story." The intended message is that a person does not think he is better than the others. Similarly, direct contradiction is avoided lest it cause "shame" through breaching the rubric of relatedness or by exposing a person's egotism.

The desire to avoid the impression of egotism extends to many practices in Pintupi life, including the ritual manufacture of sacred objects. A single individual ought not to make objects alone, lest he be thought conceited: He should be "ashamed." In this way, one denies being motivated by private will. Others become jealous of those who so promote themselves and thereby assert independence from others. When older men speak authoritatively, on the other hand, they do so as representatives of the Law, not personally. The official stance is not always accepted, of course, since younger men may recognize a personal concern involved in their ritual discipline, but the practice delineates the logic of sociality.

Aboriginal politeness is most often due to considerations of "embarrassment." People hesitate to ask strangers or distant kin for food because they are "embarrassed," afraid that such a request will be presumptuous. With very close kin, however, such considerations become less relevant, and individuals can be quite aggressive in their demands within their own camp. Beyond this circle, persons are more likely to sit and wait to be offered food than to ask for it. They avoid making the desire explicit and perhaps forcing the other party to an explicit refusal that would compromise the ideology of shared identity through kinship.

As noted in chapter 3, visitors coming to a new or distant country stopped outside the camp at which they arrived, waiting for those of the country to come and greet them and to invite them to enter the group. Visitors ought not to barge in. They waited, informants said, "to avoid embarrassment."

New arrivals in a community are not only reluctant to speak out in meetings or discussions, but they also move less freely about a camp than do long-term residents. Visitors tend to stay with their closest, most familiar kin, allowing the latter to speak for them if necessary. Full integration into a coresident community can take more than a month, and persons without close relatives may always consider themselves outsiders who should defer to others in formal situations.

Among men, sexuality represents another domain of subjectivity inflected by the concept of "embarrassment." To be sure, lusty conversation about sexual matters takes place, but men do not talk or joke about the sexual relations they have with their own wives. It is considered inappropriate even to refer to a man's wife with the term "spouse" (kurri); proper etiquette replaces such a direct allusion to sexual relations with kinship terms that pair individuals in relation to the speaker, avoiding the term "spouse." Nor would men discuss menstruation with me, because it was "shameful" (kuntangka).

Sexual relations are supposed to be private matters, not observed by others. Thus, children at the age of eight or so who become conscious of such concerns no longer sleep in their parents' camp, taking up residence in single men's or women's camps. The "embarrassment" related to sex is partly a fear of being observed in a private act and ridiculed. Much of the gossip about men's sexual adventures takes the form of laughing at outrageous and apparently shameless behavior in faraway places. One older man told me that although a young girl might be bestowed as a wife, she may be afraid or unwilling to have intercourse. In such a situation, her husband should not force her, lest she yell out or scream and he would be "ashamed." Sexual relations apparently are regarded as possessing great potential for creating disorder in the public realm. The Pintupi concern to control this potential, given that marriage acts as a vital mechanism for maintaining social order, is understandable. Thus, a number of related social relationships are also characterized by "shame," which counsels avoidance or restraint in the presence of a man's "wife's mother," "wife's father," other affines, and his circumciser (a "wife-giver"). Such relationships frequently entail use of special avoidance languages, which substitute lexemes from the avoidance language for those in everyday terminology (cf. Dixon 1971, Haviland 1979, Merlan n.d.).

Observing other Western Desert people at Jigalong, Tonkinson (1977) describes how the relationship of "shame" to sexuality appears to influence the choice of "spirit-child" explanations of the cause of pregnancy over those emphasizing intercourse or semen. Tonkinson argues that, although they do know about physiological paternity, Aboriginal men ideologically avoid this subject as well as the subject of biological reproduction, because "We are not like animals." Pintupi men also refused to talk of pregnancy and childbirth, considering them to be "shameful" matters, subjects for which numerous euphemisms abound. On two occasions when men referred publicly to the male role in procreation—saying that they "made a child appear"—others nearby giggled nervously. In application to sexuality, "shame" contrasts with a human similarity to animals, or bestiality. Unlike animals, one should be aware of "shame." The promiscuity of dogs is a subject of derision among the Pintupi, and people who have intercourse with the wrong categories of kin or who copulate indiscriminately are said to be "like dogs."

Kunta as "shame" and kunta as "respect" present two sides of the same coin. Showing respect for someone by consulting that person's wishes, by not overstepping one's bounds, or by "shyness" in stating claims, avoids embarrassment. "Respect" (or "shyness") is often expressed by a hesitation to speak out. Conversely, disrespect—such as refusing a person directly, without excuses—is "embarrassing." Pintupi speak with amazement that whites are able to refuse a person "to his eyes" (*kuru lingku*). This is to recognize no relation to the other, to assert one's total autonomy. Similarly, other uses of the concept *kunta* emphasize its relationship to respect for another's wishes, property, and rights, and a concomitant restraint on personal gain or greed. One is "embarrassed [respectful] of what belongs to others."

A Moral Order

Pintupi concepts of the emotions constitute a subjectivity that recognizes a significant identify with important others, such that these others are represented as part of the self. The self is not an aggressive, self-contained, egotistic, or entirely autonomous individual. Rather, one must be malleable to others, not "hard." One should be moved, not stolid in willfulness. When a young man at Yayayi tried to assert himself as free of obligation to others, older men chastised him in a revealing way: "Did you become a man by yourself? We grew you up. We made you into a young man!" Genuine autonomy is not a product of private will, but results only through successful negotiation in relations with others. Coming from outside the individual, this autonomy—finally established as the zealousness of upholding the Law "without sorrow"—is a representation within the individual of a socially valued moral imperative.

The cultural meaning for the Pintupi of the emotions can be read almost as a moral text against the wrongness of private willfulness. This subjectivity must be common throughout Australia, as among the Murinbata for whom Stanner (1966: 40–45) describes the mystery attached to the motivation for private will in an important myth about the "wrongful turning of life." Pintupi accept that people retain, at the core, an incomprehensible individuality, and they frequently describe puzzling behavior as simply "his own business"; or "her idea." But this selfhood is to be mediated through the social value of relatedness, something that increases throughout one's life. Acceptance of the culturally defined emotions as appropriate ways of articulating one's experience can be said to represent the society's interests, although there is no self-conscious collective representation of the "community welfare." What is interesting for the Pintupi is that sociality is constituted largely out of dyadic relations, through the emotional response of individuals to significant others, and through maintenance of a core of collectively accepted traditional regulations to which individuals

Pintupi Country, Pintupi Self

are also emotionally bound by investing the Law of The Dreaming with intimations of others. As Simmel (1950) noted in his study dyadic relations, these provide only a fragile form for continued association.

A Political Order

This is a social world dominated by the pressure of relatives, dominated by "immediacy." The cultural forms of "compassion" and "shame" constrain the ways in which Pintupi social action is organized. People protect their autonomy by hiding or removing it from sight, while in more basic ways it is "hidden" by being sanctified as a given. Pintupi structuring of the subject assumes a projection of the basis of autonomy outside the individual. This lends a particular form to social action that necessitates attributing its origins to something outside the actors, usually posited in The Dreaming.

The problem of Pintupi (and perhaps all) social order is how to objectify some relations beyond the realms of immediate subjectivity. Thus, the view of the self formulated by the structuring of the emotions has important consequences for the maintenance of order and authority in Pintupi life. As the Pintupi see it, morally binding social consensus cannot be generated by human decision-making. Rather, consensus is maintained by common adherence to a shared, external, and autonomous code: The Dreaming. What they call "the Law" is not something made by humans. Not the creation of any person or group, the Law is outside human control and cannot be the vehicle of any private interests or selfish pursuits. Those who cite The Dreaming as dictating a certain course of action are not perceived as making a personal statement of preference or desire, but rather as offering an impersonal, non-self-related precedent, divorcing themselves from any interest in the outcome. Thereby, they avoid "shame."

By following this course, one presents oneself as not trying to force others to submit to one's own will. All submit, instead, to the same transcendental moral imperative, before which humans are merely passive. Besides avoiding "embarrassment," this strategy also removes the decision from any quarrel or negotiation, from pleas for "compassion."

Human decisions can never be accorded a similar status. They lack the binding moral force as a consequence of their ontological status. No individuals possess authority or the right in themselves to create what others must follow. Authority is achieved and autonomy guaranteed instead by first identifying oneself with an external, impersonal authority—making one's authority a mediation of publicly accepted obligation rather than private will. The Law—legitimate authority—does not stem from the self; it is not arbitrary or motivated by individual interests. Consequently, for any principle or decision to gain authority, it must be objectified, projected outside of the relatedness that prevails among human actors.

Conclusion

This analysis of how the emotions define and orient Pintupi in their social world suggests why the principles used in everyday life should have a claim to existing outside the creation or subjectivity of the users, as historical and timeless truths. Both "compassion" and "shame" demand that legitimate authority be represented as external to the self and morally binding on all. This binding quality is itself generated out of the same emotions that emphasize relatedness and identity with others. The enduring constructions of Pintupi social life thus can be sustained without contradicting the fundamental image of Pintupi society as relatedness; they do so as the very maintenance of that principle.

The image and reality of relatedness are maintained through fear of "shame," effectively effacing from the public domain the egotistical aspects of individuality. The strong value on egalitarianism entails that Pintupi not seem to stress their own wishes. Rather they should appear to be emphasizing something external and objective to them—timeless, eternal principles.

CHAPTER 5

The Cultural Basis of Landownership and Its Social Implications

It is not one man that holds a country; many do.

Territoriality has been an unexamined concept in most writing about hunters and gatherers (Collmann 1982, Ingold 1980), especially in discussions concerning land tenure. In this chapter, I try to place Pintupi "landownership" in the framework of a larger political economy that accounts for the value of rights in sacred estates. As the Pintupi understand it, "ownership" provides opportunities for a person to be the organizer of a significant event and the focus of attention, albeit in a limited context. Owners of sacred sites are in a position to exercise equality with other fully adult persons, to offer ceremonial roles to others (as part of an exchange), and to share rights in ritual paraphernalia. Thus, Pintupi landownership must be understood in relationship to the emphasis on both widespread relatedness and personal autonomy in social organization.

At the societal level, landownership provides a means of projecting the significant relationships of the past into the present or those of the present into the future—in other words, of objectifying social arrangements in enduring form (Sansom 1980: 20). The process of determining who "holds" country transforms the identification among persons in daily life into a structure—embodied in the unchanging landscape—that transcends the immediate moment. The more enduring temporal formation is itself built recursively out of the raw material of current relationships. This recursive movement reifies social relationships, transforming the experiences of being "one countrymen," for example, into a social artifact: joint relationship to a sacred site that endures through time. Nonetheless, the ease and flexibility with which rights to sacred sites are extended suggests that the attempt to turn the transience of social relations

127

into a permanent form is still dominated by the overriding Pintupi emphasis on relatedness.

An individual-oriented approach is central to my analysis of the Pintupi system of land tenure. From this perspective, the existence of groups becomes problematic: No matter what their particular structure, Pintupi landholding formations are the outcome of processes of affiliation. What we find, then, among the Pintupi contrasts with the patrilineal model of landownership once believed to hold throughout Australia. In the Pintupi system, the bases on which people are able to assert their relationship to named places are several.[1]

To state the case in this way, however, does not draw attention to the positive features of the organization of relationships to "country." Nor does it draw attention to the dialectical relationship between land use and landownership. Among the Pintupi, people view "country" as the objectification of kin networks and as a record of social ties. Although the *ngurra* that is owned preexists human society, which is viewed as organizing itself around these sacred estates, *ngurra* as "camp" and as "named place" are parts of the same ongoing social process.

While I follow Stanner (1965) in distinguishing "range" from "estate" (see chapter 3), I differ from him in interpreting these phenomena as properties of individuals rather than of well-defined groups. An estate, commonly a sacred site, has a number of individuals who may identify with it and control it. They constitute a group solely in relationship to this estate.

The basis for this system lies in "identification with country," a notion rooted in the fact that place always bears the imprint of persons. Identification refers to the whole set of relationships a person can claim or assert between himself or herself and a place. Because of this multiplicity of claims, landholding groups take essentially the form of bilateral, descending kindreds. Membership as a recognized owner is widely extended, and therefore groups are not a given.

Identification is an ongoing process, subject to claim and counterclaim, dependent on validation and acceptance or invalidation and nonacceptance. The existence of such a political process has been observed by other anthropologists (Pink 1935: 243, Strehlow 1947, Barker 1976), but has rarely been treated with the importance it deserves. It enables claims of identification to be transformed into rights over related aspects of a country. Such rights exist only when they are accepted by others. The movement of the political process follows a graduated series of links or claims of increasing substantiality, from mere identification and residual interest in a place to actual control of its sacred association. The possession of such rights as recognized by others, called "holding" (*kanyininpa*) a country, is the product of negotiation.

This graded range of claims, though not well-marked by linguistic forms, is an important property of a state of affairs open to much negotiation. Thus, the Pintupi blur the distinctions between range and estate. Talk of "my country," "our [exclusive] country," and "their country" denotes a whole panoply of rights, duties, and degrees of substantiality. When necessary, however, more specified statuses toward a site and certain properties of it may be designated by a variety of terms that refer to custodians of a place—for example, *mayutju* (boss), *tjila* (big one), and *ngurrakartu* (custodian).

Landownership in the Western Desert is thus an elusive matter. Only belatedly did I come to see the mystery as part of the system itself: Ownership is not a given, but an accomplishment. Although rights over sacred sites are acquired only through political activity, this historicity is disguised by the fact that the cultural basis of claims lies in the ontological priority of The Dreaming. The contingent nature of custodianship is not culturally recognized. In the end, ownership of country—denoting close association among a set of individuals—projects into transhistorical time the valued social relations of the present, but it does so without drawing attention to the boundaries being created. Ultimately, landownership is tied to a politics that emphasizes both the claims of relatedness and those of personal autonomy.

The Cultural Logic

There are numerous reasons for referring to a place as one's "own country." If the place is called A, the following possibilities may constitute bases for such a claim:

1. conception at the place A;
2. conception at a place B made by and/or identified with the same Dreaming as A;
3. conception at a place B whose Dreaming is associated mythologically with The Dreaming at A (the story lines cross);
4. initiation at A (for a male);
5. birth at A;
6. father conceived at A or conditions 2–5 true for father;
7. mother conceived at A or conditions 2, 3, or 5 true for mother;
8. "grandparents" (*tjamu*, *kaparli*, including all kin types so classified) conceived at A or conditions 2–5 true;

9. residence around A;
10. death of close relative[2] at or near A.

One can claim identifiction with any place with which one's close relatives are identified. A fundamental link in the chain is a person's identification with his conception Dreaming and its place. He or she is, after all, its incarnation.

The Basis of Identification with Country

When they discuss the activities of The Dreaming at different places, men regularly refer to figures in these events by kinship terms (for example, "my father"). One man told me about his "mother's brother," who as a small marsupial in The Dreaming traveled past Tjitururrnga and refused to give fire to Nungurrayi, a woman also created at this spot, when she wanted him for it. A male personage in The Dreaming at Lake Mackay was yet another "mother's brother." The figure of the myth and the person conceived at the place are identified.

Because this practice is followed extensively, the landscape is personalized. Tjanya tjakamarra frequently paints designs associated with a site named Yiitjurunya, which he identified as "my grand-father's country." This grandfather, a man who was conceived at Yiitjurunya and whose Dreaming it is, is his mother's father. Tjanya has the right to paint these designs, he says, because it is his grandfather's place. Another man claimed the right to visit Yawal-yurrunya because it was his "father's Dreaming." And according to still another narrative, a man was killed at Kirritjinya in The Dreaming by the throwing sticks of *Tingarri* men. That Tjanya claims this man also as his "grandfather," a Tjakamarra man (his "father's father"), illustrates how one can be related to many places.

In Pintupi theory, an individual represents an incarnation of some figure or object of The Dreaming that was active at the conception place. The individual is said to have been "sitting as Dreaming" at this place. If the particular Dreaming traveled on beyond the place, it is said that the individual was "left," "lost," or "left behind" (*wantingu*) by The Dreaming or "set down" (*nyinatjunu*). There is little interest in what these individuals might have been like before they became persons, or whether they were "spirit children" as described for some parts of Australia or "spirit essence" as described by Meggitt (1962: 65–66) for the Warlpiri.[3] The doctrine of incarnation has its practical use in securing identity.

The Dreaming is not itself the object of speculation but the solution of another problem: Where do people come from and why do they appear when and where they do? The answer to this question also enables the Pintupi to explain the physical characteristics of individuals. For example, Maantja's peculiar birthmarks were seen to reflect his experience as part of the Euro Dreaming when he was burned in a fire.

An individual is identified with his Dreaming.[4] People are often referred to in terms stressing their identity to The Dreaming, that is, a man may be called "Emu Dreaming" or "Possum Dreaming." And just as others refer to figures in The Dreaming by kinship terms, people frequently discuss the events of their own Dreaming in the first person. In this sense, an individual is, from conception, identified with a Dreaming and through it to a place. As transformations of the same Dreaming, place and person share an identity of substance. That a person's identity is thus founded on something that is unchanging, not created by human beings, and absolutely distinctive, defines individuals to possess a degree of autonomy as part of who they are. In this theory of human substance, a part of each person is owed to no other person.

Other events in an individual's existence are also marked in space: his or her birth, initiation (if the person is male), death, and some events of lesser significance. Such socially recognized events give an individual some claim to identification with a place. They establish a sense in which the place is "his" or "hers." This relationship does not cancel out the claims of other persons to identification with the place, any more than one individual's kinship relationship to someone cancels that of other people's. They may all have their own grounds for claim. It is not unusual for several people to have been conceived at one place; they will, however, be associated with different features. The important claim to places derived by one's being of the same Dreaming but different location simply extends the logic based on the similarity of substance between a person and The Dreaming.

Place as the Image of Close Relatives

The Pintupi idea of conception reflects a world view common throughout Aboriginal Australia. What is perceived as a cosmological datum—conception seen as an event not caused by human beings—is made the basis of the social world (Stanner 1966: 19). There is a strong feeling that the place of an individual's conception really is *his* place, that those conceived at a place should remain there. If this were so, local organization would realize the plan of The Dreaming.

For instance, Timmy tjakamarra told me that his Dreaming was located near the Pollock Hills and that he had gone south "for no purpose" (ngunytji, also "insignificantly"). The implication was that he should have lived near his Dreaming-place, but in fact he lived around his father's area, Kulkurtanya. Indeed, he was usually called "the one from Kulkurtanya."[5] Such expressions of the sympathy presumed to exist between a person and his Dreaming (tjukurr walytja), his own place, are common.

People are also identified with a place through death and burial. At death, a person's name and any word resembling it become taboo for several years. Even long after the initial period of taboo, Pintupi remain reluctant to use the personal name of the deceased. Instead, they refer to an individual by the name of the place where he or she died. The man called Niwilnga tjapanangka (see chapter 3), for instance, is usually referred to as Turkurrnga, after the place where he died. Discussions of history, of dead individuals or genealogical details, usually culminate with recitals of burial places. Commonly, in the life histories, informants would talk of someone (usually employing kin terms) who gave them meat. When I tried to specify the identities of such people, narrators replied with a genealogical link to someone I knew or the person's burial place. Place, then, indexes an identity that can transcend the present.

Tjanya tjakamarra, for example, told of the travels of two mythological carpet snakes (kuniya) through Purtinkanya, where they killed and swallowed a small animal. Subsequently, at nearby Pintipungkunya they threw up; their vomit became his "grandfather," who was conceived there. This Tjapaltjarri man was, he said, "my private, really grandfather (tjamu)" because he had given his sister as wife to Tjanya's father's father. His father's father is known as Narrkalnga, from the place of death, and Tjapaltjarri, congruently, is known as Purlpurlnga, where he died. Mutual relationships among the living to these men establish a sort of descending kindred tied to place. As Tjanya noted, Purpurlnga was the father of Mara Mara tjungurrayi and the grandfather, mutually, of Tjanya and Mara Mara's son Wamitji (see Diagram 5A). In such manner do living individuals group themselves around places identified with shared kinfolk. The past legitimates current relations.

This legitimation is also embodied in landownership. Claims of identification with a place through a "close" dead relative are common. Originally from the south, Brawny tjangala's father had traveled to Marpurinya to visit his brother-in-law. Stranded in the north by the onset of summer, he died at Marpurinya. For Brawny, this fact constituted one part of his identification with the area around Marpurinya and Yumarinya. Pinga tjapanangka is closely identified with Winparrkunya, where his father, Linyarri, was killed. On a similar basis, Maantja tjungurrayi demanded apology from

Pintupi Country, Pintupi Self

Diagram 5A. Descending Kindred

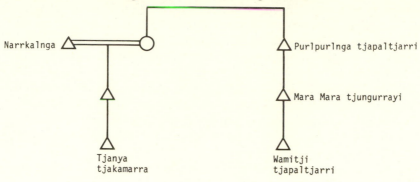

men who had gone to the place where his mother died without consulting him. Indeed, after the Pintupi moved to live in settlements, they argued their claim to residence in outstations on the basis of the death of relatives in the area.[6]

Death and the Landscape

Death, like other events, leaves its mark on the land. Thus, when an individual dies, everyone leaves the place. If a group of Pintupi are living at a temporary water hole, they move to another one. If (as most do now) they are living at a permanent settlement, they may only shift their camps away from the spot. The reason Pintupi give for such moves is that they are "griefstricken" (*yalurrpa*) and do not want to be reminded of their loss. Their grief leads close relatives to inflict injuries on themselves. In the ritualized "sorry fights" (*parnparla*) that follow a death, relatives from other communities express their "grief" in attacks upon those who were living with the deceased but failed to prevent death. The coresident relatives, they say, "did not look after him or her properly."[7]

No one should return to the site of death for a year or so. Although currently burials are carried out by white authorities or representatives of the Lutheran mission, they have had little effect on basic Pintupi ideas about death. It is now difficult for Pintupi to actually leave an area, but they avoid a specific spot where death occurred for several months. The danger is not perceived to be from spirits or ghosts. Instead, people are concerned not to provoke anger by reminding relatives of their loss and making them "grieve." Even small children observe this constraint on their mobility and show respect for an area of death.

The organization of "grief" occasioned by loss, rather than a concern about the spirit (*kurrunpa*) of the dead, constitutes the primary framework through which death is met. It is not only the surroundings where people shared activities that would remind them of the dead and cause the living to grieve. Complex arrangements are made to give away—to "distant" mother's brothers—the dead's personal possessions. Close relatives are griefstricken at the sight of things identified with the dead. Indeed, while burial now follows Christian procedures, the "sorry fight" and ceremonial transfer of personal property remain the significant features of Pintupi mortuarial activity. They serve to efface all traces of the immediate identity of the dead.

The "sorrow" unquestionably carries over into all extensions of the dead. Old men cry when they visit sacred sites, reminded, they say, of the dead who used to accompany them to these places. Their wailing resembles the keening one hears when a report of death is received. Similarly, when the design or paraphernalia of a Dreaming is shown at a ceremony, old men may be moved to tears. They emphasize that sacred objects are "dear" and invoke "sorrow" as the source of their regard. As I was told, "Those who are dead [*mirrintjanyirri*, also 'ancestors'] held them; we, who came after, we hold them now."

Pintupi beliefs about death do not focus on the recycling of spirits back and forth between a descent group (countrymen) and the land, although such beliefs are fairly common in Australia.[8] Questions about the fate of the spirit after an individual's death meet with confusing responses. Indeed, that the Pintupi were so quick to give up control of burials—they were as willing to renounce them as Arnhem Landers were insistent on retaining them (Morphy 1984)—underlines an important difference in respective strategies of social reproduction. The gathering of relatives in Pintupi mortuarial practices does help to produce an ancestral legitimation for a current group, but the gathering is a kindred. This organization is very different from the bounded patrilineal descent groups of northeast Arnhem Land (Warner 1937), for example, who take such care in recycling their clansmen's spirits through reburial.

Pintupi burial places become one more, rather short-lived, objectification of recent history. Their funerals do not emphasize lineality or descent; instead their organization on the principle of generational moieties stresses the relatedness among people in a region. Death is an affair of the whole society, as it were; close brothers of the dead are linked organizationally, for example, with genealogically and geographically distant ones. Ties of locality are largely overridden. As in initiation (see chapter 8), relatives from "far away" help those who are "close" and "too sorry" to do the work themselves. The latter lie down, wailing, at a distance from the grave while distant kin of the deceased's generation light a fire that burns away the area surrounding the grave. Through these practices, the place becomes significant to a whole network of people. If they desire to represent themselves as a group, the place can objectify their shared identity.

Attention to the fate of the spirit reflects these concerns. Accounts of traditional mortuary rites indicate that the spirit survived the body after death and remained around the grave. At the second and final mortuary ceremony, many months after the death, a fire was lit around the grave and a native curer (*maparntjarra*) dispelled the spirit. There is little attention in Pintupi belief to what happens to the spirit; what is important socially is that it somehow disappears. Some people said the spirit "finished" (died, ended), while others said the spirit went up to the sky.

Quite apart from the existence of the spirit, then, death and burial constitute a permanent and emotional identification between an individual and a place. Social recognition of this identity is reflected in naming. This identification is passed on to relatives of the deceased, who remember it along with his or her other accumulated associations and identities.

The Ambiguity of Identification

Pintupi assertions of identification, such as "that's my country" or "that's our country," are highly coded and multireferential statements. Initially, I expected that collecting such claims from numerous individuals would delineate sets of people everyone agreed were identified with a place. The isolation of finite groups proved impossible, however. Assertions of identification were also manifest in ritual contexts that stress control of rights over sacred sites. Despite the extensive verbal claims to identification with sites made on other occasions, during any given ritual only a few men were clearly in the precedence. Their positions depended on relative age, personality, and other factors, as well as the kind of claims they could make.

Claims of the form "that's my country" do not necessarily imply custodianship of the ritual associations of a place. Nor does it matter to which ritual patrimoiety ("owner" or "manager") a claimant belongs.[9] Rather, claims of identification remain ambiguous and open-ended.

Such was certainly the case with the Pintupi claims to the area around Yayayi, where they resided from 1973 to 1977. When some Aranda-speaking men from Hermannsburg argued in a land-rights meeting in 1973 that the area around Haasts Bluff and Papunya was their country, a good deal of discussion took place among the Pintupi about the security of their tenure. Prior to the Aranda claim, the area had been regarded as indisputably Loritja country. Two men of long residence explained the Pintupi position to me in terms that provide a good example of the claims people make to identification with a country. Yayayi was their country because:

1. a lot of our old people died here [in the area];
2. we grew up around here;
3. our children were "born" [born and conceived] here and it is their Dreaming;
4. it is a Pintupi Dreaming that comes through here from the west [referring to the Honey Ant Dreaming, whose travel route circles through Pintupi country and back through this area to Papunya];
5. we gave a lot of women [the Pintupi bestowed many women as wives to Aranda and Loritja men who, consequently, have obligations to the Pintupi as affines].

Despite these assertions, the Pintupi never claimed rights over the sacred sites in the vicinity of Yayayi. These were regarded as belonging without question to the descendants of the area's traditional inhabitants.[10] What the Pintupi were claiming was the unqualified right to reside at Yayayi and to use the resources of the area. This had been guaranteed them, they said, by Tjanawayi, an important ritual custodian who was in addition the Aboriginal manager of Haasts Bluff Cattle Station, which owned the country around the area. The assertions of the Pintupi were made to back up their claim and to gain the support of the Loritja and Warlpiri in Papunya as coclaimants against the Aranda interlopers. Their position had an emotional impact, or was intended to have one, that would sway support to them. There was no confusion about their relative status.

An Individual's Claims

On another occasion, Takata tjapaltjarri explained to me that the area from the Ehrenberg Range to Papunya (including the disputed territory) was his country because he "grew up" (*purlkarringu*) and became a man in this area. Yet he still continues to claim the Sir Frederick Range area to the south as his country, too. The Loritja people, who are generally considered to be traditional custodians of the country from Haasts Bluff to the Ehrenbergs, had long since left the area and gone to Hermannsburg, he insisted. According to this

Pintupi Country, Pintupi Self

position, continual association with the country is yet another criterion in claims. Other people, including the Loritja, did seem to accept Takata's claim to be one of the area's caretakers.

Takata's situation is even more informative when one considers his heritage. Ordinarily, his father was considered to be a "country-man" of Maantja (see chapter 3) and said to be from the Sir Frederick Range. However, both Ngampalaya tjungurrayi and Tjanya tjaka-marra, two men from further west, told me that Takata was a countryman of theirs. He "should have been from Purlpurlnga," they said, a permanent water northeast of the Baron Range. Takata's father's father was from Purlpurlnga but had left the area to avoid trouble for some wrongdoing. Later, Takata's father had been conceived in the Sir Frederick Range area, well to the east of Purlpurlnga, had grown up, and had been considered a "countryman" there. Takata himself was conceived and born in the area near the Sir Frederick Range, but his father was also involved in trouble, so they left that region and fled northward. They relocated in the area near Yilpilinya in the Ehrenberg Range, and his father was still alive when Takata was initiated east of the Ehrenberg Range. Not long after that, however, a revenge party from the Payarrnga area (west of Lake Macdonald) traveled northward and speared Takata's father and his father's "close brother" in the sandhills just west of Yilpilinya. The spot where they died was pointed out to me by various men on the occasions we traveled past it. Although un-mentioned by Takata himself in his claim-making, the death provided further reason why he can claim Yilpilinya as his country.

The Processual Character of Identification

It is important to recognize how the Pintupi process of identification with country is situated in personal experience. In enumerating his country for me, Jerry tjakamarra listed not only his father's "tradi-tional country" (near Lake Macdonald), but the area around Haasts Bluff as well. These were all his country, he explained, because he had seen and visited them all. Other men similarly considered places to be their country because they "knew" them, that is, had acquaintance with them. Although several forms of identification are covered in the simple phrase "my country," all derive from and indicate an emotional attachment to a place. These are expressed equally in the concepts of "knowing" (*ninti*) and also "kin" (*walytja*).

Statements such as those concerning the disposition of the Yayayi area were essentially "claims" rather than matters of un-deniable fact. In this framework, we can better understand what is being said in identifying oneself with a place. No one would or did argue with the fact that the Yayayi area was traditionally the area of other people. What was being asserted, in a clearly political context, was that some Pintupi could make legitimate claims to the place. Thus, Pintupi said, "they can't send us away like bullocks." Takata put it more certainly still: "Nobody can tell me; I grew up around this place." From this perspective, traditional ownership was simply a more stable and patterned transmission of identification over time, but it was always open to flexibility, manipulation, and change.[11]

Multiple Pathways:
The Individual Nature of Claims

In Pintupi society, there are multiple pathways to membership in estate-owning groups. Pintupi landowning groups overlap in membership and are bilateral in composition.[12] Not only is there frequently dissonance between what is said to be an individual's country and that of the father. More important, examples of recruitment to "country" directly contradict Stanner's (1965: 15) assertion that there are no cases of the adoption or naturalization of a person of one descent group into another. My subsequent argument for the flexibility of Pintupi claims depends on the point that membership involves choice.

Here, then are several cases of individual affiliation:

(a) Brawny tjangala was usually associated with the Yumari area. His own Dreaming-place was Parrkirrkanya, nearby, where he had been left by the woman Kutungu in her mythological travels. He also claimed the Pollock Hills as his country because he had grown up there. On these grounds, he argued for his inclusion on a trip to that area. For another trip westward, this time to Yawalyurrunya, Brawny identified himself with that place because it was his "father's country": His father had been conceived along the *Tingarri* route from Yawalyurrunya to Lake Macdonald, and his father had also been a resident of the area. However, Brawny's father had been residing in the north around Ngartannga when Brawny was conceived. Brawny's sister had been bestowed on a man from this region, and this was probably the reason for their residence there. When he was a boy, Brawny's family went further north to visit his father's brother-in-law, a man named Linyarri tjapangarti who was associated with the Mount Webb, Angas Hills, and Yumari area. While visiting with him at Marpurinya, summer came upon them and it was not possible to return south to their own country. Brawny's father died here during this period, and thus it is said to be his country. Others have rights to it as well, of course, but they recognize a father's death. Brawny only claims that a father's death and burial give him rights in the area, as do his own conception and residence nearby. Through his mother, on the other hand, he has residual claims to the Sir Frederick Range area. Wide-ranging as they are, Brawny's claims to identifications with country were accepted by others.

(b) Tjiwa Tjiwa tjangala and his older brother Ralyu offer another case of claims. Their father, they said, was from the south originally—from the Yawalyurru area. However, he lived in the north around Yumarinya with his wife's people, she being the sister of Linyarri tjapangarti (Pinga tjapanangka's father). Tjiwa Tjiwa's mother was conceived in this area. The father died while still in the north at Kalturanya. Tjiwa Tjiwa was conceived at Ngurrapalangunya, and Ralyu at Yawarrankunya, both of the Old Man Dreaming that traversed the area and visited Yumarinya. Both men claim the Yumari area as their country on three grounds: through their mother and her father (bearing the same personal name as Tjiwa Tjiwa), through their father who is buried there, and through their conception Dreaming links to the land. By virtue of his father's link to the south, Tjiwa Tjiwa was able to claim identification with places there, too.

(c) Miraki tjupurrula was said to have been a southerner who shifted north and became identified with Timalnga (Dakota Hills). I was told that the people of this country taught him about it and made him a "boss" of it. He resided in this area frequently.

(d) Bobby tjapangarti (see genealogy in Diagram 6B) was conceived in the Sir Frederick Range area and was said to be from this country, including Pirmalnga. Nonetheless, after the death of his father (Niwilnga), he traveled north and was looked after by people in the Yumari region. In the north he was initiated at Kuruyintinya, and he considers some men of this area to be "close relatives." He lists the place of his initiation as his country, along with his more substantial southern affiliations, as well as his mother's country (Warlungurru).

(e) A Pitjanytjatjarra man from the south who had married a Pintupi woman claimed an affiliation to the Pollock Hills area. His mother's country was around Docker River, and her Dreaming was *Tingarri*, a branch of which also traveled through the Pollock Hills. He claimed the right to visit a place because he was able to link himself to the Dreaming of the place. The logic of his claim was that he should know his mother's Dreaming.

There are, as these examples illustrate, numerous claims that an individual can assert in identifying himself or herself with a country (*ngurra*). Though all of these should have a logical basis, not all of them are given the same weight. Furthermore, not everyone agrees on the status of an individual's claims.

Conflicting Views

Accounts of relationship to country can be conflicting. Repeatedly, Tjarlu tjakamarra told me that Kirpinnga, Putarungkalnga, Walawalanya, and Yunarlanya were all his country, as well as Parliparlintjanya—further to the west—where he was conceived. He admitted that Nippy tjangala, Tjarri tjampitjinpa, and Kuniya tjangala were also from Kirpinnga and referred to them in ways appropriate for people "from one country" (see chapter 7). Indeed, they did live together around Walawalanya in the Pollock Hills and west of it.

Yet Kuniya told me that Tjarlu was *not* from Kirpinnga and Putarungkalnga. He was, rather, from the west and north of these places. Kuniya claimed that he himself had southern affiliations to the Karrkunya (Baron Range) area and the water holes stretching toward Kirpinnga in the north. In this fact there was a suggestion that he and his brother Nippy had shifted northward from where they "should have been." Nonetheless, through their fathers, Kuniya and Nippy had unassailable claim to Putarungkalnga, a Two Men (*Wati Kutjarra*) Dreaming site. Their fathers were said to have had a special sympathy with this place. Their sons have taken on this relationship, and Nippy—the elder—maintains primary control over ritual concerned with the site. Tjarri tjampitjinpa, who acts as father to these two men, grew up in the southern side of the region, but his father died at Minyinanya, in the area near these places. Further, Tjarri's own Dreaming is the *Tingarri* that passed through the area.

The disagreement between Kuniya's and Tjarlu's accounts is more specific than one about general identification with a country. It concerns, rather, ritual control. Tjarlu explained his relationship to the country by saying that it was both his father's country and that of his father's father as well. His father's Dreaming had come from this area, from Karilywaranya, the starting point for the Two Carpet Snakes who traveled west. Explicitly, he identified his father with the events of this Dreaming: "He chased the two snakes and killed them." While the Dreaming started at Karilywara, the narrated killing of the snakes occurred further to the west. So Tjarlu's father was probably conceived in the west. Tjarlu, however, emphasized the Dreaming as a whole and in this way made a claim to the starting point. Another basis for the claim was that his father died at Tjikarrnga, also in the Pollock Hill area. Generally, however, Tjarlu's claim was that he was "from the plain country" (*wirrinyingurrara*), referring to the flat, nonsandhill country running along the Gunbarrel Highway to Jupiter Well. He considered this his home area and saw it as "one country."

The issue is not fully resolvable. Tjarlu said that his mother was from the Karrkunya-Purungunya area, as was Tjarri, and this could also be a basis for his claim to be from the same country as Kuniya and Nippy. Only once did he say that Purungunya and Karrkunya were his country, however, adding that they were "from my mother's brother" (*kamurungkatja*). Generally, Tjarlu is oriented toward the north. He himself did not travel frequently in the south and continues to count most of his relatives at Balgo Hills to the north rather than at Warburton to the south. The other men associated with Kirpinnga have relatives more equally in the north and south. Nonetheless, these differing orientations seem more a matter of choice than of a determination based on "ownership" rights.

There was not a final outcome to this dissonance. No visits to the sites in question were made, nor has outward disagreement between Tjarlu and the others occurred. When I witnessed rituals related to the sites, Tjarlu participated as a significant member. But what, then, is the basis of the assertion that Tjarlu was not from this country? My interpretation of these differing views is that Kuniya was not totally denying Tjarlu's claim to identification with the country in question. Instead, he was asserting the primacy of his own claim, an assertion nobody would deny. Indeed, these conflicting claims offer an unexceptional example of the political nature of making and accepting claims.

Evaluating Claims

The primary basis on which identification is established is conception. Through such an incarnation, an individual is considered to be identified substantially with a place, as a mutual transformation of the same creative activity of The Dreaming. Yet however rooted it may be in cosmological facts, identification becomes meaningful only when validated socially. It must be actualized and accepted by others through a process of negotiation.

A single extended case illustrates the relative weight of claims and the process through which they are given form. The example concerns a journey (via four-wheel-drive vehicles) to the *Tingarri* sacred site at Yawalyurrunya in June 1974. On the way, some of the men who were led by Timmy tjakamarra stopped at a place called Kantawarranya ("yellow-ochre place"). This yellow ochre deposit on the side of a hill is held to be a creation of the *Tingarri* after the men were sent forth by the Native Cat from Yawalyurrunya.

According to the story, a man who was decorated in yellow ochre lay down there and was transformed into this hill and its mineral deposit. Timmy decided we should get some yellow ochre to take back to the settlement. Gathering the ochre was all right because this was his country and the old people had always done so. Later, however, there was a meeting of all the "custodians" of Yawalyurrunya, including Timmy's relatives from distant places. As mentioned in chapter 3, one of these men, Butler tjampitjinpa, had not been present on the trip, and he threatened to spear Timmy for violating his place. Because Kantawarranya was Butler's conception place, it should not have been touched without his permission. Other men interceded before violence was done. Although Timmy was going to allow himself to be speared, he told me he had not done anything wrong: his grandfathers had always taken yellow ochre here. The general view, however, differed from his. Most men felt that Butler should have been asked first.

The account of landownership altered after this encounter. Tjanya tjakamarra (Timmy's older brother) told me that Butler was the "number one boss" for Yawalyurrunya and that he (Tjanya) was second. This assertion of seniority had several possible bases. First, Butler is older. Second, *Tingarri* is his Dreaming and his conception place lies in close proximity to Yawalyurrunya. Third, Butler's father's Dreaming was also *Tingarri* from here, and he had been "number one boss" of the place before, with Tjanya's father as second. Prior to the episode with Butler, Tjanya and Timmy had represented themselves to me as the primary custodians.

The initial version was not, I believe, an attempt to mislead; there is no question of Tjanya's integrity. In fact, he came to me with the revised account so that I could present it in a report on the site to the Western Australia government. The experience reflects, instead, a characteristic of social action quite common among people with neither literacy nor significant social differentiation. These men were not accustomed to presenting balanced, sociocentric accounts of "ownership," listing for the benefit of an outsider all owners and the ordering among them—even though some were absent from the current field of action. The practical framework in which such accounts are ordinarily offered is one of presenting their own claims to inclusion or ownership for particular events. In these contexts, the abstract serving of "justice" is not the immediate issue; there is no third party to judge the claims. The process works because Pintupi are primarily concerned that everyone is satisfied with the results, that no one feels his or her rights have been denied. Denial and rejection, conversely, can be dangerous.

Do they have a concept
of Rights.

The ambiguity becomes even more obvious today, because reliance on motor vehicles makes the logistics of getting to sacred sites a greater problem than it was in the past. When people walked to their sites, each person could be asked prior to going. With only temporary transportation, propriety is often compromised because everyone must quickly take advantage of the ride. Further, when all the relevant parties were present in the past, the question of ordering claims—of determining who was *really* the boss, for example—did not need to be decided with the finality of an explicit listing on paper. There was room for a pragmatic political ambiguity.

How much indeterminacy lies at the core of Pintupi politics concerning "country" is suggested by the further developments in this case. Several months after the events already described, other individuals told me that Mara Mara tjungurrayi should have been the "boss" of Yawalyurrunya. To be sure, he had gone on the trip, but his role in the proceedings had been far less prominent than that of Tjanya and Timmy. How was this new assertion to be understood? According to the emerging view, Mara Mara was conceived from this *Tingarri* Dreaming; it was his "own Dreaming." Thus, as one man put it, Mara Mara should have been the boss because he "rose" (*pakantjatjanu*)[13] from Yawalyurrunya. Another man maintained that it was wrong for the two brothers to have "taken possession" (*walytjarringu*, literally "became kin" or "became identified") of this place. It was not their Dreaming: they were "from the side." They merely looked after the place their father had looked after. These informants argued that Mara Mara had been too "embarrassed" and restrained to press his claims.

Those who took this position used it as part of a larger criticism of Tjanya and Timmy, namely that they had not permitted the ceremony to be filmed. Such had been the original plan of the trip, as films had been made of visits to other Pintupi sacred sites. Because of this omission, they believed, no one had been paid for the trip, a matter of disappointment to many participants. Mara Mara would have let it be filmed.

It seems clear that the introduction of new elements into the procedure of custodianship of sacred sites—inaccessibility of sites, the separation of persons who had previously lived together into various settlements, the need to formally list "owners" for white records, concern over payment and filming, and so on—have added dissonance to the traditional context in which ownership was defined. These elements do not, however, necessarily represent an alteration in the substance of ownership. This example illustrates not only the variety of claims that can be and are made, all deriving from various modes of identification with place, but also that the organization of people in relation to place projects current political relations deeper into social space.

Claim-making and Actualization

The question of who is or is not part of a country-owning group draws our attention to the process people use to reach such a determination. There are claims and counterclaims, although they may not be voiced explicitly.

For example, Alex tjapanangka angrily contested the journey to Yawalyurrunya. He argued that he should have been taken because it was his country. In fact, he was conceived of this Dreaming, but rather close to Lake Macdonald and at some distance from Yawalyurrunya. This distance reduced the importance of his claim to identification. Certainly, none of the other men seemed overly concerned about taking him nor did they mention him in plans for the trip. After the trip he argued a modified position—that we had been wrong to travel through his country, on the way to Yawalyurrunya, without taking him along. Like others in similar situations, he used every argument he could muster to obtain support. Indeed, the ultimate goal of such maneuvering for the Pintupi intimately concerns other people's support. Not every point set forth, however, has equal value.

Many individuals maintain claims of varying sorts to a site. Because the Aborigines do try to satisfy—or, at least, they try not to affront—those with claims, people may appear to accept the claims as valid rather than openly refute them. In the end, someone may have to be quietly left out. Weaker claims are simply ignored and treated with benign neglect. This behavior conforms with the overall character of Pintupi interaction. Overt disagreement is difficult and embarrassing. The person ignored may press his claims further by threats of violence as a last resort, but the evaluation of this act will depend, as usual, on the relationship between parties. If a man is considered a relative, others may view his threats of violence with sympathy and relent. If, on the other hand, he is not regarded as having a strong relationship to people, they may respond with violence themselves.

For the most part, the determination of authentic identification eschews open refusal.[14] Negotiation takes ambiguity to heart in this way as a result of the fact that claims to land are based on identification with a place, and such identifications have multiple modes. We saw this in the varied arguments Pintupi made for the right to reside at Yayayi. As a result of claims of identity with a variety of close kin, each individual has a number of sites with

144   *Pintupi Country, Pintupi Self*

which he can claim a relationship. The countries with which one identifies, therefore, constitute a kind of record of who a person is, with whom one is identified or related, and where one has been.

A man may claim identity with all the places over which his father has rights. The problem is whether other people will accept the legitimacy of these claims and to what degree. For men this issue involves rights over the ritual associations of a place, a valuable object in the hands of a few custodians of previous generations. If those persons who control access to a place and its esoteric lore are close relatives or friends of one's father, they are likely to look on one's claims with favor. By such a process, a person may be granted a socially recognized identity with all the places his father claimed. These might include his father's father's country, his father's mother's, and so on.

One also has claims to the country of one's mother. The people who live there are not only one's genealogically close relatives, but also sometimes one's coresidents. Children are likely to live with their mother's people for periods of time and to know them well. Thus, one's mother's father, or even mother's brother, may grant access to and teach one about his places.

Two themes are outstanding. First, there is a strong ideology that everyone's identity, including rights and social identity, stems from The Dreaming. This belief is part of the ontology that perceives everything as having "become real" from The Dreaming. Indeed, the strongest claims of place identity are those that are clearly "from The Dreaming." One should, by this token, control the place of one's own Dreaming. The second theme is the importance of affective, emotional considerations in decisions about relationship to country. To some degree this dynamic is expressed in the idea of "one's own country" as *ngurra walytja*, with its reference to security, to what is known and familiar, to acquaintance as opposed to strangers.

Claims and Rights: "Holding" a Country

We have reviewed what kinds of claims to identification are reasonable to the Pintupi. But how do they become acceptable? In exploring how people manipulate such cultural forms in practice, we shall glimpse what underlies territorial organization.

Pintupi implicitly make a critical distinction in evaluating rights over country. The concepts of "looking after" (*yarntayarn-tarninpa*) and "holding" (*kanyininpa*, also "having") a country denote a special status within the broader diffuse range of identifications. "Holding" or "looking after" a country specifies rights and duties in the sacred religious domain, over the ritual and secret associations of myths, songs, designs, and objects.[15]

These concepts are important symbolic "operators" in Pintupi culture, not only articulating a special kind of relationship to place but proving critical, as well, to the meaning of kinship. The word *kanyininpa* may be used to refer to possession of physical objects ("I have two spears," "I am holding an apple") or to the actualized relationship of parent to child ("my father held me and grew me up," [*ngayuku mamalurni kanyinu purlkarnu*]). It also refers to rights over ceremonies, songs, and designs ("dead people held and lost it," [*mirrintjanyirriluya kanyinu wantingu*]). Thus, its various significations derive from the basic idea of an intimate and active relationship between a "holder" and that which is "held," as suggested in the primary meaning of physical grasp.

As "having/holding," *kanyininpa* is contrasted with another key concept, *wantininpa*, which means "leaving" or "losing" something, leaving it behind, breaking off association, or neglecting it. For example, Pintupi may say, "I left it [didn't touch], that spear" (*wantingurna kurlarta palatja*) or "I saw the fight and left it alone" (*nyangurna pika, wantingu*).

Both these concepts are used in relation to country: One "holds" a country and on death one "loses" it. Essentially, in leaving it behind, one hands it on. As Munn (1970) argues for Pitjanytjatjarra myth, this Pintupi construction relates the passage of human generations to the transmission of "country" as a social artifact. The process is represented in myth as a series of transformations from subject to object to subject: The country is an exterior object that comes to embody the subjectivity of those who "hold" it.

When they speak of "holding" a country or "carrying the Law," Pintupi represent the relationship in phrases denoting some sort of physical object as a weight or burden—a responsibility—for the holder. Indeed, the relationship is often materially represented by the holder of a country actually possessing sacred boards with the designs of the country. Although such emblems are made by men, they are said to be "left" by The Dreaming. It is men's responsibility to look after these tokens.

Little is known about how Pintupi women "hold" country. But as far as I have been able to determine, the relations of "holding" country that I am describing here are largely matters of concern to initiated men. Women have ceremonies, songs, and designs related to country and established through their own mythological traditions, to be sure. The ritual systems of men and women share a common basis in The Dreaming, and the myths with which women are concerned seem to represent complementary aspects of those controlled by men. Women do not, however, have official access to the esoteric knowledge of men about country, and to some extent men are similarly barred from access to women's esoteric knowledge.

The traditions would thus appear to be parallel, each providing rights to places in their own domain. Women's identification with country, however, does not carry the same social consequences as does men's. It does not lead to regular travel and movements to care for sacred sites. Both sexes have relations to land but they take on different values in the contexts of action. The system of relations to country among men is, I believe, more elaborated than among women because sacred sites allow for the regulation of relations among men, for whom political autonomy constitutes a major issue. This structure of action has, perhaps, unfortunate consequences for women in that their own attachments to country and freedom of movement may be compromised by the requirements of men (cf. Bell 1981, Hamilton 1979). That this brings men into conflict with women is, it could be argued, not the motivation for elaborating male cult, but the result of the actions men take among themselves.

Kinds of Rights

In Pintupi usage, the concept of "holding" includes two distinct statuses that people take up in regard to a place. As among Warlpiri (Meggitt 1962), rights over many Pintupi sacred sites are differentiated and distributed according to the statuses *kurtungurlu* (usually glossed as "manager" or "worker") and *yarriki* or *kirta* ("owners"). Whether a "holder" is one or the other depends on the nature of his kinship relationship to a place. The terms of reference themselves are drawn from the reciprocal designations of participants in ordinary language: Ego calls his mother's brother and that man's son *yarri-kirarra*, while *kirta* is used in reference to "wife's brother" and his son (Hansen 1974). Members of the "owner" moiety, however, usually refer to themselves as *wapirra*, a term designating "wife's mother's brother" and "father." The general principle plays a critically important role in Pintupi social life: Since ownership is intrinsically complementary, no one person can "hold" a country by himself, entirely to the exclusion of others.[16]

While the terms of reference are egocentric, the statuses correspond to a sociocentric division of the eight subsections into ritual patrimoieties so that "workers" are of one category (for example, ego, his father, his mother's mother's brother, and mother's mother's brother's son or wife's mother's brother) and "owners" of the opposite category. If a man is a "worker" for country X, for a ceremony of that place he should help decorate the actors, prepare the sacred objects, and so on. Those of the "owner" category should be the performers. In regard to the place itself, an "owner" should not visit a sacred site without first consulting a "worker" and should not touch the place. The sacred objects stored at sites remain under the care and custodianship of the "workers."[17]

There are four invariant subsections in each such patrimoiety, as follows (see chapter 7 for details):

Patrimoiety A	Patrimoiety B
Tjapangarti (Fa)	Tjampitjinpa (Fa)
Tjapanangka (So)	Tjangala (So)
Tjapaltjarri (Fa)	Tjakamarra (Fa)
Tjungurrayi (So)	Tjupurrula (So)

There is no technical term in Pintupi for the grouping "patrimoiety," nor are there sociocentric names for the divisions (although I have labeled them A and B). People merely talk of who is *wapirra* or *kurtungurlu* for a particular site or ceremony.

The most important point is that members of both patrimoieties have rights to the site and its ritual. "Owners" and "workers" are not in a boss-worker relationship in the Western sense: their roles are complementary and reciprocal. "Workers" may be "from the country" as much as "owners" are. They "hold" the country together.

Pintupi ordinarily explain who is *kurtungurlu* and who is *wapirra* simply by listing the subsection categories. This procedure obscures the logic of the complementarity. There are some clues, however, of a deeper logic. On one occasion, I heard an explanation of "workers" (*kurtungurlu*) as those descended "from women" (*kung-kangkatja*). This interpretation is congruent with Nash's (1980) analysis of the Warlpiri word *kurtungurlu* as meaning "woman's child." It is worth exploring the content of the less formalized explication.

Let us consider, for example, a Tjungurrayi man as being conceived at and identified with Dreaming Y. People can call this Dreaming by kin terms appropriate to the man and refer to the Dreaming as "Tjungurrayi." Tjungurrayi in turn can portray his mythological self in ritual; he will be in the actor's ("owner") role. Those who are related to the place "from women" will be "workers." That is, Tjungurrayi's sister's sons and his daughter's sons would be "workers." Indeed, this pattern would correspond to the patri-moiety division. If one imagines these rights as passed on only through men to their sons, the result is isomorphic with the patrimoiety divisions. The logic of the complementarity of rights seems rooted in the distinction of those related through men and those through women.[18]

This basis has been obscured, however, by further developments of the logical possibilities of the subsection systems. The resulting sociocentric structure offers enormous integrative potential for relating persons who live within a large region. By attaching subsections to kin types, the Aborigines have created a model for the organization of ritual activities with strangers and visitors as well. Participants need not be descendants. A "holder" of a country can invite distant acquaintances of the appropriate category to enact the role of "owner" or "worker," as the case may be. Not only does this procedure expand the "holder's" personal ties, but he can substitute distant relatives to fill the ranks of an estate group depleted of personnel. Ritual organized on the basis of such sociocentric categories represents the ceremony performed at each distinctive site as a local manifestation of a larger, total society.

"Holding" and Knowing a Country

To "hold" a country is to have certain rights to it, mainly the right to be consulted about visits to the place, about ceremonies performed there, or about revelatory ceremonies concerning its ritual associations held elsewhere. To carry out this status, one must know (ninti) the story of a place, the associated rituals, songs, and designs. What one "holds" and what one "loses" or passes on is essentially knowledge. This point is what informed Tjanya's criticism of Alex tjapanangka's claim to be a "holder" of Yawalyurrunya. Although Alex had been conceived from the Tingarri Dreaming, he had never been to Yawalyurrunya and never seen the ritual. Thus, he did not know it. Mara Mara tjungurrayi, on the other hand, was a genuine "holder." He had seen the place and knew the ritual.

The control of such knowledge provides a focus for organization, between old and young and between holders and nonholders. Many people can claim identification with a site, but they do not "hold" it unless other "holders" agree to accept the person's claim and teach them about it. Reflexively, the organization has stimulated the elaboration of esoteric knowledge. These relationships become clearer in exploring what constitutes knowledge about a place.

Those who reside in an area know much more about its local geographical features—details invariably attributed to The Dreaming. Nonresidents cannot know with similar confidence all such esoterica. Without explanation, details obliquely referred to in songs remain necessarily obscure. In any case, the words themselves in ritual songs are restrictive, often archaic and meant to obscure meaning from the uninitiated. Like the songs, an area's secret lore requires instruction. Visitors to a new region are taken around, shown some of the significant places, and taught to avoid certain sites. Later, they may be introduced to a sacred site and instructed in its secrets. Such an event is quite important and men who have been traveling invariably note the sacred sites they have seen.

At Yawalyurrunya, for example, men were able to indicate various small rocks whose color carried special meaning, a tree that was an important figure crouching, and so on. That such esoteric knowledge exists is widely attested to in the literature on Aborigines, and needs little further comment here. What does require comment, however, is that the body of such knowledge is not necessarily finite. Human beings do create—or rather discover—more. Because the creation of such "new" knowledge is unverifiable by empirical observation, it offers a suitable vehicle for differentiating older from younger men: the latter can never be certain if knowledge has or has not been withheld (Peterson, personal communication).

The unwarranted production of esoteric knowledge is checked in part by the fact of its being socialized; others must accept it. Young men, for example, are unable to make claims to special knowledge without the acceptance of elders. On the other hand, no one is sure how much old men *do* know. Who is in a position to question them? The oldest man I knew at Yayayi was reported to always eat the hearts of emus. He always got them, a young man said, "lest he stop the sun. Those old men have a lot of tricks." The tone of this comment suggested that he was not certain the old man could do so, but that no one knew for sure.

The process of this creativity depends on two elements: the possibility of the unexpected and a willingness to believe. Pintupi are quite willing to entertain the possibility that others might have access to details hidden from them. Thus, the Pintupi version of what Elkin (1944) called "Aboriginal men of high degree"—the "doctor men" (*maparntjarra*) or "clever men"—also have "a lot of tricks." They can change their form, see what is invisible to others, and cure sickness. But such knowledge is warranted only through acceptance by others. Only those who are recognized by others as knowledgeable are likely to be persuasive in offering interpretations. The threat of having one's authority challenged in public deters all but the most confident from undertaking such an account.

For similar reasons, those who reside in the area of a sacred site are positioned to claim greater knowledge about it than others.

Furthermore, they "look after" the site, care for it through cere-monies, and so on. Through such continuous interaction—and not only through conception—they qualify as *walytja* (kinsmen) of the place. As "kin" of a place, they are recognized by the spirits who reside in some sacred sites. The possibility of achieving a relationship to a place through an active process is basic to Pintupi conceptions of identity, as reflected in the idea of *walytja*. Although the word *walytja* carries genealogical implications as "kin," the core meaning of the term is "one's own." To claim that one is *walytja* is to assert a relationship of identity between oneself and persons, objects, or places. In the Pintupi view, it is possible to "become *walytja*" through prolonged association and care.

Again, the case of claims to Yawalyurrunya is illustrative. Long before the 1974 trip took place, Timmy tjakamarra dictated a letter to the people who were living at Docker River. They had intended to visit the site. His message was that they had no real rights to Yawalyurrunya, that they should not go there without him. They had not, he said, lived around the place, but had left the area as children. They had not grown up there as he had. Finally, they had not "looked after" the place as he and his father had. Because they did not really know the place, their claim to "hold" it was forfeit.

The opposite dynamic occurs when young men are initiated and subsequently taught about their sacred sites. Fathers, older brothers, and other close relatives take them to sacred sites and show them rituals. They are "introduced" (*nintinu*) to the place. This visiting and seeing the site, learning about it, become important in laying claim to control or share in the control of a site. Such instruction, then, is a crucial component of the social reproduction of ownership and through it the production of adult men.

One's own country (*ngurra walytja*) is, for Pintupi, a place of security. Here, dangerous noumenal forces are absent: One is "known" by the spirits and one "knows" the proper rituals that maintain the ongoing relationship. One's own country provides the source of one's identity. Its rituals are the substance of what one can "show" to other men; they represent that which one contributes to the totality. Through such rituals, each man has the opportunity, at least for a short time, to be a leader, to be the focus of a gathering. Ritual is, then, the performance of an individual's political autonomy as an equal among men. However important, this autonomy can never be accomplished in isolation; one still needs the help of others to put on ceremony. The ritual associated with country gives each man the opportunity to be autonomous on the condition that the same men become the audience for others.

Who "Holds" Sacred Sites?

The emphasis in Pintupi landownership is on extensiveness of rights. If pursued through persistent inquiry and observation, the resulting list of those who "own" the ritual of a site does not constitute a patrilineal descent group. However, the general rule—the first mentioned by men—is that a man holds a country "because (or when) the father dies" (*mama wiyarrinytjangka*). "When the grandfather dies and the father dies, then the son (*katja*) holds the country."

Other men articulate the process in more general terms. The explanation of The Dreaming mentioned in chapter 2 portrays the relationship of people, country, and Dreaming:

> A dead person lost it; another dead person lost it; and still another dead person lost it; and so on. . . . Finally, we hold it. . . . It is not our idea [i.e., we did not produce it]. It is a big Law. We have to sit down [live] like all those people who died before us.[19]

Men asserted that they could visit sacred sites because their fathers used to go there. In this sense, their fathers had "held" these sites before. When the ceremony associated with Putarungkalnga (near the Pollock Hills) was performed in a settlement after a visit to the place, one young man in particular was brought to watch. At its finish, the assembled gathering addressed him, telling him the story of the Two Men as he touched stones men had brought back from that Dreaming. "This is your grandfather," they told him: His father's father was conceived of the Two Men Dreaming near Putarungkalnga. Because of his grandfather's and father's close identification, this young man was instructed in the ritual and considered to have special rights.

Men think of this transmission as a vital responsibility. In old age, they speak of being "ready to die and wanting to pass on" ceremonies. They want to "give" (teach) these ceremonies to their sons. The ideas of "showing" (*yutininpa*), "giving" (*yunginpa*), and "teaching" (*nintininpa*) are, to some extent, equivalent concepts in the transmission of esoteric knowledge.

Ceremonies always involve more than a few men, and on these occasions all the younger generation men are referred to as "the group of sons" (*katjapirti*). This term should not be taken literally, not least of all because the term *katja* is the unmarked label for both "sons" and "sister's sons." Indeed, the younger men are not all actually "sons" to the older men who display and manage the ceremony. Instead, the phrase indicates a general view of transmission as "father-to-son" through the generations. However, as previously noted, rules about "holding" the country are always expressed egocentrically. All that is said is that when a man dies, his son "takes on" his country, his responsibility. The consequence of this transition is not named patrilineal descent groups.

It is significant that *katja* can mean "sister's son" as well as "son" (although it can be contrasted with *yukari*, which means "child of opposite-sex sibling"). A man's sister's sons have a claim to "look after" and "hold" his country. When I was presented with statements about *katjapirti*, further questioning always uncoverd that a man's sister's son also "held" his country. As Maantja told me:

> When the group of fathers dies, the sons [*katja*] look after it; when the mother dies, the sons look after her country. [*mamapirti wiyarrirra, katjapirtilu yarntayarntarninpa; ngunytju wiyarrirra, katjapirti.*]

Men maintain that one should "look after" the countries of one's mother (*ngunytju*), one's father (*mama*), one's grandfather (*tjamu*), and one's grandmother (*kaparli*). Since several kin types are associated with each term, this lengthy list entails even more responsibilities than it would appear.

While providing the most general rule, the formulation "father died, son looks after" does not cover every contingency and possibility, nor every outcome. In fact, as men never tired of explaining to me, "It is not one man that holds a country; many do." Many people retain an interest in a place, and many can claim some form of identification. Consequently, they are all concerned that it is looked after properly. To do so is their responsibility. At least one custodian of a sacred site drew the ire of others "because he did not properly look after the place." Essentially, Pintupi do not "own" land to the exclusion of others. As the continuous nature of Dreaming-tracks implies, every site is part of a larger, related entity. In this sense, those responsible for any part act as custodians for the larger group.

In the Pintupi view, many people should go on any visit to a sacred site. One should, it was said, "not go secretly, [but] rather go so that everyone can see what happens." Maantja reported, for example, that he and a few other men had been near a sacred site but had not visited it because there were "not enough men." This notion relates to the facts that many people have rights to a place; that they are all concerned it be treated properly; and that they may be suspicious of what others do.

The emphasis on extensiveness of rights is quite marked. Pintupi men usually serve as custodians of sacred objects and ritual paraphernalia jointly with several others, even when the men are not close kin. Sharing out the responsibility and ensuring proper care, they include others.[20] Indeed, those men who attempt to act alone on sacred matters arouse jealousy and anger. Maantja's father was killed, he reported, for making sacred objects by himself. Young men, recognizing this problem, are hesitant to include themselves in ritual until they have considerable confidence. A young Warlpiri man drew my attention to this as a serious issue. He expressed his respect for the older men who danced in ceremony. Doing so, he said, makes other men jealous and exposes the dancer to surreptitious attack. It was not so different, he thought, from Western culture: didn't we kill John Lennon?

These are manifestations of a pervasive pattern in Pintupi sociality, namely to extend ties, to include more people rather than to exclude. The Pintupi emphasis on wide-ranging relatedness among individuals in a region differs from Aboriginal forms of territorial organization that identify individuals first with a discrete group (such as a clan) and then integrate these into a larger system. Among the Pintupi, whose terrain sustains far lower population density, a primary problem is how to get enough people together to ensure continuity of knowledge and perpetuation of the cult. The duty to look after sacred sites—thus ensuring the continuity of things, making the plants and animals continue to reproduce—is mediated by a wider sociality.

Such an emphasis on extensivity provides a basis for a wealth of substantial secondary ties to land, thereby assuring a proper succession to custodianship (cf. Peterson, Keen, and Sansom 1977). This process seems critical among Western Desert people whose small groups are subject to uncertain demographic fates. There are, indeed, cases of men "taking on" custodianship of a country over which they would have claimed no primary rights. During a period of population changes and migrations from the desert, Tjarrinya tjampitjinpa claimed to "hold" Yuruyurunya. He said, "I grabbed and look after Yuruyuru, because it had become empty."

Succession is not unique to Western Desert people, but the unique form of Pintupi society is highlighted by contrasting the way succession takes place here with the process among the neighboring Warlpiri. Warlpiri describe different groups of the same Dreaming-track that are of the same pair of subsections as having a "company" relationship. Such groups are seen as substitutable, or parallel, groups that can assume each other's responsibilities. Instead of this substitutability of discrete groups, Pintupi stress that individuals of the same Dreaming-track or living nearby—no matter what their subsections—have rights because they are all "one country." The Warlpiri link two groups that are first differentiated, while the Pintupi simply extend ties in one place to a wider social sphere.

Ownership and Long-Term Adaptation

For all its flexibility, "ownership" and the Pintupi ideology of custodianship are related to territorial organization in the long term and to the regulation of resources. To understand this, one must attend to the processes that lead to shifting and temporary alterations in the shape of defined resource areas.

This relationship has two dimensions. First, the notions of "country" and "ownership" provide for extended networks of related countries and related people. A common theme in studies of local organization in desert areas has been the importance of such links in maintaining reciprocal access to resources in different territories, providing a system of "countryman" relationships overarching those based on simple kinship ties (Gould 1969a, Peterson 1969, Strehlow 1965, 1970). Since The Dreaming ancestors traveled widely, their activities may link places on a path covering hundreds of miles. The continuity of stories classifies named places into larger systems, and individuals who own a place or part of the story have a claim to be considered for other parts. For some purposes, all those places on a Dreaming path are considered to be "one country," and those who own different segments may be considered "one countrymen." Such systems of stories undergo a continual process of being reworked, providing an ever-changing charter of who and what can be identified as "one country." "Countryman" relations define potential productive ties.

Second, rights to "country" provide a basis for the localization of people in areas. The Pintupi data show that, as Peterson (1972) argues more generally for Aboriginal Australia, the emotional identification of persons with particular places leads older men to reside near their own primary sacred sites. This pattern ensures that people will return to marginal areas, to exploit the entire region, and makes for increased efficiency in a regional system, potentially supporting a larger population. The Pintupi pattern of claim and negotiation, along with extensive identification with sacred sites, contributes to this process of reallocating people to place. Because population density was low in the Gibson Desert, the group of men residing "regularly" in a range and looking after the country there was likely to be small and demographically unstable (Peterson 1983). Even two generations ago, some emptying out was occurring, followed by new people moving into the vacated area and taking over responsibility for the country.

Thus, the secondary rights to country as estate (Peterson, Keen, and Sansom 1977) provide for what was surely a predictable process of replacement of country-holding groups. The current shapes of boundaries of country ownership represent only a stage in the process by which members of one group have extended their claims and responsibility to nearby countries, essentially combining them. The fact that they are considered to be part of "one country" reflects their ownership by one group. The processes of claim, extension, and movement constitute stages in a cycle by which the resource nexus of a range will eventually re-establish itself simply from the process of following the scheduling pattern of resources (Peterson 1983).

Not Having to Ask:
Space and Pintupi Politics

There are further processes to consider in understanding "landownership" in relation to Pintupi territorial organization. These can only be understood with reference to Pintupi concepts of ownership and Pintupi politics. In discussing the content of ownership rights as the "right to be asked" (chapter 3), I maintained that such requests are unlikely to be refused, although permission might be overtly denied or withdrawn from *personae non gratae*. Nonetheless, in one's own country one does *not* have to ask.

The issue for the Pintupi is not the utility of resources, in the sense of what one could get by converting them to a product. In terms of Pintupi politics and the prime goal of personal autonomy, major value is placed on not having to ask. To live in another person's country requires that one must defer to him as the "owner." Visitors are freely extended rights to use resources, but in decisions about where to go, or how to deal with disputes, they are clearly second-class citizens.

This situation is readily apparent in people's behavior. When the Pintupi have lived in others' country, they have deferred quietly to the traditional owners. At Yayayi, Yinyilingki, New Bore, and Papunya, their influence was limited and their tenure insecure. How remarkable is the transformation in the demeanor of these people when they visit their own country, where they know the Dreaming stories best, where they know who died, where events happened, and in which they need not defer to anyone. Here, it would seem, they have what they value: the freedom to do as they please without asking anyone. It is young men who travel most widely and extensively in other people's country, precisely because deference, especially to a senior man, implies for them no decline in personal autonomy.

Consider, finally, what happens when trouble occurs in a Pintupi community. When conflict erupts, outsiders leave. In their life histories, my informants repeatedly explained how at the first sign of danger or insecurity, they went back to their "own" country. They sought protection. Personal and political relations maintain, in this way, a powerful influence on spatial organization. At times of danger when defensive needs are salient, the boundaries between groups may be significantly more marked than they are at others. Indeed, the potential of threat from attack by revenge-killers from far away may lend particular importance to the fighting prowess of men and thereby confer political value on male activities.

Summary

To fully understand the regulation of resources among the Pintupi and their organization in space, we clearly have to consider the internal structure of relations within the society. This structure does not merely reify "ecological necessities" but has taken on its own emergent values: of relatedness and personal autonomy among men. These are reflected in the dynamics of "ownership."

"Ownership" consists primarily in control over the stories, objects, and ritual associated with the mythological ancestors of The Dreaming at particular places. Access to knowledge of these esoterica and the creative essence they contain is restricted, and one can gain access only through instruction by those who have previously acquired it. Important ceremonies are conducted at some sacred sites, and other sites have ceremonies associated with them that men may perform to instruct others in what happened in The Dreaming. Because knowledge is highly valued and vital to social reproduction, men seek to gain such knowledge and to be associated with its display and transmission. It is, in fact, their responsibility to "follow up The Dreaming" (Stanner 1956), to look after these sacred estates by ensuring that the proper rituals are conducted. Men acquire prestige when other men defer to their knowledge in the telling of a story or the performance of a ceremony. They may convert control of knowledge into authority over younger men and women.

Since knowledge and control of country are already in the hands of "owners," converting claims to an interest in a named placed requires convincing the owners to include a person in knowledge and activity. Identification with a country must be actualized and accepted by others through a process of negotiation. This process objectifies social relations among persons into an enduring arrangement of sharing an estate.

Around each significant place, a group of individuals can affiliate. The groups may differ for each place considered; the corporations forming around these sacred sites are not closed. Instead, there are descending kindreds of persons who have or had primary claims to sites. Of all those "identified," only a portion actually "hold" a country and control its related rituals. These primary custodians are the ones who must determine whether to teach an individual about it; they decide on the status of claims. Men are rather congenial to teaching "close kin" about their country and to granting them thereby an interest in the place. For claimants who are remote genealogically, or not coresidents, there is less persuasiveness to claims. These processes make it likely that claims of a patrifilial core will be acceptable. Because at the height of a man's influence he is likely to live in his own country, it is predictable that he will pass it on to his sons. Rights are also passed on to sisters' sons, who are frequent coresidents. If such persons or those with other sorts of claims take up residence in an area and convince the custodians of their sincerity, they can become important custodians, too. Conversely, failure to maintain some degree of regular association with a place is likely to diminish one's claims. These are processes whereby one sort of "one countryman" status may be transformed into a more enduring one.

The fact that men seek to gain access to rights for many countries leads to extended associations of individuals with places, surrounding a core of those with primary claims. Among the Pintupi, there are numerous individuals with extensive estate rights. Individuals also establish widely varying personal constellations of such rights. The necessity of continued participation to validate rights to a country means, however, that any person's influence must be limited. His valid "holdings" will objectify for the future the scope of the political relations he has established with others.

Consequently, Pintupi territorial organization is best understood not in terms of local groups, but only by placing it within the larger sociocultural system that imbues "country" with value for people. Inevitably, the structure of this system presents itself through time.

CHAPTER 6

Relatedness and Differentiation

It was just like army all the time.

A s with relations to land, a negotiated quality characterizes much of Pintupi social life. Relationships among people are not totally "given" in the defining rules of landownership, residence, or kinship. Instead, relationships must be worked out in a variety of social processes. This represents a political side to Aboriginal life that stands in marked contrast to the icy formality of the elaborated structures of kin classification.

The politics of Pintupi life, however, should not be confused with an aim to dominate over others. Such a motivation is, I think, entirely strange to them. The roots of Pintupi politics lie in the emphasis placed on shared identity with others as a basis for social interaction *at all*. They seek to sustain a degree of autonomy within the constraints demanded by relatedness to others.

Both residential and estate-owning groups are open to the expansion and negotiation of boundaries on the basis of claims to shared identity. In this way, general relatedness remains the necessary, superstructural condition for any groups. Pintupi constantly maintain as much in their view of the society as a totality, not as a set of segmentary units like bands as building blocks, but as an expansive, overlapping set of individual networks of kin. One can go anywhere, they say, because "it is all one family." The Pintupi system emphasizes, first, an extensive and wide-ranging relatedness among individuals in a region. As with the concept of "one countryman," the larger regional system (the relationships between different localities of the total area) is built out of egocentric or dyadic links among individuals.

Particular groups are crystallized out of these categories by events in time. These aggregations provide in turn a basis for future organizational improvisation, but each person also has other links to exploit and to maintain. The emphasis on sociality has its costs.

159

Relatedness comes to dominate the ability of any group to define itself as a bounded entity.

The problem of territorial organization is only one manifestation of a more general order of social relations: What occurs within a residential community exemplifies the same structure as the supralocal relations. In some respects, the actual dispersion in space represents a response to the social limitations of sustaining autonomy and relatedness within a community through time. That is, people come together or move apart in accord with the values defined by a social logic. Pintupi place great value on sustaining their relations to others. Their concern in social action is to maintain the immediate occasion itself, to find some basis on which to ground current relations, but also to reproduce wide-ranging relatedness among individuals. This shared identity exists in relation to the threat of conflict and differentiation.[1]

Differentiation

A tension between "relatedness" (being *walytja*) and "differentiation" (as expressed in conflict and violence) defines the basic lived problem of Pintupi life. Although shared identity, compassion, and the like constitute genuine, basic features of Pintupi social life, their opposite is also a fact of life. Violence, conflict, and threat exist, on the one hand, as well as a willingness among those threatened to stand up against these.

The Pax Australiana has not stilled the fear of revenge expeditions approaching in the dark of night. When deaths have occurred for which members of the local community are believed responsible, Pintupi often dream they see revenge parties. Dogs growling at the impenetrable darkness beyond the fire may alert people to danger, and men shoot their rifles into the night to drive away the feared killers (*tjarnpa*) who cloak themselves in invisibility.[2] If such precautions are common even now, it is not surprising that some Pintupi remember the past as "like army all the time."

Both men and women are proud of their fighting prowess and speak of past fights with animation. Pintupi do not desire a quiescent life: fights provide drama in lives lived entirely in public. Indeed, one motive for drinking alcohol in the contemporary settlement society is the excitement of the violent engagements that follow. Discussion of these incidents continues for days afterward.

My own realization of the value Pintupi place on fighting came as I watched the dramatic and excitable Tjarri tjampitjinpa. His son, though still uninitiated, had set off a brawl with a man, and the boy was winning until the victim's brothers violently intervened

Pintupi Country, Pintupi Self

to demonstrate the unacceptability of a boy fighting with a man. Tjarri had been observing the brawl impassively from his camp until the punishment to his son became too much for him to bear. The transformation was instantaneous and remarkable. His demeanor took on the convention of violent engagement. His carriage shifted to the fluid bearing appropriate for dodging spears. Bellowing his outrage, he called on his son's opponents to attack him, picked up his spears, and rushed out to the fray. I remember thinking that he had slipped into this mode as comfortably as one puts on a well-worn glove. Several years later, when his preadolescent nephew was confronted and threatened by an angry woman for making her son cry, Tjarri's nephew promised to get protection. Through the tears of humiliation, he spoke firmly with pride, "My uncle Tjarri is a great fighter, too!"

But these are not warrior people; fighting represents not so much an attempt at dominance as an assertion of autonomy. It is the ever-present possibility of conflict—what I call "differentiation"—that gives relatedness its special value.[3] Ultimately, they are two different trajectories of autonomy.

Conflict and attempts at intimidation are regular occurrences in Pintupi communities as individuals try to influence others. In my experience, the ability to sustain relationship to others in the face of this possibility is rather a remarkable achievement. This ability is accompanied by a great tolerance for the sheer qualities of individuality. Conformity is not desired, only consideration for others. People are not ostracized for temporary, erratic, or even violent outbursts. "That's his business," Pintupi say to the peculiar behavior their comrades exhibit from time to time. On the whole, motivation goes unremarked and there is no sense that things could be otherwise.

The tie between conflict and the concern for relatedness is clarified in the example of a middle-aged man who sought to have a girl bestowed upon him. According to the general opinion, she had already been "promised" by her relatives to his younger brother. In addition to spearing this brother in the leg for opposing his claim, the older brother also threatened the girl's elderly parents for breaking their alleged promised to him. The girl's resistance to him, and the older brother's insistence, led the younger man to renounce his claim, but the older brother still did not succeed. For days, he wreaked havoc in the rhythms of camp life. When a group of men sought to sing together at night, he brought the occasion to a halt by a volley of spears. To prevent the girl's visiting other communities, he forcibly intervened, dragging her off a vehicle and threatening those who supported her. On another occasion, he broke up an evening's entertainment at the community school, fearing she would use the occasion to meet other men. Throughout the period, he created so much difficulty for others that some thought of encouraging the bestowal to bring his trouble-making to an end. Ultimately, she married neither brother.

This attempt to alter a bestowal offers a good illustration of the availability of Pintupi "determinations" (Sansom 1980: 24) to re-negotiation. Closure, in the form of a final or definitive account, is unusual. Just as with landownership, so also can promises of bestowal be changed as current relations alter. Often, it is difficult to find out from men who is bestowed upon whom.

Obviously, making trouble can be a means of influencing people. It tends to be rooted more in self-regard, however, than in a desire for power. Isolated as he had become in the community, what the older brother wanted was not simply to marry the girl. Her bestowal would have signaled that he was "loved" and supported by relatives. Thus, his challenge for people to demonstrate their support extended beyond his interest in the girl. His unusual actions pressed others to act as relatives, to "help."[4] Indeed, a man cannot marry without help from others, so it is not uncommon for men having difficulties with bestowal to behave in this way. The results, I think, confirm the meaning of their actions. In three cases I witnessed, failure to gain a bestowal was followed by a period of temporary psychotic dissociation. Their "madness" (rama, "deafness"), real enough for the time, dramatized these men's separation from others.

The man in the first case regarded reluctance to arrange the marriage as a rejection, just as the bestowal would have been proof of acceptance. He challenged the community to show its concern for him by granting his desires. Despite their displeasure with the upheaval he was provoking, few men openly denied his wishes or relatedness. At the same time, even when his spears or boomerangs flew about them, men sat stolidly in their place, unperturbed and unwilling to be intimidated. By ignoring his outbursts, they forestalled open conflict. Pintupi often respond to requests and threats in this way: they neither refuse nor accept. In this case, the parents might have relented but for the girl's steadfast refusal to accept the man. She exercised her own autonomy and put an end to the whole affair. The pressure on her abated, and the man withdrew even further from active involvement with others.

To live in such a "self-help" society, individuals must be capable of both compassion and strength. Another example is exceptional in its forcefulness, but telling: A man widely known for his ferocity and intimidation forcibly raped a woman at gunpoint. As she was his classificatory "sister," the crime was especially horrendous. Her outraged relatives pursued the assailant and would have killed him on the spot, had not the police intervened. The man was jailed, but he swore to kill her parents and "get her" again when he was freed. In light of his reputation, this was not an idle threat. When he was due for release, she joined her parents and came to live under the protection of her brother, Tony tjampitjinpa, in a remote community. Only fifteen persons lived there, and in the dark nights every sound of a vehicle represented the threat of this man's approach. Throughout it all, Tony remained prepared to defend his relatives, defying the threat of violence with his own autonomy and courage.

Despite the threat of violence, in Pintupi social life relatedness is the primary, almost primordial, value. Differentiation is experienced as a breach in that value, as fighting is the opposite of smoothly running relations among kin. In addition to the emphasis on shared identity in the cultural formulation of emotion, the value of wide-ranging relatedness is embodied as well in the extended classificatory kinship system, in subsections, and in the numerous named, ceremonially constituted relationships. These institutions transpose relatedness to the widest social field. Much public life, especially ceremonies and public meetings, conforms to a fundamental image of sociality. One avoids the appearance of egotism, self-assertion, or private willfulness (all considered shameful) and accepts identity with others as part of the self.

Critically, as a person grows older, the field of those considered to be relatives increases in breadth and complexity. This is of great significance because relations are the source of most valuables in Pintupi life, including food, a spouse, rights in ceremony, and protection. A person's relatives are likely to be found in all geographical directions; the network will involve persons who do not consider themselves to be related. This dispersed quality of the social field is a source of strain. One cannot afford to reject or ignore ties with some neighbors to concentrate only on a few other relations.

A talented young man explained to me why he did not want to work for an Aboriginal organization in Alice Springs, the regional center. Because so many people come to Alice, there would be too many obligations at once; one could not satisfy them all. If he did work there, he could only last a year.

Sustaining a Center?

The crux of the difficulty is that being a relative requires regularly demonstrating the relationship. Creating and maintaining relatedness demands interaction, reciprocity, and exchange. Unfortunately, this is not always possible. If, for example, a man kills a kangaroo,

In the men's boughshade, Pintupi men prepare their spears for a tense "sorry business" confrontation after a death. (Papunya, 1981)

he must choose who among his coresidents will receive a share. Frequent neglect is regarded as a rejection of relatedness, and those neglected may complain about "not being loved." One particular source of conflict lies at the periphery, with people who live far away. Such conflicts present the most potent danger because fewer opportunities exist among those who do not live together to alleviate disputes with exchange.

But the danger of conflict is not merely with such people, not simply between local groups. Within local groups, as well—which, after all, materialize out of quite variable and changing ties— considerable social energy is devoted to sustaining the appearance of all being related, of being "from one camp" (*ngurra kutjunguru*). As "one camp," they should help each other. Although, in a sense, they do stand as a group in contrast to other similar residential groups, this corporate identity remains contingent rather than enduring. As Sansom (1980: 259–67) noted elsewhere in Australia, the aggregation of individuals into a significant "mob," an expression of local autonomy, takes place through sharing of activity. Thus, as soon as some Pintupi moved from Papunya to Yayayi in 1973, they asserted their autonomy with respect to Papunya by organizing their own initiation and assembling their own football team. Pointing with pride to the marks of an initiatory gathering, Yayayi people

Pintupi Country, Pintupi Self

stressed that people from several other communities had been invited: Yayayi was "level" with these groups. "Everybody knows this place now," they told me. The shared activity of the Yayayi people in organizing the initiation had created a group with social recognition. The establishment of a group in this way excludes others as outsiders, as "nothing to do," but the formation is only temporary. To build such a formation represents a genuine social accomplishment, and local leaders gain prestige by sustaining a "mob" at their location.

An individual's social identity is not entirely subsumed by such a group. First, residents of any local group have relatives in other groups and these people have claims on them. Second, members of any such group are only temporarily part of this group; they might as easily be living elsewhere and, expectably, over the course of time they will associate themselves with other such units. The significance of this internal differentiation is most clearly demonstrated when someone dies: relatives in other communities "attack" (usually in ritually circumscribed ways) the residents of the local group who should have "protected" the relative.

When trouble occurs in a community, all its members are considered to share an identity with regard to the problem. They will be known, for instance, as "the people from Yayayi." Those who attack on one occasion may be coresidents, at a later time, with some of those they attack. Further, people from close neighboring groups may identify themselves for some activities in segmentary fashion as "from one camp" with the Yayayi people, in opposition to those from far away.

Given the available external alternatives, to live with certain people is a positive choice. Thus, the residential group is sustained primarily by the positive feelings—embodied in exchange—among participants, a system maintained by egocentric ties. These are often too fragile to sustain large gatherings for long; when tensions and conflict erupt within a residential group, people move apart and join other local groups. Through dispersal, time and geographic distance work to subdue memory of the conflict. Eventually, it is expected, dissension gives way to renewed recognition of shared identity.

The problem of managing relatedness is apparent in the lives of older men, who talk about how to delay ceremonial obligations to one set of people while satisfying another. Such situations of conflicting and delayed obligation are referred to as "trouble." While men of prominence are skillful in managing complex relations over time, one cannot ever satisfy all demands. Therefore conflict, division, or differentiation are inevitable, although people work to reduce the instability, to suppress distinctiveness, by making choices less insulting (or less obvious) to others.

The Tyranny of Distance

Although the Pintupi social system operates to sustain relatedness at the widest possible extent, with people far away as well as close, centrifugal tendencies persist. They exist as byproducts of the very emphasis on relatedness.

There are two significant but contradictory tendencies in Pintupi social organization. One is the logic of expansiveness, the principle that everyone in the region is related (*walytja tjurta*), that they are "all one family." The other is the distinction between "close" relatives (those with whom one regularly interacts, "one country-men") and relatives from far away, with whom one camps less frequently. In a variety of ways, the logic of Pintupi sociality attempts to overcome distance as a threat to relatedness. While they do, in fact, manage to establish wide-ranging relatedness among individuals, the Pintupi do so partly at the expense of preventing any social center from emerging. Local groups cannot isolate themselves as units from individuals who claim ties. Without firm boundaries to determine who has an interest and who does not, action is subject to ongoing negotiation as the membership of local groups changes. The practices followed by any set of people represent, in a sense, their own particular consensus. The entry of others into that social field may, as in the bestowal case, change the result.

This lack of social closure, as a basic condition of activity in the Western Desert, has often been apparent in dealings Pintupi have had with whites. For several years, Pintupi men were involved in commercial painting on canvas of the ceremonial designs of their sacred sites. The men insisted the designs were important, because they were "from The Dreaming," but they justified painting them for sale in that they were not the most sacred, "dangerous" ones. They claimed the right to do so, confidently: men painted the particular designs for which they were custodians, through their fathers and so on. Trouble arose when an exhibit of these paintings on display in Perth was seen by Pitjanytjatjarra men from Warburton Range. These men had similar sorts of ceremonies and actually shared some Dreaming tracks with the Pintupi. They charged the Pintupi painters with exposing secret designs that were owned by all of them. The Pintupi accepted the complaint and made restitution for their "trouble" with an offering of sacred objects.

Such constraints mean that a sense of insecurity and uncertainty underlies any action that may later be exposed to further judgment

Pintupi Country, Pintupi Self

and reassessment. Accountability therefore poses a problem. People are concerned with determining who is responsible for a course of action. For these reasons, Pintupi take care to assure themselves that others assent to a course of action.[5] Elders, unlike younger people, seem to have greater certitude about what can be done. They often act confidently, but many of them are said to have made errors, to have "trouble." When there is trouble, individuals take care to dissociate themselves. Thus, they may say, "It wasn't my idea" or "I had nothing to do with it."

The sheer fact of distance imposes its own constraint on Pintupi social life. With people moving frequently, and often separated for extended periods, how is it possible to have all significant "relations" present to decide an issue? Trouble may be inevitable. Besides, when people live far away, one is less likely to have regular contact with them. If there are recent genealogical links, to be sure, one can expect to share in the informal relations of coresidence and sharing. As with immediate camp life, however, one cannot maintain exchange and interaction with everyone at once, and distant ties may be neglected in favor of the immediate.

Thus, accusations of sorcery and other grievances such as killings and wife-stealing are most common among people who live far apart. Unexpected deaths were usually attributed to sorcery by outsiders and prompted responses of countersorcery or retaliatory revenge expeditions (*warrmala*) to kill the suspected guilty party (*kuurnka*, also the word for "ripe," "uncooked"). Such expeditions of ten to twenty men often traveled hundreds of miles, well beyond the areas individuals knew from their foraging pursuits. Periods of grievance between groups alternated with periods of more amicable relations until a new incident sparked off trouble. During turbulent times, people tended to return to their "own" local areas. As a result, distance is a marker of social boundaries. Revenge often prompted counter-revenge, so that strangers and visitors from distant areas were treated with suspicion. Despite their sociability, Pintupi felt most secure in the company of their closest relatives and most frequent coresidents. These were people they knew, whose intentions and motives were understood.

Warrmala

The threat of revenge expeditions insinuated itself deeply into traditional life. One middle-aged man, Linyarri tjapaltjarri, described what happened when, some thirty years earlier, his camp had suspected a revenge party was in the vicinity. Still uninitiated, he and his cousin Tony tjampitjinpa were old enough to travel on their own for extended periods, in the vicinity of their parents. They were doing well until they saw that their relatives had set a big fire to signal their attention, alerting them to the danger of a revenge party in the area. Their relatives were afraid the boys would be speared. The two boys put barbs on their spears and prepared themselves, but continued to hunt during the days. At night, they returned to their own base camp at Piruwatja to cook the day's hunt and climbed up on the hills to look for smoke. In the next few days, they looked for a sign of smoke, trying to make their way back to their relatives. Finally, they headed toward Yumari. Here they came upon an unusual set of tracks. There were no women in the group, and many of the tracks they did not recognize. So they climbed up on the nearby rocks and waited for people to return. No one came, but they saw a smoke to the west that they thought had been set for them and decided to go there the next day. In preparation they straightened their spears and put wood shavings (*kukulpa*) in their hair ("like men do"), lest the revenge party kill them. Courage deserted them, however, and they decided to go back to Piruwatja, where they kept a fearful lookout. (The whole organization of revenge parties seeks to generate such fear; the wood shavings worn in a man's headband, Linyarri said, frightens people and makes them "get stuck.") Next they fled northward to a less obvious claypan, where they sat awake all night, afraid the revenge party would sneak up. Back and forth they went, searching for their relatives and at the same time frightened of crossing the path of the *warrmala*. It was with considerable relief that the boys eventually saw their band's fires east of the Gordon Hills. Everyone cried for the two when they saw them.

Not all such incidents ended so happily. Kanawa nangala's first husband was killed by a revenge party. She was a young woman at the time, with only one child, Tjangkiya nepaltjarri. She remembers seeing a group of men. As she told me:

> The revenge party stood there, a group of men. I said, "Hey, there's trouble . . . look, an attack." His name [her husband] was Rintja, Tjangkiya's father, she was the only child, very small. I tried to warn him; that's how I tried to tell him. I stayed there all day, saw the whole thing.

Kanawa remembers her own actions in detail:

> I took spears, a firestick, a spearthrower. Swiftly—alone—I crawled away, carrying Tjangkiya, crawling. I felt my way along. There were no trees to hide in, no scrub, only spinifex. They did not see me; I was lucky. What happened? I became magical [laughs], truly! . . . I tried to tell him.

According to her story, Kanawa crawled and hid at the side of a sandhill. From there:

> I saw them come forward, all those men, with spears. They burst in. They descended on the camp. I left a rabbit cooking in the fireplace. It just kept cooking. I spoke to the child, "Look out!" Tjangkiya was crying, her stomach was bad, from the way I had carried her. I said, "Look out, we'd better leave." . . . He was just a young man, only a young man.

The revenge expedition killed Kanawa's husband and tossed his body on the fire. She did not think the men would have speared her; they might just have sent her back to her own people. In any case, she thought, they did not see her. She remained hiding at the base of the sandhill, barely sheltered from the cold, while her daughter cried. They had no fire. Darkness fell, but it was not until the moon rose that she went back to the camp, gathering coals to start a fire. She made a firestick and left, returning to her own relatives. No revenge party was sent out by her relatives; instead, sorcery was used to square back the killers, from far away.

I asked her why the revenge party had sought her husband. Her answer suggests just how uncertain the Pintupi world could be:

> I don't know. Maybe there was a death over there [where the killers came from]; or maybe for no reason, or maybe something happened in a ceremony. At a recent one, I had stayed behind with my relatives because I was sick.

One should note how these events cut across loyalties. Among the party was her own mother's brother, Katji tjapangarti, who had acted as a guide, showing them the way.

Revenge killings and violence were commonplace. This was not the only such killing Kanawa saw. Her attitude, not at all disapproving, reflects a Pintupi view that violence is an expression of feelings. When she was still a girl, a young man had been killed by a *warrmala*. His mother, overwhelmed with grief, cursed her husband (not the boy's original father) for failing to prevent the death. Aroused to anger by her swearing, the husband speared her through the side, nearly killing her. Fearing revenge, he fled back to his own relatives in the south. His wife's kin and those of her dead son, however, reached him by means of sorcery, bringing about his death. The injuries did not stop there, either. Men grow angry at the death of a relative and give expression to their sorrow by spearing those who "should have protected" him or her. After the killing in Kanawa's group, a wave of such expressive spearings took place among her relatives. This was proper.

There is a dialectic between "relatedness" and "differentiation" that can never be permanently resolved. The "strangeness" of distance is reduced and partially overcome by periodic ceremonially sanctioned gatherings and marriage exchange. Ritual, marriage, and the production of "social" individuals with ceremonial relationships to each other are essential components of the superstructure that opposes the centrifugal tendencies. Paybacks and revenge expeditions do, however, leave a history of disputes. People remember well the background of deaths and injuries that shadows the present. When conflict surfaces in daily life, one hears mention of past events that are usually shrouded in silence. The brothers and sisters of a woman who was killed by her husband, for example, do not forget that "that mob" killed their sister. Yet other ties bind them into continuing residential association. This tension exists at all levels of the system, not just between local groups.

The Idea of Exchange

Whether it is shared identity or conflict that is expressed in social action, Pintupi expect that reciprocity and equivalence will be the guiding principle. Giving, they say, should not be "only one side." Instead, it should be "level," "square and square," or "*ngaparrku*," signifying equal return in the opposite direction. This rule of parity is as important in revenge expeditions as it is in marriage bestowals. Those responsible for the death of one's close relative must be "paid back." And those who receive a wife are responsible to help the giver(s) obtain a wife in return. Violence and compassion are each transformations of this invariant principle of equality, respecting the autonomy of others.

Relations among kin are defined by the expectation of reciprocated help, an image of things flowing back and forth. In this sense, social relations that are differentiated hierarchically feature some similarity to those between equivalent statuses: One should help one's mother's brother as a return for his nurturance. The Pintupi do not so much weigh and measure the value of objects against each other; exchange value is hardly elaborated in an economy such as theirs. But an expectation of exchange marks every form of social transaction, often satisfied by demonstrations of concern for the welfare of the other. Thus, when two of Kanawa nangala's relatives cried for her dead husband, she gave them emu eggs she had collected.

Living in Pintupi communities provides a regular instruction in the dynamics of give-and-take. One day as I sat with an informant, he asked me to give him my shoes. I refused (they were my only pair), only to be reminded that several days earlier he had given me a packet of cigarettes. He implied that he had done something for me, and, therefore, I should do something for him. This was not quite the same as suggesting I was in his debt to some specific amount. He phrased his claim, rather, to remind me of his action and to move my feelings to reciprocate. Similarly, because my friend Tjarlu tjakamarra was only paid every other week, on off weeks I usually gave food to his family. When his food stocks were in abundance, he insisted on my eating meat at his camp. Relationships, he instructed me, should be "level," that is, two-sided. Most Pintupi find great satisfaction in being able to do this.

Maintaining a fairly balanced account in one's transactions is thus important. People grow testy and grumble if those whom they have been feeding do not obtain meat to share with them. Older men complain that younger men, their sons and sister's sons, "rob them" of money and food and never pay back anything. Young unmarried men rely on their relatives to prepare food for them. In settlements, where hunting is infrequent, they sustain this relationship by giving money to their fathers, mothers, or mother's brothers in return for provisioning. At paydays, one can watch the borrowing and repayment of money in accordance with such claims.

Fights are also understood as occasions for equal exchange. If one man spears another, the former should offer his leg to be speared in return (ngaparrku). This return brings an end to the action, a parity with no "trouble" left. When this did not occur, observers expressed the feeling that "it is no good only one side." Those who have not been able to square back an injury often promise that they will get even at some future time.

Grievances and quarrels are resolved by squaring of accounts. While the Pintupi were living at Yayayi, Joe tjampitjinpa killed a man in a fight. According to traditional law, he should have offered himself to be speared in the thigh by classificatory "brothers" of the dead man. He failed to do so. The aggrieved relatives of the deceased from other settlements maintained that this would make things "clear" (kili, "a clear account"). After Joe's removal from the settlement (he went to jail), a ritualized fight of reconciliation (parnparla, "sorry fight") was carried out, and Joe's younger brother offered himself to be speared to even the account. This recognition of the right to get even was supposed to bring an end to the "trouble," to forestall a revenge attack against the community.

If blood is drawn from one party in a fight, Pintupi say that the other should be made to bleed. Such "squaring back" provides some emotional satisfaction for the grievance, just as a child may cease to cry after striking the dog who knocked it over. In the absence of

Diagram 6A. Reciprocity and Non-Reciprocity

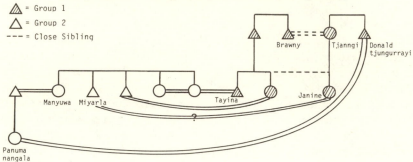

courts to enforce a judgment, the resolution of grievances depended (and still does, to a degree) on a feeling of emotional satisfaction, that enough has been done.

Conversely, unfulfilled expectations of a return often lead to conflict and social disturbance. The following narrative illustrates the sort of conflict that occurs between people from different localities:

> Miyarla tjapangarti had been "promised" Janine nampitjinpa as a wife when she had grown up. Miyarla's sister's daughter, Panuma nangala, had been bestowed as wife on Donald tjungurrayi, Janine's mother's brother. The plan clearly aimed for an equal exchange of sister's daughters as wives, "square and square." These arrangements had not been made by the men themselves; instead, they represented an equivalence between their respective kin networks. Previously, Miyarla's two sisters had been bestowed on Janine's close brother, Tayina tjampitjinpa, and Tayina's sister had been given to Miyarla's brother (see Diagram 6A). Miyarla had been giving money for some time to Janine's mother and mother's husband (Brawny married Tjanngi after her first husband, Janine's father, died). Brawny, however, had other intentions and delayed the bestowal. In his frustration, on several occasions Miyarla invaded the camp of his mother-in-law and swore at her. He had, he shouted, paid a lot of money in growing up this girl. Nonetheless, Janine was bestowed on another man. In consequence, Miyarla's sister "took back" her daughter from Donald, and there were threats of taking Miyarla's sisters back from Tayina. His close kin said that they had been giving "too one-sidedly" and were getting nothing back. There had been "no square and square." Panuma stayed with her mother for a week and they talked of moving to Yuendumu and giving Panuma to a man who would give her uncle a wife. Nothing came of the threats, however, and eventually Panuma returned to her husband. With the loss of this bestowal, Miyarla lapsed into the sort of

Pintupi Country, Pintupi Self

psychosis that seems to follow rejection. He recovered, but only temporarily. A few years later, Miyarla murdered Panuma's father (his brother-in-law) in his sleep. He was, people said, still distraught because the latter had not helped him get a wife.

The basis of this conflict was a breach in the expectation of reciprocity that underlies marriage bestowal and affinity. The actual politics of bestowal vary considerably, but to the Pintupi imagination the ideal is an exchange in which brothers-in-law receive each other's sisters "square and square." With or without such a reciprocal bestowal, receipt of a wife entails enduring obligations between a man and his affines.[6] They should "help" each other. Failure to do so—by providing support in a conflict, for example—may result in attempts to break up the marriage. In the Pintupi view, a man must defend his wife's brothers, because "he has their sister." On no account may he quarrel with them. Thus, the Pintupi felt that they could not be asked to move from Yayayi since the custodians had married "our women."

Marriage represents only one sign in a larger but correspondingly organized framework of reciprocal exchange. Male in-laws are involved in each other's ritual as well. If anything, the ritual life is even more devoted to formal exchange than is daily life. The exchange of sacred objects between men makes the principle into a goal itself. One man (or a group of brothers) may give a sacred object to another. In the course of time, the latter must "square back" the original giver(s) with other sacred objects or with items such as spears, shields, or boomerangs. If the recipients do not make a return, it is expected that the givers will become angry and retaliate with killing or sorcery. Frequently, when they have returned from lengthy trips through the bush to areas of specially valued spear wood, Pintupi men have manufactured spears and sent them to men with whom they have obligations. Through the return gift, they become "clear" (kili) or "free," without the constraint of obligation. As a result of the exchange, however, something is gained in the form of continuing relations among these men. A sense of mutual identity and responsibility endures through time.

A man's status relates directly to his capacity to take part in such reciprocal exchange. The ability to exchange in parity with men, to be "level," depends on a social entitlement that differentiates adults from their juniors. Not surprisingly, initiation and socialization focus on increasing this capacity.

A sense of exchange is also involved in social relations that are not "equivalent." Though relations between juniors and elders are expected to manifest efforts at a return, their exchanges are of a sort that can be described as transformative and hierarchical: One's parents "grow one up," and in return one offers obedience. What is exchanged is not similar in kind or value, and as a result of such asymmetrical transactions there is an increase in value on the part of the junior and an obligation that can never be repaid. The resulting identity such transactions create between a senior and a junior show these kind of exchanges to be a way of regenerating cultural value through time (Weiner 1980: 71).

Often these asymmetrical relationships concern women as items of exchange. While reciprocity is necessary, bestowal creates a hierarchy between giver and recipient—between a wife's father and his son-in-law. This is precisely the conception that informs the role of the circumciser for an initiate. Because he inflicts pain on the novice, the circumciser should help the young man get a wife. Therefore, the ideal circumcisers are persons in the class of "father-in-law" (waputju, who are also sister's sons) or "wife's mother's brother" (tjukurnpa).[7] These men are brothers-in-law to each other, and in agreeing to perform the operation, they accept the responsibility of providing the initiate with a wife.[8] There is, as always, the requirement that relationships be "level" or reciprocal, but there is hierarchy, too. The men should show restraint in each other's company, and the recipient should defer to his father-in-law. His subsequent obligation to his in-laws never ends either, since he is supposed to support them with gifts of meat as long as they live.

All stages in the acquisition of important ritual status seem to be accompanied by the novice undergoing an ordeal and pain, as a kind of payment. This process makes ritual knowledge, as some Pintupi say, "dear." The right to make sacred objects follows on having fingernails pulled out and holes stabbed in one's palms and inside one's elbows. In this way, older men "give" knowledge. An instructee, returns this prestation with pain, meat, and obedience, but he cannot offer the genuine equivalent of what he is given.[9] He becomes more than he was, now having the right to make sacred objects himself.

Going through initiation provides the means by which young males become able to exchange with older men, a step in the direction of equality. Initiation entitles them to take control of the sacred knowledge that is necessary for the performance and direction of ceremonies. This control is a token of their personal autonomy, but the central theme of Pintupi sociality remains, that one cannot be autonomous by oneself. "Freedom" requires the help of other men. As we shall see, it does not quite come as a gift.

Becoming "free" means that a person has fewer restraints on movement and the expression of identity. Only after his initiation,

Pintupi Country, Pintupi Self

for example, can a male actually fight with other men (parallel to the prohibition on sex for noninitiated males). Boys who *do* attempt to fight with initiated men are likely to provoke a corporate response from those who have been initiated, a defense of privilege. At the same time that this movement toward increasing autonomy involves participation in higher levels of exchange, it is also a step toward taking responsibility for those who are, as yet, unable to be equal. As boys become men, they become responsible to look after others. This is a transformation of their point of view.

Reproducing Relatedness

Marriage constitutes one means of reproducing relatedness among individuals in a region. The logic of this practice is similar to that discussed in Lévi-Strauss's (1949) well-known treatment of marriage alliance, but the Pintupi prescription that spouses should not come "from one country" cannot be reduced to the sociocentric formulation of marriage into a different band or descent group. Marriages take place, rather, among webs of kinfolk. Distance is the key, as one young Papunya man made clear in explaining why he could not marry a girl he admired from his own settlement. They were, he said, "from one *ngurra*." In the Pintupi view, they are "too close" (*ngamutja*, "from nearby"), and one's spouse must be "from far away" (*tiwatja*).

The convention of marrying only those who are not currently considered "one countrymen" assures (in the next few generations) renewed contact, visiting, and coresidence among those who are kin to each spouse. This arrangement renews, as well, rights to use the land, and maintains thereby a regional network. A current generation's affines become the next generation's "one countrymen." Pintupi marriages do not represent a pattern of long-term, repeated, and continuing alliances between groups, as do marriages in North Australia (cf. Goodale 1971, Hiatt 1965, Shapiro 1969). They serve instead to reproduce a more general relatedness among individuals within a region.

Indeed, as the data on landownership show, people over an extremely wide area jointly share rights in each sacred estate. A general relatedness is therefore instantiated at each site.

To make this argument concrete, let us consider the genealogy in Diagram 6B (of Tupa tjangala), as an example of how people of several different local areas are united as kin, as "one family." Relationships were traced back a few generations before the present, to key grandparental figures. For this grouping, Niwilnga tjapanangka[10] is a focus. He was the father of Tjarlaku tjampitjinpa's wives and

Diagram 6B. Genealogy of Tupa tjangala

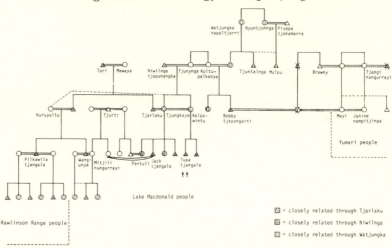

adopted grandfather to Pilkawilanya and Wangunya tjangala. Pilkawilanya is reported to have gone to live in his wife's country in
the south. His children are now considered to be associated with
that area around the Rawlinson Range. They remain, nonetheless,
important relatives to Wangunya's children and other people identified with Lake Macdonald. Visiting is frequent. Further, all these
people are associated, via their joint relation to the long-deceased
Niwilnga 'tjapanangka, with the children of Tjarlaku tjampitjinpa,
the ceremonial custodians of Lake Macdonald. Bobby tjapangarti, a
son of Niwilnga, but having a different mother than did Tjarlaku's
wives, is associated with the south through his father, to Lake
Macdonald through his brother-in-law and sisters' children (Tupa,
and so on), and to Kintore through his mother's brother (Tjuntalnga
tjupurrula).[11] It is noteworthy that when Bobby married, his wife
came from none of these regions. Instead, she was from a more
northern area, the Yumari region, adjacent to his mother's country.
Some of his close relatives (Wangunya, Jack tjangala, and Partuli
nangala) also married others from the north: the children of Tjurti
tjapaltjarri, who used to travel with Tjarlaku's group. Their siblings
married in other directions, creating an impressive network of ties.

Through marriage, Pintupi reach out, reintegrating diverse people into their kin networks. Indeed, with more complex genealogies
(often nearly unreadable ones), it becomes clear that some repetition
of marriage patterns occurs after a few generations. When one
examines kinship relations charted out in space, the Pintupi assertion that they are all family takes on a historical reality.

Pintupi Country, Pintupi Self

Marriage is not, of course, the only institution that reproduces this sort of relatedness. As aspects of a single total process, we shall see marriage, ceremony, and socialization are all symbolically related.

Ceremony

A foraging economy in a harsh desert requires both a geographical dispersion of population and its integration into a regional system. Localization, therefore, has been the major source of differentiation to which ritual responds. Ceremony provides a forum in which "difference" among people can be addressed and converted to "relatedness." In fact, this is one of the principal consequences of rituals such as male initiation, which prescriptively bring together people of geographically separated social areas. Autarky is prohibited: a group should not initiate its own people.

The sequence of initiatory events as a symbolic process shows how this works. To focus on the geographical dimensions of ritual process, a short description of initiation will suffice (see chapter 8 for more details). The process begins when an initiate is sent to gather people of far-flung localities that are still part of the Pintupi social universe. These are "different" people, potentially hostile, but the novice's party is protected by a widely recognized right of free passage. Just where the youth goes is a product of lengthy preliminary discussion among his senior male kin. Diversity is important; he ought not to follow the same direction as his brothers. When these visitors return with the novice to his country, they approach the gathered "countrymen" in strict formation, spears pointed down to indicate friendly intent, while the host group waits in similar formation. The visitors run past, handing the boy back to the hosts, who then run past the visitors, and the men run together to the ceremonial ground. Then the visitors are given food, symbolizing a shared identity. After eating, visitors with grievances or disputes against the host announce them. While often these grievances lead to spearings and genuine injury, the intent is to reach satisfaction and reconciliation before the ceremony proceeds. When the initiatory singing takes place among the men, it seems to convert the opposition between those socially differentiated by geography to rivalry and then to complementarity between generational moieties (categories that transcend local groups). Finally, complementarity between moieties is transmuted to that between males and females.

The result of most ceremonial proceedings in the Western Desert is the participants' sense of themselves as "all relatives."

Further, enduring ceremonial relationships are established among various participants; for initiation, the boy becomes affinally related to people who were previously only "distant" kin. Those who have participated jointly in an initiation become, to some extent, related. These dimensions of ritual address the inherent threats to the fabric of Pintupi social life.

The Self and the Other

The Pintupi societal emphasis on relatedness is reflected powerfully in the concern individuals show to complete themselves through identity with others. This dimension of Pintupi life is most strikingly evident in the situation of "orphans." The very term "orphan" (*yapunta*) is itself used for anything that has been lost or has lost its relationship of belonging. No one is entirely an orphan, of course, in that if one's parents die, others will take over the role. Often they treat a child as really their own. On the other hand, when a parent dies, Pintupi find the condition of orphans to be full of pathos. "Poor thing, he has no mother," they say. Thoughts of a young man who had lost all his close relatives occasioned special compassion because "he is only one, now."

Many of the Pintupi who have lost a parent in childhood show adjustment problems, an anger that is not appeased. One very intelligent young man I knew had been raised with love by his parents' siblings, yet he seemed unable to settle himself in a community. He took to drinking heavily, and under the influence was expressive of his difficulties. "I have no mother, no father, nothing," he cried. "I can die, no worries."

Some orphans turn to antisocial activities, testing their ties to relatives. These are the young men who most directly embody the wildness of youth, of fighting "live or die," as if no one cared. In recent years, the most active petrol-sniffing children among the Pintupi have been those who have lost parents or who have been emotionally neglected. Their surly attitude attempts to build a self-reliance in the face of a devastating loss. They may often be individually quite pleasant; indeed, they seem on the lookout for close ties with others. But there has been a blow to their confidence in being loved.

Such children are likely to place great demands on others. These demands, however, manifest a pattern all Pintupi children show in tantrums. Children must, in fact, assert themselves to get caretakers to act. Adults do not presume to know what is "good" for a child; they expect to be "asked." There is often, then, a test of wills between children and their mothers. Adults will give in eventually, but they do so in their own good time, preserving their autonomy as beings separate from the child. Through tantrums, children attempt to coerce others to satisfy them, to demonstrate their will. Such willfulness seems intensified by parental loss.

The problem of being "alone" represents, moreover, a threatening situation for everyone. Men, especially those who are faced with trouble, emphasize that they have lots of relatives. Thereby, it is implied, they can get help if they need it; they are not alone. For example, the eccentricities of Tarawa tjungurrayi—pursuing his own business too much—had rather isolated him from others. Even his wife would no longer cook for him. He seemed to feel the threat of this situation when his wife deserted him for a time. All our conversations seemed inevitably to return to the same theme: "No one can touch [harm] me. I have a lot of relatives." He stressed also that he was a great fighter and had no fear of anyone. His importance was also secure, he implied, because he had important sacred sites: "I can handle it." Here, certainly, was a case of protesting too much. Underlying the protests was insecurity and fear that people did not take him seriously.

In this regard, women seem little different. When Kawinya napaltjarri's daughter died from poisoning in Alice Springs, she was devastated with grief. She grew angry with her sisters when they did not rush to her side immediately. According to her, they should have come and stayed with her, looked after her. "They must have boyfriends who are more important," she proclaimed witheringly (and falsely), and "that's why they do not help me."

Conclusion

Among the Pintupi, conflict and relatedness define each other structurally as values (cf. T. Turner 1984a). There is a dialectical relationship between violence and diplomacy. Indeed, if we are to fully understand Pintupi social life, it is necessary to come to terms with the significance of violence. In suggesting that differentiation and relatedness are two trajectories for autonomy, I would argue that violence offers a way of sustaining and producing an image of the self. As such, it is tolerated as an acceptable form of action. Nonetheless, identity with others constitutes the primary condition and expectation of life, deeply embedded in personal experiences. When the capacity to complete oneself through relationship with others is threatened or prevented, the resort to violence establishes one's own will. At the same time, the ever-present possibility of conflict lends enormous value to sustaining shared identity as a precondition for social action.

Chapter 7

Kinship: Models of the Pintupi Social Universe

He's really my father. He looked after me, grew me up.
We are all family, from all the brothers.

The extraordinary classificatory bent of Aboriginal societies, incorporating all individuals into a system of kinship, has always stimulated particular anthropological interest. Increasingly, it has become clear that the elaborations of such structures of classification reflect Aboriginal concerns with constituting a sociality beyond the local group (Maddock 1972, Munn 1973a, D. Turner 1980). In their cultural emphases on "continuity" and "permanence" (Stanner 1966), on a "stable anchor of identity" (Munn 1970), or on identifying "what is" with Eternity (Róheim 1945, Strehlow 1970: 132), the institutions of kinship and estate-ownership are thematically consistent.[1]

We have seen that every named place is part of an encompassing structure of places, and rights to sacred estates are not simply exclusionary rights but rather a placement of individuals into a larger order of relations. Every ritual related to land is an instantiation of a societal whole. Each part, each local "unit," can be produced only through the cooperation of other components of the larger structure. The organization of ceremony, requiring participation of others from far away, provides one way of constituting Pintupi society as a whole.

The necessary participation of others beyond the immediate family in the production of individuals as full, social adults is basic to the system that anthropologists know as "classificatory kinship." Thus T. Turner (1979a, 1979b) argues that "socialization" is one of the principal productive activities in small-scale societies. The particular elaborations of Pintupi kin classification reflect his view that "kinship" should be understood as a system concerned with reproducing the conditions for the elementary social units or family.[2] The relations involved in the total process of "socialization" serve as critical components of any system of reproduction. Kinship systems categorize persons by the role they can perform in relationship to the process through which the elementary units of social life are reproduced.

In the Pintupi case, kinship coordinates the complex relations of social reproduction that needs people from far away to sustain life in local groups. Marriage exchange, initiation, and cooperation in band activities are equally components in this process of social life.

A general theory of kinship is not, however, this book's immediate concern. Before discussing the structure of social reproduction we must first discern what is at issue in Pintupi kinship. The precise meaning of Pintupi kinship is not readily apparent because, in a sense, they have *two* systems of kin classification. The more formal and elaborate of these alternatives bases itself on the distinction between brothers and sisters. It specifies kinds of distance and potential in-law categories by differentiating those related through siblings of opposite sex. When one attempts to elicit the terminological system, Pintupi are most likely to provide these terms. And to be sure, the system is commonly in use.

The pragmatics of kinship regularly departs from this model, however, when Pintupi collapse the distinctions of the formal system into one with fewer categories. This second model is of fundamental importance in understanding Pintupi sociality. As in the organization of estate-ownership, the way Pintupi apply kin terminology is greatly influenced by their political and diplomatic recognition of others and their mutual involvements. In practice, therefore, Pintupi use terms that stress the closeness of the relationships between those engaged with each other, ideologically suppressing the existence of differences among themselves.

This underlying structure in classifying social relations, actually a "typical" Western Desert Aluridja form (Elkin 1940), is rooted in the continuing primacy of extensive "one countryman" relations. Aluridja terminology, distinguishing only affinal status, generation, and sex, opposes the shared identity of people who coreside with the affinal status of people who are "distant."

The main line of my analysis is that the generational (Aluridja) model should be considered the encompassing one in Pintupi social thought, embodying the concepts of hierarchy and equivalence in social relations. It seems closer to the Pintupi view of a region as "all one family," relatively undifferentiated by locality. This generational ordering of the social world maintains an image of continuity and permanence, seen as the passage of generations and the transgenerational transmission of The Dreaming. Secondarily, I would consider the significance of the more formal model as another ordering of the relations within a region, providing some limitation on the political pressures to acknowledge relatedness.

Kinfolk

For any Pintupi individual, the social universe is culturally divided into the categories of "kin" *(walytja)* and "nonkin." By describing the latter as "not men" or "different men" *(munuwati)*, Pintupi represent them as being in the deepest sense unrelated. Those who are "relatives" belong together or share identity, while those who are not truly "relatives" have little or no interaction.

The category *walytja* does not define a closed set of people. Rather, who is considered to be a "relative" varies situationally, depending on whom the speaker is viewing as in contrast with "relatives." For example, all the people who lived at Yayayi were often specified by speakers from Yayayi as "relatives" over and against the wider community that included the neighboring settlement of Papunya. In these contexts, many Papunya people were said to be "nonrelatives" who had little claim on the events at hand. But in the context of the whole central Australian Aboriginal community, Pintupi would often stress that Papunya and Yayayi were really "one country." After all, they were very close and much visiting took place. Thus, when they visited Alice Springs, Papunya and Yayayi people often camped together and defended each other as "relatives." It would be highly unusual, indeed insulting, for Pintupi to call anyone with whom they were actively engaged a "nonrelative."

Within this overall similarity, Pintupi recognize different varieties of shared identity, differences that constitute the system of kin classification. The contrasting relationships that may exist between a person and an other are discriminated in terms of the nature of exchanges that take place. Both kinship models categorize individuals egocentrically according to what they contribute to the production of social persons. The importance of socialization as a component of social reproduction makes kinship an appropriate idiom for human relationships in many small-scale societies.

Subsection System: Sociocentric Categories

The most noticeable way in which the Pintupi divide their social universe is that of subsections, allocating every person by birth to one of eight categories. Each of these categories is further marked linguistically for male (initial *tj-*) or female (initial *n-*). As systems of reference and address, subsection terms and kinship terms are not identical, although a relationship exists between the two forms of classification. Built on principles implied in the system of egocentrically defined kinship relations, the subsection system casts these principles into a society-wide model of relationships among enduring sociocentric categories. Subsections are not social groups.

This system of classification is similar to that found among the neighboring Warlpiri (Meggitt 1962: 165), although the Pintupi probably adopted it more recently. According to Fry (1933), the Pintupi he met at Mount Liebig in 1932 were just beginning to adopt the eight-subsection system in place of the four-section system. For their part, the Pintupi insist that the system was brought to their country by the *Tingarri* travelers from The Dreaming, journeying down from the north.

The subsection system classifies a number of kin types into one category, and it systematically relates these named categories to each other through principles drawn from the egocentric kinship system: affinal exchange, filiation, and generation. The categories serve as a shorthand for more specific kin relationships. Within a single subsection category, an individual may locate persons of more than one kinship relationship and kin type to himself or herself. For example, the same subsection category includes those ego calls "father" (*mama:* F, FB, MZH) and those he calls "sons" (*katja:* S, BS). Because of the abbreviated character of this classification system, for more important considerations the Pintupi resort to the finer points of genealogical reckoning and their concomitant kinship terms.

What is significant about subsection categories is that, unlike kinship terms, they are sociocentric rather than egocentric. Everyone belongs to one of the subsections, and the categories are ordered in relation to each other in terms of the expectations of kinship behavior among them. Thus, one subsection is always "mother's brother" or "mother" to a certain other subsection. For organizing activities among people who do not know their precise genealogical relationship—as occurs with the large-scale ritual gatherings[3]—this dimension offers obvious advantages. If individuals know their respective subsection categories, then they understand what sort of behavior is appropriate among one another.

Furthermore, the system enables replacement of individuals within categories. Men of a subsection may substitute for each other as "brothers." Thus, any man of the Tjakamarra subsection may act as "sister's son" for men of the Tjapanangka subsection. A greater number of individuals is thus available to fill the roles necessary for organized activities such as ritual. The system also implies that relationships exhibited at any one place or ritual are merely instances of a larger, society-wide order, such as the help Tjakamarra men provide for their "mother's brothers." Individual relationships are portrayed, in other words, as manifestations of an enduring total structure.

As a matter of etiquette, subsection terms are generally used in preference to the personal name that grandparents give an individual. In daily life, the former are common both as terms of address ("Hey, Tjakamarra, come here") and as terms of reference ("Tjakamarra told me . . ."). Subsection terms are not relative with respect to a speaker—any ego calls a man of the Tjakamarra subsection "Tjakamarra"—but they are part of a structure that does implicitly express a series of relations between the social categories. Because these relations are understood by speakers, when a subsection term is applied to an individual, its use specifies this person's expected relationships to individuals of other social categories—what can be anticipated in the sense of kinship obligations.[4]

Relating Subsection Categories

Because the subsection system operates as a self-contained whole, with each category defined in terms of all the others, anthropologists have often been bewildered and intrigued by the different sorts of cycles possible: matrilineal, patrilineal, same generation, and so on. These cycles are of less concern to the Pintupi themselves, for whom the subsections have a sort of "added-on" quality. It is preferable to stay as close as possible to the way Pintupi conceptualize the system. For them, the relations among subsections reveal principles, intriguing possibilities of order, as much as they can be said to represent them.

The essential reference point of the Pintupi subsection system is that persons of the same category are considered to be siblings, either brothers or sisters, to each other. A second point is that the children of women are distinguished from those of the women's brothers. That is, children of men of a category belong to a different subsection than the children of women in the same category. (The alternate Pintupi structures are contradictory on this point; but it is this differentiation of opposite-sex siblings as linking kin that enables kinship classification to subsume affinal relations systematically. At a certain distance, consanguineal links define categories of affinal relationship.)

Diagram 7A. Principles Relating Subsections

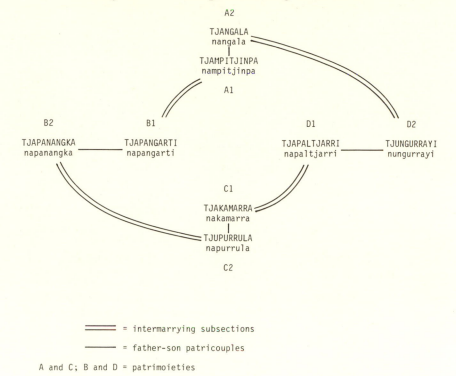

```
                              A2
                          TJANGALA
                           nangala
                              |
                         TJAMPITJINPA
                          nampitjinpa
                              A1

    B2            B1                        D1            D2
TJAPANANGKA   TJAPANGARTI            TJAPALTJARRI    TJUNGURRAYI
napanangka     napangarti            napaltjarri     nungurrayi

                              C1
                          TJAKAMARRA
                           nakamarra
                              |
                          TJUPURRULA
                           napurrula
                              C2
```

```
        =========  = intermarrying subsections
        ─────────  = father-son patricouples
A and C; B and D = patrimoieties
A2, D2, C2, B2 = generation moiety
A1, D1, C1, B1 = other generation moiety
```

According to the subsection system, members of a category should obtain their spouses from the specific category with which they are paired as potential spouses. The eight subsections are organized into four such intermarrying pairs. There is a strong preference for marriage to members of this opposite category (which will include children of MMBD and FFZD), although marriage with the alternative category that includes first cross-cousins can be an acceptable secondary choice.

These principles relating the subsection categories are illustrated in Diagram 7A. As the diagram indicates, a Tjapanangka man should marry a Napurrula woman; a Tjupurrula man should marry a Napanangka woman, and so on. The subsection of children differs from that of either parent but is determined by theirs. Members of the categories that are supposed to intermarry both call members

Diagram 7B. Father-Child Couples of Subsections

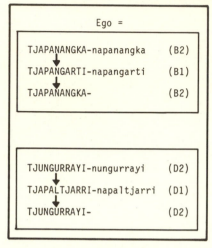

Ego =

TJAPANANGKA-napanangka (B2)
↓
TJAPANGARTI-napangarti (B1)
↓
TJAPANANGKA- (B2)

TJUNGURRAYI-nungurrayi (D2)
↓
TJAPALTJARRI-napaltjarri (D1)

TJUNGURRAYI- (D2)

Patrimoiety BD

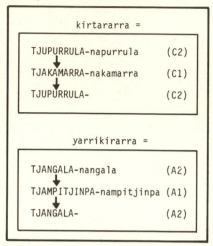

kirtararra =

TJUPURRULA-napurrula (C2)
↓
TJAKAMARRA-nakamarra (C1)
↓
TJUPURRULA- (C2)

yarrikirarra =

TJANGALA-nangala (A2)
↓
TJAMPITJINPA-nampitjinpa (A1)
↓
TJANGALA- (A2)

Patrimoiety AC

of the same third category "son" *(katja)* or "daughter" *(yuntalpa)*. Tjapanangka men and Napurrula women call all Tjapangarti men, for instance, "son."

There is a potential problem in assigning a child to a subsection when a marriage does not follow the preferred ideal. The Warlpiri say that the mother's subsection should be the important consideration in assigning the child to a category; in cases of irregular marriage, the father is "thrown away" (Meggitt 1962: 61). Pintupi men, however, regard a child's subsection as depending on the father as well. The Pintupi solution is pragmatic: The child may be called by the term naming the subsection that contains children of the father, by the term naming the subsection containing children of the mother, or people may speak of the child as being "two ways, mix-up." In the last case, they name both the subsection appropriate for the mother's child and that for the father's child. A man may be known, for example, as "Tjapangarti/Tjapaltjarri mix-up."

Male speakers usually treat a child's subsection as a product of the father, apparently conceptualizing subsections in father-child couples or cycles, as shown by Diagram 7B. Indeed, in explaining the principles relating the subsection categories, men usually described which subsections should marry and which subsections are related as father-child pairs. These couples are grouped further into two unnamed patrimoieties.[5] Such patrimoieties are only partially realized by the Pintupi. They do not see them exactly as sociocentric halves, but instead appropriate a dual division in egocentric terms.

Men refer to these patrimoieties in reciprocal terms that denote the ceremonial complementarity of rights and duties: They use the term *wapirra*[6] to refer to the relationship among themselves if they are themselves of the "owner" moiety, and the terms *yarriki* (the combination of "mother's brother" and "mother's brother's son") and *kirta* (the combination of "sister's husband" and "sister' son") for the patricouples of the other moiety if these others are "owners." They use the term *kurtungurlu* to refer to the moiety that acts as "manager" or "worker."

We should not ignore the fact that the system of reference is egocentered. It reveals what is significant about subsections as an intellectual construct that offers the intuition of higher, more comprehensive orderings of social life. In my experience, Pintupi men seemed to find it difficult to present the subsections systematically, with cycles and so on. In comparison with a Warlpiri man who once offered to sketch the subsections on paper for me, the Pintupi are more egocentered in conceptualizing the system. They tend to think of who is what in relation to some reference point rather than grasping the principles abstractly.[7] Although this is not at all problematic in terms of the practice of organizing, the higher levels of order—such as patrimoieties—appear more opaquely in this frame.

Actually, patrimoieties constitute a form of systematizing mainly for ritual organization, and are rarely spoken of otherwise. In phenomenological terms, this organizational category represents an emergent level of ordering in social relations that participants come to realize through the activity of ritual. The production and realization of such hierarchical orderings is partly what makes ritual of such interest to Aboriginal people: It coordinates sets of egocentric orderings on a sociocentric grid.

Finally, subsections are organized conceptually into a parallel set of endogamous, alternate-generation moieties. These are presented in Diagram 7C (using only the male terms for subsections). The generational moieties are reciprocally named in egocentric terms, "us" (*nganarnitja*) and "them" (*yinyurrpa* or *tjanam-iltjanpa*).[8] The generational classification holds importance in both marriage and ritual contexts. Far more than patrimoieties, this form of order is an essential and pervading feature of the Pintupi model of the social universe and will be treated in detail later.

Subsections and Kinship

Although subsection categories are understood as being related to kinship principles, they cannot substitute entirely for the latter.

Diagram 7C. Generational Moieties

```
┌─────────────────────────┐      ┌─────────────────────────┐
│  Yinyurrpa ("Them")     │      │  Nganarnitja ("Us")     │
│                         │      │                         │
│     TJAPANGARTI         │      │   TJAPANANGKA (ego)     │
│                         │      │                         │
│     TJAMPITJINPA        │      │      TJANGALA           │
│                         │      │                         │
│     TJAKAMARRA          │      │      TJUPURRULA         │
│                         │      │                         │
│     TJAPALTJARRI        │      │      TJUNGURRAYI        │
│                         │      │                         │
└─────────────────────────┘      └─────────────────────────┘
        Moiety 1                          Moiety 2
```

Given the variety of different identity relationships in a single subsection—"younger brother" (*marlanypa*), "older brother" (*kurta*), "grandfather" (*tjamu*, FF), and "grandson" (*tjamu*, SS) within one's own—considerations other than subsection category may determine the kin term that is applicable. (Diagram 7D presents a grouping of kin types by subsection.)

As others have pointed out (Meggitt 1962; Munn 1973a), the value of subsection classification lies in another direction. Subsections provide a shorthand model of kin relationships, a metalanguage that permits the systematic ordering of relationships on a society-wide scale. Munn writes that the kinship terminology is egocentrically defined, whereas the subsection system, a higher level of sociocultural order, "makes it possible to project egocentrically defined kinship relationships on a generalized sociocentric grid that locates them in terms of the over-all social structure" (Munn 1973a: 217). The subsection system, then, represents a society of dispersed bands as an enduring totality built on a set of basic principles. These "decentered categories" (T. Turner 1973) define people as same or different, as interchangeable social entities no matter whose point of view is taken.

"Kinship," Lévi-Strauss (1949, 1963) and others have argued, is a language. They have reified its rules, however—or, at least, they have failed to see the rule-oriented dimensions of language in relation to the concrete individuals who use it. On can hardly forget this after watching Aboriginal organization in process. To the extent that kinship becomes, as with sections and subsections, a self-defining structure detached from ego's point of view, that is surely a fact of phenomenological importance. Munn's account of the

Diagram 7D. Distribution of Kintypes to Subsections

```
                    Ego = TJAPANANGKA subsection

TJAPANANGKA   = YB, EB, FF, SS, FFB, BSS,...

napanangka    = YZ, EZ, FFZ, SD, BSD,...

TJAMPITJINPA  = MB, MMBSDS, MBSS, FFZDDS, FZH, DH (m.s.),...

nampitjinpa   = M, MBSD, MMBSDD, FFZDDD, SW (m.s.), FBW,...

TJAPANGARTI   = F, S, BS, FFF, SSS, MH, MZH,...

napangarti    = D, FZ, FFFZ, MBW,...

TJANGALA      = FZS, MBS, DS (m.s.), BDS, MF, FMBSS, MMH,...

nangala       = FZD, MBD, MFZ, DD, FM, BSD, DDH,...

TJUNGURRAYI   = MMB, MMBSS, FFZDS, ZDS, DDH,...

nungurrayi    = MM, MMBSD, FFZDD, ZDD,...

TJAPALTJARRI  = MMBS, ZDH, MFZS, MBDS, WMB,...

napaltjarri   = MBDD, MMBD, ZSW, WM,...

TJAKAMARRA    = ZS, FFZS, WF, MMBDH, MBDDH,...

nakamarra     = ZD, FFZD, MMBSW,...

TJUPURRULA    = MMBDS, WF, ZH, FFZH, FFWB, FFZSS,...

napurrula     = MMBDD, FFZSD, W, WZ, ZHZ,...
```

Warlpiri stresses the importance of subsections as a mediatory code, a system that can, on the one hand,

> ... be translated into the more specific egocentric code for kinship;
> ... on the other hand, it serves to name and express the semimoiety
> [father-son couples] and moiety relationships that are the widest
> categorical division of the whole society. (Munn 1973a: 21)

Munn interprets the subsection system as a semitotemic device. It identifies the general types of kinship relationships between Warlpiri patrilineal descent groups and defines the position of a single group with respect to all the descent groups of the society. Thus, certain descent groups, such as a Tjakamarra/Tjupurrula pair, are likened to others of the same subsections as being "company." These groups can marry other groups and participate in each other's rituals in the same way.

Kinship: Models of the Pintupi Social Universe

Pintupi use the same subsection categories as do Warlpiri, but they do not have patrilineal descent groups of similar definition to those described by Munn. In the Warlpiri system, a preference for community endogamy (Meggitt 1962: 56) implies that members of patrigroups marry within a restricted set of localized descent groups. The subsection distinctions (along with the differentiation among community members established through opposite-sex siblings as linking kin) defines acceptable distances for marriage within such a community (D. Turner 1980: 38–71). This arrangement leads to fairly regular relationships of alliance and descent among members of a community's patrigroups. Instead of preferring such community endogamy, Pintupi expect marriage with people from "far away." Among Pintupi, then, subsections organize relations among people from all over a region, integrating them into a structure that articulates the society not as a coordinated ordering of distinctive local groups, but as a set of related categories. In a sense, they transcend locality in favor of broader categories, extending participation on a systematic society-wide basis that seems detached from locality.

Despite the differing societal implications, the subsection system provides the Pintupi with a satisfactory symbolic ordering of social life within a region. The more comprehensive structure is modeled on more immediate levels of the system—on the mutuality experienced in the division of labor in the camp. The distinction whereby a man's sister's son and his own sons have complementary but separate roles in many ceremonies (that is, *kurtungurlu* and *wapirra*) becomes the basis of a sociocentric organization of ritual. The ceremony for each sacred site is thus organized by ascribing sets of subsections to each of the two complementary roles. These sets are the implicit patrimoieties. Pintupi will say, for example, that for the site of Yumari the patricouple of Tjangala and Tjampitjinpa are *wapirra* (with that of Tjupurrula and Tjakamarra being derivatively *wapirra*), while the father-son pairs Tjapanangka and Tjapangarti and Tjapaltjarri and Tjungurrayi are *kurtungurlu*. This system consistently images the society as constituted of opposing but complementary and cooperating categories—those "descended of men" (patrifilial kin) versus those "descended of women" and affines.

Between people of these categories, relations are those of complementary exchange: *kurtungurlu* manage the occasion for the *wapirra* and receive food (ideally meat, and now often money) as payment for their "work." The meat is formally given to the *kurtungurlu* but ends up being distributed among all the older men who jointly sanction the performance. From ceremony to ceremony, the roles may be reversed but the patricategories remain invariant, always "manager" and "owner" to each other. Munn argues, in her Warlpiri analysis, that the exchanges between categories replicate structurally the relations of the family camp—the exchange of men's products for women's (1973a: 26). In this way, the subsection system articulates principles of the egocentric kinship system—marriage, filiation, and the division of labor by sex—into a model of the society itself as ordered by an enduring framework of complementary exchange.

While these principles operate in their ritual, too, Pintupi are not nearly as intrigued by these correspondences as are Warlpiri. Pintupi rarely invoke the *kurtungurlu* and *wapirra* distinctions as the defining feature of their attachment to a place. Nor do they make as much out of the differentiation of categories based on opposite-sex siblings. Other features predominate in the Pintupi appropriation of this system.

Subsections do provide one representation of the regional system, an objectification that has meaning in contrast to the egocentrism of kinship itself. The other structuring of the broadest society, however, is modeled on a different set of immediate relationships, between parents and children. A more detailed examination of the underlying principles of kinship will reveal these elements of the Pintupi theory of social relations.

Kinship Terminology

Diagram 7E illustrates the Pintupi principles of kin classification, represented on a genealogical grid. [9] It is presented for convenience of reference, but such a distribution of kin terms does not in itself explain the cultural rationale of classification. The deeper meaning of Pintupi kinship can be grasped through recognizing that relationships that are distinguishable terminologically may still be alike in important ways. It is easy to overspecify the distinctive kin roles; Pintupi tend to see similarities. Analytically, the terminology itself is a surface realization of basic, enduring conceptions. That Pintupi can use alternative models of the kin universe relies on this fact.

Goodenough's (1969: 317) rethinking of "status" and "role" can help us recognize similarities between culturally articulated relationships. The distinction between identity relationships and status relationships is critical. First, statuses are "collections of rights and duties" rather than categories or kinds of persons. Second, a status may be part of different identity relationships. Thus, Goodenough concludes, a "culturally ordered system of *social relationships*" is "composed (among other things) of identity relationships, status

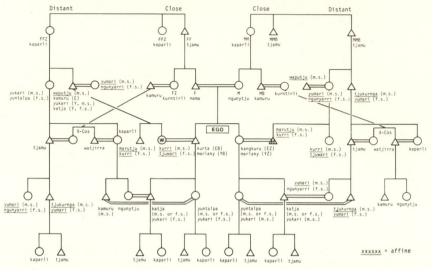

relationships, and the ways in which they are mutually distributed" (Goodenough 1969: 317).

The relationship terms applied between two individuals (such as "father" and "son") define the appropriate relationship between them as two social identities, marking a specific allocation of rights and duties (Goodenough 1969: 316). When claims are made on people that derive from status relationships, Pintupi usually resort to kinship terminology to highlight the basis of the claim. Thus, a man will command his niece, "Sister's child, go and get some water."

As I came to understand, the identity relationships between generations share a common status relationship. Though differentiable as "father," "mother's brother," and so on, all relationships with those in the parental generation are articulated through the concept of "holding" (*kanyininpa*), combining nurturance (a duty) and command (a right). Viewed from another perspective, the concept of generation is one of the most basic principles of classification that determines the distribution of rights and duties. The differences among people of a generation, such as those proposed in the subsection system, remain secondary.

Pintupi kinship classification thus starts from a premise quite different from the European model. They stress that the children of "brothers" or of "sisters" are "family," or "really siblings" themselves. This point was repeatedly and explicitly urged on me. In presenting genealogical information, Pintupi commonly list a set of apical siblings in perhaps the first ascending generation, naming them in age order and making a vertical mark in the sand for each. Under these lines they similarly record the whole set of offspring of the siblings as a single group. These, they say, are all siblings.

People represent themselves as close siblings in the same way, referring to various dead individuals by joint relationship terms that strongly link the living. The use of possessive pronouns, especially exclusive and inclusive forms, is as subtle in implying relationships of solidarity and distance as the distinction between *tu* and *vous* in French. This was certainly part of the message, for example, when two elderly women stressed their shared identity in claiming a man as "our (*ngalimpa*, first-person–dual inclusive–possessive) mother's brother." Their claim of another person as "our father" (*mamalampatju*), using the first-person plural exclusive (-*lampatju*), similarly stressed the idea of brother or sister sets and their descendants. When I asked informants to tell me who really were their siblings, they frequently included the offspring of the parents' same-sex siblings (that is, of father's brothers, mother's sisters). Even when requested to limit the list to "those from one father" (*mama kutjungkatja*), Pintupi are inclined to name such siblings. The reason they do so is apparent when personal histories are considered. Because a person's siblings "look after" (*kanyininpa*) his or her children in the event of his or her death, parental siblings are interactively close.

This "sibling set" constitutes a basic unit in Pintupi kinship reckoning. It lies at the heart of the kinship system's classificatory nature. The extensions quickly compound. Ego's "mother" may have several successive husbands, all of whom are "father" to ego and whose "brothers" are "father" to ego, and so on. Ego has a similar relationship to all their camps, in that "fathers" are expected to feed and protect "sons." Individuals can certainly distinguish actual genealogical kin such as *pater* from *genitor*, and for certain purposes they may do so. However, the cultural emphasis usually overrides this discrimination in favor of the aspects of social experience related to sibling sets. There is an affective basis to this representation of one's identity as well as a diplomatic one.

One example of genealogical thought in its local form suffices to demonstrate the place of sibling sets. An informant, as frustrated as I by my incomprehension, thought he had explained to me what a Pintupi genealogy was. The significant fact, he admonished me, was that "all of these people [a number of Tjungurrayi men who were related] come from a set of brothers." They are "one family." He was referring to people he called "brother," explaining that they came from a group of Tjapaltjarri men who were brothers to each other. Were they, I asked, brothers because all men of the same subsection category are brothers? "Look," he said peevishly, "Tjarlu tjakamarra has five sons. Their children will be siblings, all the brothers." Eventually, they also would produce another set of siblings, "all the brothers."

The premise of sibling sets extends back through time, so the people of the Yumari area, I was told, were all "one family." They were descendants of three Tjapangarti men (Linyarri, Katji, and Yiitjuru) who are said to have been "brothers." In what genealogical sense the three men (all born around the turn of the century) may have been "brothers" is unclear and irrelevant. Possibly, they were descended from "brothers," but any differences among them have been rendered socially unimportant. As perhaps the longest surviving of a larger group, these three men, remembered as having "looked after" the surviving descendants, are represented as a sibling set themselves because of their shared relationship to descendants. This sort of information and expectation is effectively coded in subsection categorization. Thus, among people of the same category, there is always the notion that, although genealogical details may be hazy, a link exists.

Such a view reflects pragmatic expectations about individual life spans and the possibility that one's children may be looked after by one's younger siblings in the case of one's death. If carried through logically, the focal point of the "brothers" criterion is the grandparental generation that produced "brothers." An alternative Pintupi explanation for the inclusion of an individual as "close kin" or "family" is, accordingly, that he or she shares the same grandparent. In this respect, it is significant that the terms for "grandparent" (*tjamu* for male, *kaparli* for female) are used for all second ascending generation kin. Any person who may have been involved in marriage exchanges that resulted in ego is considered a "grandparent" (see Diagram 7E). Regardless of subsection, which might appear to categorize some as "cross-cousin" and others as "mother's mother's brother," Pintupi regard all related people of this generation as "grandparents." Notice that this identity awards no recognition to membership in differing patrilineal descent groups: one's father's father and his brother-in-law, for example, are both *tjamu*. Their descendants are all considered to be close kin by ego, and unmarriageable. They are, as well, "one countryman" claimants to the country of the shared grandparent. Potential in-laws should be descendants of grandparents who are considered "distant" rather than "close."

Prolonged and regular coresidence effectively determines the social significance of any sibling links. Thus, the male children of three closely related Tjangala men from Yumari (Tjiwa Tjiwa, Ralyu, and Tjanyinti) were usually listed as "all the brothers" and perceived as constituting a group, a sibling set apart from other Tjampitjinpa men. The assertion that they were "really brothers" was based on the culturally significant consideration of descent from "brothers" or from "sisters." They cooperated as a group in the organization of bestowals, projecting their social identity into the future. Further, these Tjangala men had several sisters, and the women had many daughters. The children of these daughters were themselves still a defined group of siblings in Pintupi eyes. The importance of the group was sustained by the coresidence of the descendants.

In practice, the people who consider themselves "brothers" are usually those "from one country." Their expectations of coresidence and a shared interest in some of the same rituals and sacred sites underlie the continuing closeness among brothers (and sisters) and the closeness of their offspring as siblings. Therefore, Pintupi may equally well use the residential association of locality as a cultural representation of these groupings: The identity of the loosely defined set that Pintupi recognize as "the Yumari mob" can be traced genealogically or residentially. This sort of co-implication reflects what Bourdieu (1976) called a "habitus." A set of practices conjoins the different codes of kinship and locality as manifestations of a single logic.

Locality

In deciding how to classify individuals in kin terms, Pintupi regularly make a distinction between "close" and "distant" kin that has an important impact on classification. This distinction effectively makes locality another criterion of the kinship system.

The isomorphic relationship between being "close" and being "family" is explicit. "Close" (*ngamu*) refers to geographical or spatial proximity, contrasting with "distant" (*tiwa, warnma*) or "far away." In the Pintupi conception, close kin are precisely that; they are one countrymen with whom one frequently lives in one camp. Kin who are "from close" are typically assimilated to appropriate categories of consanguinity because they are *walytja*. By applying this consideration, persons of each genealogical level are seen as being grouped into sibling sets.

For example, the term *tjukurnpa* denotes the kin types MMBS or MFZS for a male ego, but if the alter is "from one country," the Pintupi substitute "father" (*mama*) for the former term. A real *tjukurnpa* is a potential "wife's mother's brother," one of the people involved in marriage bestowal, and this term is applicable only to a man who is from "far away." Classification reflects the expectation that "close kin" live together, and that one must marry those from distant localities (local exogamy). I initially learned this from a man who camped with his family adjacent to me when I was first at Yayayi; he was my *tjukurnpa*. In a good mood one day, after a few months of my living there, he informed me, "Tjapanangka [my subsection]! I'm your daddy. I call you *katja*." The look of puzzlement on my face made him convulse with laughter, but eventually I understood his point: we were from one camp.

Diagram 7E illustrates that a *tjukurnpa* is always the son of one called *tjamu* (grandfather), especially of a distant MMB (*tjamu*). The diagram distinguishes between "close" and "distant" *tjamu*. Children of the former are considered "close kin" and are classified in consanguineal categories: such a man is called "father" (*mama*) rather than "wife's mother's brother" (*tjukurnpa*).

Similar thinking converts those "close kin" of the types MMBD and MFZD (*yumari*, "wife's mother") to the category of "father's sister" (*kurntirli*). Those of the kin type MMBDD or "spouse" (*kurri*, male speaking), MMBDS or "wife's brother" (*marutju*, male speaking), or "husband's sister" (*tjuwari*, female speaking) are all assimilated to the category of "cross-cousin" (*watjirra*). As "family," they are classified with consanguineal terms. [10]

This common practice of reclassification makes clear that the separation of in-law (distant) categories from consanguineal (close) ones represents a fundamental principle of ordering. Pintupi consistently reserve the terms *yumari* (WM or MMBD), *tjukurnpa* (WMB or MMBS), *kurri* (spouse or MMBDCh), *tjuwari* (HZ, BW, or MMBDD), and *marutju* (ZH, WB, or MMBDS) to refer to in-laws or potential in-laws. [11] If a person belongs to one of the kin types that may be designated by these terms but is considered to be "family," she or he is classified by the appropriate consanguineal terms, as close kin rather than distant. Distant kin are potential in-laws, while close kin are, in terminological usage at least, "fathers," "mothers," "mother's brothers," "father's sisters," siblings, "close-cousins," and grandparents.

In this way, social and physical space are mnemonics of each other. Pintupi kin classification represents the band, the one countrymen, as a "family," with locality as a distinctive feature of grouping. The kin terms adequately define participants' relationships to each other in terms of exchanging products, labor, and women—the relationships of production and reproduction.

It is worth noting the resemblances between Pintupi kin classification and the system Elkin (1940) discussed as Aluridja-type (southern Pitjanytjatjarra) and by Hamilton (1979) for Janggundjara (cf. Scheffler 1978: 88–118). All these systems are found among speakers of related Western Desert dialects, and they share with Pintupi many lexemes in the classification of kin. The historical connection between the systems seems obvious.

According to Elkin (1940), the only classification of consanguineal kin of ego's own generation level is "brother" or "sister." Genealogical cross-cousins (MBD and so on) are classed as "brother" or "sister." The Aluridja distinction clearly marks off consanguineal or "close" kin from potential in-laws. The latter are referred to by terms indicating this contrasting status.

The comparison is valuable in indicating the content of the Pintupi categorization of the children of "brothers" or "sisters" (and of any mixed sibling set) as themselves siblings or "family." In this way, the systems distinguish "close kin" from in-laws. The Aluridja system classifies the cross-cousin of ego's mother as a mother's sibling; his or her child is thereby sibling to ego and unmarriageable. While Pintupi usage does not classify parental kin in this way, it shares the notion of "cross-cousin" as a sort of sibling and gives primacy to proximity in defining status.

Siblings of Opposite Sex

The foregoing considerations of the criteria that lead to merging of categories bring us to another important feature of kin classification: the distinction between "brothers" and "sisters," founded on the distinction between males and females. Similarity and difference between siblings of opposite sex is implied in the distinction between males and females of the same subsection category via prefixes on the same root. The kinship terminology is complex in regard to this classification. The valence of the brother-sister pair is critical in differentiating the way in which social reproduction takes place among the Pintupi—where it is focused on husband-wife pairs as a unit—from that among people for whom patrilineal descent groups are important. Among such other Aboriginal peoples—for instance, the Warlpiri, the Yulngu of Northeast Arnhem Land, and the Ngaringman of the Victoria River area (Rose 1984)—brothers and sisters seem to constitute a cultural reproductive unit.

In the Pintupi system, ego distinguishes older siblings in regard to their sex. "Elder sister" is *kangkuru* or *yayi* while "elder brother" is *kurta*. Younger siblings are classified by the unmarked term *marlanypa* (*marla*, "behind" or "after"), according with the cultural significance attached to relative age in deciding the polarity of authority relations. Older siblings have authority over ego and the

Nosepeg Tjupurrula entertains his young son at their camp. (New Bore, 1981)

responsibility to "look after" him or her. Another term, *nyarrumpa*, refers to a cross-cutting category of "sibling of opposite sex." A man's *nyarrumpa* is his sister and a female's *nyarrumpa* is her brother.

The provisional nature of the distinction between siblings of opposite sex is manifested in the case either of them is "linking kin" to the descending generation. Here we find three sets of terminological possibility, different levels of generalization that people may select.

Level one. Male ego may call his sister's children *yukari*, and a female ego may call her brother's children *yukari*. Each calls his or her own children and those of same-sex siblings "male child" (*katja*, often rendered "boy" in pidgin) or "female child" (*yuntalpa*). Unlike Warlpiri usage, where the terms a brother uses for his sister's children are the same as those she uses and vice versa (Meggitt 1962: 84; Scheffler 1978: 331–32), among Pintupi it is husband and wife who use the same kinship terms for their children. The Pintupi discriminate between "own children" (children of same-sex siblings) and "children of siblings of opposite sex." The term *yukari* marks only the relative sex of linking kin and not the sex of the child.

This distinction has relevance for a number of organizational domains. Siblings of opposite sex are the foundation of the complementary ritual statuses in many ceremonies, between "those from

Pintupi Country, Pintupi Self

men" ("owners") and "those from women" ("managers"). A man's "son" and his "sister's son" assume different roles, and "cross-cousins" (*watjirra*) are similarly differentiated in contexts of marriage and ritual as being descended from a pair of opposite-sex siblings.

We have seen that, on one terminological level, a man differentiates his own children from his sister's children.

Level two. On another level, however, men and women can also call the children of *any* sibling by the terms *katja* or *yuntalpa*, neutralizing the distinction formed between opposite-sex siblings. For this reason, I have glossed *katja* and *yuntalpa* as "male child" and "female child," respectively. The specification of an individual as a child of an opposite-sex sibling is not necessary in all contexts. Indeed, as the unmarked category, emphasizing simply filiation from ego or ego's siblings, the "child" terms are the primary.

These terms are, as well, the only "child" terms used by the Aluridja (Elkin 1940: 215), who have no special terms to distinguish "sister's children" from a man's "own children." Thus, Elkin (1940: 376) argues that in the southern area "the [kinship] terms do little beside indicate sex, generation level and marriage relationship."

The cross-cousin distinction is not absolute, either. An informant, for example, described a cross-cousin who was his close relative as an "elder brother" (*kurta*). The other man, he said, was "from the woman" (that is, born from a Napanangka) and he himself was "from the man" (*watingkatja*). Though specifying their descent from an opposite-sex sibling pair, his usage neutralized the distinction.

I have heard Pintupi describe members of the "cross-cousin" category alternately as "like a sibling" and sometimes as "like a spouse" (or spouse's brother). The ambiguity parallels the alternative classifications between the children of opposite-sex siblings as "siblings" or as "cross-cousins," the latter indicating "distance." In the four-section systems used by other Western Desert peoples, which classify "cross-cousins" in the same section as "spouses," close cross-cousins are considered unmarriageable (Tonkinson 1978: 48). They are like siblings, whereas spouses should be "distant," that is, not descended from those who consider themselves to be siblings.

Level three. A third usage, at the highest level of categorization, makes it clear that the relationship of generation levels is more central to Pintupi kinship terminology than the distinction between opposite-sex siblings as linking kin. These terms emphasize the importance of relationships among people undifferentiated by lineality, and give priority to generation level and "closeness."

Ego's "father" (*mama*), "mother" (*ngunytju*), "mother's brother" (*kamuru*), and "father's sister" (*kurntirli*) all may call ego *ngayum-parnu*, which I gloss as "child." This term is unmarked for sex or relative sex of linking kin, designating only consanguines of the first descending generation. Reciprocally, ego calls all of these people and their siblings *ngayupula*, a term similar to "parent" but extended to parent's siblings. In effect, Pintupi recognize the essential similarity in status relationships between a person and all his or her "one countrymen" of the preceding generation. The reciprocal use of the terms designates a "closed, polarized set of relationships" (Goodenough 1970: 89) in which the elder looks after the younger and the younger defers to the older. Divorced of marital possibilities, differences in kin type thus become insubstantial in defining social identity.

The lexeme *ngayu-* is the root of the first-person singular pronoun. Thus, the construction *ngayupula* conforms to a typical teknonymic pattern, the form "... pula." One may speak of "Bobbypula," referring to Bobby's father, mother, or wife. To do so specifies someone closely identified with whatever name is given. *Ngayupula* is, then, "one related to me." Usually the term is applied only to persons in the first ascending generation. (I have no similar linguistic data with which to gloss *ngayumparnu*, but its contexts imply something like "one from me.")

Both egocentered categories are realized materially in important life-crisis rituals. The persons whom ego calls *ngayupula* (F, M, MB, FZ) are also in the special relationship of *yirkapiri* to him or her, a categorization relevant to initiation and mourning. At a man's initiation, for instance, his male *yirkapiri* lie down to one side, separately, taking no active part in the proceedings. They are "too sorry." The initiate's close relatives who consider themselves to be really *yirkapiri* also camp together. Likewise, at mortuary rituals the *yirkapiri* are terminologically and behaviorally distinguished from other categories of relatives, but not on a principle of lineality. One's *yirkapiri*, in fact, come from throughout the region.

Alternative Orderings

The preceding analysis makes it clear that Pintupi have two ways of categorizing the brother-sister "space" of the relationship domain. One of these emphasizes simply "relatedness," generational succession, and (somtimes) the sex of the referent or addressee. The other marks generational succession and descent from opposite-sex siblings, emphasizing the distinction between males and females as linking kin.

These differences make "cross-cousins" somewhat ambiguous, close on one scale and more distant on the other. The distinction between males and females of a sibling set is maintained on all levels of the relationship terminology except that of cross-cousin. All these are classified under a single term, *watjirra*, discriminating neither sex of alter nor relative sex. It indicates, rather, "ego's generation" and "descent from parental sibling of opposite sex." The absence of such a category in the southern Aluridja system corresponds to a lack of terminological distinction there between one's own children and those of siblings of the opposite sex (Elkin 1940). Pintupi retain the sense of the Aluridja system by insisting that if opposite-sex parental siblings are close relatives (such as from a "group of brothers"), the resulting cross-cousins are "like brothers" or "like sisters." Often they use sibling terms with each other (as one would in the Aluridja system). Such cross-cousins should not marry, nor should their children marry, although the latter will be in the appropriate subsection categories for marriage.

If Pintupi relationship terminology offers two alternative schemes of organization, how do they differ? The first emphasizes a model of generational succession basic to the Aluridja-type system—one that functions not "to trace and represent genealogical relationships, but to show genealogical level, sex, and affinal position" (Elkin 1940: 378). Such a system yields no basis for some genealogical relationships to prevail over others, treating all active relationships simply as equal. Because all parental-generation people are essentially alike (*ngayupula*), as are all people of one's own generation of siblings and so on, the generational model reflects a principle of general, nonspecific "relatedness" among individuals in a region. This is why, perhaps, the Pintupi emphasize the fact of being *walytja* itself, instead of delineating different roles within the class. If one is related at all, only sex and generation matter. As in the Aluridja case, Pintupi practice and use of kinship terminology emphasize local exogamy. They confine the class of potential in-laws to geographically "distant" persons, while assimilating genealogically but geographically "close" persons to relationships of consanguinity and unmarriageability.

The second scheme is concerned with distinguishing roles and statuses defined by the complementarity of opposite-sex siblings. In practice, this principle is employed in many contexts of men's ritual where "sons" and "sister's sons" assume complementary roles, and in contexts concerning marriage and bestowal of women. In all likelihood, the distinction is relatively recent, along with the adoption of sections and subsections in the Western Desert.

What does the distinction do? In systems like the Warlpiri one, according to D. Turner (1980), it is a constituent of a structure through which alliances are established within a geographically bounded, intermarrying cluster of patrigroups. People are differentiated within this "community" (Meggitt 1962: 51) in terms of distance through application of the brother/sister difference. These marital arrangements are coordinated with ritual organization. Pintupi, however, continue to place emphasis on marrying people "from far away," although they do also apply the further distinctions of marriageability, entailed by the distinction between brother/sister links.

By distinguishing extra categories within ego's generation, the separation of those descending from opposite-sex sibling pairs reduces the range of "brothers" who will be competing for a particular category of "wives" (cf. Shapiro 1971). This narrowing may enhance integration by reducing conflict among men. In theory, at least, a man will not be competing with those he calls *tjamu* (MMBSS, FFZDS) or with his male cross-cousins for wives.Men of these categories are precisely the ones who are supposed to help one get a spouse. A marriage to one in the wrong subsection category is seen as removing a potential spouse from another man. When Pintupi complain about "wrong" marriages, they often specify that "it is no good to rob another man's wife." Possibly the differentiation of kinds of relatives may also reduce potential conflict over bestowal rights between patrilateral and matrilateral relatives of a woman.

Another concern is male ritual. The southern Pitjanytjatjarra, who do not distinguish between "men's children" and "women's children," also do not organize male ceremony by complementary patrimoieties. Generational moieties provide the structure of their ritual life. The Pintupi, eclectically, have some ceremonies organized on generation and others organized on the distinction between the rights and duties of a man's children and those of his sister's children. Thus, they not only distinguish the classes of kin defined by opposite-sex siblings, but base all the ceremonial organization concerned with landownership on the resulting "owner"/"manager" distinction. Yet they do not, as do the Warlpiri, emphasize stretches of a Dreaming-path as associated with a patricouple of subsections. The Pintupi ritual groups have not become patrilineal. Whatever their purposes elsewhere, these distinctions in Pintupi ritual merely intensify, albeit in another pattern, the sense of mutuality and shared concern (the integration of autonomy within relatedness) evident throughout their activities.

The distinctions may have deeper consequences, of course. Hamilton (1979, 1980) speculates that the formation of patriline-based men's ritual groups, in contrast to the birth totemism that

Pintupi Country, Pintupi Self

once prevailed among Pitjanytjatjarra, establishes a priority on ties through men and offers them leverage in sexual politics. Subsections (and presumably the sibling distinction) enable men to increase their control over women by consolidating themselves in patrilines around sacred sites. Insofar as "sons" and "sister's sons" both continue to remain important in Pintupi ritual, one wonders if "patrilineality" is truly the variable Hamilton should be using. An increasing reliance on filiation in establishing the transmission of ritual rights—in contrast to conception or birth as prevailed among the Pitjanytjatjarra—may create a political realm that gives added value to men's relations with other men and to the formation of more discrete groups. In the Warlpiri case, perhaps, the descent orientation and the distinction of kinds of kin lend some impetus to the emergence of more locally autonomous patrilineal groups that are integrated in a larger system by recognition of shared Dreaming-tracks and cognatic ties between their members. Such is not the case for the Pintupi, who have in many ways assimilated the brother-sister distinction to their own pattern of overall relatedness. The distinction of siblings remains significant and often quite visible behaviorally, but in a deep sense Pintupi stress the common identity of descent from a set of siblings and the similarity among people within a generation.

Generation

The classification of persons into two genealogical levels, "us" (*nganarnitja*) and "them" (*yinyurrpa*), constitutes the endogamous generational moieties that are absolutely basic to any consideration of Pintupi social relationships and terminology. Their significance is more than a simple sorting of kin types. The meaning implicit in such a classification makes generational moieties a dominant symbol of Pintupi social structure. Among Jigalong Aborigines, for example, Tonkinson has noted that:

> Most terminology reflects the existence of generation levels, in that members of the same grouping . . . use identical reciprocal terms in most cases, which express the openness and *high degree of equality* in their relationships. On the other hand, people in adjacent level groupings (all members of the first ascending and descending generations) are usually addressed by non-identical reciprocal terms, which indicates that there is a difference in status between the two people concerned. (1974: 50, emphasis added)

The contrast of equality and hierarchy holds for the Pintupi, too.

The "us" category includes ego, all of his or her siblings, crosscousins, and potential spouses and their siblings. It includes all individuals of the second ascending and descending generations (who call each other, reciprocally, *tjamu* and *kaparli* for male and female alter, respectively). The "them" category includes ego's "father," "mother," their siblings and cross-cousins, and ego's children, children of his or her siblings, and children of ego's cross-cousins.

Although the moieties are not named—merely labeled with the deictic terms "us" and "them"—the categories are sociocentric. Every person is a member of a single category, *nganarnitja*, whose members act together on occasions such as male initiation and death. These moieties also define the acceptable marriage alternatives. For Pintupi, the most important condition of marriage is to find a spouse within one's own generational moiety. Criticism of "wrong" marriage, accompanied by expressions of disapproval and disgust, reaches its most forceful level when people violate this rule.[12] Informants emphasize the prohibition against marrying *yinyurrpa* rather than specifying that particular relationships or kin types are unacceptable marriage partners. Bad as it might be, marriage to the wrong kin type in one's own generation is more permissible than marrying a person of the alternate generation.

First Ascending Generation

The full significance of generational categorization is revealed in the way Pintupi actually use kin terms, assimilating persons of one's own generation to sibling terms. Kinship terminology as a whole is concerned with defining identity relationships for a variety of activities and social domains. In this sense, as Stanner (1966: 37) remarks for the cultural orderings of the Murinbata, Pintupi terminology represents merely a working toward a unified system and coherence. We see this when the domain is restricted to a group of "one countrymen," those who consider themselves to be "close kin."

In the first ascending generation, all "close kin" are referred to by parent or parent-sibling terms. The general rule for such a merging (actually a neutralization of the sibling of opposite-sex features that distinguish within a broader class of kin) is that a parent's cross-cousin is classified with that parent's spouse category.[13] Thus, a father's cross-cousin is classified as a "mother" (if female) or a "mother's brother" (if male). A mother's cross-cousin is classified as a "father" (if male) or a "father's sister" (if female) (see Diagram 7F).[14]

As an example, let us posit as ego a man of the Tjakamarra subsection. By strict subsection relationships, ego should use the

Diagram 7F. Classification of Parental Cross-Cousins

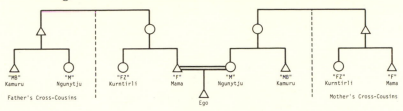

"MB"	"M"	"FZ"	"F"	"M"	"MB"	"FZ"	"F"
Kamuru	Ngunytju	Kurntirli	Mama	Ngunytju	Kamuru	Kurntirli	Mama

Father's Cross-Cousins   Ego   Mother's Cross-Cousins

term *tjukurnpa* to address or refer to a man of the Tjangala subsection whose kin type is MMBS or WMB in the ascending generation. The term is reciprocal. Frequently, however, male individuals refer to such persons as "father" (*mama*); Tjarlu tjakamarra explained that he referred to Nippy tjangala as "father" because they were "from one country" and the latter had looked after Tjarlu when he was a boy. A true *tjukurnpa*, he said, should be from far away (see Diagram 7G).

Similar merging occurs in the case of Tjangala's sister, Nangala. If she is a person Tjakamarra considers to be "family," he calls her "father's sister" (*kurntirli*). Nangala is ordinarily of the kin types MMBD, MFZD, or WM to Tjakamarra, and is expected on subsection grounds to be a *yumari*, or mother-in-law. When she is a close relative, however, she is assimilated to the "father's sister" (*kurntirli*) category as a mother's cross-cousin. Such a person is said to be "too close" for Tjakamarra to marry her daughter. Therefore, she is not a "wife's mother." She is classified out of an in-law category and into a consanguineal one (see Diagram 7G).

The classification of father's cross-cousin is more complex, but it follows the same principles. In terms of the subsection system, such people are in the category that male ego usually considers as "sister's children" (*yukari*) and female ego considers as "own children" (*katja* and *yuntalpa*). When persons of this category are older than ego or if they are close (as true cross-cousins of one's father or coresidents), they are called "mother" (*ngunytju*, for female alter) or "mother's brother" (*kamuru*, for male alter) (see Diagram 7H). The main reason given for such reclassification—following the principle of categorizing parental cross-cousins with that parent's spouse category—is that the person "looked after" ego or "grew him up."

When people of this kind are "distant" kin, however, with whom one has relatively little interaction, one uses the "sister's child" term. With distant kin, there is no conflict between the expectations of seniority by relative age and the connotations of juniority implicit in the "sister's child" term. Among close kin, it

Diagram 7G. Classification of "Close Kin" by Tjarlu tjakamarra

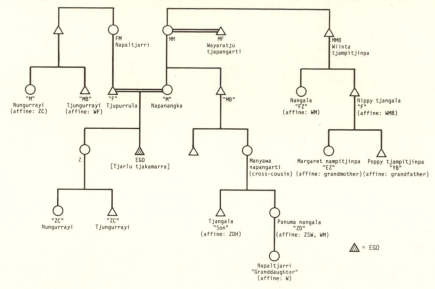

is generational succession that is maintained, representing the people with whom one is living as like a family.

First Descending Generation

The distinction between "own children" (*katja*, male child; *yuntalpa*, female child) and "opposite-sex sibling's children" (*yukari*) provides the basic grid on which the principles of classification operate with this generation. However, these terms account for only part of the space in the first descending level. There are also the children of those one calls "cross-cousins" (*watjirra*). These may be classified as either in-laws or consanguines. The schema can be represented systematically as follows for cross-cousin's children who are consanguines:

Female Ego	
Male cross-cousin's child	= "own son" (*katja*)
	= "own daughter" (*yuntalpa*)
Female cross-cousin's child	= "brother's son" (*yukari*)
	= "brother's daughter" (*yukari*)
Male Ego	
Male cross-cousin's child	= "sister's son" (*yukari*)
	= "sister's daughter" (*yukari*)
Female cross-cousin's child	= "own son" (*katja*)
	= "sister's daughter" (*yuntalpa*)

Pintupi Country, Pintupi Self

Diagram 7H. Generational Classification
of the Close Kin Universe

Close Consanguines

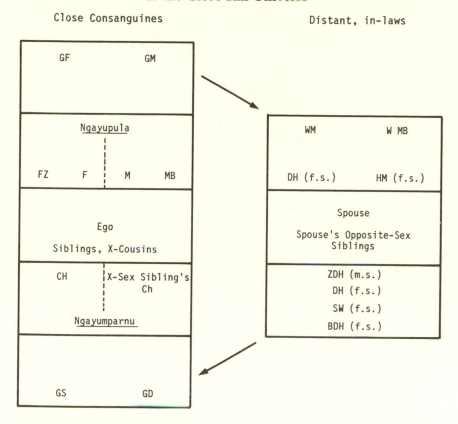

Panuma nangala was Tjarlu tjakamarra's MBDD, his female cross-cousin's daughter. According to subsection categories, Nangala is "wife's mother" (*yumari*) to Tjakamarra. This relationship would indicate he could marry her daughter. When I asked him about this possibility, Tjarlu said that she was not his mother-in-law. He called Panuma, rather, "sister's child" (*yukari*) because they were from "one country" and he had helped "grow her up." Had she been older than he, Tjarlu would call her "father's sister" (see Diagram 7G).

It is not necessary to explicate these terms in greater depth, as they represent the inverse of the treatment of parental cross-cousins. What is important is the fact that all close consanguines in the first descending generation are assimilated to "own children" terms or "children of opposite-sex sibling" terms.

I must, however, draw attention to an anomalous difference in usage by male and female. The anomaly, simply put, is that a female ego calls her MMBS a "mother's brother" if he is close, while she calls his sister (her MMBD) "father's sister." The man thus called "mother's brother" calls the female ego "sister's child" (*yukari*), but he calls her brother "own male child" (*katja*). Although Tjarlu tjakamarra called Panuma nangala "sister's child," he called her brother "own male child." Brothers and sisters thus apply different terms of reference to the same man: he is "father" to the brother and "mother's brother" to the sister. The male usage follows the general Pintupi pattern of classifying parental cross-cousins with the parent's spouse category, but the female usage follows the Aluridja pattern of classifying a parental cross-cousin with the parent or parent's sibling. When I pointed out this anomaly, no one seemed to be concerned; it did not seem to matter. The more important feature of the classification is that those who are considered "close kin," from one country are classified as parents or parents' siblings if in the ascending generation, and as "own" or "opposite-sex sibling's children" in the descending generation.

Own Generation

In the case of "close kin" from ego's own generation, the categories are collapsed by reclassifying distant kin types as siblings. At this level, there are really only siblings and in-laws. Because cross-cousins resemble both siblings and in-laws, they present an ambiguity for reclassification, but one resolved pragmatically.

For example, those of the kin type MMB or MMBSS may be reclassified as "brother" (*kurta*, "elder brother" or *marlanypa*, "younger sibling"). This merging is most common if such a person is close kin and similar in age to ego. The merging follows the outlines of a four-section system, in which ego, MMB, MMBSS, SS, and ZDS are all included in a single section (cf. Tonkinson 1974). Although as a general rule, men of the Tjakamarra subsection call those of the Tjampitjinpa subsection "grandfather" or "grandson" (*tjamu*), the terms for "brother" may also be used. The explanation they offer is that they are "from one country" and are "family": "We lived together" (*nyinangulatju tjungu*). Because they are from one country, Tjarlu tjakamarra calls Poppy tjampitjinpa "younger brother" (*marlanypa*). At the same time, Tjarlu calls Poppy's father, Nippy tjangala, by the term "father," while Nippy had been likewise a "brother" to Tjarlu's real father (see Diagram 7G). On the same grounds, a male Tjakamarra calls women of the Nampitjinpa subsection, if they are close, "sister" instead of "grandmother" or "granddaughter" (*kaparli*). Grandparental terms are held most applicable for those who are two generations distant or who are from "far away."

The next case differs from that of classifying in the parental generation.[15] "Close kin" of the cross-cousin type (that is, MBChild, FZChild) may be called "brother" or "sister," rather than "cross-cousin" (*watjirra*). The basis of this merging is the idea of sibling sets. As cross-cousins (descendants of a pair of opposite-sex siblings), individuals may stress either the fact of their descent from a pair of siblings and a common grandparent—as "brothers," for example,—or they may stress the distance of descent through the opposite-sex pair.

It is on this basis, possibly, that a man refers to his female cross-cousin's (his "sister's") daughter as his "opposite-sex sibling's child" (*yukari*). For a Tjakamarra man, such a woman would be of the kin type MBDD and in the Nangala subsection. If distant, she is a potential "wife's mother" or "sister's son's wife" (*yumari*), that is, an affine. If close, she is a "sister's child" and her daughter is called "granddaughter" (*kaparli*). In subsection terms, the last individual would be of the Napaltjarri category, with whom marriage is appropriate for Tjakamarra men. Pintupi insist that such a person should not be called "spouse" (*kurri*) but should be assimilated to a consanguineal category that simply indicates generational distance. The underlying idea expressed in these reclassifications is that if persons are "close kin," they must be either siblings or descended from sibling sets.

This brings us to the final case of reclassification. For males, MMBDD and FFZSD are the kin types for potential spouses (*kurri*). If these persons are from one country, they should not marry. Instead, they regard each other as consanguines and call each other "cross-cousin" (*watjirra*). Occasionally, they may even use sibling terms. The focal point of such a unit is a shared grandparent or grandparental sibling set, which makes them a sibling set. They are classified in accordance with this.

The concerns of consanguinity override concerns with identity relationships specified by categories derived through the differentiation of siblings of opposite sex. Within the consanguineal universe, what is maintained is rather a concern for genealogical level and for the distinction between consanguines and potential in-laws, between those who are "close" and those who are "distant." Despite the patterning of subsections and the influence they exert on the terminology as a whole, the consanguineal system focuses on sibling sets and descent from these sibling sets. These sets provide the foundation of the classificatory principles.

The Pintupi model presents the universe of "close kin" as a set of cooperating "one countrymen." It is composed of five categories, as follows:

1. Second ascending generation—"grandfathers" (*tjamu*) and "grandmothers" (*kaparli*)
2. First ascending generation—"fathers" (*mama*), "father's sisters" (*kurntirli*), "mothers" (*ngunytju*), and "mother's brothers" (*kamuru*)
3. Own generation—siblings ("elder brother," *kurta;* "elder sister," *kangkuru;* "younger sibling," *marlanypa*) and "cross-cousins" (*watjirra*); ego cannot get a spouse from his or her own country
4. First descending generation—"own sons" (*katja*), "own daughters" (*yuntalpa*), and "children of opposite-sex siblings" (*yukari*); all these may be called "male child" (*katja*) or "female child" (*yuntalpa*)
5. Second descending generation—"grandsons" (*tjamu*) and "granddaughters" (*kaparli*), terms designating relatives of two generations' distance (see Diagram 7H)

Generation is perhaps *the* significant factor in classifying close kin. At a higher level of categorization, generational succession is emphasized even more overtly. Thus, those of the first generation may all be *ngayupula* ("parent") to ego and the first descending generation all *ngayumparnu* ("child"). The resulting model is quite similar to that of the Aluridja system, marking only genealogical level, sex, and affinal status (Elkin 1940).

When the social universe is narrowed to "family," the terms and categories dropped are those designating in-laws, as follows:

yumari—WM, ZSW (male ego); DH (female ego)
tjukurnpa—WMB, ZDH (male ego)
kurri—spouse
marutju—WB, ZH (male ego)
tjuwari—HZ, BW (female ego)
ngunyarri—SW (male or female ego), HM (female ego)
waputju—WF

In the "family" context, grandparent and cross-cousin terms are retained, but with a more restricted meaning than in the full-blown subsection classification. Within the "family," grandparental terms are applicable only to persons who are two generations distant, whereas in the subsection system they may be applied to persons of one's own generation (such as MMBSS). Among "close kin," Pintupi maintain genealogical level and classify such persons as "brother." The classification accurately discriminates their relative role in the activities of band life and estate-ownership.

The Aluridja model, as a whole, categorizes people in terms of what they contribute to the production of social persons. Categorization occurs through a set of cultural concepts that are more widely ramified throughout Pintupi social life. This model of kinship recognizes, therefore, the social value placed on "nurturance" versus "equivalent exchange" (mapped onto distinctions of generation level), on "distance" versus "closeness" (mapped onto the distinction between potential in-laws and "one countrymen" who share residence) and on the division of labor (mapped onto the distinction between male and female).

In the perspective sustained by the "close kin" model, the Pintupi subsection classification appears in a new light. With subsections, both grandparental and cross-cousin terms are used for a further, more comprehensive purpose. They indicate points at which descent from opposite-sex sibling pairs can be significant for creating distance, either in the second generation above or the first above (for example, MM and MMB produce children who are cross-cousins to each other). The terms mark genealogical distance, setting limits to consanguinity that can be exploited in establishing in-law ties. Further, they are clearly linked to the differentiation of roles in male ritual. In this sense, the opposite-sex sibling distinction seems to synthesize relations of marriage and ritual relations into a single sociocentric structure.

Kanyininpa: "To Have and to Hold"

Subsections and patrimoieties, drawing their articulating force from the distinction between brothers and sisters as linking kin, create an image of society as an integrated totality of parts. But this model represents only one way of coordinating the relationship between the kinship system and that of local organization. In its own way, the Pintupi system of landownership already accomplishes such a coordination through emphasizing the extensiveness of ties. Thereby, many individuals throughout a region have their own claim to a site. The model of society as a succession of generations reflects this organizational structure within a region. What differentiates people is generational precedence, reflecting the obligation to nurture those who, as the Pintupi say, "come after." This model presents their society as a series of successive generations, each one "holding" and "looking after" (kanyininpa) the next. Grounded in the experience of social life as essentially supportive, and articulated with poetic force, this construction constitutes the Pintupi cultural representation of hierarchy: authority is the result of nurturance.

The metaphor of "holding" (*kanyininpa*), as the Pintupi invoke it, is rooted in a powerful experience: it derives from a linguistic expression describing how a small child is held in one's arm against the breast (*kanyirnu yampungka*). The image of security, protection, and nourishment is immediate. Extension of this usage characterizes a wide range of relationships as variants of this mixture of authority and succor. An older woman who oversees and looks after the younger girls and women in the single women's camp is said to "hold" them. Most fully, the concept designates a central core of senior persons around whom juniors aggregate and by whom they are "held."

A person's relationship to all those she or he calls *ngayupula* (parents and their siblings) is identical in one dimension of status: they all "hold" or "look after" her or him. The performance of such a relationship inclines Pintupi to call someone "father" rather than "wife's mother's brother" (*tjukurnpa*). Senior generation people who frequently live together in small communities or bands jointly "hold" those they call "child," by feeding as well as offering protection and security. They are all "parents" in "growing up" (*purlkarninpa*) children.

Such interaction with more distant kin actualizes or intensifies the relationship. A man becomes "really father," therefore, when he looks after you. The meaning of such a relationship is exemplified by the case of Lirru tjungurrayi, and a young man, Jim tjapaltjarri, who was his wife's son by a previous marriage. Jim had been in a car that had crashed on the road from Alice Springs to Yuendumu, killing two occupants. The relatives of the dead men held him accountable. In fact, a story circulated that he had killed the dead men with a tire iron. Released by the police, Jim feared for his life and fled to the outstation community where his mother and Lirru lived.

To protect him until the aggrieved relatives had calmed down, Lirru and his wife secretly traveled with their son to Putarti, a permanent spring far from any settlement. Though elderly, they took only some flour, tea, and sugar, and weapons with which to forage. Lirru's spears would be their protection. After a few days, the family returned to their home community. Jim seemed much chastened already, and humbled by his dependence on his "father's" knowledge and courage. Lirru and other senior men began to arrange for a "sorry business" in which Jim could be speared and the matter ended. Jim, however, was frightened that he would be killed, and he kept trying to postpone the event. Lirru urged him to follow his advice; otherwise, the relatives of the dead might seek revenge by killing him in the camp. Throughout this whole period, when people felt real danger, Lirru accepted the responsibility to protect his "son." Though previously well-versed in the ways of the white world, there was a visible change in Jim. He became quiet in the presence of Lirru and other senior men, showing them a sort of respect he never had before. He accepted their judgments and recognized his dependence on the knowledge and strength of his "father." Jim's deference was the real recognition of Lirru's performance in "looking after" him.

This is what Pintupi mean when, explaining their affection for and deference to elders, they say, "He is really my father, my old man; he took me over, looked after me." Rooted less in command than in responsibility, the relationship of "holding" not only defines the juniors, but it is the very basis of the status of seniors (cf. T. Turner 1979b, 1980a). Being an adult is defined by the capacity to "look after" others.

To "look after" someone constitutes as important a criterion of fatherhood as the actual procreative role, what Pintupi call "making appear" (*yutininpa*). All the people who "look after" a child are held to share rights and duties for him or her. A young man explained this to me when a boy was about to be initiated: "They can't initiate him until my father arrives from Yuendumu. He grew up (*kanyirnu purlkarnu*) that boy." The boy had lived for a long time at another settlement. The old man who "looked after" and fed him there became, thereby, a "father" with special concern for the boy. His actions were recognized in the special status he shared with other "fathers" and "mother's brothers" at the initiation.

The responsibility to "look after" a person does not fall solely to one's genealogical parents, but to parents' siblings as well. As in many other activities, Pintupi acknowledge their shared identity by emphasizing that many people "grow up" a child. Men who consider themselves "brothers" often refer to their offspring as "our son" (*ngalimpa katja*). Potentially, the whole senior generation are parents. It is common to hear Pintupi talk of how first one old man, then another, and another "looked after" them, until at last, they say sadly, there is no longer one to "hold" them.

One virtue and function of the classificatory kinship system, then, is the ease with which an individual can attach herself or himself to "fathers," "mothers," "mother's brothers," or "father's sisters." The kinship system is portable and reduplicable in numerous locations. In both the traditional lifestyle as well as that which prevails now, individuals reside or travel with kin other than their "real" parents. What one boy said characterizes Pintupi attitudes: "I might go to Jigalong; I have too many [that is, a lot of] daddies there." He could expect to be fed by the husbands of his dead mother's sisters.

Hierarchy and Equality

The Pintupi model of society emphasizes generational moieties and the succession of generations. On the one hand, the model denies the importance of distinctions among people within a generation. On the other, it coordinates equality with hierarchy.

The relationship of "holding" someone is a relationship of senior to junior. In the Pintupi view, older people, those from "before," look after those who come "behind." This is usually structured along the lines of generational seniority, although other persons can be said to "hold" a person. An older brother or sister, for example, may "hold" or "look after" and grow up a younger sibling, until that person becomes independent.

A sociocentric model of "before" and "after" exists in generational succession, providing a more apt image for the whole social structure than the relationship of older to younger sibling. In many contexts, siblings of the same sex are equivalent or in competition (which amounts to the same thing). Such is never the case in relation to members of the other generational moiety; as regards the ascending generation, siblings occupy a similar status. Principally because it is an egocentric criterion, relative age cannot generate discrete social categories whose members share responsibility.

Relative age itself is an important feature primarily within generational level, organizing relations among roughly equivalent persons in terms of authority and initiative. Nonetheless, there is rough equivalence within a generation, as expressed by the lack of restraint or "shame" among "brothers." In contrast, relations between a man and his father, or a man and his mother's brother, are expected to show the deference of inequality. Brothers may camp together and discuss any topics, without the circumlocutions expected in discussion with alternate generation people. Similarly, fights are expected to occur within a generational moiety, although affines (WB, ZH) should not be struck or threatened. Fights between brothers are "no trouble," but one should never hit a "father" or a "mother's brother." If one does hit a "mother's brother," he should not strike back, however. Rather, the offender's own "sister's son" (a "grandfather" to the "mother's brother") will hit him, to "square him back." Brothers, who are considered to be of equal status with

Diagram 7I. View through the Generations

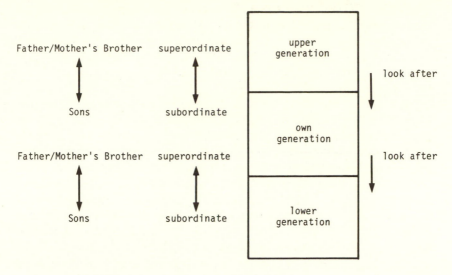

each other and undifferentiated by intergenerational hierarchy, should square each other back directly, thus restoring a sense of social equilibrium.

As a symbol, the generational moiety is complex, condensing both societal and individual meanings. Considered at the societal level, it characterizes people throughout a region as "the same," reflecting in this way the wide-ranging relatedness among individuals in a region. This meaning emerges in contrast with the neighboring Warlpiri: For the Pintupi, generation treats status with respect to patrilines or locality as unimportant. The assertion of equivalence among those of a generation overrides distinctions between local groups, reintegrating their members as unified within a category that is "translocal."

For individuals, one's own generation represents both equality and, in another sense, autonomy. Intergenerational relationships have a common conceptual basis, defining rights and duties largely through the status relationship of "holding." This is illustrated in Diagram 7I. Social relationships between adjacent generations are those between "parent" *(ngayupula)*, who "looks after," and "child" *(ngayumparnu)*, who owes a measure of respect, help, and obedience. Concerns with the specific rights and duties of "fathers" as opposed to "mother's brothers" arise only in quite specific contexts. Thus, "holding" marks a hierarchical difference.

Relations between persons of adjacent generations are characterized by the affective considerations associated with the simple generational model. This rather "Hawaiian" structure of kin classification resembles strongly the situation Hamilton (1979) reports among southern Pitjanytjatjarra, where all males of the first ascending generation are called "father" except for the real mother's brother.

The generational categorization combined with the notion of "close kin" constitutes and conforms to a model of one sort of social relation, expressed throughout Pintupi folklore. In a well-known myth, the character of a death adder is said to "look after" two young carpet snakes: "The old man 'held' those two *(yinalu-pulanya kanyinma)*." He provided them with food and instruction. Correspondingly, the two young carpet snakes were obliged to heed the death adder's advice. Nor is it surprising that Pintupi men refer to a spear-thrower as "father." It "protects" *(kanyilpayi)* them, they say, when used to parry the spears of attackers.

The "looking after" model of social relations, it should be apparent, is a hierarchical one, contrasting with the egalitarian model of intragenerational relationships. The Pintupi classification of the social universe into generational moieties provides a two-fold model of social relations, encompassing the concepts of inter-generational succession (hierarchy) and intragenerational equality. This model informs most of Pintupi social behavior and underlies the two kinds of status relationships that can be called, respectively, "hierarchical exchange" and "equivalent exchange."

"Holding" implies a vulnerability on the part of the junior and a responsibility by seniors to protect and nurture. Authority is represented as necessary for the welfare of subordinates. Hierarchy, in the Pintupi sense, thus leads to the eventual autonomy of subordinates. The image of "holding" *(kanyininpa)* as restraint in the form of guidance identifies authority in social life with a parent's concern for a child.

The concept is of the form that V. Turner (1967: 30) called dominant symbols, combining both a "physiological" referent (nursing, feeding) and an ideological or social referent (protection, knowledge, authority) to the relationship between generations. This conjunction of "abstract moral values" with "sensory substance" (V. Turner 1967: 54) informs the Pintupi understanding of authority itself. The effect, especially, of combining other forms of hierarchy with processes of generational precedence and kinship is to present the reproduction of society as a part of nature itself rather than as a human construction.

Conclusion

One of the basic conditions for social life anywhere is knowing whom one is dealing with. Among the Pintupi, as with most Australian Aborigines, the code for defining social relations is drawn from the domain of kinship. Like all systems of classification, the Pintupi system organizes the variety of human relations into a finite set. Viewed regionally, by assigning individuals to a set of differentiated but interlocking statuses the broad extension of kin classification provides yet another means of transcending the immediate (see chapter 2). In this sense, it not only represents the social universe as portable and reduplicable in any temporary location, but it portrays the organization as a functional one. The significance of nurturance makes it clear that kin classification identifies individuals in reference to the structure of Pintupi social reproduction.

This classificatory system is not just a sorting system. It is also a semantic device that constitutes a meaning to the social world (Geertz 1973: 360–411), a symbolic operator more inclusive than the restricted notions of kinship (Buchler 1978: 132–33). The formal classifications are encompassed by the larger metaphor of kinship as "amity," and the categories themselves are reduced in practice to a very simple model of social life among "family." The social world is represented as a succession of generations, each "holding" or "looking after" *(kanyininpa)* the ones that follow.

There are parallels between the structure of relations found at the lower and higher levels—family and region—of the social system, the latter modeled on the former. The broader categories represent transformations of the infrastructural relations of production and reproduction. Two such forms can be cited. In the first, the patrimoiety organization represents the most encompassing structure of regional integration so that Patrimoiety A : Patrimoiety B :: Brother : Sister :: Husband : Wife :: Male : Female. In the other, more prominent in Pintupi culture, the emphasis is on the shared identity among people in a region, differentiated only by the capacity of some to help reproduce the system by nurturing (socializing) others. The metaphor of "looking after" is extended to the most encompassing levels of societal integration, coordinating equality and hierarchy as Generation Moiety A : Generation Moiety B :: Parent : Child :: Mother : Baby.

The system is a whole "generated from the reproduction of the family" (T. Turner 1979a: 162). In it, however, the higher levels (communal institutions) become more valued than the elementary units. This is the ultimate source of hierarchy. It is not, of course, a characteristic of Pintupi alone that they are concerned with reproducing sociality itself. This domination of kinship over economics may be, as Godelier (1977) noted, common in small-scale societies. Widespread relatedness among people, as the necessary condition for reproducing the family, must first be itself maintained for the productive units of "bands" to exist. Insofar as these "bands" work well below carrying capacity, economics remains in the service of kinship or relatedness. Occasions of resource abundance, therefore, become for Pintupi not moments for leisure but rather opportunities to intensify social life.

CHAPTER 8

The Cultural Content of Hierarchy: Politics and Value

Who will look after us now?

*T*he Pintupi do not recognize an explicit domain of activity that could be called "politics." Except for the recently introduced Village Council, neither specific governmental structures nor true "leaders" exist. The Pintupi interpret their society as the continuation of a preordained cosmic order, The Dreaming; it is the human responsibility to follow this up, giving little theoretical importance to negotiation, human transaction, or decision in organizing their affairs.

Like most Aboriginal societies, the Pintupi have a gerontocratic bias (Rose 1968). By this I do not mean that a council of elders "rules" or exercises command over communities. There is no formal governing body of elders. Pintupi are more or less free to come and go in daily life, to participate in fairly equal fashion. If they are unhappy with their situation in one community, they move to another. Nonetheless, a noticeable, if informal, deference characterizes the behavior shown to older people. It takes the form of allowing elders priority in discussions and in respecting the right of "the old men" (*tjirlpi tjurta*) to speak for community affairs. Younger Pintupi frequently suggest that deeper knowledge of important matters and responsibility for them lies in the hands of "all the old men."

A "hierarchy" of sorts therefore can be said to exist. But how is it conceived? On what is it based? Indeed, what do Pintupi have in mind by such statements? One of the most illuminating discoveries of my fieldwork was that the prevailing idiom of men's relationships in the initiatory cycle was "looking after" (*kanyininpa*), just as in the domain of kinship per se. The metaphor is not

fortuitous. Pintupi culture proposes that hierarchy and the reproduction of the social order are fundamentally connected.

The existence and cultural content of hierarchy in Aboriginal
Australia constitute a general problem for anthropologists. Most
accounts of Aboriginal politics and hierarchy assume a certain view
of what represents "value" in Aboriginal societies—ecological
knowledge, women, or ritual—and treat this value as a scarce
resource over which various actors compete for control. This kind
of analysis does not explain "value"; it only takes it for granted and
interprets hierarchy as its monopoly, as dominance. Most transactional approaches, for instance, follow Barth's formulation (1966) of
the mechanism relating value and hierarchy: Hierarchy is political
in the sense that it is an expression of the attempt to increase one's
share of this value.

Critics of transactionalism argue that value lies in the expression
of relations within the structure of a social totality (Dumont 1982).
In this view, hierarchy is an integral part of value and may be
instigated not by struggle and competition for scarce resources but
by different roles in the larger whole. This interpretation of social
value seems more relevant to the ethos of Pintupi hierarchy, which
carries a tone of support rather than of coercion. Pintupi exhibit
little interest in domination; the most prominent quality of their
hierarchy is, rather, its contrast to the free, unrestrained, almost
anarchic quality of daily life.

My analysis of Pintupi "politics," by which I mean the processes
involved in the regulation and allocation of social value, starts with
their conception of hierarchy as "looking after" (kanyininpa). This
cultural construct is basic to politics as locally understood. The
view—and legitimation—of male hierarchy as nurturant depends
on the capacity of older men to transmit valued ritual knowledge
to younger men. That older men *do* "look after" subordinates,
contributing to their social development by transmitting valued
ritual knowledge, is a major theme of male ritual. Yet the idiom of
nurturance is an ideological form that takes for granted the processes
on which it is based, ignoring or concealing them. The possibility
of representing hierarchy as "looking after" depends on the prior
allocation of social value to knowledge. This chapter tries to explain
why and how Pintupi society projects the source of autonomy and
authority outside itself, onto The Dreaming. This projection is
nothing less than the creation of Society in Durkheim's terms
(1912), the objectification of certain principles and relationships as
standing outside of individual choice, as nonarbitrary. What is

interesting about the Pintupi case is that it shows how difficult such an achievement is.

This objectification is the work of symbolic processes. As we have seen, the important cultural concept of "looking after" is used in a variety of domains, including child care and generational succession as well as serving to justify male hierarchy as nurturance. The persuasive force of such a political formulation lies in representing these heterogeneous activities as similar. The symbolism of nurturance provides a means of sustaining hierarchy within an essentially egalitarian framework (cf. Myers and Brenneis 1984, Read 1959, Rosaldo 1980), investing social value in elder males while denying this process to be the result of individual will. Through an examination of the relationship between the cultural construction of authority and the processes of Pintupi social life, it is possible to address the functions and limitations of Pintupi politics.

The traditional Pintupi understanding of authority has been extended to new sorts of relationships in contemporary life. The category "boss" now is also used in reference to the Aboriginal Village Councillors, who are the elected representatives of the Aboriginal community to the Australian government and (in theory) the legislators of community regulations; and in reference to whites who employ Aborigines or otherwise stand in relationships of authority to Aborigines. The problems accompanying the application of Pintupi concepts to these domains, as discussed in the next chapter, reveal the organizational limitations in this view of hierarchy.

Ritual knowledge constitutes the widest, hierarchically encompassing sphere of exchange among men within a region. The transmission of knowledge not only differentiates older from younger, but comprises a critical element in reproducing the regional system by increasing the ties of "overall relatedness" which an individual has with people from far away. This hierarchy is established in the social production of persons. Such hierarchy in Pintupi life assures that "relatedness" does not have to be totally recreated anew by each individual. Shared identity already exists, as it were, not merely as the product of individual arrangements but inscribed in The Dreaming, objectified in the landscape from which persons come. Consequently, shared identity is maintained at a higher level of the social system as well. The token of relatedness—rights to country—is passed on from generation to generation. Through subordination to the hierarchy of ritual apprenticeship, one comes to operate these tokens for the next generation.

Hierarchy: "Bosses"

My recognition of the nature and basis of Pintupi politics derives more from personal participation than from a priori theorizing. As an anthropologist, I struggled during my fieldwork to avoid being considered a "boss" (*mayutju*). Their primary experience of whites as government representatives (especially in the early seventies) led Pintupi to expect all whites to be "bosses." Like most ethnographers, I preferred to distinguish myself from administrative authorities. Ironically, it was my realization of how the Pintupi persisted in conceptualizing my role as a "boss" that led me to understand their view of hierarchy.

A key turning point was a confrontation between a member of the community and myself. While I was recording a story at my "grandfather's" camp, a late arrival berated me for writing down his name and "looking" at him. Despite a protest from my Pintupi associates, no explanation satisfied him, and so I left the group. The two men who accompanied me were, appropriately enough, a "mother's brother" and a "cross-cousin." One of them consoled me in the following terms: "That's too bad. He should not speak to you 'cruel way' (threateningly); you look after Aborigines. You help us." He mentioned other considerations, too. Injury to me, he feared, might lead to repercussions from whites and there were so many of them! What he stressed, however, was that I was one who "holds" Aborigines. The other offered his view of my situation by saying, "You help us with language (English), you explain for us, get our money from the government. You are the one who stays here with us, and the notebook is your work." The implication was that people should allow my work in return for my "looking after" them.

I was defended, therefore, not as a kinsman in the narrow sense, but rather as one who did things for people. I was—and I recalled how frequently the Pintupi had described me to visiting Aborigines as "one who freely gave" (*yungkupayi*)—the "generous one."

This is an important quality of the hierarchical model of social relations. The common view, apparently, was that people should show me consideration, respect, and cooperation with my wishes— as one should for one's "father," "mother's brother," "mother," and so on. Months later, as I prepared to leave the field in 1975, a number of people expressed their sense of loss to me in a similar way: "Who will look after (*kanyilku*) us now?" they asked. Perhaps, they wondered, I might consider staying to be their "boss." In these last moments at Yayayi, my tacit understanding of how Pintupi do things became an explicit recognition of the significance they ascribe to "looking after." The aptness of the term stems from its ability to articulate both control and responsibility into a moral order. The hierarchical model expressed in the categorization of kin by generation is a manifestation of a deep and pervasive structure in Pintupi culture that informs all their constructions of authority. A "boss" (*mayutju*) is one who "looks after" his subordinates.

Explicit connections link the general notion of a "boss" with kinship relations. For example, one's "father" and "mother's brother" are often referred to as one's *mayutju,* as those persons who can tell one what to do. Furthermore, people in these categories, as well as "mother," are a girl's "bosses" in regard to bestowal. One's duty is that "one should work" for all those of the parent category. They tell one what to do, but it is also expected that they will be generous.

Terminology is informative about the meaning of these relationships. Both "father" and "mother's brother" are addressed by the same respectful terms meaning "old man" (*tjirlpi* or *yina*, referring to the grey beard of an old man). (These words are not limited to the relationship terminology, but also can designate any elder man.) "Mothers" and "father's sisters" are similarly conjoined in a single term of address as "old woman" (*ulkumanu*). Such uses reflect the expectation that elders possess authority over juniors. Pintupi speak of the "old men" (*tjirlpi tjurta*) as the locus of authority within communities, recognizing them to possess autonomy vis à vis younger people. On that basis, such terms of deference are regularly extended to whites in authority.

The Pintupi idea of a "boss" does not, however, correspond to an office of authority or formal leadership. When I asked two informants whether they had "bosses" (*mayutju*) in traditional times, one clearly contrasted that period with his experience of government authority: "No, we could go wherever/however [anyway] we liked." Almost simultaneously, the second man added "only father [*mama*], or older brother [*kurta*] or own mother's brother [*kamuru*], those who gave us meat." The second speaker's elaboration—that there are no general "bosses," only one's particular "bosses"—implied that a person becomes a "boss" only insofar as he or she acts like a "boss" by "looking after" individuals. Pintupi understand authority as a right that corresponds to the duty to "look after," to "grow up," and to transform ego.

Transformation and Hierarchical Relations: Levels

Authority for the Pintupi is morally based on the expectation of reciprocity. The "boss" does more, contributes more of value to the junior. Authority is acceptable if these social relations transform the junior party, developing and adding to the junior in a way that cannot be fully reciprocated. Inequality follows, it appears, as a sense of indebtedness to those who "look after" one.

In Pintupi life, this inequality is essentially inscribed in the framework of relative age. Pintupi regard elders as "looking after" the rest of the group; their authority is legitimized by the way in which they "hold" those who follow. Far from being absolute, such authority is situated primarily in the domains of ritual, sacred sites, and marriage where older persons can look after younger ones by passing something to them. In these particular domains, elders have considerable power over their juniors, but outside these areas, social relations are more egalitarian, access to natural resources remains relatively free, and there is no monopoly of force (Maddock 1972: 183).

Authority is not recognition of ability to dominate through coercion as much as it is appreciation of what is given. What establishes older people with this capacity is that the young cannot become autonomous and equal without their help. Ceremonial knowledge is necessary to become fully adult.

The experience of difference between elder and younger—a "value" in the Saussurean sense—should be considered in systemic terms as well. The inequality of younger and senior men is founded on their participation in the communal institutions of a male cult. These communal institutions regulate the movement of individuals through the statuses of a more elementary social unit, the family, from dependent to responsible. Thus, the social relations embodied in Pintupi ritual life should be understood as "superstructure," intimately connected to the relations within the family.

Pintupi themselves attribute the value of ceremony to its revelation of The Dreaming, to its metonymic association with that period, and to the fact that their ancesters (mirrintjanyirri, "dead people") held it before. But other discernible features that accompany this transmission of knowledge hold enormous societal significance. The sheer fact of the male cult's being "communal"—a shared activity involving people from a broad region—is important. Ceremony is the only institution that operates so fully at this regional level. Participation in ceremonies among those sharing a Dreaming-track provides, for Pintupi, the widest range of relatedness among people. As among "countrymen," so also this relatedness established in ceremony must be maintained by exchange. Equality and shared identity among men throughout a region is constituted and coordinated through the exchange of ritual knowledge and revelation. In this fashion, ritual relations establish a level of regional organization that subsumes other levels. This is one sense of "hierarchy," corresponding to Dumont's (1982) interpretation as the principle by which parts are related to the whole.

Wide-ranging relatedness does not exist as an automatic entailment of Pintupi beliefs. It must be produced in social action. Pintupi thus make participation in the male cult—close relationship with men from far away—a precondition of sexual reproduction, creating a differential between those with knowledge and those without it. This differential provides a basis for "hierarchy" in a second sense more closely related to that most political anthropologists have discussed.

If food and protection constitute the raw material of nurturance within the family, the hierarchy of the superstructure is experienced in terms of transmitting ritual knowledge as the substance that makes development possible. Elders "make men." That which differentiates the seniors from the juniors is precisely what is transmitted. Through accepting the authority of seniors, one eventually becomes autonomous oneself. This transmission acts as a kind of delayed exchange or "replacement" (Weiner 1980). One's inequality is therefore only temporary, since one eventually becomes a senior "looking after" the next generation. Though one makes a return—gifts of meat, deference, and labor—a person cannot reciprocate with equal value. Thus, in Pintupi eyes, the presentation of ritual knowledge is an unparalleled "giving" *(yunginpa)* from elders.

Ritual

Ritual is the activity, more than any other, that defines men as men *(wati)*. Yet its social value and cultural meaning are not to be found simply in the most obvious "symbols" within the ritual itself. Pintupi themselves focus largely on the politics of ceremonial ownership and the revelation of controlled esoteric knowledge (that is, what happened in The Dreaming). A major concern is to ensure the continuation of The Dreaming, so that those who come after will hold the Law as their ancestors did. They regard the enterprise of ritual, in large part, as a form of social production, a significance captured in the pidgin characterization of ceremony as "business."

This quality of ritual has presented an obstacle to some forms of anthropological understanding. Eliade's (1973) and Róheim's (1945) attention to the cosmology represented in the symbolism of Aboriginal ritual, for example, depends on the consideration of narratives lifted out of their context of local ownership, revelation, and apprenticeship. In contrast, anthropologists following a structuralist bent (Lévi-Strauss 1962, 1966) have accepted the Aboriginal emphasis on the land-based quality of religion, but they expand the frame in which this is considered. Stressing how the continuous myths and ceremonial complexes relate "totemic [local] units" into a single system, they point out that the mythological events constitute "differences" along a shared dimension. Because each group owns, is defined by, and presents a part of the whole complex, the experience of these entire ceremonies is of society as a structured whole.

What deeper meaning Pintupi themselves find in a given ceremony or a myth is alway difficult to discern. Inevitably, of course, the corpus of events communicates something of resonance. The principal message may be just the unquestionable mystery of things, as Stanner (1966) suggested. Most often, Pintupi cite Dreaming stories to demonstrate precedent for current activities. Because it was done this way in The Dreaming, they say, that is how we do it now. Beyond the narration of an event, the ceremonies *may* offer a variety of "metamessages." Among the Warlpiri, for example, Munn (1964, 1973a) reports how individuals drew attention to the extra meanings offered by the signifying media of ritual decoration. To the Warlpiri, the circles of body decoration that directly represent the water holes of myths were also vaginas, and the lines that represent travel were penises.

This sort of cosmological ordering through metaphor and multivocality—e.g., male : female :: line : circle :: travel : camp—is potentially a property of Pintupi ritual, too. Pintupi appreciate the aesthetic expression of what they sometimes call "pictures," but this is not the most prominent feature in their exegeses. More often they explain of a ceremony that "it is true," that "it comes from The Dreaming," that "it belongs to so-and-so," or that "it is part of such-and-such a Dreaming-track." Such comments hint at the indexically relational dimensions of the symbolic form.

The pattern of segregating males from females, which characterizes most daily Pintupi activities, manifests itself in ritual as well. Most of men's ritual is performed out of sight of women and children, at secluded spots—often obscured by trees—a few hundred yards outside the main camp.[1] Another kind of ceremony *(pulapa)* is performed at night by firelight, with men, women, and children singing while dancers march before them. At the end of such performances, the women and children are covered with blankets while the dancers perform secret dances with ritual paraphernalia that only initiated men may see. Men and women each have their own distinct corpus of ceremony, with only some of each sex's ritual involving interaction with the other. My knowledge of

Pintupi Country, Pintupi Self

women's ritual is quite limited, and the comments here refer to men's ceremonial.

Because it requires the cooperation of a large number of men and much time, ceremony *(turlku)* is only an occasional activity. Today there are usually enough men in a community to perform ritual, but the considerable demands for labor and coordinated activity mean that it tends to occur in relatively short bursts of enthusiasm. Before contact with white society, the opportunity to aggregate large numbers of people was exploited for the performance of ceremony *(turlku)*. Considered to be entertainment, as well as serious "business," ritual is the substance of sociality in Pintupi communities.

The primary classes of male ritual performance are *ngalungku* (initiatory, including several different song cycles), *tingarri, pulapa, tjuyurtu* (sorcery), *yilpintji* (love magic), and *warntapi* (cf. Moyle 1979: 17–32). As Moyle remarks, a number of other important ceremonies do not seem to be part of a larger class. *Kurtitji* and *yarritjiti*, for example, both important in the initiatory process, are not considered to be *ngalungku.*

All Pintupi rituals require the cooperation of more men than is the case for other activities. This is particularly true for the two most important ceremonial undertakings: initiation and the lengthy seclusion of postinitiatory novices for instruction in the *Tingarri* ceremonies.[2]

At "*Tingarri* time," the custodians of sacred sites all along the *Tingarri* Dreaming-tracks cooperate in the transmission of this knowledge to novices *(punyunyu)* of various stages. Throughout the seclusion, the young men regard themselves as more or less under the authority of "the old men" *(tjirlpi tjurta)*. It is a period (sometimes extending for six months) of strict discipline and rigidly maintained segregation from women while novices sleep at the ceremonial grounds throughout the time. Regularly, the novices are led dramatically around the outskirts of the main camp at sunset, surrounded and protected by older men holding leafy branches and shields, while women and children hurl burning sticks at them. A young man typically completes several such seclusions, the finish of each marked by his coming to stand in the smoke in front of his "mothers" and "father's sisters." Men expect to "stand in the smoke" *(puyu kanturninpa)* several times before they are considered to be fully adult.

The decision to perform a ceremony is usually made by middle-aged and older men, at the instigation of a few. Only the proper custodians can decide whether to show a ceremony. Those most interested go about setting it up, calling on friends to help. Lack of enthusiasm may bring a halt to the proceedings before they really start, but those already involved playfully exhort the reluctant, teasing them for their preference of engaging in sex over ceremony. Usually other men arrive during the course of preparation, some materializing only at the end to see the actual performance in the late afternoon. Preparations frequently take as much as six hours, and the pace is very slow. Most of the men sit, converse, play cards, work on tools, and sing periodically, while a few work from the outset. As time presses, more join in the preparation.

These performances are ritualized reenactments of Dreaming stories. The performers are decorated with ochres, vegetable down, and headdresses of various sorts, each myth cycle having its own distinctive designs. They dance their prescribed roles while other men chant the associated songs. The actual performance rarely takes more than five or ten minutes. Such ceremonies are, on the whole, similar to those of the Warlpiri (Meggitt 1962) and the Aranda (Spencer and Gillen 1899). It was exceptional, in my experience, for ritual to take place even weekly, but some periods were marked by daily performances. For example, during a three-month period of *Tingarri* performances in 1974, ceremonies were often held on consecutive weekday afternoons.

Initiation

A focus on the relationship between equality and "looking after" is central to male initiation, the premier cultural event in Western Desert life. Directed to the "making" of individual men, at the same time the ceremony symbolically constitutes the society as a structure of reproduction. Pintupi initiation reflects the process of growing up, coordinating several dimensions of the self with respect to "relatives." The production of the social person involves an elaboration of the ties of relatedness to others, the creation of a public self that takes priority over its private qualities, and the development of the ability to "look after" others. Such themes are significant throughout the male cult as well as in the female life-cycle. In initiation, the strands of Pintupi social life are brought together at the fulcrum of the system: the construction of related individuals.

The goal of the cult—to make boys into men through circumcision and instruction—derives from The Dreaming, from a mythological cycle that traveled very widely across the Western Desert. The cult is a corporation of *all* initiated men, contrasting itself to women and children. This cult and its songs, the most dangerous and sacred possessions of men, are considered the true markers of male identity. To reveal them to the uninitiated is punishable by violent death. Because, as Pintupi stress, all men together own the cult, no one has the unilateral right to dispose of its secrets.

Pintupi men desire that the details of cult practice and their cosmological symbolism remain secret, restricted to initiates only. Therefore this discussion treats only features that are generally known by Pintupi of both sexes. The initiatory process is quite complex, involving a whole sequence of ceremonial revelations. The description that follows focuses on only one portion, the critical transformation from "boy" to "man."

Initiation emphasizes the development of a young male toward the positive aspects of being a "man," of equality and a wider sociality. The first ceremony of manhood, culminating in circumcision, dramatizes a man's becoming responsible for himself. It proceeds through a negation of being "looked after" (kanyininpa) by "parents" to the beginning of attachment to a geographically broader society, as symbolized by the acquisition of affines, men from distant countries, and their importance to the initiatory process. Unlike the initiation of Warlpiri men (Meggitt 1962: 306) or the Yulngu in Northeast Arnhem Land, Pintupi initiation does not mark a boy's incorporation into a distinctive patrilineal descent group. Pintupi emphasize instead the primary attachment to the widest translocal cult of men itself, an institution independent of kinship relations. This is what it means to be a "man" (wati), to wear the red ochred headband (yiruwarra) made of hair-string.

The ritual of initiation is also part of a larger social process. Like many ceremonial forms, it addresses the problem of differentiation among people who live in geographically separated areas. The symbolic action of the initiatory process, prescriptively including people from "far away," converts difference into relatedness.

The main process of initiation begins, essentially, when a boy is "seized" (witirnu) by young men of his own generational moiety. He is taken to a camp that is removed from women, from uninitiated males, and from all members of his parents' generational moiety. At his disappearance, his "close" relatives of the senior generation (especially his mother and father) wail as they would at a death, because they have "lost their boy." These people are known as yirkapiri (called "Mourners" by Tonkinson [1977: 58]). After some planning by the older men, the boy is sent on a journey (tjilkatja), accompanied by ritual guardians of his own generational moiety to gather people from far-flung localities that are still part of the Pintupi social universe.[3]

The night before he departs, Pintupi stage the Kurtitji (shield) ceremony, a ritual learned from the Warlpiri (Meggitt 1962: 284). All the residents of his camp—men, women, and children—attend this sociable event, with the novice sitting in a separate windbreak under the tutelage of his "brothers-in-law," who act as guardians during the entire initiatory process. Throughout the night, men sit in a large circle and sing the *Kurtitji* cycle, beating boomerangs on shields, while women dance in a line. As daybreak approaches, the novice is prepared by his "brothers-in-law," covered in red ochre and fat, and adorned with a hair-string belt *(naanpa)*. This symbol of manhood marks him as a pre-initiatory novice *(malulu)*.[4] Not long before dawn, the hair-string is placed around his waist. Thus readied, he is led to the group of singers and taken to each of the men who considers himself to be a "father" (usually his "real" father and "father's brothers"). In turn, he is seated on each of their laps. As the "brothers-in-law" lead the novice away again, the Mourners *(yirkapiri)* wail. When the sun comes up, the novice and his guardians depart with instructions to find men to take part in the initiation.

The journey of the novice's party may take as little as two weeks or as long as two months. When the party encounters other groups, joint initiatory singing and ceremony take place. This process constitutes part of the boy's instruction. Most of the ceremony, however, takes place on a single day after the return of the novice and visitors. When the participants return with the novice to a preappointed place in his own country, they approach his gathered countrymen in a strict formation. The spears of the visitors are pointed downward to indicate friendly intent, while the host group waits in similar formation.[5] Women, children, and all those who consider themselves to be Mourners are seated to one side of the linear formation of armed men. The visitors trot between the standing men and the seated group, casting leaves on the covered heads of the Mourners. As the visitors hand back the novice to the host group, they run past; then the hosts run past the visitors. Finally, the men run together to the cleared ceremonial ground, usually within a hundred yards.

At this point, all return to the main encampment where the visitors are given food prepared by the novice's kin. This sharing of food symbolizes the new relations among those joining in ceremony. Those who have arrived with grievances against the hosts announce them. Violence may erupt, but the customary "sorry business" *(parnparla)* is intended to encourage reconciliation among the participants before the ceremony proceeds.

When the disputes are settled, the women and children are sent away a distance sufficient to keep them out of earshot and sight.

Pintupi Country, Pintupi Self

The men retire to the ceremonial ground where they sit in two circles, each facing inward. Each circle is composed of men from a single generational moiety, one to the north and the other south of it. The novice lies unclothed, prone, and passive on the ground, beside his own generational moiety. His head rests in the lap of a "brother-in-law" who comforts and protects him. Men of the parent category who are "close kin" (including "fathers" and "mother's brothers") recline near their own generational moiety. These Mourners take no active part in the proceedings because they are "too sorry." Their sorrow, expressed in silence, restrained behavior, wailing, and close cropped hair, has been evident since the boy was first seized.

After arriving at the ceremonial ground, the men begin to sing the distinctive and stirring songs of the Dreaming cycle associated with circumcision (Moyle 1979: 25, 102). The moieties alternate in the singing of verses, becoming competitive in intensity and loudness. "Antagonism" is also expressed in teasing between members of opposite moieties. After a few hours of singing, the main dramatic performances begin, and numbers of men from each moiety retire (each to its own area) to decorate themselves. Their performances, usually several in number, reenact the distinctive events of their Dreaming ancestors' travels. The novice's eyes are uncovered and he may watch the reenactments passively, but little is explained to him. These performances are finished shortly before sunset.

By late afternoon, the men return to the main camp and the novice is taken by his "brother-in-law" guardian back to the secluded camp. In the main camp, while the men await the return of the women and children, the novice's "brothers" select a circumciser for him, after consultation with the boy's "father" and "mother's brother." There may be more than one circumciser designated. The boy's "older brother" designates the choice by placing a vertical line of white ash on the circumciser's forehead. By accepting this role of ritual operator, a man promises to help the boy obtain a wife. Usually, a circumciser is a "wife's father" or "wife's mother's brother" to the novice. When the women arrive, food is distributed among the men, and a fire is built in front of the circumcisers. Men line up on either side of these operators so that the circumcisers and the "mothers" of the boy face each other at opposite ends of the double column. Then the circumcisers are pointed out one by one to the women.

Next, all the men, women, and children walk to the ceremonial ground where small, dim fires are lit. The men walk onto the cleared space, but the women remain to one side, as the men begin to sing again from the Dreaming cycle. During this sequence, "sisters" of the novice dance in the loose-kneed, shuffling step known as *nyanpi*. Young boys are instructed to run toward the waiting group of men where they are tossed into the air, caught, and sent running back. This process marks them for future initiation. After the tossing, the novice's "brother-in-law" brings him running out from the far dark corner of the ceremonial ground and places him prone on the ground near the fire. Seeing him, the Mourners wail. From the darkness comes a low rumbling sound that signals the women and children to leave. They run off hurriedly and in disarray, dispersed by a hail of burning sticks hurled through the air and by the intimidating shouts of men.

The men again arrange themselves in circles according to generational category and continue to sing. This goes on for about half an hour, until enthusiasm has reached an intense peak: in the song cycle, they have reached the events of circumcision. At this point, all those of the generational moiety opposite to the boy's leave, with the exception of the circumcisers. Singing resumes among this company until—in fairly short order—the boy is circumcised. Dazed from his ordeal, he is told, "You're a man *(wati)* now, like all of us." He is informed by his older brother of the identity of the operators and then led away by his "brother-in-law" to the secluded novice camp. Here his hair is bound up into a chignon *(pukurti)*, a sign of his status as a man prior to subincision.

The young man remains secluded for some time as a *wankarrpa* ("with wound"). When he is healed, he is known as *pukurtitjarra* ("the one with a chignon"). Until his seclusion is formally ended with a ceremony of reentry, usually the *Yarritjiti*, those of the opposite generational moiety are prohibited from visiting him. The symbolism of the *Yarritjiti* is clearly of "birth" through men to manhood: The novice dramatically "appears" *(yutirrinpa,* the euphemism for birth) like a newborn infant, covered not in the mother's blood but in that of men. He gains the full status of manhood only after his subincision and further instruction.

As with most ceremonial proceedings in the Western Desert, one consequence of initiation is the participants' renewed sense of themselves as "all relatives." The sequential process of the ritual seems to transform the opposition between those socially differentiated by geography (that is, hosts and visitors) to rivalry and then to complementarity between generational moieties, categories that transcend local groups. Finally, the complementarity between moieties is transformed to that between males and females, as the group of initiated men as a whole oppose themselves to women, driving them away from the circumcision.[6] The sequence of categories offered in symbolic action—host/visitor > generation A/generation

B > male/female—constitutes a model of society in the Western Desert as fully translocal.

The shared identity becomes more than the euphoria of a moment. Those who participate intimately in the performances have ceremonial relationships with each other that endure throughout their lives. Men who, at one stage, press the shield to the boy's chest in the *Kurtitji* are know thereafter as *kurtitjitja* ("from the shield"), and they should be given presents of clothing and blankets. The men who take part together in a single *Kurtitji* become *pilayarli* to each other, just as an initiate's "fathers" and "mother's brothers" all become *pilayarli* with his circumciser. Such relationships are marked by circumspection in behavior and by special "respect" registers of speech, which Pintupi sometimes describe as *tjamay-itjuninpa* (the word for "talk" in the register).[7]

For the novice, initiation creates affinal relations with people who were previously only distant kin as well as establishing a special relationship to those initiated in the same ceremonies. The latter, known as *ngalungku* or *yalpuru*, are addressed also in respectful speech. Other people also remember those with whom they joined for an initiation. Ever after, it remains significant to one's social identity that one sat as *yirkapiri* together with a set of people. The shared activity of ceremony becomes a basis for relationships in the future.

An initiation is itself one moment in a larger cycle of exchanges among geographically disparate people. Those invited to an initiation by another local group should reciprocate by sending one of their own initiates to that group.

Freedom and Responsibility

Though limited, the details in this account suggest the ideas implicit in transforming Pintupi boys into men. The principal themes are equality (as the bearing of responsibility) and the ability to "look after" others (as a product of extended relations). A Pintupi man's life involves increasing ties of shared identity with people from far away. The men's cult offers the primary medium of such widespread relatedness. Indeed, older men are observably proud of being known by others from "far away."

Typically for Pintupi ceremony, these ideas are signified as much by the organizational forms of participation as they are by esoteric symbols. The organizational themes are five-fold:

1. The division of the group into the generational moieties *(yinyurrpa* and *nganarnitja)* and their complementary relationship throughout the ritual

2. The ultimate equality of all men
3. The initiate's relationship with his own generational moiety, with his "brothers," "brothers-in-law," and "sisters"
4. Specification of potential affines, that is, readiness to take on the full responsibilities of manhood
5. The translocal organization of circumcision, bringing men from different parts of the region together into a single structure of relatedness

The first three themes merit special scrutiny because much of male ritual is organized not around generational moieties but around complementary patrimoieties. The patrimoieties emphasize inter-generational continuity and the passage of ritual knowledge through time, while initiation is concerned primarily with the transforma-tion of individuals. Both are concerned with ordering relations among men within a larger region, but they offer different models.[8] Generational moieties represent the wide-ranging relatedness among individuals in a region: everyone in a moiety, like everyone in a region, is the same. Like the cult of men, these moieties are intrinsically translocal.

It is men of an initiate's own generation who "seize" him for initiation. To be sure, they must first ask his "fathers," "mother's brothers," "mothers," and "father's sisters"—the *yirkapiri* of the parental generation. But the initiative stems from his "older broth-ers" *(kurta)*, and these are the people who organize the ceremony. The symbolism of "seizing" denotes a separation of the boy from those of the ascending generation, who "looked after" or "held" *(kanyirnu)* him.[9] Novices remain separated from members of the alternate generation moiety throughout the initiatory process. The Mourners *(yirkapiri)*, taking no active role and speaking seldom (they are "too sorry"), follow the convention of behavior appropriate for a dead child. It is taboo to speak the initiate's name.

At the same time, the novice is being incorporated into his own generational moiety. Men of his own generation are the ones who instruct him in the duties and knowledge of manhood. He is identified operationally (V. Turner 1969a) with those he calls "brother" *(kurta)* and "brother-in-law" *(marutju)*. These relations emphasize equality of status. "Brothers" are equivalent and substi-tutable in many senses, while a "brother-in-law" is the epitome of equivalent exchange. "Brothers-in-law" have one's "sisters" as wives, as one has their "sister" as wife, and each is obliged reciprocally to help the other. In initiation, these characteristics of "equality" are drawn on symbolically, in contrast to the hierarchy of relations with alternate generations. By emphasizing relations of

Pintupi Country, Pintupi Self

equality, the initiation proclaims itself as an event in which all men are equal, as all men are like brothers. In contrast to the revelatory structure of patrimoiety ritual, older and younger men participate as equals.

The social relations of boyhood are thus expanded and transformed. Until the *Yarritjiti*, it is still "same-generation" men alone who instruct the novice in the duties and knowledge of manhood. The symbolism stresses autonomy but a wider relatedness as well. Fittingly, it is an affine, the "brother-in-law," who takes on the role of teaching the responsibility toward the wider society that is embedded in the youth's new identity. Parents continue to have no contact with the novices, who become dependent, therefore, on others to bring them food. Sustenance is passed to initiates through the "brother-in-law." One's dependence on others besides parents is given immediacy by this combination of privation and affinal help. Extrafamilial ties come to dominate, representing the social identity the new adult will develop.

As a man, the initiate will be engaged in ritual and other transactions with men from distant places, and this is the implication stressed by choosing as guardian one who represents the wider social network constituted by affinal ties. In this regional system, the young man will begin to participate as one of generally equal status. He will retain a specific kinship identity toward alters (as "mother's brother" or "sister's son" and so on), but such relationships will be contextually delimited rather than a permanent feature of social identity. The symbolic initiatory emphasis on one's own generational moiety is a statement and model of the type of relations governing behavior among those who, as men, share in the same cult.

Pintupi men stress the identity among those who are part of this male cult (denying differences between men) and their contrast with the uninitiated: "Nobody owns the [initiatory cycle] Dreaming; nobody is boss. Everybody was made a man by that one. Everybody holds this ceremony." Unlike the patrimoiety-organized rituals, no individuals claim primary rights to this ceremony. The very concept of an "owner"—the occasion to demonstrate personal autonomy and difference—conflicts with the themes that "we are all men" and that the male corporation "united us."

Initiation is a step toward the possibility of exercising such autonomy. It entitles a man to have sex legitimately, to marry, and to participate in ritual. Pintupi initiation guarantees a unity among men in a region prior to the possibility of difference. Initiatory markings such as circumcision and subincision demonstrate that one is a man. "With this," I was told, "we can go anywhere."

Totemically interpreted, this regional unity among men is accomplished as shared identity through joint ownership of a particular ceremonial cycle, the initiatory Dreaming. Difference is inflected through subsequent identification with specific sacred sites in other Dreamings (more often patrimoiety-organized). Thus, a special identity with other men is the precondition for the exercise of autonomy. An individual's own autonomy depends on the provision of society, represented in the form of ritual "knowledge" as an object of exchange.

Thus, initiation is a dramatization of a man's becoming responsible for himself, developing autonomy and capacity to look after others through relations, and a negation of being "looked after" by elders. The initiate becomes one among equal men, capable of entering into reciprocal exchange with others. Before initiation, a boy cannot fight with a man, cannot assert his autonomy in a characteristic fashion. Hereafter, he begins to be concerned with his obligations to potential affines, people from "far away," giving them gifts of meat. These introduce long-term relations of exchange, prototypically involving the circumciser, who "cut" the initiate and who must repay him for the injury with a wife. In return the initiate must give meat and otherwise help his circumciser. Though the young initiate is no longer barred from the activities of men's ritual life, he enters as passive and subordinate.

A person cannot develop this new autonomy for himself. Men taunt the overly proud young by reminding them of their dependence on others: "Did you become a man by yourself?" they ask. [10] Pintupi realize that "making a man" requires a great outlay of time and energy. They regard it, rightly, as their central social enterprise by which most of social structure is established. The translocal, communal relations between people who live at a distance are embodied in the institutions for "making men."

The Increase of Value

Initiation ushers in a young man's participation in ceremonial life. Within the overall group of initiated men, Pintupi distinguish several relative, hierarchical stages of development. Each ranks as subordinate to the next higher stage and superordinate to those below. Higher categories are defined by their ability to look after the lower ones. It is usually men of the next higher status who actively interact with novices and who "hold" and train them. Gradation is based on knowledge of myth, ceremony, and song. Each man experiences the Law through members of the next higher category, which is for him a mediation of The Dreaming and a restraint on his freedom.

The following stages represent the male life cycle as Pintupi describe it, largely in terms of progression in ritual knowledge:

tjitji	child
kipara	"turkey" (bush bustard), the key mythological figure of the tooth evulsion ceremony that is the first rite of passage for adolescents
yulpuru/malulu	a boy who has been seized for circumcision
wati minu	a circumcised man
wati/puntu	a man who is circumcised and subincized
katayarra	"long hair," a recently subincized youth
punyunyu	novice in any postcircumcision ritual cycle, usually referring to one secluded for *Tingarri* instruction
wilangkatja	one far along in *Tingarri* instruction, possessing a *wila* necklace as a symbol of several seclusions
kuntingkatja	one possessing a ceremonial decorated stick, symbolizing completion of *Tingarri* instruction
tjarnpa	one who directs activity of young *Tingarri* novices, usually leading them on ceremonial hunts
marpanpa	"sinew," middle-aged mature man, emphasizing full physical maturity and strength
tjirlpi/yayu	old man, grey hair, a senior man [11]

One's progression through the life cycle takes place only through performance and participation in ceremonies. It thus depends on other men and their willingness to teach. One moves from being "looked after" (or "held") by seniors to "looking after" and instructing others.

Marriage represents a significant stage in the life cycle, but it is controlled by progress in the ritual sphere. Biological reproduction is, therefore, subordinated to the coordination of relations among men. A man should not marry until he is well along in *Tingarri* instruction. Effectively, he may do so any time after subincision, that is, after he has been incorporated into the translocal cult of men and acquired significant relations with people from distant countries. A "long-haired" novice (*katayarra*) is still unmarried, traveling widely around the region. Though his sexuality, now symbolized by long, uncut but bound hair, is developing, it is already subordinated to the constraints through which society is reproduced.

Older Pintupi men are frequently nostalgic about their postinitiation days when they were "wild" and still had little responsibility. They stress the exclusiveness of their relations with other men: they had nothing to do with women. And as traveling men, they were free and unfettered. This period seems to represent a virility not yet channeled into reproduction but under the guidance of the larger society as embodied by older men. Although they have become partly "free," young men are not considered ready for the responsibility of "looking after" others. They must be tempered by further instruction, strengthened by more Dreaming revelations.

Young men in seclusion today often refer to these periods of seclusion as "high school" or as "prison," emphasizing both the tutelage and the restriction of personal freedom. Again, as in initiation, *Tingarri* novices are stripped of their clothing, and their movements and food are controlled by others; they surrender their autonomy. Instruction and revelation of ceremony provide the immediate focus for all activity, and after each revelation the young men are required to hunt meat for the senior men who "give" them such knowledge. Novices are passive participants, likely to be awakened at any hour of night and sent off on a hunt. In this highly conventionalized activity, the young men are marched in single lines, their heads bowed in recognition of their subordination and passivity. They still require help and direction from others; in procuring the ceremonial gifts of meat, *kunartinpa*, they are aided by the slightly older men who "look after" them.

Throughout the seclusion period, novices are expected to subordinate themselves to those who look after them. Talking, inattention, misbehavior, or insolence can result in beatings and threats of dire consequences. Over time, the combination of discipline, physical ordeals (tooth evulsion, nose-piercing, circumcision, subincision, fire ordeals), and revelation of sacred knowledge produces marked changes in personality.

The energies of virility are directed into the social forms of ceremony. Men are enthusiastic about their immersion in ritual. As young men, elders told me, they had sung all the time. One should not pursue women or sex in camps, but instead devote oneself to ceremonial activity. Relations among men should mediate relations with women. The private (or intrafamilial) can only be pursued within the framework of a prior commitment to the extrafamilial relations among men.

The young are only controlled, it seems, by these requirements of ceremonial discipline. Otherwise, their lives are full of passionate assertions of autonomy. Men speak freely of the fights, trickery, and exuberance of their youth. Once married, one man explained, he became concerned that "I might lose my life, and I have a family." "If I were single," another man said, "all right, I can die no worries."

As a consequence of initiation, however, young men develop obligations to exchange with other men. The autonomy they achieve is immediately countered by the responsibility to sustain a set of relationships with other men from distant areas. It is only after spears and hair-string have been given to a circumciser that one can see him or move freely in his presence. Through these repayments one becomes "free" (kili), looking forward to an enduring relationship of exchange when the circumciser bestows a wife. Afterward, men enter regularly into similar cycles of debt and resolution based on ceremonial activity (Moyle 1979: 64–65). The ability to sustain such exchanges successfully becomes a measure of a man's worth.

In Pintupi life, autonomy is inseparable from relatedness. The two are coordinated through initiation. With marriage, sexual intercourse becomes legitimate and men assume full responsibility for "looking after" others. This is expected of middle-aged men, who have developed the endurance and power associated with "sinew" (marpanpa). Contrastingly, young men cannot settle down, cannot stay in one place. They are believed to lack the persistence and concentration of older men, as most young men admit freely. With pride, they told me, "I can't get married; I'm too much of a traveling man."

The young are viewed as wild, uncontrolled, and somewhat antisocial, but they are also admired. They represent the passions of human nature. The adventurousness of the unmarried mythical Two Men (Wati Kutjarra) makes them glamorous to Pintupi men. Filled with magical power, these two youths traveled all over the Western Desert, destroying many dangerous, threatening demons.

Such passions are not considered evil, but they must be controlled. Older men have learned to channel their energy, sexual and otherwise, into social forms, especially ceremony, that sustain their autonomy while assuring the reproduction of a wider relatedness. One takes up domestic life only after demonstrating attachment to the larger structures of social order. The societal intensity that Pintupi seek to sustain provides the occasion on which a man's importance can best be showcased. The reproduction of relatedness is not their reason for participating, to be sure; it is rather that involvement in activities with those from "far away" demonstrates a man's importance. For example, when an important, very secret, and new cult known as "the Balgo business" (tjulurru) was performed at Papunya in 1981, with people attending from as far away as Broome, Maantja tjungurrayi exercised his knowledge and skill to demonstrate himself proudly as its "boss." In thus capping a distinguished ceremonial career, he asserted that he had the full ability and strength to "handle" its dangers and responsibilities.

Young men who have finished their instruction and other mandatory ceremonial obligations describe their growing autonomy as that of "free men," as the absence of imposed restraints. Autonomy is expressed in the capacity to make decisions about when and where ceremonies will take place, about who will be instructed, and about who will take part. Men who have passed through the Law can enter into equal relations with other men, exchanging ritual prerogatives and sacred objects. Participation in this domain is a source of prestige, accomplishment, and personal pride. Predictably, men are zealous about protecting their rights to speak or to be consulted, and proud of bearing their responsibilities successfully.

Pintupi experience the life cycle as a continuous progression toward autonomy and potency, a progression toward greater identification with the most encompassing dimensions of the moral order. Younger males consent to the authority of the older in expectation that there is value to be gained—both for them and for the entire society. To carry the Law is something they do for themselves, but something they do also for the continuation of life itself. Women, too, recognize the social value of male initiation and accede to its necessities. The power and authority of older men in this context are considered necessary to make everyone conform to the cosmic plan.

What men display is the ability to "look after" people. Of course, at the same time, they define what it means for men to "look after" others: One does so by carrying and passing on the Law. Ultimately, what older men give to younger is the ability to participate with other men as equals. Although this autonomy is not usually viewed as personal aggrandizement, the Law that they pass on as value still serves as the instrument of their power. Through it, men exert authority without accusation of being egotistical. They only mediate The Dreaming.

Knowledge

Esoteric knowledge is the value on which the developmental cycle of Pintupi social reproduction is built. It is significant that Pintupi conceive of such knowledge as originating outside human society. Knowledge derives from The Dreaming and is passed from "all the old men" (tjirlpi tjurta) to "all the boys" (katjapirti), from "older" to "younger," from "before" to "after," endlessly through the generations.

Hierarchy is therefore not perceived as a human creation. Instead, it is simply the form taken by the transmission of something of extraordinary value that predates human relations. Authority and responsibility are passed on to younger people, embodied in an object ("the Law") that is not their product. In the Pintupi view, the capacity for authority does not reside within the person. In this transmission, subordinate and passive juniors become superordinate and autonomous seniors. This feature of social life is the foundation of the way in which Pintupi conceptualize their physical environment and the larger cosmos.

In her analysis of Warlpiri and Pitjanytjatjarra myth, Munn (1970) describes the structural similarity between the intergenerational transmission of authority and autonomy and the cosmological transformation in myth of subjects (the ancestors of The Dreaming) into objects (country and sacred relics). Both the landscape and the social order are culturally represented as externalizations of autonomous beings to which others must accede. Both the cosmos and social life are conceived as a chain of subject-object transformations. Thus, Munn recognizes in Aboriginal myth the cultural form in which a society is, in Berger and Luckmann's (1967) analysis, "objectified."

The Pintupi view is that one "follows up" The Dreaming, submitting receptively to a given order of things. The country, an object, reflects a previous transformation, an externalization of the activity and creative power of the ancestral figures of The Dreaming. These figures must be viewed as subjects whose actions constitute a reality to which all descendants must submit. As Munn argues for the Warlpiri, The Dreaming leaves something of itself, its subjectivity (from "inside"), at a place where it becomes part of the contemporary objective environment. Pintupi believe that what is left behind (wantingu) still contains the transformative, active potential of The Dreaming.

These figures and their objectifications are really the creations of human activity, although this connection to human historicity is denied in their projection outside of social space. These constructions are depersonalized, instead, as Law—their connection with the subjectivity and will of living persons effaced. No one submits to the personal will of another. This is the significance of objectification, a transformation into an imperative reality to which everyone can submit. Mythical constructions, in other words, are projected outside of society onto the landscape, whose physical enduringness metaphorically reinforces their significance. Ultimately, by identification of the self with this "given order of things," mediated by the country as an object, Pintupi individuals experience The Dreaming as self-objectification and are, on this basis, autonomous and potent toward their juniors.

"Knowledge" is experienced in precisely this fashion. Pintupi culture recognizes it as something a man is "given" and which he "holds" in his stomach, "inside," with his "spirit" (*kurrunpa*). It passes from "outside" to "inside." Acccess to this knowledge, which eventually enables a man to act as an equal among men, is carefully regulated by the stages of cult life.

Juniors, then, experience the authority and autonomy of The Dreaming as mediated by their seniors. Through their own acquisition of knowledge, they move toward a similar autonomy vis à vis their successors. The metaphor of "holding" and "passing on" the Law, conceived of as an object, mediates the relations between generations, just as the country forms the middle term in the experience of the cosmos: subject (ancestors)—object (country)—subject (people).

This sort of homology between social order and ideational forms is a common quality of ideology (R. Williams 1977: 100–107), "naturalizing" the historically created social order. What goes unremarked among Pintupi, as a result of this "naturalization," is the initial projection of potency outside of society, the process of social objectification itself.

Symbolically, the ontology of The Dreaming reflects the structure of the male life cycle. In this sense, the ontology of The Dreaming accurately represents empirical reality as Pintupi experience it: it is "true." At the same time, The Dreaming provides the basis for the relations among men it represents. The mythological order is both "type" and "token," a representation of society that is itself the product of society. As in an Escher drawing (Hofstadter 1979), the relations for reproducing The Dreaming are represented in the symbol itself.

This self-positing of a system is an inescapable quality of sociocultural reproduction. What is significant here is that hierarchy both obscures and validates itself in such a construction. Social theory is familiar with this kind of social artifact. Impersonal and enduring through time, The Dreaming resembles what Marx called a "fetishization," a reification that appears to have a life independent of the concrete relations that create it. Its structure still represents, however, the social relations that produce it. [12] To say this is not to denigrate the construct as unreal but rather to understand the processes that make The Dreaming appear to exist independent of human action. The basis for Pintupi hierarchy, the capacity of older men to "look after" younger, is therefore reproduced reflexively and indirectly.

Imperative models for human relations, the forms of The Dreaming constitute a sort of social consensus. The projection of these artifacts of consensus outside the human order allows them to be mediated to human society through the "nurturance" of senior males. The constraints on behavior they impose are not arbitrary injunctions placed on a person's actions by another. As long as the elements of social value that these men are able to offer—in the very occasions of expressing authority—provide the essential basis for the social development of subordinates, the system reproduces itself and its values. That is, in the process of social production, knowledge of The Dreaming is itself reproduced as the basis for autonomy and the prime source of value. The Dreaming is experienced as the essential foundation to which human beings must conform.

The particular notions captured in the Pintupi metaphors of "holding" (nursing) and "losing" (relinquishing, as with death) represent the permanence and continuity of society's ground rules in terms of the processes of biological reproduction. These metapors emphasize not the creation of a hierarchical ordering of rules, but its perpetuation and reproduction.

The split in the cosmos, *tjukurrpa* and *yuti*, corresponds to the hierarchical organization of cult: Just as The Dreaming is the source of the present, so are the older men the source of the younger. The inequality among men, albeit temporary, is justified as the means through which society reproduces itself and through which younger men themselves move to greater autonomy. Succession to authority is essentially an acceptance of the responsibility to "look after" others.

Taking Responsibility

Participation in ritual life has a deeply human, immanent character. An outsider should not mystify what it means to Pintupi men, because its more metaphysical meanings are built up out of more intimate ones.

I was fortunate to learn through my own experiences how pride in accomplishment and a concern for others lie at the center of the sacred life. I was about to take leave of Yayayi. Tony, the man considered the "boss" for that community, was a "mother's brother" to me, that is, a man responsible to "look after" me. Like most Pintupi men, he was usually restrained in his expressions of

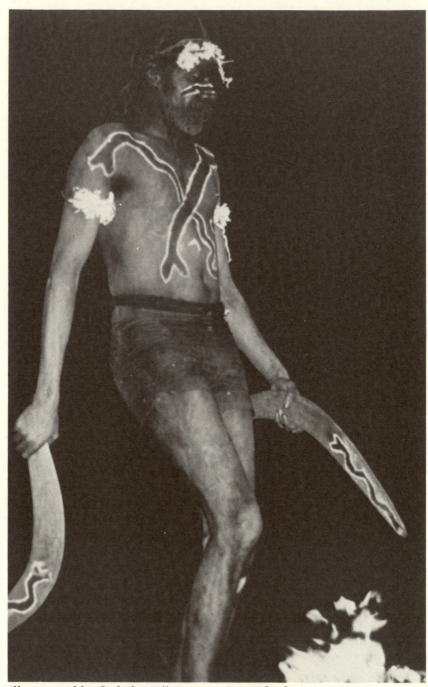

Illuminated by firelight, Jeffrey James Tjangala dances in a Rain Dreaming ceremony. (Yayayi, 1974)

sentiment. He was difficult and demanding, but I believe he treated me fairly in the way one should treat a "nephew." Though we had been closely involved in each other's lives for months, I was still surprised when he decided to show me the storehouse that had been built to house the sacred objects of Pintupi men. These belonged to many more men than those residing in the Yayayi community itself. This decision was an intensely emotional and meaningful action on his part, truly taking up the relationship of "uncle." To reveal these objects was more than a great trust; it was also a demonstration to me of who he was. "These," he told me, pointing to rows of sacred objects, "are your uncle's (that is, his). You might think your uncle is nothing. No! I am the boss of all this. I have a lot." Thus, he told me, the responsibility of looking after the men's objects made him important. He would stay in the area to care for them, and his knowledge and these boards would attract "millions, thousands of people." They would know him.

Dangerous knowledge and sacred objects provide men with the opportunity to demonstrate their quality through autonomy. One thereby becomes important, known to others, and visited, and one demonstrates the ability to undertake responsibility. Compare this attitude with an older boy's demand for attention when he returned from visiting relatives in Jigalong, many hundreds of miles away: Sitting at his parents' camp, he attempted to describe his experience, to be the focus of attention. "Mommy, mommy," he cried, "listen to me, listen to *me!*" For boys, such assertion cannot occur outside the comfortable context of "close kin." Men act in a larger arena, but the occasions for such autonomy in ritual are embedded in the larger set of relations among men that itself reproduces relatedness.

Developing maturity is not, therefore, simply a slipping of the chains of constraint. It also involves learning to carry a heavier load with intelligence, to manage the complexities of social relations. The other part of moving through the life cycle is the ever-increasing establishment of relations with others. Most of these new ties derive directly from participation in ritual: They include the people who went through initiation with a man, those who taught him, those he himself taught, and so on. At each stage he reaches, a man experiences both a wider domain of autonomy and a greater responsibility. Not only is this sense of responsibility a psychological product of the periods of seclusion, ritual discipline, and subordination; it also derives from the very construction of a social identity that is increasingly related to other men through exchange and shared participation in events.

Taking on responsibility has political ramifications in Pintupi society, as a means of advancing one's personal position. Those who desire to enhance their reputations and esteem do all they can to "help" others. In contemporary life, the typical arena for such activity is in white-Aboriginal relations. An aspiring leader will offer his abilities to translate for other Pintupi into English, and to translate English into Pintupi, thereby voicing their concerns and interests to the representatives of the government and explaining the latter's concerns to the Pintupi. He may show initiative in requesting help for individuals, interceding with whites for them. In the cases I observed, men of previously low esteem gained much credence for their opinions by shouldering such responsibility; people listened when they spoke at meetings. Such initiative led one man to be considered, as a result, to be a Village Councillor (see chapter 9). Another man, during the fifties, became spokesman for and "king of the Pintupi" by helping others, deciding where he and his people would camp and guiding their relations with whites. His position declined, however, when people began to suspect that he was not really "looking after" them.

For important reasons, these sorts of "patron-client" relationships differ from Dreaming-derived authority relations. The former involve special abilities for dealing with whites—a skill of restricted distribution. Traditionally, the only similar specializations were those of older men regarding The Dreaming and those of "parents" to feed their children. What "politics" there were derived from the maintenance of a monopoly on ritual knowledge.

Putting oneself forward and taking responsibility become important dimensions of an older man's identity. They are the privileges of full adulthood. But the possibility of asserting oneself too much is fraught with danger. This limitation holds true both in ritual, as in the case of men who attempt to produce sacred objects on their own, and in other domains. A leader of one Pintupi community, for example, came to be perceived as someone who thought he was better than others, who made decisions on his own. People criticized him for always sitting in his own camp and for taking the privilege of riding in the front of community motor vehicles. When he died suddenly during an initiation, there was widespread belief that he had been sorcerized. The suspicion that he had acquired some sort of "trouble" by asserting himself, or by acquiring ceremonial obligations that he had been unable to make good, exemplifies the dangers faced by those who put themselves forward. One should assert one's autonomy only in ways that do not threaten the equality and autonomy of others.

Tony, the "boss" of Yayayi, hoped that the existence of the sacred storehouse would enhance the status of his community and encourage a substantial population to remain there. He expected to build a "mob" there in whose activities he could take a leading role. Many other men, however, found this situation undesirable. Older than Tony and unwilling to defer to him, they chose to live in communities where their autonomy would not be diminished. Their remaining with him would have required a downplaying of his own role. In the end, the community dispersed.

The formulation of hierarchy in the transmission of sacred knowledge does not have these limitations. It is able to sustain hierarchy within the overall rubric of relatedness among people. The geographical, dispersed basis of the structure is critical. Many men each have a turn in "revealing" knowledge, in showing their country. In deferring to elders, younger men obtain the means to become autonomous themselves. In this way, hierarchy and equality coexist.

One moves through the stages of ritual development only through demonstrating concern for others. This dynamic creates a sort of hierarchy that remains essentially egalitarian, the hierarchy itself represented as necessary for men to reach equality and to sustain social life. Simultaneously, by projecting social norms outside the creation of men—they are only *mediated* by seniors— social consensus is maintained for important social regulations. The social order and the prevailing power relations are secured through presenting the political order as the social organization of esoteric knowledge, with the dominance of males posited as a result and mainstay of the cosmic order. This view of authority depicts as natural and necessary the protracted immaturity of younger males while they pass through the ritual cycle, enabling the older men to keep the women for themselves while providing them with a domain in which to exercise their authority.

The superordinate's obligation is to "look after" the subordinate, in return for which the subordinate owes his "boss" deference, respect, and a degree of obedience. Pintupi ideology and experience view these conditions as being "naturally" met through the ger- ontocratic mediation of the plan of The Dreaming, on which the welfare of future generations depends. The authority of elder males is legitimized as acceptance of a responsibility to "carry" and "pass on" the Law and to "look after" those who follow. Thus can we regard "holding" as a dominant symbol in Pintupi social life, a schematic image of social order.

One can appreciate this symbol's particular value for the Pintupi. The image of "holding the child at the breast" *(kanyininpa yam- pungka)* refers to nursing as a primary experience of social concern. My argument that this concept extends to the hierarchy of elder males seems to lend some credence to Róheim's (1945) analysis of male initiation as a symbolic declaration that, henceforth, it is men who will be nurturant and protective. Through control of The Dreaming and male ritual, senior men "look after" and "hold" younger men.[13] In his discussion of details of secret men's ritual, Róheim (1945) draws attention to the rather transparent symbolic emphasis on male "motherhood" (his term, not theirs) in men's ritual. The special facility of Pintupi conceptions of hierarchy is that authority and control are presented in the guise of concern and nurturance. In the Pintupi conception of these "opposites" there is a necessary unit, a mature and transcendent grasp of the complexity of social life—similar to the Ndembu notion of matriliny as simultaneously nurturance and authority (cf. V. Turner 1967: 57–58).

Women and Sexual Politics

Thus far, I have considered hierarchy mainly as it exists among men. Between men and women, the nature of relationships is more difficult to untangle. These relationships cannot be so directly interpreted as "hierarchical," especially insofar as men and women occupy rather autonomous domains and older men do not mediate ritual knowledge as value to women as they do to younger men. Women's own pursuit of autonomy is a prominent feature of life. Nonetheless, the social significance of Pintupi men's wide-ranging relatedness does constitute an asymmetry, a more diffuse hierarchy of sexual politics.

Thematically, the life cycle of Pintupi men develops toward the potential of personal autonomy in two dimensions. There is not only an increasing elaboration of ties of relatedness to others, but also a change in point of view: One moves from being "looked after" to "looking after" others. Both are mediated by knowledge as an object. In this process, the intrafamilial relations of a child are replaced by the establishment of extrafamilial ties. These new ties with people from far away are seen as necessary to taking up the new intrafamilial position of a parent. Like the ties of kinship, of "one countrymen," these relationships with people from far away are constituted by exchange, but in these more extensive ties, knowledge and ceremony—rather than food and labor—are the stuff of exchange. For men, the ties to affines created by initiation are prior to marriage. Consequently, sustaining relatedness is necessary to achieve greater autonomy.

Pintupi women pass through a cycle of development similar to men's: from passive to autonomous, from nurtured to nurturing. For women, however, childhood is followed directly by marriage and childbearing. Women develop their status directly by "looking after" children. Young women, like their male counterparts, are not able to do so on their own. They obtain supervision and help from older women. For the most part, women develop in this way without the abrupt discontinuity of immediately breaking their relationships to the natal family and their mothers. Since a young married couple resides with the wife's parents, the wife's mother oversees her actions to ensure that children are cared for properly. Much of the cooking for the new family of a young woman takes place in her mother's camp.

Women begin instruction in women's ritual and a wider cycle of sociality only after bearing a few children, having demonstrated in this way their capacity for nurturance. Like men, they also move toward increased social value, autonomy, and power of decision through "looking after" others. The autonomy women experience derives from the segregation of men's and women's activities. Pintupi believe that there is "men's business" and "women's business," and that it is inappropriate for either sex to intrude on the proper concerns of the other. Not only do women take little notice of men's advice on how to conduct their affairs, but they are recognized to have considerable power in their own domain.

On occasion this authority has been quite tangible. Several years ago, a young man reported finding an ominously fashioned bone under the dirt in an area of the Yayayi camp restricted to men only. The bone was marked with a set of grooves placed by human activity. It was shown to some knowledgeable older men for their assessment. They thought that the object was a "pointing bone" (sorcery object) of some sort, and the marks a record of killings. This interpretation gained credibility when a man who frequented the area where the bone was found became agitated, assuming he was being accused, and he began to protest violently. Contrary to his intention, this behavior made others suspicious that he *had* been engaged in sorcery. Claiming knowledge of the appropriate procedures, one of the older men destroyed the bone by smashing it with stones. He did not really know what it was, but he enjoyed taking precedence in the situation. There is always a risk in such responsibility, and the truth came out the following day: the smashed bone had been a ritual object belonging to the women. The young man—slightly deficient mentally—who had "discovered" the object had actually stolen it from the women's ceremonial camp, only claiming that he had found it at the men's area. Men became worried about this breach. They thought that the women would punish the young man's desecration with their own sorcery. That was his problem; no one could do anything about that. But the old man who had smashed the bone had to make compensation to the women, which he did with grave concern. To his relief, the women accepted graciously.

In their relations with men, however, women's autonomy diminishes, especially in marital bestowal. It is common for young women to resist being detached from their natal family. Perhaps, as Bell (1981) and Hamilton (1980, 1981) argue, marriage represents a reduction of autonomy for women. Certainly Pintupi expect that young girls who are being bestowed will resist. Often they run away from camp or refuse to have sexual intercourse with their husbands. According to the older women, such behavior is hardly a contemporary development. The quite elderly Kanawa nangala told me that as a girl she had had no interest in being married and was not attracted to men. When her parents tried to bestow her, she told me laughingly, she fled the camp and hid in the bush. After a long search, her kin relented and postponed the marriage. Older women explained to me that young girls tend to be "a bit wild." The relatives of one unhappy girl who had been promised to an older man thought they might circumvent her resistance by driving the pair out into the bush and leaving them there for a few days, so she could not run away. When they attempted to bestow her in camp, she ran screaming from her husband, and he was unable to intercept her. Sobbing hysterically, she maintained distance between them as the whole community watched detachedly, until she made her way to her mother's camp where he could not approach.

Men recognize women's autonomy as an obstacle to their own desire for a wife. Bride service itself, as Collier and Rosaldo (1981) have pointed out, is a means of getting a women's relatives to influence her. If this is not sufficient, men may employ "love magic" ceremonies *(yilpintji)* to make women assent. These ceremonies offer a way to overcome women's autonomy: by making men attractive, by preventing women's sexual development and attractiveness to other men, and by spells that circumvent the will. One may reach a woman through her dreams, and she will not know what drives her toward the man who cast the spell. A conflict of wills is central to the relations between men and women depicted in Western Desert myth (White 1975).

It is not so much men per se that women resist, but rather undesirable marriages. Indeed, women employ their own ceremonies to make men desire them. Individual women may regard marriage bestowal as a form of subordination, a reduction of their autonomy. If they resist and cause a lot of trouble, they may be able to prevent a marriage they do not want, while men try to overcome their resistance.

Despite its negative impact, marriage for women (as for men) is a step toward greater autonomy through the display of nurturance. There is no conflict between motherhood and Pintupi women's autonomy (contra Collier and Rosaldo 1981). All women that I knew, young or old, thought motherhood extremely important. Although younger women often resist the full responsibility of child care, mature women are proud of their ability to nurture children. Raising children is a crucial stage in women's development, and people feel "sorry" for those who have no children.

As with the men, women ritual leaders are those who have moved to some extent beyond the intrafamilial level of relations through their part in the reproduction of social persons. When a boy is initiated, women participate in two basic categories, as "sisters" or as "mothers" and "father's sisters." The former play an important role in organizing the event, preparing food, and dancing for the boy. When Maantja's grandson was initiated, his older granddaughters were prominent in the event. These women are equal to their brothers in a sense, but opposite-sex siblings have different relationships to the reproduction of their kin group. Not only do sisters' marriages help a brother get a wife, but sisters' husbands become his closest affines. More important, sisters' dancing and organizational work indebts a brother to them throughout his life: They helped him become a man. This increase in their importance, however, takes place within the context of making men, in an institution dominated by men as their own "business" and stressing men's importance. In producing their own value, women contribute as a sort of surplus to the social value of maleness.

The "mothers" and "father's sisters" who nurtured a novice are Mourners (yirkapiri) at his initiation, the same category occupied by "fathers" and "mother's brothers." These women are granted a special privilege when he is reintroduced to the community. Alone among the women, they stand behind the fire as it is approached by the young men who took care of him in the bush. The men come to stand in front of them, in the smoke of a smoldering fire, and these women are able to see the men's ritual designs on their backs and allowed to take and keep the hair-string wrapped across their shoulders.

Women, like men, also develop special relationships through their participation in the man-making process. Through the Yarritjiti ceremony, for example, by which a new young man is returned to the community, the man and his mother form a relationship (known as pampulpa) with a special set of women who danced for him at night. These women are of the "mother-in-law" category, but the ceremony changes that. In the morning, when he comes to "sit in the smoke," these women rub his back and twist his shoulders, then giving him the tea and damper (bread) that symbolizes the affinal exchange relationship he can now take up. When the ceremony ends, the "mothers" and the new *pampulpa* exchange blankets. The young men have a commitment to help these women with meat and protection in fights.

Distance, Dominance, and Hierarchy

Though the cycles of both men's lives and women's lives emphasize increasing personal autonomy, the course of social reproduction is not without contradiction.[14] Because of the way they intersect each other, the development of men and women are not simply parallel courses. Indeed, such contradictions lie at the heart of anthropological difficulties in characterizing gender relations in hunter-gatherer societies as "equal," "complementary," or "male dominant."[15]

The problems of "distance" and "threat" offer some illumination of the relations between men and women in Pintupi social life. Inasmuch as wide-ranging relatedness constitutes a basic feature of this social system, men's violence represents the greatest threat to its reproduction. In the Western Desert, male-centered initiatory ritual is the idiom of most of the regional activity through which the broadest relatedness is established. The most elaborated ritual complexes among men are concerned with sustaining relatedness among men throughout a region.

This fact does not deny that Pintupi women exercise power, nor does it deny their own experience of autonomy, but women's power is not identical with men's. By all accounts, women's ritual is not merely privatistic but is addressed to varieties of social dissonance, largely those within the residential group (Bell 1980a, Hamilton 1981). While these traditions may secure the social system at certain levels of relationship, the conditions of Western Desert life impart greater societal value to the interlocal relationships managed in men's ritual. Pintupi do not, on the whole, compare the value of men's ritual to women's. Certainly, I have never heard men ridicule women's ritual, although sometimes men joke uncomfortably about what women might be doing in their rituals. Nonetheless, a difference in relative value is manifest in the labor organized by each sex's ritual.

Social life is not altered much to permit women to have their ceremonies. Men's ceremony, on the other hand, involves a wider inclusiveness. Their ritual plans affect everyone: They determine the aggregation of large groups, including both men and women, and dictate the movements and labor of women for extended periods. The respective rituals of each sex have a different integrative scope,

Pintupi Country, Pintupi Self

and those of men seem far more concerned with relations of distance than are those of women. Initiation, after all, is for males the incorporation into a group transcending local and kinship relations. It is such relations with people from far away that quintessentially define adult men, while women accede to adult status through nurturing other ties, especially those with children.

Since men's violence presents the greatest threat of differentiation, this allocation of spheres is not surprising. Presumably, a decline in the value of relationships of distance could alter the situation of men and women. Generally, men have a greater number of relationships established through ceremony with other individuals from afar than do women. They are more concerned in daily life, as well, with the sustaining of distant relations. Men's violence is a serious danger. Women are certainly capable of violence. Indeed, they speak with as much pride about their fighting ability as men do, but their weaponry (clubs) limits the damage they can inflict. Spears and spear-throwers are far more dangerous. Thus, Pintupi men say, women are "harmless." Though fights including women are common, I have no record of deaths inflicted by women's weapons. Men, on the other hand, are responsible for the deaths of women as well as of men. Thus, the serious violence and threat that follow on "differentiation" (or mismanaged choice) are ultimately men's business. When a group is under threat of violence, or when a women feels threatened, people congregate and travel with male kin for protection.

These patterns, identifying men and women with different domains of social life, continue to be important in contemporary Pintupi communities. Women tend to associate their activity with the "single women's camp," a residential and cooperative work group consisting of their close kin. In my observation, women identify most strongly with the group of their immediate kin, while men articulate the broader relationships. Men are likely to congregate in larger groups that transcend this differentiation and in which the forms of speech stress the relatedness of all there. The larger, more permanent congregations in recent settlements may have increased men's influence in these communities (cf. Bell 1980a), but this possibility only proves the point of what defines the value of activities.

Conclusion: The Problem of Hierarchy

The concept of "looking after" (kanyininpa) mediates between relations of equality and those of inequality, both important concerns in Pintupi social life. Generational categorization, especially, sorts relationships in this way. Indeed, the formulation of the emotions in Pintupi culture reflects the concern with equality and autonomy: One should be cautious ("shameful") about the appearance of assertiveness and command.

At the level of the most basic material processes of subsistence, there is no ground for inequality among adults. Access to unharvested resources is relatively free, and each woman or man has the capacity to manufacture the tools and to carry out the tasks of feeding herself or himself. There is no question here of controlling scarce resources—such as land or labor in agricultural societies, or animals where pastoralism provides the subsistence base. The prevailing ethos of autonomy and equality among Pintupi reflects this capacity for primary production.

Between adults and children, as evidenced in the kinship system, there is inequality founded on the expectation that the parental generation will feed and protect, that is, "look after" the younger. This inequality—presented in the authority parents have over children (the authority between adjacent generations)—is based not in simple material production, but rather in what we might call "social production." Children cannot "produce" themselves. They must be nurtured by others who are capable of material production.

While there is no basis in subsistence production for inequality among adults, this is not true of the larger process of social reproduction. One can feed oneself, but it is easier to do so in concert with a larger, cooperative group—a "band." Furthermore, living with a larger group offers some protection from the danger of attack. Finally, the division of labor makes it important for men and women to have access to each other's labor. Thus, marriage is desirable. All these activities require sustaining one's relationships with others.

The formation of such relationships—critical dimensions of the living activity of material life—is essential to Pintupi social production. Creating and maintaining relationships requires work and planning. The consequence of such processes is, to follow the Pintupi usage, relatedness. In relation to social production, people are not equal. Older people are identified with this hierarchically encompassing level of organization, insofar as relatedness is the condition necessary to subsistence production as adults. Yet the difference between senior and junior, the deference marked in authority, is produced only in the process of "nurturing" those who are junior, of preparing them for equality.

This inequality is identified with another construction of hierarchy by which The Dreaming is objectified as a timeless, enduring structure outside the lived world of human events. A person's

Pintupi Country, Pintupi Self

movement through the life cycle—especially of youth constrained by elders as a stage in moving to greater autonomy—has the same structure as the general relationship of human life to The Dreaming. Both seniors and The Dreaming are experienced as existing, objectified realities that constrain one's autonomy but whose acceptance is necessary for completion and well-being. The value of these institutions is comprehensible in relation to the experience of social life as contingent, serving to objectify social arrangements in an enduring form that denies them to be products of human choice and will. The Dreaming externalizes social facts into binding normative rules in a way that human consensus never can. It constitutes impersonal models for reality, to which everyone must submit: ground rules beyond negotiation.

This surely is Durkheim's *conscience collective*. Substantially, the continuity of The Dreaming as narrative provides a framework of shared identity among people that is the very condition of their mutual participation with each other. In that sense, it replicates both the relationships among elders that sustain the range in which social reproduction can take place, and elders' hierarchical differentiation from juniors.

Knowledge of The Dreaming thus acquires its value not just as a timeless cultural ideal but in terms of the opportunities it offers for recipients to engage in the wider structure of exchanges in Pintupi society. It has a sort of "transcendental value" (Iteanu 1984) because the wider structure of relatedness is the precondition of Pintupi social life. Ritual knowledge provides the medium in which the performance of autonomy is carried out in a framework of relatedness. Hierarchy is rooted in the process of creating social persons, in which ritual knowledge is necessary to social development. Thus, despite the constraints of subordination to elders, men regard participation in ritual life with enthusiasm.

Ritual knowledge is anything but false coin offered by old men in justification for underlying, more real material interests and relations of power. The issue of "coinage," connecting "signs" (signification) and value, is appropriate. Like all ideologies, The Dreaming is a structure of valuation, but it takes for granted the processes on which it is based, ignoring or concealing them. It acquires value in relation to the processes that Pintupi articulate as "looking after."

CHAPTER 9

Time and the Limits of the Polity

It's only their idea. They are just men, like me.

The most visible feature of contemporary Pintupi life is the problem of the community, rooted in the way Pintupi articulate the relations among people who live together as *walytja*. I have talked repeatedly of the pressure on individuals in a residential group to maintain the smoothly running, cooperative relations of mutual help that recognize shared identity.

Our understanding of such Aboriginal polities has been obscured by a positivistic emphasis on geographically based local groups. Strehlow, for instance, grasped that there was no jurisdiction encompassing the segments of the Aranda-speaking area, but his treatment of the Aranda polity still stressed the existence of authority and leadership within local areas. He writes of ceremonial chiefs and elders with "very considerable powers" (Strehlow 1970: 129).

Such a "building-block" view ignores the concrete relations among those who are temporarily coresiding. For Pintupi society, lacking the particular basis of localization (that is, distinctive boundaries and membership) essential to Strehlow's analysis, these relations constitute the real stuff of the polity. Among Pintupi, the polity is not a reflex of authority and is not identified with a permanent, concrete grouping. It is better understood as a temporary jurisdiction of relatedness among autonomous equals.

There are, to be sure, contradictions in this form of social order. When individuals have the capacity to choose which social relations to sustain, such relations tend to be fragile. On the other hand, Pintupi personal autonomy depends upon sustaining relations with others. Thus, the temporary polity must be continually renegotiated among the autonomous actors who are involved with each other. Mediation of this opposition in daily life depends on the regional emphasis and land-based quality of Pintupi sociality. In this sense, the social system as a whole embodies a constant relation to time and space (cf. Bateson 1979: 107), unfolding as a regional system through time. The spatial distribution of people in small, labile groups—rather than aggregation in large and permanent communities—enables the intermittent autonomy of living with just a few close associates.

Autarky is not by any means the goal of Pintupi action. On the contrary, they prefer to live with others. The question is whether any particular aggregation of persons can endure. Thus, the relief with which older Pintupi describe the traditional movements out from the large, fixed gatherings at summer water holes to small, autonomous family groups is paralleled by contemporary events. Since establishing the early outstations in 1973, Pintupi continue to move centrifugally outward from the large settlements, where conflict and tension have been marked, to smaller and relatively more peaceful outstations.

The Pintupi system of organization places little emphasis on maintaining the structure of any residential community, finding its duration in other social forms. The relations that endure, objectified in the reproduction of "country," are those of the broader translocal social structure. What it preserves, rather than community integrity, is individual autonomy. But the structure assumes the possibility of mobility among people who live in small and changing local groups. These have not been the conditions of the large, sedentary Aboriginal settlements of the past fifty years. Yet now that increased possibilities for self-determination present themselves, such fragile polities are the forms of sociopolitical organization that Pintupi action is reasserting.

The critical feature of Pintupi politics is the continuing emphasis on individual autonomy, that sociality is reproduced without an individual's subordination to a higher-order social unit such as a "community." Bateson's (1972: 107–28) contrast of Iatmul and Balinese social systems offers a precedent for this kind of interpretation. The Pintupi, in other words, are not communal. Society is not accomplished through an individual's duty to a corporation of which he or she is a part, but by obligations individuals have to each other. In such a kinship-based social order, these relations are defined egocentrically.

Both communally and individually oriented action may reproduce society as a system of action, or provide for the "general welfare." But they have, as Weber (1947: 121) stressed, quite different implications. Pintupi sociality implies that one's obligation to the necessary categories on which society (as a whole) depends must be objectified outside the dyadic relations that constitute life in temporary localized communities.

The Problem of the Community

Over time, conflict, disagreement, and disputes are likely to arise within any group of people living together. Under the seminomadic conditions of a hunting-and-gathering regime, Pintupi did not have to continue living with their opponents or with people who were quarreling. They could respond to an increase in tension by moving; as Lee and DeVore (1968) put it, they voted with their feet. Nor was the solution to conflict an increase in the social restraints on individuals. With mobility, there was little of the in-group sorcery or witchcraft that anthropologists have associated with communities where individuals come into conflict but are bound together by indissoluble ties (Douglas 1966). Perhaps the most significant social consequence of the temporary quality of the Pintupi "community" is that individuals are not subordinated to a construction of the residential group as a whole.

As described in chapter 8, hierarchy exists for the Pintupi as a means of preserving the basis of relatedness among individuals in a region. The ritual, land-based organization of men into a totemic system of differences within an encompassing framework of connectedness is a fragile form of integrating individual autonomy into a societal whole. Pintupi understand the performance of these ceremonies as "the Law." The constraints such a hierarchy imposes on individual behavior are not great. There are few community sanctions on action, for example—few occasions on which the community (or some representative of the whole) takes punitive action against an individual. Most departures from acceptable custom are countered by the self-help of others. To sustain the temporary communities evidenced in Pintupi life histories, this emphasis is sufficient.

Collective sanctions that demand the participation of even an offender's close kin focus mainly on protection against "sacrilege." Thus, according to Pintupi, men act collectively to punish those who reveal initiatory secrets. Punishment of this sort is "without compassion," without recognition of the relationship one might have with the offender. This is what Pintupi mean when they say that it is a "hard Law." Such collective action can be viewed as protecting the basis of the larger structure of regional integration. In other words, no local group is free either to ignore or to punish an offense according to its own determination alone.

An important Western Desert custom illustrates, however, that such collective action is not easy to accomplish. When a person is accused of serious sacrilege, a "fire stick" is sent from local group to local group to inform men of the region about the "trouble." This procedure is necessary to gain legitimacy from the relevant polity for the sanctions appropriate as Law. The custom reflects the diffuseness of the traditional authoritative body, the breadth of those who have a right to be consulted. Authority does not reside in any actual residential group.

There seems to be no basis for similar action to preserve the basis of any concrete community. Neither formal ostracism, as one finds among the Eskimo, nor collective action against trouble-makers, as Turnbull (1961) described for Mbuti bands, has a place in the Pintupi repertoire of social control. Pintupi "trouble" is resolved less often by collective action and subordination of individual autonomy than it is by a reaggregation of people in space.

Pintupi remember the large aggregate communities that once formed around the few available water sources in summer months as exciting and socially intense. However, their descriptions also testify to mounting tension and conflict when coresidence had to be sustained for a long time (cf. Mauss 1904). During these larger gatherings, ceremony was the effective means of integrating cores-idents into a more comprehensive community by coordinating autonomy and relatedness. Insofar as ritual requires large numbers of people, this correspondence was obviously more than a felicitous coincidence.

The large and semipermanent quality of contemporary Pintupi communities makes them similar to the temporary aggregations of Western Desert summers. Indeed, throughout the Northern Territory, observers have commented on the tension, conflict, and strain that settlement life imposes on Aboriginal people. The sequence of developments at Yayayi followed this pattern.

The Aboriginal people who came to live at Papunya attempted to integrate themselves as "one countrymen" by traditional means, through marriage exchange and shared ritual. But the problems presented by the increased social scale and the permanence of sedentary life proved too great to surmount except by fission. This was the origin of the Yayayi community, one of many Pintupi attempts at separatism. In May 1973, Yayayi had an initial population of more than 350 Pintupi, mainly people who had moved away from the large Papunya settlement dominated by other linguistic groups. They emphasized a common identity as "all one family, the people from the west." Yayayi was to be their place, free of Papunya control and an expression of their distinctive identity. This collective identity was not to last either. By the end of my first stay in May 1975, the population had dwindled to well below 200. Increasing tensions led some Pintupi to pressure the Australian government into providing resources for another outstation, at Kungkayurnti (Morice 1976).

Even after Kungkayurnti was established, the Yayayi population continued to shrink as conflict, frequent drinking, and outbreaks of violence increased. One such occasion resulted in a murder. Yayayi was not, people said, a "happy place." After the death of an important leader in 1977, the Yayayi group split further still into two outstation communities: one remained at Yayayi (with eighty persons) and the other located itself at Yinyilingki (forty-five persons). Yayayi shrank again after another homicide, when some of its residents decided to join relatives at Balgo Mission in Western Australia. Hardly anyone was left by 1979.

Yayayi's gradual devolution suggests how the organizational problems of a large, permanent community remain beyond the reach of traditional Pintupi means of resolution. The very basis of integration limits the numbers it can manage. The expectation among Pintupi coresidents is that they are "one countrymen," that they should help each other. When the number of people is large, however, too many claims are made on one's relatedness. Though conflict and differentiation are inevitable, it has been more difficult for people to move. At the same time, there is little means of regulating an individual's behavior to sustain the commonweal.

The problem of the community is the limited power of the objectifications through which Pintupi reproduce their social life. Pintupi social constructions are suited to sustaining a regional system through time, rather than to stabilizing a permanent settlement. Pintupi communities have nothing like an "office," for example, that stands for an accepted level of organization and endures through time. What is the "Yumari mob," after all, when individuals may identify with several such aggregations? Such social groups are not given, not structures objectified beyond the events in which they are constantly "realized" or reproduced. The objectifications related to residential groups are usually temporary. A gathering of people is justified by the purpose of ceremony or visiting—they are "one countrymen" or "share one Dreaming"— but the gathering itself does not persist.

These constructions maintain social continuity in the face of flexible movements and individual autonomy, but the Pintupi community remains a fragile and temporary polity. Now, as in the past, the necessity of sustaining relatedness among autonomous equals in a world where boundaries are ambiguous lends social value to particular forms of action.

Communities

All contemporary Aboriginal aggregations depend on the permanent water provided by bores and the availability of food transported from the outside. The cash economy predominates for both food and clothing, with most food being purchased at the community store. Education for children is encouraged as well, with teachers supplied by the Northern Territory Department of Education. It is the availability of these goods and services that makes large, sedentary populations possible in the desert. Indeed, for decades the concentration of these resources in a few settlements restrained the growth of smaller, decentralized communities. On the many occasions that the Pintupi have discussed relocation, they have worried explicitly about water, transportation, teachers, and medical services. Until these provisions were guaranteed, they did not move.

In the early days of contact, Aboriginal settlements in the Northern Territory were administered by Australian government representatives through an appointed superintendent and a white staff. Since 1968, settlements have had elected Village Councils, constituted primarily of middle-aged Aboriginal men. [1] These institutions exist by policy of the Australian government. After the election of a Labour government in 1973, they became the organizational basis for Aboriginal "self-determination." Optimistic government advisers, administrators, and others seem to have expected that a local council of democratically elected representatives would come to express the "collective will" of the Aboriginal community. [2] Yet the very idea of a permanent corporate community as representing the welfare of its individual members conflicts with the Pintupi view of Aboriginal control. They stress individual autonomy.

The Village Councils are separate institutions removed from the integrated totality that characterized traditional Pintupi society. Obviously, such a mechanism carries out functions imposed by the settlement context, standing for the settlement community as a whole. Each council is supposed to act as a community's official representative in dealings with the government and other outside bodies. In an era in which Aborigines are financed largely by the federal budget, control of the settlements and the funds for their operation are in the hands of the Village Councils. They are expected to oversee the allocation of funds, to make employment decisions, to regulate use of community-owned property, and to represent the local community to outside agencies. Among the most valuable property owned by communities are motor vehicles, which are usually controlled by the most prominent councillors.

Though officially the council serves as the representative of the community, the political integration of settlements relies equally on other measures. In the Papunya area, whether at Papunya itself or at outstations, the Pintupi lived on land that belonged to other people. Thus, Pintupi justified their association with the larger Papunya community and the traditional owners of the land on the basis of shared Dreaming-tracks, deaths of Pintupi in the area, intermarriage with landowners, and work for the government in building the settlements. In doing so, they countered the obstacle of permanent settlement on someone else's country by asserting their rights as "one countrymen." Although the Papunya situation was exacerbated by the fact that the Pintupi had come from far away, a similar problem is common to contemporary settlements.

The Pintupi emphasis on extensive sociality among individuals, once rooted in the requirements of a hunting-gathering economy, has proven important to settlement life, sustained by the dependence on intermittent welfare payments and limited access to motor vehicles. To some extent, settlement conditions have also allowed people to elaborate the ties of relatedness that are valued in and of themselves. There has been an increase in social production.

Village Councillors

While the advent of sedentarism has led to many changes in the material conditions of their lives, the Pintupi have sought to integrate the new domain with the old. They conceptualize the role of Village Councillor in terms of their own understanding of hierarchy: "Bosses" should "look after" their charges. However, there are inherent contradictions in this model, specifically in its capacity to represent a higher, communal level of social structure.

Because they "look after" people, councillors are expected to prevent fights or to break them up. This responsibility becomes especially important when people are drinking heavily and unable to take care of themselves. I have seen residents ignore the actual protagonists and criticize the councillors for failing to "protect" people. Certainly "bosses" should not contribute to conflict. Nonetheless, councillors are sometimes drawn into the fray, either because they are drunk themselves or because they find it necessary to take sides. Doing so provokes criticism in many camps, but refusing to help close relatives can also antagonize others.

Leaders explicitly use the same concepts as their critics and

Pintupi Country, Pintupi Self

followers. When disputes emerged concerning his position as head councillor at Yayayi, Brawny tjangala justified his right by pointing out that he had obtained money, tents, and vehicles for the community. "I look after all this mob," he asserted convincingly; therefore, people should treat him as befits a "boss." This meant that they should not fight with him, that they should allow him priority in speaking, and so on. Brawny's apparent success in obtaining resources for the people at Yayayi (he was president of the council when the government awarded a grant) did win him a good deal of respect.

Eventually, Brawny was deposed temporarily from the council. He had taken the council truck belonging to the Yayayi community and driven to another settlement for some time to settle a personal dispute. The people at Yayayi had been left without transportation for food or medical help. In his absence, they complained that he was "not properly looking after the people." For their part, the other councillors resented his lack of respect for their rights, complaining that he had not asked for their permission to take the vehicle. In their view, it did not belong to him alone; he was too forward, "too jealous for the truck." When he returned, Brawny was fired from his position. While previous threats to dismiss him had never materialized, the presence of the Community Adviser on this occasion seemed to make a difference. This "outsider" enabled the other councillors to give their decision an objective status: They told him to write to the government that Brawny was no longer president of the council. This tactic made the responsibility for the decision ambiguous. Did the government fire him or did the people do so?

The patron-client conception of the rights and duties surrounding authority inevitably undermines a councillor's ability to organize the community. Brawny's malfeasance was egregious, to be sure. However, in the absence of prior social agreement about what constitutes appropriate action, the "common good," or even a "community" itself, the expected duty of a Village Councillor—namely, to look after his people—remains essentially ambiguous. The duty seems to counter the practical effects of council authority over community property. The episode just described was not the first or last quarrel over Yayayi's truck. By denying someone the use of a community-owned truck, a councillor opens himself to the accusation that he is not helping them. "That's not his private truck," I heard people complain; "it belongs to everybody." The right of the councillor in his social identity is that he be asked for use of the truck. Pintupi recognize that it is a councillor's job to "hold" the truck. But his duty, it seems, is to grant its use.

There are parallels between the ways the Pintupi construe landownership as the right to be asked and their understanding of hierarchy. Yet a construction of authority as morally based in a "boss's" contribution of value to a junior and responsibility for that person's well-being involves functional priorities and limitations that differ from those intended for the Village Councils. Instead of defining individuals in relation to a higher-order social unit such as a "community," Pintupi practice continues to award priority to personal autonomy. Traditional hierarchy has as its goal the production of equality and relatedness; a Village Councillor's responsibility to the level of organization embodied by the "community" as a whole may conflict with his obligation to individuals.

As with other uses of the hierarchy model, so also for the Village Council being a "boss" consists more in reserving a certain priority and respect than in exercising the ability to exact compliance. As "bosses," the councillors are free to talk to government representatives, to take priority in meetings of a current political nature, and to make decisions. One should "ask" the council before moving to a settlement. But the council has no real power of sanction or denial, and few feel obliged to follow or to police decisions if their own interests are in conflict.

Within the Pintupi communities at Yayayi, Yinyilingki, New Bore, and Papunya, the council's chief responsibility has been to break up fights, to control liquor use, and to oversee work and wages. The regulations relevant to such matters, agreed to in "meetings," are rarely obeyed. Although the councillors frequently threaten to send the disobedient to other settlements, they seldom do so. They have few sanctions available to them. Occasionally, the wages of a lazy worker have been reduced, but this sanction causes so much anger and dispute that most councillors are seldom willing to use it. Better to give in to the pressures of the immediate context.

One intelligent and literate young man declined the position of community manager. His refusal surprised me, because it would have ensured that Aboriginal people were more fully in control of their own affairs. This job, however, would have required him to register people's work hours and therefore to dock their pay. Fully recognizing the likelihood of conflict, he told the councillors that "I don't want to end up in the cemetery." Faced with the threat of violence, it is not surprising that Pintupi find it difficult to be "hard" in upholding their decisions. Nor is it easy to resist the claims on their sympathy by relatives who ask for "one more chance." When it is necessary to avoid the claims of sympathy and

Pintupi Country, Pintupi Self

compassion, they characteristically prefer to shift the responsibility by delegating such jobs to an outsider.

This person tends to be the Community Adviser, who usually relays council decisions about work and wages to the accountants in Alice Springs. As the individual who actually sends the letter, a Community Adviser may be held responsible for the action. His position often becomes quite difficult, because a decision to terminate a worker may not be made by the council as a whole. Individual councillors with personal reasons for wanting to remove a worker may simply tell the adviser to do so. In the end, the local community may opt to sustain its internal cohesion by replacing an adviser whose "actions" have angered people.

Hierarchy, Autonomy, and Public Goals

Two issues seem particularly crucial to the nature of Village Council hierarchy. The first concerns the problem of equality and inequality: the status and meaning of "bosses." At best, respect for a councillor's authority is more a product of his personal relations with individual followers than a consequence of his representing a level of organization that transcends individuals. Such authority is sustained by generosity in providing access to valued resources ("looking after"), not by withholding them for a greater good.

A second issue is the ontological status of council actions—of "the community." This points to the problem of hierarchy as an encompassing level of organization. A council's capacity to manage the affairs of settlements that are both larger and more permanent than traditional encampments is opposed by the overriding concern of individuals with relations of equality. Those who disagree with decisions may simply defy the council.

While accepting a Village Council's right to act as the representative of the settlement in relations with the government, Pintupi do not authorize these assemblies to make policy and regulations binding on them. No matter how much respect councillors might enjoy as individuals, their decisions are usually viewed as without authority when they attempt to impose new regulations on community residents. At one point, the Yayayi council agreed that alcoholic beverages would be prohibited in that settlement. One man's reaction was indicative of the issue: "It's only their idea," he insisted. "They are just men, like me."

Insofar as such determinations are viewed as encroachments on one's autonomy, Pintupi treat them as egoistic, coercive, and self-willed. When the Yayayi council did seek to impose sanctions, for example, by proposing to send away a young man who took a council vehicle without authorization and smashed it up, the other dimension of moral authority proved to be lacking. They agreed to give him another chance. Claims on their sympathy made it difficult for them to be "hard" and uphold the Law.

Pintupi will accept an elder's actions in sustaining the higher level of organization they call the Law as a form of "looking after." Such is clearly not the case for actions intended to sustain "the community." The authority of a "boss" does not include the right to create laws that impinge on other people's autonomy, but only to mediate determinations that are already accepted. No direct mechanism exists for objectifying political decisions into guiding principles. To do so would require removing from the actions of men their identification with subjective personal will, interest, and responsibility. In the context of the Village Council, an acceptable resolution of hierarchy and equality is thus difficult to maintain.

The traditional Pintupi construction of authority accomplishes its resolution of hierarchy and autonomy outside the consciousness of actors. The projection of artifacts of legitimate social consensus to a realm of being divorced from subjectivity—The Dreaming— enables these norms to be mediated to human society through the nurturance of senior males. Such norms are not perceived, consequently, as arbitrary injunctions placed on one's actions by the will of others. Furthermore, as long as the elements of social value that these men are able to offer in the very occasions of expressing authority (that is, ritual knowledge and the right to take part in exchange with other men) constitute the essential basis for the social development of subordinates, the system reproduces itself and its values. Thus, knowledge of The Dreaming is experienced as the basis of autonomy and the prime source of value. Subordination becomes temporarily necessary to achieve the full autonomy valued in egalitarian society. The authority of seniors is thus not their "own idea" but rather a mediation of the transcendent authority of The Dreaming.

As with many undifferentiated societies, inequality is represented as deriving from powers exogenous to the social system (Atkinson 1984: 66, T. Turner 1980b). The "higher" level of society (in the Pintupi case, The Dreaming) is not understood by participants as a product of human activity, although it is human social action that reproduces it. Instead, the genuine ontological difference that the higher level presents to individual consciousness is articulated as the presence of a self-sufficient reality on which the realm of human life depends.

Village Council decisions and rules, contrastingly, lack this ontological resonance. Because council decisions are clearly perceived not as principles transcending time, but as human products, they lack legitimacy. Rarely do such decisions stand. The problem is that the councillors are not mediating an authority that exists outside of themselves. Indeed, this lack is precisely what they try to remedy by representing their decisions as coming from the government or the Community Adviser.

Substance of the Polity

In pre-contact life, legislation was not a significant dimension of Pintupi political action. It is difficult to believe that the Pintupi had frequent occasions to make binding collective decisions. Given their productive system, few "public goals" had to be established that demanded compliance from individuals.

An important domain in which this did occur was that of men's ritual. The decision to hold an initiation, for example, still obliges the participation of a novice's relatives in prescribed ways. While individuals must forego some autonomy in the process, they do so as a matter of following The Dreaming. Effectively, decisions in this domain consist of pursuing a plan long established, whose legitimacy is assured. Elders discuss their plans in terms of what is the Law, not in terms of what an individual may want.

What to do is not the problem. This framework is provided by already objectified, legitimate solutions that carry compelling moral imperatives.[3] The problem is, rather, with whom to do it and when. Indeed, the substance of political relations, of public goals, is essentially the maintaining of relatedness among people in a region. It is almost as if the medium—the particular ritual or myth, the object—that unites people does not matter; it is a relator.

We know that innovation does occur among Pintupi, even in the norms. The Dreaming has been constantly revised and elaborated through dreams, strange encounters, and mystical experiences, but innovation took place in the idiom of The Dreaming itself. Even in revising, Pintupi seem to perpetually search for the precedent outside themselves that accounts for current arrangements, although objectification is understood to exist prior to the event. What is most important is that acceptance of these norms built a relationship among those who shared the Law: they became "one country, one Dreaming." In this way, the Law objectified a form of association that linked people through space.

Many of the organizational problems that emerge in contemporary Pintupi life have a collective dimension. Settlements depend on community property that is not easily replaced (trucks, bores, water tanks), as well as on wages and store food that cannot be procured by each individual. Sedentarism, larger population, and the effects of drunkenness on coresidents make conflict more frequent, while "fission" has become more difficult. These matters seem to demand communal regulation, but the Pintupi resolution of hierarchy and autonomy makes it difficult for them to produce binding consensus through their own deliberate activity. A call for support for the good of the "community" remains without persuasive force, because individuals do not regard themselves as members of a joint undertaking to which they all have a responsibility.

Pintupi feel that organization at the communal level is the problem of the Village Council. When they no longer like what is happening at a settlement, the most common solutions are to move or to fire the councillors. Residents expect the councillors to "look after" them while simultaneously expecting to do little themselves toward maintaining the community. After all, the council "holds" the community. But to whom can the council turn? Not only is the Australian government, in the end, unwilling and unable to provide legal support for council regulations, but the white personnel who administer settlements often unconsciously impose their own ideas of "democracy." They are inclined to view emergent leaders as too pushy or as unrepresentative of the entire Aboriginal community. Attempts by councillors to exact compliance through withholding resources or jobs are subverted by government regulations and by an imposed sense of "fair play."

Councillors face the problem of convincing people to accept decisions, to gain legitimacy for them as public goals. When these are seen as contrary to the desires of individuals or groups, the leader is considered to be no longer looking after them: Hierarchy is exposed as non-nurturant and rejected.

The objectification of new organizational forms has not, on the whole, emerged from the action of Village Councils. Innovation has taken instead a characteristic Aboriginal turn: The spread of regional religious cults through the Western Desert has provided a means of objectifying the conditions that now underlie social life. At one level, the sharing of these cults, especially that known as "the Balgo Business" (Glowcewski 1984, Kolig 1979, Myers n.d.),[4] can be interpreted as a form of action that unites the people from various areas—from Broome and Jigalong to Yuendumu, Lajamanu, and Kintore—into a single "moral community." Improvement in transportation has brought Aborigines from distant areas into regular contact with others. Mythologically, this new association is projected into recently revealed connections between the Dreamings that traveled all over the area. Practically, the people whom contemporary life has brought into association are related through sharing the one "business." The expansion of regional cults thus represents a new kind of protonationalism among Aboriginal peoples, an identity they share in opposition to whites.

As significant as their geographical extensiveness is the focus of such emerging religious forms on "the community." Both the Balgo Business as well as the Christian Pentecostalism that the Pintupi at Kintore have absorbed from southern neighbors emphasize frequent, regular congregation within settlements for communal singing. At Kintore in 1982, Christian singing occurred almost nightly (B. Clark, personal communication). Both movements overtly stress the goals of making people happy and reducing conflict. This form of "community" is deeply rooted in traditional forms of articulating social relationships through ritual. Furthermore, community is constituted by collective adherence to an authority objectified outside of human relations. In both cults, human misbehavior is sanctioned by watchful supernatural action.

Those proselytizing for the Balgo Business emphasized its moral character and disciplinary aspect. They maintained that it would stop drinking and violence, drawing young people away from personal sexual pursuits and rock and roll ("guitar") into communal ceremonial activity. Generosity and mutuality would prevail among participants.

Pintupi Christianity, similarly, seems to have caught on strongly with the young as well as the old of both sexes. One of its delights is the beautiful communal singing of hymns in Pintupi, giving substance to the relations among coresidents. A major concern of this new Law is alcoholism. Christians, Pintupi believe, do not drink. In the past, considerable Pintupi drinking took place under pressure from relatives. Given the importance of sustaining relationships, individuals found it difficult to remain aloof. When they did, they were accused of not liking the drinkers. The effectiveness of Christianity in the context of Pintupi culture is that it provides an authority outside the individual subject on which he or she can base a refusal to participate in drinking. "I can't drink; I'm a Christian" has become an acceptable form of refusal. Former alcoholics articulate their abstinence as adherence to an authority outside themselves. Fittingly, the Pintupi versions of hymns stress how God (Katutja) or Jesus "looks after" (kanyininpa) them. He is their "boss" (mayutju).

Pintupi have also responded to the stresses of permanent settlements by attempting to establish a number of small new outstations. Though many people were living at Kintore in 1983, several groups were awaiting the provision of new water points further west.

Within a year, they began to set up small autonomous communities throughout the desert, each established around a few senior men who regarded themselves as close countrymen. Such men talk now of "my outstation." Through this gradual process of decentralization, Western Desert people are reinhabiting the desert they once left behind.

Consensus and Relatedness

For Pintupi, the fabrication of binding authority is not the means for organizing a community. Their concern for individual autonomy opposes that sort of development. They sustain the community not by legislation or subordination of individuals to an institution that represents them collectively, but rather by continually renegotiating their relatedness in consensus. This dynamic complicates the problem of "meetings," an important forum of Village Council political action. In the Pintupi view, meetings (*wangkinpa*, literally "speaking") include any significant group discussion with an agenda or a common concern. Gatherings to discuss plans for initiation or other ritual matters, inquests relating to death, and the like are all described as meetings.

In illustrating how this polity functions, I present a case that led to the Pintupi moving back to their own country as a way of sustaining their own autonomy. Similar processes underlie the contemporary trend in many Aboriginal settlements of movement to smaller and more remote communities.

As reported for other societies (Brenneis 1984, Frake 1963, Lederman 1984, Rosaldo 1973, Weiner 1976), Pintupi meetings rarely result in decisions or plans for concerted action.[5] I initially found this perplexing. But the power of meetings to create binding determinations is limited. Instead, the illocutionary force of speech in meetings lies in sustaining the context of relatedness among participants.[6] The actions of meetings (decisions, deliberations) do not have a status hierarchically superior to other forms of social action (that is, as principle to case or as rule to application). Meetings tend to deal with idiosyncratic threats to relatedness among those whose lives impinge on each other. Thus, the subjective, moral dimensions of shared identity are notable in speaking.

The process embodied by the Pintupi strategy in meetings bears a significant resemblance to the moral movement of The Dreaming. A speaker presents his own position as representing that of an external, authoritative source. For example, a man who was reluctant about a proposed move from the Papunya area to Kintore referred

Pintupi Country, Pintupi Self

to the opposition that had been expressed by officers of the Department of Aboriginal Affairs. He did not deny relatedness by committing *himself* against the sense of a gathering. Similarly, it was common for Pintupi councillors to present their decisions as ideas coming from the white Australians employed as Community Advisers and thus to abjure responsibility for them. Though advisers served at the council's behest and were without authority, council members used them as convenient representatives for an authority that stood outside the Pintupi social world.[7] The strategy is quite widespread, according to what I heard about a Central Land Council meeting to determine who had traditional rights to an area. One speaker justified his claim on the grounds that the Land Council had written his name down.

Political strategy in Pintupi meetings aims at sustaining the relationship among speakers rather than encouraging antagonistic debates about policy. The formal features of speech reflect the meeting's function of constituting the polity.[8] Thus, in meetings Pintupi emphasize their concern with "shame" and show themselves as recognizing shared identity with others. They avoid direct refusal and open contradiction of other speakers as shameful. Seeming self-important, willful, or lacking in control are similarly unacceptable. Maintaining respect dictates that individual assertiveness should be downplayed in public speech. So speakers are likely not only to be self-deprecatory but also to present their own contributions as depersonalized, as "that word."

In these and other ways, Pintupi speech reflects the characteristic orientation to this world's events as conforming to an already objectified, external authority or "law." Interruption and depersonalization contribute to making a meeting's outcome "anonymous" (Liberman 1981), detached from the egotism, will, and responsibility of individuals. Because the outcome—the consensus no one opposes—appears to come from outside, no one's autonomy is diminished. Indeed, the polity is established as those who accept it. This reflexive property of meetings makes "consensus" as important in constituting a polity as it is in formulating a policy.[9] Certain talented speakers gain prestige from bringing meetings to this sort of fruition, sustaining a focus within a general framework of "anonymization."

The substance of Pintupi strategies is clarified in the way meetings end. They typically appear to end in assent. A speaker catches the drift of the main sentiments and phrases them for the whole group present. Strangely, however, nothing may come of it.

The more I observed such meetings, the more I was convinced they are an end in themselves: the meeting *is* the polity. Yet this form of temporary polity has limited organizational capacity. In addition, the constraint of sustaining relatedness with others makes the distribution of people in space critical to preserving autonomy. The encounters between the Pintupi and the Papunya Village Council actually led to the final movement of Pintupi out of the Papunya area and the founding of a settlement in their own country in the Kintore Range.

Until 1981, the Pintupi lived mostly on outstations around Papunya, on land identified with some of the residents of Papunya who controlled the Village Council. Although the Pintupi outstations were granted their own funds by the government, they were administered through the Papunya council. This created a problem when members of the Papunya council fired a mechanic who worked for them. The outstation people liked him and voted to hire him themselves. When the Papunya people refused to permit this, some of the outstation men threatened violence. This infringement on their autonomy was the last straw for the Western Desert people, and many began to speak among themselves of plans to separate from Papunya. This would enable them to achieve control over their own affairs. Yet when joint discussions took place between the Pintupi and the people from Papunya, speakers found it hard to press the issue of disagreement. The Papunya spokesmen emphasized how they help their relatives in the outstations and how they should be "all one council." For all their previous talk of separation, many Pintupi were reluctant to assert their wish for autonomy by contradicting such sentiments.

The issue of separation surfaced again in a confrontation over the use of a truck during an initiation. The meeting took place at Papunya during a gathering for a ceremony, an event involving people from all the surrounding outstations. The impending ceremony required the participation of people who lived a few hundred miles away, and some suggested sending the truck used for supplying the outstations. Peter, a white Australian employed by the outstation council, was responsible for this store truck. He was reluctant, fearing that the long drive would disable the vehicle on which the outstations depended. He also expected the truck to be essential for the Pintupi move to Kintore.

Previously, the Papunya council had prevented the outstation people from taking the truck to Balgo for a meeting with relatives there to discuss a settlement at Kintore. The council had argued then that there would be no vehicle to look after the people left behind. Peter had supported the Balgo trip, viewing it as an organizational step toward satisfying the Pintupi aspirations for establishing a settlement in their own country. In this case, Peter insisted that he would do whatever the "outstation people" wanted. However, because there were differences of opinion, he was not sure it was really their wish to use the truck.

Those opposing Peter (and who also opposed the plans to move west) then sought support from members of the Papunya council, in whose jurisdiction the outstation Pintupi were "guests." Somewhat unusually, given traditional patterns, the main speaker for the Papunya council on this occasion was a young woman, whose status was based on her knowledge of English and Australian culture. She attacked Peter's hesitation by saying that he should not try to control a vehicle that was "for Aboriginal people." In addition, she pointed out, the business concerned "initiated men." Thus, she excluded Peter and emphasized his inferior status. Finally, she represented him as being "jealous" (selfish) about the vehicle.

Peter's attempt to call a separate meeting for the outstation people to decide for themselves was seen as asserting an unacceptable separation of interests between Papunya and the outstation people. The latter did not yet want to make the division overt; to make differences public would be to insult their "relations" in Papunya, where they were staying. Even if they did not want to use the truck, they could not make this a public issue while residing in Papunya. Consequently, they implored Peter to rejoin the main group. A Papunya man's speech to the group was explicit: Clearly offended by the suggestion of Papunya interference, he said that the Papunya councillors had not wanted to involve themselves (that is, had not been unduly assertive), but that their help had been requested. Then, referring to how Papunya regularly helped the outstations, he threatened to withhold future aid if the outstation people persisted in their negative view.

Such emphasis on the unity of Papunya and the outstations was common in joint meetings at the time. Usually, as such a meeting progressed, Pintupi men who had once spoken privately for separation and autonomy stood and assented to the view that they were all "from one country, one council," and therefore did not desire a split. To do otherwise would have been to deny the shared identity and mutuality of being related—the only basis on which coresidence and association (or "meeting") could continue.

Such assertions of the "relatedness" or identity that underlies social interaction can be a significant constraint on any meeting. Where consensus cannot be reached in actuality, it is not disagreement that is publicly announced. The emphasis remains on producing or sustaining a sense of shared identity, or of having "one word" (cf. Liberman 1981, Sansom 1980). Those who are capable of bridging dissension in difficult situations—usually men of considerable oratorical skills—are highly valued and sought out.

Given the Pintupi view of residential groups as a temporary product of individual affiliations, a meeting is the polity and defines it, however momentarily: It is the domain in which consensus can occur. Communities exist only as long as people view themselves as related. Therefore, this polity is not a structure that should be taken for granted, nor is it an enduring accomplishment. Severe opposition and debate would deny the very basis on which resolution could take place at all. Recognizing this, Pintupi would rather not have a meeting until at least some of the opposition has diminished. To do otherwise would invite violence, what they call "setting up" a fight.

The appearance of agreement is important to meeting participants, leading speakers' positions to vary with the context in which they act. The next case followed on the strain in relations between the Pintupi and other Aboriginal groups in Papunya and was, despite appearances, a step toward moving back west to their own country in the Kintore Range.

Upon deciding they were going to move from Papunya to a new, autonomous outstation, the Pintupi requested help from the Department of Aboriginal Affairs. At the resulting meeting to discuss their plans, the agency representatives told the Pintupi men not to hope for much financial support from the government and stressed the difficulties of a move. Most of the Pintupi had already been talking of moving, yet as the meeting progressed one of those previously most vocal about the need for a move stood to tell the meeting that they did not want to move west: "We have to stay here." His remarks were clearly addressed to the source of power at the meeting, the white "bosses," and he was phrasing what he took to be the inevitable conclusion of the meeting. Just five minutes later, he spoke to me in a fashion that indicated he still planned to move. Nonetheless, he had undoubtedly enjoyed his moment in the limelight.

In this way, individual leaders focus an event, but what they create is an artifact of the moment, not an objectification to which people must submit through time. Holding a meeting represents in itself a social achievement, a recognition of some common level of sociality. Because that fact dominates the event, the appearance of disagreement is uncomfortable. In this egalitarian structure, the actors must work to sustain the context of relatedness that underlies the possibility of continued interaction.

What the meetings sustain is the sense of shared identity among people who are coresiding. When this fails, communities fall apart. Participants seem to understand this. When members of the Papunya council spoke against Peter, he was upset that no one defended him by confronting the opposition. Afterward, however, individual Pintupi explained that there was nothing to worry about because the Papunya people could not fire Peter: it was "only talk." The Pintupi silence was not assent to criticism or willingness to allow Peter to be dismissed; rather, their silence sustained the continued association with Papunya that was still necessary and desirable. Agreement in a meeting thus recognizes one's relatedness to those present but does not compromise one's autonomy outside the context.

Participation and Its Consequences

As previous examples illustrate, speakers in a Pintupi meeting often seem less concerned with a particular outcome than they are with taking an appropriate part in the event's production. Demonstrating the right to be heard seems quite close to what participants in meetings perceive as most important. These demonstrations provide the real protection of their autonomous status. Such common features of Pintupi meetings as the repetition of what has already been said and the concern to be the one who phrases "shared" sentiments can be understood in this light. As in other societies with egalitarian tendencies, there is little motivation or power to coerce others.

A resulting problem is that a speaker may get to be heard, but what he can say is heavily determined by the immediate context. This is the difficulty imposed by life in large groups. When many people are present, one's self-direction is compromised. The need to maintain identity with those whose interests are at stake is a major constraint on Pintupi action and helps explain why many forms of political activity follow an extreme path of negotiation. A sense of looseness, negotiatedness, or temporariness is prominent in Pintupi social action. Very little ever seems "settled."

As I pointed out in the cases of estate-ownership, in Pintupi culture one should "always ask" rather than merely assuming the right to act. If the claimants are living in the same community, people are unlikely to dispute each other's claims even if they are considered questionable. When individuals are accused of acting in disregard of the claims of others, they seek to mollify their accusers and to excuse themselves as not having intended to negate others' rights. They try to assure the accusers that they regard them as "relations."

One can never be certain who might extend a claim to be included. Pintupi avoid the unnecessary differentiation of others as unrelated or, as they say, "nothing to do" (*mungutja*). The recognition that one's rights rarely exclude those of other people makes consultation an essential part of daily life. This requirement is especially true when one needs the recognition of others to sustain claims of one's own. Further, the threat of violence by one whose claim might otherwise be regarded as weak—as with a marriage bestowal—could lead to acceptance.

Thus, the conditions that permit genuine autonomy are, as they always have been, restricted to life in relatively small groups or to frequent travel. Not surprisingly, these conditions have become the aspiration of contemporary outstation movements: available transport and numerous small homeland communities. As soon as the Pintupi had moved en masse to Kintore, smaller groups began to plan their own desert outstations. Many Pintupi still see any "community" as contingent, expecting that they can go elsewhere if events should turn against them.

The limited jurisdiction of a meeting and its precarious achievement in terms of decision and regulation are obvious when one considers residential aggregations in a longer temporal perspective. The point of a meeting's consensus is more the recognition of the rights of the participants than the content of agreement. This situation poses yet another limitation on the objectification of a decision: at best, consensus is only the account of those present. Because it must remain sensitive and responsive to the entrance of new persons into the social field, consensus offers only a poor mechanism to sustain communal institutions.

A Community and Self-Determination:
The Medical Service

In their meetings, therefore, Pintupi do not objectify a "community" into a reality that exists independently of them. Yet clearly some institutions represent the commonweal, as does the medical service. Pintupi maintain such communal institutions without renouncing individual autonomy, by treating them as essentially outside Aboriginal society. This does not mean they regard medical care as unimportant. High infant mortality and adult sickness make health a serious and recognized problem in Aboriginal communities.

In 1980–81, Papunya's independent medical service was officially controlled and administered by the Village Council. Operating costs were provided in grants from the Department of Aboriginal Affairs, to whom the council was accountable, but the selection of employees was a local matter. The medical service consisted of a doctor, two nursing sisters, and a number of Aboriginal "health workers." These last workers were the only employees drawn from the local community and the only medical personnel able to speak Aboriginal languages. While some of the health aides worked at a clinic housed in Papunya, others provided emergency care and administered a stock of medical supplies for people at the distant outstations. These remote settlements were visited by the doctor or nursing sisters on a regularly scheduled basis.

The white Australian doctor was extremely capable and dedicated to the political ideal of Aborigines administering their own medical services. This was his understanding of "self-determination" when he arrived at Papunya in early 1981. He hoped to educate the community to the health dangers they faced, so that they could take responsibility for corrective and preventive action. The percolation of medical knowledge to more accessible and culturally sensitive local workers would place health care more strongly under Aboriginal control. While recognizing that medical specialists would be needed to treat acute conditions, the doctor hoped that an "Aboriginalization" of the health service could achieve the self-reliance that would free them from dependence on white outsiders. To accomplish this goal would require not only that Aboriginal health workers be able to diagnose and treat a variety of recurrent ailments, but also that they be willing to undertake the responsibility for such care. Yet this sort of self-determination proved to conflict with local values.

Most of the Aboriginal health workers were women, and usually younger women. This situation reflected the facts of education, the primary Aboriginal identification of medical activity with children's sicknesses ("women's business"), and the fact that the nursing sisters were usually women, whose aides would naturally be of the same sex. According to the doctor, many of the health workers showed considerable skill in diagnosis. To improve their abilities to relate diagnosis to treatment, the teacher in charge of bilingual education was asked to prepare a visual chart and a set of mnemonics to serve for instruction. The workers' intelligence, combined with this training and their familiarity with the common sicknesses in the area, it was hoped, would lead them to take over responsibility for a significant portion of health care. Unusual cases could be handled by conferences over the medical service radio channel or by flying visits or evacuation. If the major obstacle to Aboriginalization were a combination of white domination and Aboriginal lack of confidence, these steps would lead to "Aboriginal control." In other words, the local people would take over running the health service, along the lines of the Chinese village medical program.

During the first several months of 1981, I was able to observe this sytem in Papunya and at the outstations. Despite the diligent efforts of the white staff to transfer responsibility to the Aborigines, long-standing patterns persisted. Rather than going to the health workers for care, local people continued to seek out the nursing sisters even for such simple remedies as pain tablets. Reluctance by the white staff to take on duties a health worker could provide was interpreted as unwillingness to "help Aboriginal people." For the most part, the health workers were viewed as "translators" or "interpreters" rather than as health experts. They themselves seem to have found the jobs attractive primarily because the pay was good. Knowing that they were hired and fired by the Village Council constituted the health workers' understanding of Aboriginal control. The doctor's model—that they were working for the good of the community—was not theirs.

The health worker at one outstation, a young woman with one child, is illustrative. She was considered highly intelligent and competent by the doctor and nursing sisters, and she performed well in their presence. However, the local community found reason to complain about her performance. She was a reluctant worker, often attempting to have my wife and me carry out local health care. When an infant was badly burned early one Sunday morning, for example, she refused to get out of her blankets to treat the child. When she did try to hold clinics for the ailing at regular times, people persisted in visiting her whenever they wished, arguing that she had to "help" them. As such demands for "help" threatened to hamper considerably the pursuit of her own concerns, she became less responsive. Traveling and daily foraging activities—important concerns for her as for others—began to interfere with her medical duties.

With the exception of ritual duties, the sacrifice of an individual's interests and personal obligations for the continuing performance of a task supposed to contribute generally to "community welfare" has little precedence or significance in traditional Pintupi life, with its simple division of labor. The specialization embodied in the health workers' role was quite unusual.

It is not surprising that health workers were most responsive to close relatives—people who had an immediate and prior claim on their help. Conversely, criticism from neglected others in the community—and the predictable threats to have the workers sacked—

sometimes led workers to withhold medicines and treatment. These issues were rarely resolved fully, but they were frequently addressed in meetings both of the outstation council and the Papunya council. The rhetoric of these discussions, emphasizing that workers must "help" people, was consonant with the expectation that coresidents should act as "relatives." But such "help" was expected at the individual level and not as duty to a larger entity. That local people often directed their complaints outside, to the white staff, is instructive about how internal segmentation is overcome and "community" enforced.

In Papunya, absenteeism among health workers was common, often to the distress of the white staff when emergencies arose. Sometimes the health workers simply found their medical responsibilities to be in conflict with other obligations—especially obvious when ceremonies were under way. Viewed as "flexibility," this is precisely the quality said to be valued or desirable by Aboriginal people (Nathan and Japanangka 1983b: 165). This policy leads to high staff turnover. On the other hand, the most dependable Aboriginal workers appeared to labor out of a personal sense of obligation to a "boss," from whom they expected a reciprocal special relationship in turn. In these terms, quitting or taking leave from the job was a personal matter, not based on considerations about the state of the medical service or the community's need.

The chief issue in the case of the health workers, then, was whether they took responsibility for the medical service's operation and continuation as a whole. At Papunya the expectation was that it would continue whether or not an individual took part. While there was an Aboriginal obligation for the workers to "help" people, this was not represented as an obligation to sustain the particular institution in which this "help" could be transacted—especially when one's energies were required elsewhere.

The Council and the Health Service

Similar perspectives on the medical service underlay the Papunya Village Council's position. The council was not interested in the service's day-to-day affairs nor did it feel accountable for its failures. Indeed, one dedicated nursing sister quit when the council refused to hire another sister to help her with overload work. They refused as well to give her a place to live, after having turned over a medical flat to a relative of one of the council members. They seemed unconcerned that she might leave.

The council did not think of itself as having to sustain the medical service. Hadn't there always been medical care? That they might even use some of their own funds or resources for the health service was inconceivable: This agency was sustained from outside, although local people could control its action as it affected them. They viewed the service as separate in some sense, as a "different business" rather than as an institution for the general welfare of an autonomous community. This view was consonant with the ways in which hierarchy is created within Pintupi society, by projecting a form of organization outside the framework of interpersonal obligations.

The Australian doctor interpreted this unwillingness to take on "responsibility" as a product of living in the "total institutions" of government settlements (citing Goffman 1961, in fact). This condition would take time to dispel, he thought, because Aborigines were used to having whites deliver services for them. Reasoning further that those with authority in the community had not been sufficiently involved in the medical service, he asked an older man, whom he believed to have "traditional authority," to head the medical service. While this man was able to give the doctor good political advice, he had neither a basis for authority over the health workers nor the desire to command them. The doctor's goal of "Aboriginalization" meant making the medical service "represent" the community. However, the concepts of "representation" and of "community" were themselves elements of a different cultural tradition.

Aboriginal Control

To the local people, "Aboriginal control" did not require an all-Aboriginal medical service. To be sure, they thought it important and useful that white staff could understand their language and culture. However, they found it advantageous to have whites operate the medical service. The employment of outsiders to assume responsibility for the health service was the mechanism through which they managed to objectify it while preserving their own individual autonomy.

They did have respect for medical knowledge as "white-fellow" business and simultaneously doubted the abilities of their fellow Aborigines, but this dualism was not the sole basis of their attitude. Rather, as outsiders, whites do not have a primary identification with any particular segment of a settlement, which encompasses people of different languages and kin networks. Therefore, whites can be approached equally by everyone for help and trusted to deliver on their responsibilities no matter who asks. What matterd to the local people was their ability to fire a white who was not doing the "right thing" or not "helping Aboriginal people." This view extended to all relations with whites on a settlement. By placing responsibility for a community on some person outside the internal network of relations, Aborigines avoided the vulnerability to criticism from relatives inherent in service positions. Whereas the doctor (and others) wanted the community to perceive the medical service as *theirs* and thought this would necessarily mean a desire to take over the responsibility for medical care, local ideas of "control" had a different interest. They were content to have whites embody the responsibility for them as long as the whites did not exceed their authorization.

The doctor learned this when he opposed a proposal by Village Council members to appoint the pastor's wife as a nursing sister, arguing that she would return to the old pattern of white control and introduce dissension as well as domination by the mission. The council regarded his speech as interference in their control: They would decide who was employed, and they valued the mission, against which it was not his concern to speak. Indeed, there was talk of sacking the medical service. He was a good doctor, it was said, but he ought not to tell Aborigines what to do.

In view of their own experience, the Aboriginal belief that medical care will always be provided seems realistic. That they should have to do something to sustain that possibility, they did not recognize. But if Aborigines did not recognize a necessity to take over responsibility for this social reproduction, how could they sustain a service? And with what consequences?

The people of the Papunya area were quite content to let a white staff run the health service as long as they did "the right thing" as defined by the Aborigines. Much of the responsibility for sustaining the service—in terms of both labor and accountability to Aboriginal culture ("helping" the people)—fell on this staff. When matters did not proceed as the local people wished, they would simply replace the current whites with a new set. "There are," I heard it said, "plenty more whites."

We can see how this arrangement satisfies the conditions of "Aboriginal control," but it may endanger the very autonomy that the Aboriginal people seemingly seek to preserve. Because the blame for failure or difficulties is laid on the whites, is it possible for the Aboriginal people to recognize basic problems, or will selection of new whites simply reproduce the same underlying structure? To some extent, control of this sort is an illusion, since the Aborigines do not control the means of its reproduction: The money for health services is produced by others and by political activity in an arena beyond the settlement. Obviously, Aborigines' ability to control the policy of, for example, the Northern Territory government is limited. These problems may eventually drive Aboriginal people to seek political control at a higher level of organization. Even without that, however, what seems open for Aboriginal reevaluation is the relationship between relatively low levels of health care and the significance of personal subordination to a larger entity.

Outsiders: Pintupi and the Government

On the whole, Pintupi understand the Australian government and its representatives as largely autonomous "bosses," to whom deference and obedience is owed. In turn, the government is obliged to "help" and "look after" the Aborigines. Their interpretation of past government behavior convinces Pintupi that their view is appropriate. They reason that the government gave them food; that the government gives pensions to the old; and that it has said, repeatedly, that it wants to "help" Aborigines. Finally, others tell them the government should help and is not helping enough. In these ways, Pintupi assimilate government actions to their indigenous political theory. In accord with their expectations, Pintupi alter much of their behavior in the presence of whites so as to show respect, as befits a "boss."

In their own eyes, Pintupi have maintained their side of the relationship in reciprocal obligations. Thus, their responses solidify their expectation that the government should "help" them. Interestingly, they do not seem to feel their autonomy is significantly diminished by having white "bosses."

The theme of reciprocity is a common one that Pintupi explore in assessing their relationship to the encompassing polity. Two informants, for example, described to me the historical basis of Pintupi-white relations. Sometime in the thirties, when they were children, a white missionary met them and their group near Mount Liebig. He offered them wheat flour and rice; in return, they gave him various kinds of Aboriginal food. This transaction, they said, formed the foundation of a reciprocal relationship between whites and themselves. These men and others told me (in 1975) that they should get pensions and that the Pintupi should be allowed to stay in the area of Haasts Bluff and Papunya (not their traditional country) because they had built these settlements by providing labor. The government should "look after" them.

A more complex case of miscommunication resulted from the trip to Yawalyurrunya in 1974 (see chapter 5) to visit the sacred site. While requesting the trip for themselves, the Pintupi believed they were doing something for the whites and the government by

Pintupi Country, Pintupi Self

"showing" their country. They expected that the government would henceforth "hold" the site for them, reasoning on their experience of the responsibilities entailed by initiation to ritual secrets. These claims were not at all clear to the whites, but the Pintupi men nevertheless expected to be paid for going on this trip. Remuneration had been involved in previous trips to sacred sites, when the men had been paid for the filming of their rituals. For the Yawalyurru pilgrimage, however, the custodians of the country had prohibited filming. Contrary to their hopes and expectations, there was no pay for their work as "guides." As the idea developed over the weeks following the expedition, they decided that in return for its representative having been taken to the site, the government should put a well nearby and establish a settlement there. Nothing happened for several years, but when (eventually) a bore was drilled in the Yawalyurru area, Pintupi interpreted it as a product of their 1974 trip.

The implication of these cases is the same: We helped the government and they should help us. Unfortunately, this code is not often shared by the whites, who take a different view of the same social relations.

The particular conception of reciprocal and enduring obligation ultimately informs the Pintupi category of "boss" and the appropriate relationship implied by this designation; thus, their view of "work." Men often asked the Community Adviser at Yayayi (employed by the government but said to work for the Aboriginal community) to drive them to Papunya, the nearest resource center. If he refused, men sometimes asserted that the "boss" should help them because they had worked for him: "I helped you build that fence." All such workers had received financial compensation, but in their view the relationship was not simply economic. It consisted of an ongoing series of obligations that extended beyond the work domain. Just as they would listen to a father's advice, Pintupi men will accept criticism from white bosses that they would not tolerate from equals.

This acceptance is not simply a fear of repercussions. A strong emotional attachment of Pintupi to their "boss" is commonly grounded in this sort of conception. People remember their former "bosses" with a genuine sentimentality. [10] Similarly, they accept the term "boy" to refer to a worker—a boss's "boys"—because it matches the pidgin translation of *katja*, the term for "son" or "nephew." These are categories of kin who must work for fathers and uncles. In line with this conception, Pintupi go to a "boss" when they need food or have a broken-down car. Those who fulfill the expectations of this role are liked and respected. But it must be emphasized that in the worker's eyes, he has already earned the help.

It is striking how the Pintupi have been reinforced in their view of the government as responsible to look after them and to maintain communal institutions. When they worked at Haasts Bluff some thirty years ago, men were paid very small wages—called "pocket money"—and were given government rations of food and clothing along with other services. The government (and before that the mission at Hermannsburg) bore the responsibility of maintaining settlement property, which was therefore outside the immediate control of Aboriginal people.

At some time before the move to Papunya in 1960, wages were raised but still remained rather low, and at Papunya everyone was fed at the government kitchen. Due to changing ideas about Aboriginal development that characterized the sixties, the government began to adopt a program emphasizing self-reliance and self-determination. Wages were raised and rations cut off; people were expected to take care of themselves. Most capital provisions, however, such as the hospital, the vehicles, and the bores, still were provided by the government. Many Pintupi continue to believe that white people's houses in Melbourne have been given to them by the government.

Despite the official policy of self-determination, in 1973–75 many Pintupi thought of their wages as "pocket money," to be spent on personal luxuries. They found it hard to understand that they ought to use these funds for the necessities of life. Though settlement vehicles had been turned over to local, Aboriginal control, people had to provide their own fuel. In the view of many Pintupi, the government was thus expecting them to use their own "private" money. They wondered why rations had been cut off. They felt they were being cheated and that the government was not properly looking after them. [11] To them, of course, the government is not their representative; it confronts them as truly "other" and "outside."

Once, a Precedent

Because it does not explicitly recognize negotiation, Pintupi political theory encounters limitations in comprehending white-Aboriginal relations. Pintupi do not recognize an autonomous political order, and the concepts through which they articulate political activity incorporate many implicit assumptions and expectations that, one might say, experience has not differentiated. Thus, they try to project each important event into a model or precondition for subsequent activity: an objectification of social activity similar to that constituted by The Dreaming. Men's expectations that they should be paid for being filmed or photographed exemplifies this attitude. "That," they say," is Law."

A visitor to the community characterized this view as "once, a precedent; twice, a tradition." Pintupi try to find a "once and for all" (Stanner 1966) to which they can conform. Although in relationships among themselves Pintupi do make changes, the process is not explicit. New relationships between Pintupi in the Papunya area and those in other areas were formulated as "following up" a Dreaming tie that had only just been discovered. The emerging political unity of the contemporary Aboriginal community, made possible by increased transportation, is still understood as part of the unchanging "order of things." Similarly, when Pintupi seek to improve their situation, they usually try to find a better "boss" to look after them. Seeking a "boss" serves their own internal requirements for an outside realm on which to objectify the broader community and sustain their own autonomy.

Because a "boss" is someone outside the community, his decisions are similarly beyond the system of kinship. During my stays among the Pintupi, decisions made by the Village Councillors, even though they were conceived of as the heads of the community, were frequently taken to the white boss for ratification. If these decisions came to have unfortunate consequences—when a worker was fired from his job or his wages reduced for lack of work—the blame could be shifted to the white boss.

The advantage, indeed the necessity, of having such a "boss" is obvious. Outsiders become the instruments of the local system; the councillors can simply claim they are mediating, enforcing a white boss's rules. In the past, if a councillor wanted to be sure that a vehicle was not used by anyone in the community, it was the white boss whom he would ask to hold the keys. A Pintupi person, bound in the web of kinship and his or her duty to look after others, cannot refuse a request, but a white boss can. Consequently, it would appear that white bosses are used as a medium for the projection and transformation of decisions into an externalized object to which human subjects must conform, a Law that must be followed.

Conclusion

How is it possible that subjective meanings become objective facticities? (Berger and Luckmann 1967: 18)

I would depict the Murinbata as valuing continuity both for its own sake and for the sake of the aesthetic appeal of its symbolisms, but also as making it a rational principle. Their mentality had what might be called an Adrasteian mould in that it imposed on time and change an image of persistence as the main character of reality. It would not deny Chronos but gave Adrasteia the triumph . . . they welcomed change insofar as it would fit the forms of permanence.
(Stanner 1966: 168)

*I*n showing the essential foundation of Pintupi transcendentalism in the lived world of their daily experience, I have aimed at providing what might be called a social ontology. Ethnographically, this project links two components. One concern is the relationship between the negotiated quality of Pintupi daily life and a regional system based on extensive individual ties of shared identity. The emphasis in Pintupi social action on negotiation and sustaining relatedness contrasts strongly with the clarity of "rules" and "norms" as reported in ethnographic descriptions of other well-known Aboriginal groups. In this respect, Meggitt's (1962) presentation of the Warlpiri in terms of a structural-functional framework provides an important case. Not only does the contrast between "negotiation" and "rules" highlight genuine ethnographic differences in the apprehension cultural subjects have of their own system, but such variation reflects differences in the means through which polity is achieved. The Pintupi evidence suggests that the social achievement of rules—an indigenous objectification—should be analyzed further. The second concern of my ethnography, therefore, has been with how reification or hierarchy—transcendental value—is secured in such a social world.

The relationship between the transcendental and the immediate is dialectical. Initially, these two domains seem opposed. The transcendental, as expressed in The Dreaming, constitutes the very image of "permanence" and "continuity." This is a general characteristic of religious forms in Aboriginal Australia, where, as Stanner (1966) wrote of the Murinbata, they appear to make of continuity a rational principle. Contrastingly, the world of Pintupi daily life—in residence, landownership, and decision-making—is one of politics, negotiation, and considerable individual flexibility.

Social Value and Social Logic

For both Stanner (1966) and Munn (1970), as well as for the insightful Róheim (1945), a central problem is how to situate the "image of permanence" in the reality of Aboriginal life. All reject the view that the timelessness of The Dreaming reflects an absence of history among Aboriginal people. I follow them in this sense of what is at issue: Continuity is a fundamental Aboriginal concern. The differences in our accounts stem from the social logic we conceive to underlie The Dreaming.

Stanner and the others are inclined to understand the Aboriginal value on timelessness and permanence in general existential terms as a manifestation of a longing for enduringness. Stanner's emphasis, especially, is on the genuinely religious qualities of this view: "The strongest symbolisms may be read to say that cosmic necessity was the datum of social necessity" (Stanner 1966: 139).

Similarly, Munn and Róheim present the image of permanence as a solution to a longing for order, though each comes closer to grounding this desire in specific social or psychological considerations. Róheim (1945) attributes the Aboriginal emphasis on eternity to compensation for "separation anxiety." Munn (1970) analyzes The Dreaming as resolving a problem for individual subjects, providing a "stable anchor for identity" and socializing these subjects into an intersubjective order. Though she devotes little emphasis to the broader material context of Aboriginal lives, Munn intends these issues to be understood as particularly important for seminomadic foraging people.

On these points, my analysis of the significance of The Dreaming as a cultural form in Pintupi life agrees with Munn. In my view, however, the social value of a timeless, eternal order owes equally as much to its opposite—the necessary submission to the implicit politics and negotiation of relatedness in daily life. Because I begin with the social logic as encountered by individuals, the formulation of Society appears as essentially problematic. I have aimed to present a dynamic and pragmatic view of the meaning of The Dreaming and various substitutes for it as embedded in the processes of Pintupi social action. The Dreaming secures an objective framework of sociality outside the individual and outside any temporary local group.

The dialectic of Pintupi social life consists of the opposition between "overall relatedness" and "differentiation," the two possible trajectories of individual autonomy. This opposition is transcended, or synthesized, by The Dreaming, which serves at once as the guarantor of individuals' autonomy and of sociality. Here lies the source of this cultural form's social value.

There is, I believe, not cause but a dialectic more like coevolution in this formulation. The Pintupi interpretation of their world constructs reality as an objective order outside themselves, to which they must adapt: Symbolically they formulate conditions as cosmological data, as a given Law. But why? The emphasis on individual autonomy and the immediate relations among people leads Pintupi to represent enduring relationships among individuals as deriving from an order outside themselves. This strategy sustains a regional system that extends beyond any current aggregate of persons. Social reproduction consists essentially of maintaining this structure through time. In this view, The Dreaming is not a symbol that has intrinsically a "meaning"; the meaning it assumes in social action, I suggest, changes in time and from region to region.

In Dumont's (1980, 1982) theory of value, the subordination of a changeable political world to a higher religious level of order would represent no conceptual difficulty. The changeability of daily life is embedded in a hierarchically encompassing level of social structure. To some extent, the Pintupi construction of The Dreaming works in the ways Dumont suggests—by focusing attention on the basis of claims in The Dreaming rather than on the immediate lived experience of negotiation itself.

So it appears—if structure is taken for granted. From the perspective of the Pintupi lived world, structure takes on a different aspect. The creation of structure, the principle by which parts are related to a whole, is both problematic and motivated. It is problematic insofar as Pintupi social structure imposes limitations on any actual community. It is motivated in that the "encompassing level" of structure bears a significant relationship to lower levels of the system. This position can be argued theoretically, as T. Turner (1984a) has recently undertaken in relation to dual organization. Here I have presented the case empirically. According to what I am able to perceive of the processes of Pintupi social life, the selection of this particular transcendental value is motivated by the contradiction internal to Pintupi sociality—the opposition between relatedness and differentiation. If this analysis of Pintupi transcendentalism is correct, then one could expect structures of similar logical form, appealing to exogenous domains, to exist in other small-scale societies, where people need each other without being bound to any specific others.

Two Cases of Transcendentalism

Basso's (1984) account of the moral significance of "place" in Western Apache discourse exemplifies the same social logic. Among Apaches, where respect for individual autonomy is great, elders depersonalize and objectify their criticism of inappropriate behavior by channeling it, indirectly, through the landscape. Mention of a place where historic or mythic events took place leads listeners to search for connections between their situation and these events. The message, called the "arrow," comes later, but the critic has not impinged on the other's autonomy.

Lee's (1984) account of !Kung San trance dancing suggests the fruitfulness of treating trance as a social artifact. Like Pintupi ceremonies, !Kung San trance dances provide a major arena of sociality among those who live together. The division of labor symbolizes as much, with women singing while men dance and enter trances (Lee 1984: 110) to drive away that which threatens the members of the group. Curing is done for the residential group, constituting the band as a group among whom people show concern for each other. According to Lee, trance dancing became a major focus of the !Kung in the 1960s, an increase in performance that coincides with the pressures of sedentarism—just as ceremonialism has increased on Aboriginal settlements.

!Kung sociality is constituted as deriving from a source outside the present, immediate world. The emphasis in these dances, the stuff of band sociality, is on the capacity to see the invisible //gangwasi, the spirits of the dead. These are the main agents of illness and death, and they are "dealt with" by mature men who gain this ability by going into trances. The content of social relations in !Kung bands is, according to Marshall (1961), "sharing, talking, and giving." The threat to relations among band members comes not from "ancestors" (as Lee inappropriately calls them), but rather the recently dead.

Significantly, the focus of //gangwasi concern is conflict among the living. Lee (1984: 107–8) quotes an informant as saying, "When you are quarrelsome and unpleasant to other people, and people are angry with you, the //gangwasi see this and come to kill you. . . ." Not only are the spirits of the dead understood as attracted to conflict, they are symbolically identified with social negativity: These are the beings whose recent ties of shared identity with their own living relatives (a positive valence) have been broken. As an old women told Lee:

> Longing for the living is what drives the dead to make people
> sick. . . . They miss the people on earth and so they come back to us.
> They hover over the villages and put sickness into people, saying,
> "Come, come here to me." (Lee 1984: 109)

In banishing the recently dead, trance dancers are banishing the ties of the past in favor of those of the present.

Far from suggesting that Aborigines, !Kung San, and Apaches are the same, a theory of value offers a finer means of differentiating and comparing them. The Dreaming is a specific cultural form, with its own semiotic properties and its own autonomous implications for social life. Among the cultural implications that make Aboriginal people distinctive is the geographical extension of The Dreaming. The !Kung San trance dance, for all its sociality, is a reflex of the band alone and, like that impermanent unit, represents its focus as those who recently departed from this group. If the impermanence of this form of objectification is dramatically different from the temporal continuity projected in "ancestors," the trance dance also lacks the geographical link to other, distant people emphasized in Pintupi ceremonialism. The trance dance is not part of a wider regionalism. In this respect, the societal intensity of Aboriginal hunter-gatherers, even in the arid Western Desert, is not matched by the foragers of the Kalahari.

Time and Space

An emphasis on the broader, extensive social relations within a region constitutes the structural conditions that underlie the reproduction of Pintupi society. These relations are essential to understanding the nature of Pintupi residential groups. Finally, however, the temporary residential aggregations are the limiting moment of the social process.

Meillassoux (1973) portrayed the social relations in hunting bands as lacking in temporal depth and durability. Because the means of production are freely available, a hunting mode of production (as he calls it) emphasizes cooperation among producers, culminating in an immediate distribution of their product. Thus, he argues, social relations based on a spontaneous exchange of the products of joint labor with no long-term investment in other persons, an "immediate return," contrast with those found among horticulturalists and other food producers. The critical feature of food-producing societies, in this view, is the descent group that endures through time. According to Meillassoux, because food producers invest labor in preparing the land, their social relations are characterized by a temporality of "delayed return."

Many hunting-and-gathering peoples place considerable importance on long-term relations of exchange (just as many horticulturalists invest little in land). Aware of such variation among hunting societies, especially those in Australia where Lévi-Strauss (1949) formulated the notion of long-term exchange, Woodburn (1978, 1979) suggests that Aborigines differ from other foraging peoples because they "farm women."

In fact, Aboriginal societies demonstrate the insufficiences of any notion of immediate return. Woodburn and Meillassoux both assume that the "band," a residential group, constitutes the basic structure of hunting-and-gathering sociality. Rather than investigating the significance of reproducing the social relations within a region (which may be the precondition for any actual bands), their position implies that relations of production are all that need be considered. Analytically, they ignore the necessity of what I have called social production.

Unlike the ideal typical "hunters" of Meillassoux's model, Aboriginal peoples are enormously concerned with continuity through time. However, permanence is not located in the residential productive units; on that count, Meillassoux is assuredly correct. Where his model is misleading is in the equation of hunter-gatherer sociality with the "band." Nor, in the same vein, is the critical material process of such societies simple production. Production is not the main difficulty for these small-scale societies. If anything, such societies are chronically underproductive in a strictly economic sense (Sahlins 1972).

The Pintupi case illustrates that the relations enduring through time are those of the broader translocal social structure. Thus, the production of social persons is concerned specifically with the reproduction of the condition of widespread relatedness among people. However much actual bands may coalesce and disperse, an underlying nexus of relations must be sustained. On the one hand, individuals do not identify entirely with or subordinate their autonomy to the band they are currently living with; on the other hand, they must sustain the possibility of entering into productive relations with others not included in the current residential group. With the ironies so characteristic of history, the enduring dimension of Pintupi structure reflects regional organization as the condition on which any concrete residential community can exist. Broader ties, in turn, limit the continuity of any residential group. Meillassoux neglects this dimension.

For all its flux and flexibility, Pintupi society maintains a structure that can be reproduced in the face of the pressures of immediacy represented in production. Pintupi did not simply move to where the food was, but rather scheduled their movements so as to use available resources in pursuit of their own social values—to initiate a boy or to exchange ceremonies.

What seems important about the Pintupi is not that they "adapt," but that they create such societal intensity while managing to conform to the ecological constraints of a harsh region. Life is not ever simply life in a small band. Particular groups, in the past and in the present, have represented only temporary manifestations of a society that people continually work to reproduce. Understanding Pintupi organization requires looking beyond local groups, adopting the Pintupi view of their society as a wider, totalizing, less bounded structure. It necessitates, furthermore, giving attention to the emergent structures and processes by which a regional system maintains itself. These materialize only over time.

The Social Basis of Negotiation:
Ethnography and Theory

Some readers may wonder at the weight I have placed on the negotiability of Pintupi daily life. One school of anthropological interpretation emphasizes process—in contrast to juridical models— as a central feature of social organization everywhere. Versions of transactionalism (Bailey 1969, Barth 1966, Kapferer 1976) have not resolved how the contexts in which individual "strategy" is elicited are themselves generated. Indeed, the structural significance of negotiation and politicking may vary from society to society (cf. Comaroff and Roberts 1981). In this perspective, the meaning and content of "politics" in small-scale societies becomes fully problematic: It has no universal content (power) or function (social order). Neither is it necessarily distinguished from the symbolic, potentially hegemonic, activities of constituting meaning. Instead, the political must be interpreted as part of the overall structure of social relations.

In these matters, ethnography becomes something like the proverbial one-eyed man who guides the blind. What it sees is clarified only in comparative perspective. Ethnographers are guided by the experiences and understandings their informants reveal of their social world and its workings. These concern the world as it "appears" to them. While these local understandings may in some sense represent their experience of what is important, they are also only parts of a complex, largely taken-for-granted social structure. Finally, what is taken for granted must be accounted for as well, relating the events in which people participate to a larger structure.

This study has been concerned particularly with the relationship between "event" and "structure" in Pintupi society. I have given priority to a phenomenological condition: the observable inclination of acquiescing to the pressures of immediacy. Starting here reveals the special problem of constituting and sustaining a polity, a challenge faced and managed by participants in any residential community. This ethnographic inquiry may provide a new consideration with which to confront other ethnographies: Is it possible, for example, that the emphasis on "rights" is a specific dimension of the Warlpiri social system (Meggitt 1962, Munn 1973a), just as the sense of "negotiatedness" and the maintaining of "relatedness" are embedded in the particular structure of Pintupi social life?

My sense of these issues has a personal basis. I well remember asking a Pintupi man to sing some "love magic" (*yilpintji*) songs for me. He assured me that it was all right for me to tape them. "Women can hear them," he said. Immediately having said this, he turned to an older man and asked him, "Is it okay?" Since my friend was a man of ritual standing who knew the Law, he was not merely asking for information from an elder. Rather, he was making public his intention and displaying an awareness of another person's rights. This sort of negotiation seems to be reflected in a more general cognitive rejection of systematizing, in favor of a perspective placing primacy on first-hand experience. Platitudes about Aboriginal people "philosophizing" about kinship are a commonplace of introductory anthropology courses, but Pintupi did not seem interested in reflecting on their organizational categories as an abstracted object. People preferred to point out someone's identity in relation to me or to themselves, leaving the overall organization for my reflection late at night. My contacts with Warlpiri were considerably different; as informants, they were inclined to treat kinship, local organization, and language in more systemic terms.

Evidence of the difference between Warlpiri and Pintupi people in regard to "systemizing" does not depend on my impressions alone. A genuine variation in the quality of self-perspective is reflected in the way Warlpiri exegesis of graphic art emphasizes correspondences between levels of meaning (Munn 1973a) and in the Warlpiri success in organizing themselves via à vis whites (Meggitt 1962: 331–40). Indeed, when traveling through the Warlpiri community of Yuendumu in 1982, I noticed a sign for a basketball game of *Yapa* (Aboriginal people) vs. *Kartiya* (whites). They seem quite comfortable in acknowledging differences and integrating them into a higher level of structure.

Contrastingly, Pintupi insisted first and foremost that I see and experience things, hesitating to present information analytically or schematically. In response to questions, they were likely to say, "You'll see it," or to point out with irritation that "You've seen that" (so why are you asking?). I have taken this as a vital form of metacommunication.

In this sense, we might classify the Pintupi as phenomenological rather than structuralist in their approach to cultural forms. Their emphasis on the emergent form of cultural artifacts made me aware of how precarious an achievement their political arena was: organizing an initiation or a meeting was a considerable accomplishment. Without offices or defined social groups, they must continuously produce the contexts in which organization can take place.

It is intriguing that such differing emphases—on "rule" or "process"—occur among peoples who, like Warlpiri and Pintupi, share a good deal culturally. Far from being distinctively Pintupi, the value on relatedness is reported in many descriptions of Aboriginal social life and elsewhere in the world. What differs is the field to which this value may apply and the way in which it can be employed; that is, the way this value is situated in a larger structure.

Value and Structure: A Comparison

Whereas Pintupi relatedness is maintained at a regional level and definite social boundaries that would distinguish local groups are lacking, other Aboriginal groups have more definitively formed and bounded social units. Among Warlpiri (Meggitt 1962, Munn 1973a, Peterson et al. 1978), the patrilineal descent group is the basis of ritual and ownership of sacred sites, albeit a system in which women have rights as well as their brothers. There are other claims to landownership than those of patrilineal descent, to be sure. But when one asks Warlpiri who "owns" a place, they respond with definitive listings quite unlike Pintupi claims. Coordinately, the emphasis of Warlpiri male initiation is less on entry into the translocal corporation of men (as it is for Pintupi) than on full inclusion into a distinctive clan (Meggitt 1962: 306). This difference is reflected in the contrast between patrimoiety as the organizational focus of Warlpiri men's ceremony—which aggregates patrilineal groups into larger categories—and the Pintupi emphasis on generational moieties, which transcend the differentiation of local groups in favor of other criteria.

In discussions of land or ritual—fields in which the extent of mutuality in claims is more restricted among Warlpiri—the group of "owners" is more defined than for Pintupi. The greater definitiveness with which Warlpiri groupings are made implies that some rights may be asserted by them without fear of abridging or rejecting relatedness among people. It is as if these distinctions were not matters of personal will and rejection, but rather were already achieved understandings to which one assents: objectifications. Furthermore, an overall relatedness is achieved in Warlpiri society through various mechanisms of reintegrating "distinctiveness." This constitutes a different sort of overall relatedness, however, than that of the Pintupi.

In contrast to Western Desert people, among the Warlpiri the complementarity of what are known as "owner" and "manager" relations to land is extended to coordinate a wider, regional sociality. Integrating children of male members of descent groups and children of female members, respectively, at one level of organization, this same principle relates descent groups themselves into wider categories of social order, effectively into the patrimoieties. A whole series of descent groups are categorically "managers" to a category of "owner" descent groups. Since the statuses of "owner" and "manager" are defined by different, complementary sorts of rights and duties over sacred sites, a focus on rights and duties could become more prominent for the Warlpiri as the very means through which relatedness was sustained. In other words, this differentiation provides another way of denying one's exclusive, egoistic control (Maddock 1972: 36–42), although accomplished differently than among Pintupi. It is important to understand that this relatedness is achieved through a specific set of structurally based differentiations that vary from society to society. Thus, the concern to maintain relatedness by considering the claims of others is not as characteristic for Warlpiri as for Pintupi. The limits on what is "negotiable" are different.

It is illuminating to bring this analytic focus to the Yulngu of Northeastern Arnhem Land (see Warner 1937 on the "Murngin," Shapiro 1969, Morphy 1977, van der Leeden 1975). Here the region is integrated, politically and ecologically, through alliances between patrilineal groups ordered into a system of named patrimoieties, *Yiritja* and *Dua*. The dependence of the structures of alliance on arranged marriage leads to a concern with temporal continuity, with the reproduction of these relationships through time, as evidenced in elaborate mortuary ceremonies and clan differentiation. Thus, meetings and determinations are often held within the jurisdiction of the clan alone (Williams 1973). In contrast, the Pintupi system is predicated on the denial of repeated and defined particular political relationships in favor of overall regional integration. Consequently, among Western Desert people, social attention to temporal continuity in terms of mortuary, clan structure, or even the reproduction of alliances is insubstantial. The social concern with an individual's marriage, so vital to alliances in the north, is far less pronounced in Pintupi life.

Finally, the phenomenological style of Sansom's (1980) analysis of Darwin fringe dwellers also has a social basis, albeit a different one from the Warlpiri focus on "rights" as perceived by Meggitt. As Sansom writes:

> fringe-dwelling Aborigines lack perduring corporations. They have instead their mobs and each mob is an association of the living that depends for its continuing existence on a flow of propitious events or "happenings." (Sansom 1980: 20)

The emphasis Sansom places on the "negotiatedness" of the social order in fringe camps seems less a theoretical act than a recognition of the practical consciousness of a people who are aggregated on the basis of a multitude of ties escaping the subtler integrations of the traditional order. Thus, "the sociology of the corporation, of hierarchies, and of the propertied familial grouping must be put aside" (ibid.). In fringe camps, negotiation becomes a prominent and recognized feature of daily life.

The Pintupi situation becomes most comprehensive and distinct through this comparative lens. There is an enormous value placed on relatedness in terms of a whole region, not structured as the integration of lower-level units. So important is overall relatedness that local units at the lower levels of the system are not clearly bounded. In the absence of boundaries, in the Pintupi view they "are all family," and relatedness is not achieved through the integration of units as much as through the relation of all to all. This makes the questions of who is and who is not "related" always problematic and never taken for granted. Without a basis on which one can legitimately refuse or exclude another, avoidance of overt differentiations and an attempt to sustain the rubric of overall relatedness become essential to most forms of social action.

Especially critical is the level of social organization on which a value (like relatedness) or an event (a "meeting") appears. Differences in the level and manner of inclusion have important consequences for other cultural dimensions and dramatically affect the experience of the participants. The fact that overall relatedness is the structure which is reproduced through time, rather than the structuring of differentiation (as in Arnhem Land), is responsible for very different emphases on the part human beings can play in creating, altering, or affecting their environment. Because relatedness is not constrained within a higher level of structure in Pintupi society, it has

Pintupi Country, Pintupi Self

no limits of application. Thus negotiation is never fully concluded and decisive choices are rarely made.

Pintupi society offers little opportunity for people to accumulate value from generation to generation. For one thing, value is inscribed in the land and is not, in the end, portable. And given the flexibility of estate-group boundaries, individuals can easily relocate themselves in more promising venues. Thus, the dispersed underlying structure tends to reemerge through time. The low population density of the Western Desert has undoubtedly been a factor in this system. In Arnhem Land, where population density is higher, marriage alliances are regular and repeated in a way they are not among desert people, and value is controlled through time by the supraindividual units of clans. These conditions impose themselves structurally on the individual's freedom.

In the Western Desert, there are no enduring corporations of this sort. Only The Dreaming remains as a control, a structure beyond individuals and binding them to itself, but it is, correspondingly, felt more intensely as an imperative here than elsewhere in Australia. Although individuals in other parts of Australia appear more constrained by membership in a group and political alliances of the past, they are freer in the invention of song, dance, and innovation. Western Desert people are known throughout Australia for their conservatism and the strength of their adherence to the Law.

On the whole, anthropologists have given little consideration to structural differences in the political organization of small-scale societies, yet these variations are crucial. The comparative perspective shows Pintupi personhood, transcendentalism, and regional organization to be linked systemically, dominated by the structural limitations of their fragile and temporary polity.

Notes

Introduction

1. In all, I collected six life histories of men and one of a woman, all of whom had spent considerable periods of their life in the bush. They remembered this life in extraordinary detail, and their narratives were recorded simultaneously on cassettes and in my notes. I worked with single informants in Pintupi (the language of daily life), for two hours each day, for several weeks in succession. The number of interviews with each ranged from eight (with the woman) to thirty-five, averaging around twenty. They were paid at the rate of two dollars per hour for this work during 1973–1975 and four dollars per hour later.

These informants were selected on two bases: their willingness to talk with me; and their traditional countries. I chose five male informants who were, I believed, representatives of different local areas. The sixth male came from the "same country" as one of the others and was chosen to provide data on the comparative range of individuals from "one country." Interviewing the female helped me check for sex bias in life histories.

I purposely left these interviews as unstructured as possible, telling the informants only that I wanted them to tell me of their life in the bush, their travels from water to water, whom they encountered, and what happened. I hoped this approach would not encourage them to attempt to deliver the sort of content I "wanted." To some extent, the strategy succeeded, and I learned much that I could not have foreseen about life in the bush.

Although I had intended to study women as thoroughly as men, in my initial fieldwork I was unable to do so. In the Pintupi view, men do not socialize alone with women, except with their wives and mothers. Therefore, I talked with women only in the presence of their male relatives and this unfortunately did not allow me to collect data from them in any systematic or extensive way. In subsequent field trips, when I was accompanied by my wife, it was possible for me to spend much more time with women. The imbalance of my work was partially rectified, but I would certainly hesitate to regard it as definitive on Pintupi women's point of view.

In addition to life histories, interview sessions were also employed to collect narratives of Pintupi myths of The Dreaming and interpretations of associated song cycles reflecting the Pintupi conception of the country in which they lived. I particularly concentrated on the sacred *Tingarri* cycle of stories because it was said to be *the* Pintupi Dreaming; because I had witnessed a period of *Tingarri* ritual performances; and because it was considered to be "not dangerous," and despite its secret associations it could be heard by women and children.

CHAPTER 1

1. Myers (1976: 41–46) presents compositional data for the Pintupi bands encountered by Jeremy Long, E. C. Evans, and other observers. Other bands have been reconstructed from unpublished census notes on immigrants to Papunya.

2. Those whom I present as "the Pintupi" are part of a large, culturally related set of peoples that R. Berndt (1959) named the "Western Desert bloc." Numerous able ethnographers have worked with one or another set of these peoples, usually

referred to by locally recognized dialectal variations. The Berndts' work at Ooldea (Berndt and Berndt 1945) resulted in a pioneering early ethnography. Later important studies have examined the Pitjantjatjarra (Munn 1970, Elkin 1940, Yengoyan 1968, Mountford 1976, Tindale 1972), the Janggundjadjara (Hamilton 1979), the Ngatatjarra (Gould 1969a), the Mardudjara (Tonkinson 1974, 1978), and the Gugadja (R. Berndt 1970, 1972, 1975).

Although the ethnographic literature was once full of dispute about whether there were named "tribes" within this bloc and what the names were (R. Berndt 1959, Tindale 1974), most current researchers are suspicious about the significance of the social boundaries that such names might imply. Enormous similarities exist among the peoples represented in these studies. At the same time, we have only begun to explore the nature of the subtle differences among the groups who have lived in different regions of the Western Desert (cf. Hamilton 1980).

These are not the only relevant comparative materials. The near neighbors of the Pintupi to the north and east are the Warlpiri, represented in well-known, excellent monographs by Meggitt (1962, 1966) and Munn (1973) and the subjects of some theoretically significant recent land claims (Maddock 1981). Somewhat further to the east are the Aranda, known from the ethnographies of Spencer and Gillen (1899), Strehlow (1947), and Róheim (1933, 1945). The Warlpiri in particular offer the possibility of some intriguing intradesert comparisons.

Surprisingly, few comprehensive ethnographies exist of Western Desert people. This book offers the first full-scale ethnography of the Pintupi, though Strehlow (1965, 1970) and especially Róheim (1945, 1950) both did valuable research with the Pintupi as well as the Aranda. Tindale worked with the Pintupi for short periods on several occasions. Long (1964a, 1964b, 1971) used his tenure as patrol officer and representative of the Welfare Branch to do some valuable research, and Thomson studied a small band of people he called Bindibu (1964, 1975) with some fanfare, describing the water hole at which he found them as "Shangri-la." K. and L. Hansen (1978) have been studying the language for the Summer Institute of Linguistics. Hayden (1979) undertook archeological research, mostly lithic analysis, in the early seventies. Moyle (1979) has published a study of Pintupi music, based on research that was contemporaneous with my first period at Yayayi.

3. Róheim (1933, 1945, 1950) did research with some of the Pintupi who stayed at Hermannsburg.

4. Duguid (1963) describes his experiences of a young Pintupi boy known now as Wartuma tjungurrayi.

5. This pressure is clear in the reports sent to the Northern Territory Administration:

So long as the land/population ratio was not seriously disturbed (i.e., by overpopulation and/or drought) these natives were able to maintain themselves in accordance with their own custom. . . . Periodic droughts gave rise to minor crises in respect of water but once rain had fallen the bush dwellers would return to their nomadic way of life, and the pressure on available food and water resources at Haasts Bluff and on settled areas in the neighborhood would be relieved. (Northern Territory Administration 1961a)

6. At the end of this period, Donald Thomson encountered a Pintupi group that had been stranded for several years by drought in an area north of Lake Mackay (Thomson 1975). They had been unable to return to their traditional country.

7. The radical nature of the break between settlement life and traditional life is far more marked in central Australia than in Arnhem Land, where outstation movements have been based on the abundance of game and the land's capacity to

support semisedentary populations (cf. Meehan 1982). In central Australia outstation movement cannot rely on nature's resources to the same extent.

8. Yayayi's organization of 209 persons in 47 living units in May 1974 was fairly typical of Pintupi communities:

6 living units = women's camps, pop. = 47;
8.8 persons/unit;
6 living units = single men's camps, pop. = 30;
4.8 persons/unit;
35 living units = married camps, pop. = 132;
3.8 persons/unit.

9. Based on a sample of 47 camps, the main categories of interdomestic association at Yayayi can be described as follows:

(1) close proximity between camps of brothers-in-law	16 camps (in 7 groups)
(2) married couple living near wife's parent(s)	8 camps (3 were parents-in-law)
(3) married couple living near husband's parent(s)	7 camps (3 were parents-in-law)

CHAPTER 2

1. This perspective is rather like the naive empiricism of Azande witchcraft (Evans-Pritchard 1937).

2. Interestingly, Pintupi creative beings are never plants. When their activity ends, however, they may turn into plants, especially before they enter the human realm.

3. See Eliade's (1954) discussion of this feature of cosmology.

4. I am indebted to Daniel Maltz for formulating the problem in this way.

5. To whom one is speaking is an important factor in the use of place-names. Just as I might describe myself as "from near New York City" when I am abroad and speaking with those unfamiliar with local distinctions, so do the Pintupi pick out salient and better-known features when communicating about locale.

6. Sometimes, though the meanings are less transparent, the names come from songs associated with the place and The Dreaming there. Thus, Lake Mackay is known as Wilkinkarranya. These terms are rarely heard in ordinary speech, but initiated men, older women, and sometimes even children are usually able to give the derivations of a name from songs or stories. I have no data on their comparative abilities to do so, but one would expect that women would be unable to derive the names of places known through ceremonies restricted to men.

7. See, for example, Gould (1969a), Strehlow (1970), and van der Leeden (1975).

8. What is meant by *Tingarri* presents an interpretive problem. Considerable confusion surrounds the label because of its polysemy (cf. R. Berndt 1970, Gould 1969a, Petri 1970). A broader discussion of these issues can be found in Myers (1976).

9. The version presented here is derived from repeated sessions with two informants and gathered over the course of a year, including a visit to the main place mentioned.

10. The fluff (*yutalpa*) extracted by crushing the stems of certain plants is used interchangeably with the down taken from birds, such as eagles, to place designs on the bodies of performers and on ritual objects in many kinds of male ceremonies.

11. This is what is meant by the term "increase" ceremony in the anthropological

literature, made famous by Spencer and Gillen's (1899) description of Intichiuma rites.

12. It is possible that men are excluded from some sites associated with women, as Bell (1980a) has reported elsewhere in central Australia. Although I have no information to indicate that "women-only" sacred sites exist among the Pintupi, women do control certain details about The Dreaming from which men are excluded.

13. Lévi-Strauss's (1966: 239) argument about the value of sacred objects as guarantors of authenticity in totemic systems is borne out by this material.

CHAPTER 3

1. Tindale (1974) has continued to maintain, however, that land as economically productive of food is also "owned" by a corporate descent group.

2. Given these uses, vegetable foods are categorized into four types: *nyuma*—seeds that are ground by stone mortar and made into cakes (*nyuma*) cooked in hot ashes; *lungkunpa*—seeds ground by mortar and, with water added, made into a paste; *tirnu*—fruits pounded and pulverized into a thick paste, then rolled into a large ball for storage; and *naru*—fruits with inedible seed cores that must be removed.

3. This argument follows, in part, Sahlins's (1972) treatment of the limitations of a "domestic mode of production."

4. These were often "increase" ceremonies, of the type described by Gould (1969a: 126) for the Ngatatjara, Spencer and Gillen (1899) for the Aranda, and Meggitt (1962: 220) for the Warlpiri.

5. He had been living at Haasts Bluff and Papunya settlements since 1948, moving to Yayayi in 1973.

6. This usage is informative. According to the subsection system, which is discussed in chapter 7, this man would be a *tjukurnpa*, a potential affine. The fact that his status is shifted to "father" indicates that he was considered close kin and a regular coresident.

7. Some anthropologists have apparently taken similar conceptions to refer to people who occupy one bounded territory or to a sociocentrically defined group. Thus, the "Yumari mob," for example, would be treated as a corporate group. Sansom's (1980) discussion of "countrymen" in Aboriginal fringe camps in Darwin, however, shows an egocentric focus similar to that of the Pintupi. In the fringe camps, a "countryman" is anyone who has shared common experiences.

8. See Myers (1976: 92–96) for supporting evidence of bilaterality in residence pattern.

9. Strehlow (1970) offers a variant of this "ecological function" in his discussion of Aranda sacred sites as refuge areas for game.

10. This fact has important consequences for Lee and DeVore's (1968) model of hunter-gatherer conflict resolution as simply walking away. At those times of the year when !Kung San conflict was worst—summer—resources restricted movement (cf. Lee 1979: 383–85, 389). I am indebted to Randy White for pointing out this parallel.

11. Balikci's (1970) account of the Netsilik offres a parallel in the relief of leaving large gatherings on the winter ice and the breakup into smaller groups.

12. For a comparable argument, see Williams (1982).

13. Attention to resources and the process of band formation can be instructive

concerning the meaning of Pintupi territoriality, esepecially in indicating some variation in permeability of boundaries for different items. Maantja described large congregations, including people from far away, near Lake Macdonald at seasons when *mungilpa* was available. Growing in large quantities near claypans filled with water, and abundant in August and September, this resource supported large populations, often gathered for ceremony. At such times, people with relatively distant ties might come to exploit the resource, conforming to Dyson-Hudson and Smith's (1978) model that unpredictable and dense resources are exploited through information-sharing and a high degree of nomadism. At other times of year, however, when water becomes a scarce resource and only a few well-known permanent waters are available, the data indicate that people returning to their "own country" operate in more localized, separate groups in what Dyson-Hudson and Smith describe as a "home-range" form of resource utilization.

CHAPTER 4

1. The problem of alienation this analysis presents is a fundamental issue for anthropology, related to the recent concern in the humanities with "decentering the subject" (Derrida 1978, Lacan 1981, Ricoeur 1970). The existential attempts to address the problem are, I believe, vital dimensions of religious activity. In anthropology, the critical difference between an individual and his contingent subjectivity has not been given the attention it deserves. Victor Turner's (1969b) discussion of "anti-structure" offered one attempt to explore the problem of a socially constituted subjectivity.

2. My appreciation of the philosophical problems entailed in analyzing the emotions owes a great debt to Ronald Rubin, although he might not agree with the positions I have taken.

3. Emotional concepts do, in Pintupi theory, possess objective referents: that is, they do describe internal states that the Pintupi may alternatively refer to as conditions of the "spirit" (*kurrunpa*). To be afraid, for example, is to have a "wet spirit." However, these phenomenal responses derive from subjective evaluation: They depend, in other words, on the perception and definition of various kinds of situations. It is not merely that, as Levy argues, " 'feeling' becomes associated with cultural understandings which designate the cause of the feeling and what should be done about it" (Levy 1973: 322–23). One must emphasize that these "cultural understandings" may themselves give rise either to a "feeling" or to a sense of its appropriateness. In this sense, the determination of when one ought to be angry, when sad, when sorry, when lonely, and how to act, is largely a cultural matter.

4. Although she has been recently criticized for imposing a Durkheimian framework on Warlpiri culture (Dubinskas and Traweek 1984), Munn is ethnographically correct in arguing that the functioning of this self-related orientation, this linking of "the interior subjectivity of the person with the external world," provides a key structure in social control.

5. V. Turner (1969a) and Munn (1969), along with many other anthropologists, have noted how inward states may be treated as subjective evaluations of social conditions.

6. A more extensive discussion of the ritual process involved in ceremony and how it expands the system of "relatedness" is offered in chapter 8.

CHAPTER 5

1. Since I first proposed the notion of multiple pathways to landownership among the Pintupi (Myers 1976), extensive study of other Aboriginal groups' traditional claims to land has found the principle to be widespread. This is especially true in the importance given to *kurtungurlu* ("sisters' children") as equal but complementary parties to ownership in the later Warlpiri and Alyawarra claims (Bell 1980a, Maddock 1981). The inklings of this system can be found in Strehlow's (1947) discussion of individual ownership of *churunga*.

2. The notion of "closeness" is discussed in chapter 7.

3. Tonkinson (1977) presents an interesting discussion of the difficulties he encountered with other Western Desert people when asking about where babies came from.

4. Pintupi frequently say that a person was left by a Dreaming and that subsequently he "became a vegetable food" (*mayirringu*) or "became a meat animal" (*kukarringu*) or became some other physically existent animal. Usually, then, this animal was killed by the mother or father, or vegetable food prepared, and eaten by the mother. Occasionally, individuals attribute this item as their Dreaming, saying that they are "Desert Oak" Dreaming, for example. The physical feature should be interpreted, however, as a "sign" of the action of The Dreaming. In every case the referent can be traced back to The Dreaming itself.

5. It is also possible to see this comment as an expression of conflict between two historically competing structures of land tenure, one based on conception-totem affiliation and the other based on patrilineal inheritance (Hamilton 1979, 1980).

6. For the Tiwi, Goodale (1971: 99–100) describes a similar passage of rights to the country in which a father dies. Since a father should die in his own country and his countrymen would give his children rights without question, this transition would look like patrilineal inheritance while being based, in fact, on burial place.

7. The Pintupi notion of "losing" a relative is expressed by the word *wantininpa*, "to leave, leave behind, or to lose." It is also expressed in the description of a parent whose child is dead as "empty" (*yurltu*).

8. Strehlow (1947: 55), Spencer and Gillen (1899: 127), and Pink (1935: 280) have described an Aranda ideology of "reincarnation," in which the living individual's spirit comes from The Dreaming and returns back to it when he or she dies. This ideology is directly related to the process of "claims" in relation to land. The Aranda model, like that of the Murngin (Warner 1937), places greater emphasis on the cycling of patrilineally controlled spirits back to the land and from thence again into the visible world. The expectation of the Aranda was to be conceived in the country of one's own patriclan, and such conception was seen as an entitlement to rights to this Dreaming. Conception outside one's clan territory, however, raised questions of ownership and acceptance of such claims depended on those who controlled the ritual paraphernalia. Acceptance or rejection of a claim seems to have depended on an individual's persuasive powers. Pink (1935: 286) reported that such claims often were not accepted.

9. The question of ritual patrimoieties has become significant in recent discussions of landownership. First given detailed treatment in Meggitt (1962) for the Warlpiri, the complementary relationship between two categories of relationship to sacred sites ("owner" and "manager") has proven difficult to translate into Western terms of ownership. Maddock (1981) offers a general discussion of the problem.

10. Later, of course, I learned that some of these "traditional" inhabitants lay claim to the Yayayi country through the same sort of flexible processes illustrated

in this chapter. Nor were their claims entirely beyond dispute. One traditional owner's father, for example, had been a migrant to the area!

11. It is worth noting the ease with which Warlpiri expanded northward into Gurindji country and made it, for a while, their own. The same is true, I would argue, for the extension of Warlpiri claims southward to Winparrku (as noted in conflicting accounts by Mountford 1968 and Tindale 1974: 139).

12. In this way, they resemble patterns of landownership that are widely distributed in Oceania. See, for example, Scheffler 1965, Davenport 1959, Goodenough 1955.

13. The word translated as "rising" or "getting up" (*pakarninpa*) refers to the fact that the *Tingarri* men were sitting in a hole in the ground at Yawalyurrunya. From this hole they "arose" on their journey. Mara Mara was conceived on this journey, but the assertion here is that he was one of these men. In other words, he had been at Yawalyurrunya and had risen from it on this trip. On this basis, he identified with the place.

14. As I have argued elsewhere (Myers and Brenneis 1984), this kind of interaction is common in societies where basically egalitarian relations prevail. In Rosaldo's (1973) view of the Ilongot, political encounters between individuals are rather more like "courtship" than confrontation.

15. By asking "who holds country X?" (*ngaanalu kanyininpa X?*) or "what country do you hold?" (*ngurra ngananya nyuntulu kanyininpa?*), one elicits different responses than by asking "whose country is X?" (*nganaku ngurra?*). The first questions refer less ambiguously to rights and duties over ritual association.

16. The Pintupi system is, in this sense, one variant of the pattern Maddock (1972) describes as widespread in Australia, whereby the "parochialism" of local groups is opposed by a cultural emphasis on "universalism."

17. For examples of ritual organization, there are two films made by Roger Sandall for the Australian Institute of Aboriginal Studies, *Pintubi Revisit Yumari* (1967) and *Pintubi Revisit Yaru Yaru* (1969).

18. This distinction is common in nonunilineal descent groups elsewhere in Oceania (cf. Huntsman 1971).

19. "*mirrilu wantingu, mirri kutjupalu lutjamilarnu, marla kutjupalu lutjami-larnu, . . . Marlalpi . . .* Not *nganampa* idea: Law *purlkanya.* We got to same way *nyinantjaku* like all those dead people."

20. The restricted nature of such sacred information forbids discussion in detail.

CHAPTER 6

1. The Pintupi do not find this condition of immanence to be tragic. They share an acceptance of "what is" with other Aboriginal people. Stanner's brilliant analysis of the Murinbata miming of a buffalo in its wallow as an incipient perception that "at the centre of things social, refuge and rottenness are found together" (1966: 44) suggests this is something mysterious to the Aborigines themselves.

2. These "feather-feet" (*tjinakarpilpa*) killers (Tonkinson 1978: 139) are known as *kutaitcha* throughout much of central Australia. Through special techniques, it is believed, men are able to become invisible and to leave no tracks. Thus, they can kill their victims without leaving any trace of their activity. *Tjarnpa,* as the Pintupi call them, are greatly feared, and people who dare to wander around in the night are warned about the danger of being strangled.

3. Sutton's account of Cape Kerweer people similarly considers the dialectical relationship between violence and diplomacy (1979: xiii–xiv).

4. When this man threatened me, for writing his name down in my notebook, people thought it appropriate that I reminded him of all the help I had given him. His behavior was reminiscent of women who have lost children, who become demanding and edgy while testing one's feeling for them.

5. This corresponds to the importance Sansom (1980: 79–113) gives to the social activity of "witnessing."

6. The temporal perspective of the Pintupi implies that these exchanges are parts of the process of replacement, as discussed by Weiner for the Trobriands: "Inherent in the replacement process is that payment received has long-range expanding effects. What one individual gives to another not only creates obligations between giver and receiver, but eventually involves other kin . . ." (1980: 78). Thus, replacement allows for the regeneration of social relations through time.

7. See chapter 7 for an analysis of Pintupi kin terminology.

8. Similarly, a young man whose broken leg had been repaired by surgery in a hospital expected that the doctor would pay *him* because the latter had "cut" him.

9. Burridge (1969) interprets this "debt" at growing up as a universal quality of life in society that must be met with some means of "redemption."

10. See Maantja tjungurrayi's mention of this man in his life history, chapter 3.

11. See chapter 3.

CHAPTER 7

1. The most familiar version of this argument is Lévi-Strauss's (1966) analysis of "totemic systems," interpreting social structures as sets of homologous, related transformations.

2. See also Gregory (1982: 29): "The term 'reproduction' is used here to refer to the conditions necessary for the self-replacement of both things and people. As it is a wholistic concept which includes production, consumption, distribution and exchange as its principal elements, the concept of reproduction in general must weld eight elements—the production, consumption, distribution and exchange of things on the one hand; the production, consumption, distribution and exchange of people on the other—into a structural whole." Gregory (1982: 31) goes on to point out that the material process of "consumption" can also be seen as one of "personification," a process by which the consumption of things is turned to the production of human beings. This process takes on special analytical importance in "clan-based" societies.

3. See the description of such an encounter between Pintupi and Ngalia Warlpiri in Fry (1933). The word *papulanyi* refers to the formal introduction of people.

4. These terms convey sufficient information so that further aspects of a person's identity may be unnecessary in deciding what behavior is appropriate.

5. Scheffler (1978: 507) is disinclined to consider these formations patrimoieties because they are unnamed and lexically constituted only in egocentric terms drawn from the kinship system. Perhaps some sort of distinction needs to be made between this sort of construction and more conceptually overt moiety systems. The problem arises in treating such moieties as enduring, univocal features of social classification. For the Pintupi, at least, they are not. The categories are principally evident in ritual activity. The divisions remain, nonetheless, quite distinct behaviorally.

6. *Wapirra* is a Warlpiri term for "father," but also the Pintupi reciprocal term for

"wife's mother's brother" and "sister's daughter's husband," that is, a person of one's patrimoiety but of a different patricouple.

7. This difference is ethnographically real. Meggitt reports that Warlpiri "speak contemptuously of the Pintupi who even yet have not fully grasped the principles underlying subsection affiliation" (1962: 169).

8. White (1981) discusses the importance of generational categories in Aboriginal societies within a comparative perspective. It has been noted by many students of Western Desert societies, most recently by Hamilton (1979) and Tonkinson (1978).

9. Diagram 7E outlines a system in which cross-cousin marriage is prohibited and marriage with distant second cross-cousins is permitted. One point of complexity should be explained. The chart shows FFZD as being called "sister's child" (yukari). Since FFZ is of the same subsection as ego, the FFZD can be called "sister's child" by a male ego on this basis. As she is likely to be older than ego, alternatively the FFZD may be called "mother" if relative age is being emphasized. The same is true for FFZS, who may be called either "sister's child" by a male (or "own son" by a female ego) or "mother's brother," depending on whether the latter is younger or older than ego. He may be called "wife's father" (waputju) by a man if he is a potential affine. The chart gives priority to contexts that emphasize marriage relationships—in which case FFZD is considered a "sister's child" (yukari) and FFZS a "wife's father." The terms that emphasize relative age are appropriate for "close kin," however. In that case, the seniority and respect of the ascendant generation term are used. The same pattern (in reverse) holds for MBSD and MBSS.

10. The principles underlying the classification of "close kin" are discussed later in this chapter in the section on "generation." Here attention is focused on the concept of "closeness."

11. A similar principle is obviously at work in the Pitjanytjatjarra differentiation of siblings (close) from cross-cousins (marriageable). Summarizing Munn (1965: 7, 7A), Scheffler writes that sibling terms "are extended collaterally to all kin of ego's generation. Alternatively, the children of mother's 'distant brothers' and father's 'distant sisters' may be designated as watjira. . . . These 'cousins,' but not the children of mother's 'close brothers' and father's 'close sisters,' are marriageable (Scheffler 1978: 97).

12. This situation offers a case of what Shapiro (1971) has described as the categorical separation of the potential wives of "fathers" from those of their "sons."

13. The merging of relatives into a few broader classes of kin supports the existence of the "superclasses" and "subclasses" inferred by Scheffler (1978). He argued that many distinctions of kin classification were understood by Aboriginal people as being "like" or derivations of other types. For example, in some systems "brother" and "grandfather" are linked as members of a superclass, while in other systems a "grandfather" is like a "cross-cousin."

14. This classification differs from the Aluridja system, in which parental cross-cousins are classified as either parents or parental siblings (Aluridja: MMBS = MB; Pintupi: MMBS = F).

15. Parental cross-cousins are reclassified as that parent's spouse or parent's spouse's sibling.

Chapter 8

1. Privately, many older men admitted to me that as children they had spied on some men's ceremony, with some trepidation. Pintupi are not very sanctimonious,

and they realize that similar indiscretions probably occur now. Apparently, their greatest concern is that they not have to take official notice of it. If they did, their responsibility to the entire male initiatory cult would force them to take punitive action.

2. Tindale (1974) describes a gathering for a Western Desert initiation in the Tomkinson Range that involved as many as 500 persons. *Tingarri* ceremony corresponds to the Aranda *Engwura* (Spencer and Gillen 1899), a large-scale organization of men and novices from throughout a region for sustained series of revelatory rituals.

3. There is usually serious discussion among the boy's relatives about where to send him. They are guided by an obligation to reciprocate the visits of novices from other groups, to avoid "trouble." Since several such obligations are frequently outstanding, this presents an opportunity for persuasive political performance and subtle judgment.

4. He will wear the *naanpa* during his travels as a material form of the invitation for others to join him. At times, the belt itself symbolically stands for the initiate: For example, the belt may be sent to a local group in place of the boy as an invitation. While the belt is often made by a novice's mother, this is not a necessity. Men stress, rather, that a "brother-in-law" must put it on.

5. This kind of agonistic ritual of "greeting" is widespread in central Australia. See, for example, Spencer and Gillen (1899) and Fry (1933).

6. This analysis of initiation owes much to V. Turner's (1967) interpretation of Ndembu male initiation.

7. Speech to a *pilayarli*, and other ceremonial relationships, is the same as that to a "wife's mother's brother" (*tjukurnpa*). This differs from speech for "brothers-in-law" (*marutju*), and both differ from ordinary speech.

8. T. Turner (1984a) suggests that moiety forms represent transformations of the organizational principles of lower levels of the social structure. Differences between patrimoiety organization and generational structure seem significant in this regard.

9. Joking occurs throughout a ceremony on the theme of separation of the generations. Thus, men address their "mother's brothers" as "brothers-in-law" (*marutju*), a misrepresentation that causes men to laugh. Members of each generational category sit in their own circle for singing, and the initiate lies beside members of his own generational moiety. Members of each moiety refer to their own group as "all the brothers."

10. Burridge (1969) discusses the problem of "indebtedness," "redemption," and "integrity" as integral to social life generally.

11. These terms, it should be understood, are descriptive rather than titles of status. Other terms are often used to refer to the same relative statuses, employing various distinctive features of the status. In addition, some categories are overlapping, such as "middle-aged" and "old man," having no distinctive markers. Often all post-*Tingarri* men are referred to as "the old men."

12. T. Turner's view (1973, 1980a) is that such reifications can be understood as transformations or "invariant" principles of lower levels of a social system.

13. The symbolism of male nurturance—of men taking on a role homologous to women as mothers—is actually even more powerful, in that men's blood becomes nourishment for "growing up" boys during ritual seclusion. As the subject is a matter of ritual secrecy, I cannot go into the details.

14. Convincing accounts of women's autonomy were presented in the works of female ethnographers as early as Kaberry (1939) and Goodale (1971).

15. These issues are discussed in Begler (1978), Bell (1980a, 1980b), C. Berndt (1974), Hamilton (1979, 1980), and Leacock (1978). Various explanations of Aboriginal gender relations have been offered, depending largely on whether these relations were interpreted as exemplifying male dominance or female autonomy. Women's role in producing the bulk of subsistence has been used, on the one hand, to explain male control and male elaboration of ceremonies as an ideological mystification (Hamilton 1975, Bern 1979) and, contrastingly, to account for the greater autonomy of women in hunting-and-gathering societies (Leacock 1978, Martin and Voorhies 1975). The question for anthropologists should not be to "determine" the monolithic presence of either men's dominance or women's equality. We should examine instead how men and women impinge on each other's lives and how their activities are integrated within the total structure of social life (Weiner 1976). Doing so reveals how sensitive relations between men and women in Aboriginal societies are to historical conditions (see Barwick 1974, Bell 1980b).

Chapter 9

1. On the subject of all-male councils and the general decline of women's autonomy on settlements, see Bell and Ditton (1980) and Bell (1980a).

2. The meaning of "representation" is a complex problem in political theory, indicating how much of a cultural concept it is. Pitkin (1967) has analyzed various meanings the concept has taken in political theorizing.

3. In some respects, this analysis resembles Lévi-Strauss's (1966) distinction between the "bricoleur" and the "engineer."

4. Though there have been some publications on this cult, the Pintupi consider it to be a matter of great secrecy. Consequently, I do not feel free to discuss it in any detail.

5. In a somewhat different context, of course, this is exactly what Bell and Ditton (1980) argue about the problem of representation when Village Councils in contemporary Aboriginal communities are made up entirely of males. Not only do these councils have a "wider ranging jurisdiction than any body [traditionally] enjoys in Aboriginal society" (Bell and Ditton 1980: 13), but councils of male elders "did not constitute the only decision-making mechanism in Aboriginal society and probably did not exist in any formal sense in the past" (ibid.). In this way, Bell and Ditton emphasize the limits on the jurisdiction of any such gathering.

6. Austin (1962: 99–100) describes an "illocutionary act" as the "performance of an act *in* saying something as opposed to performance of an act *of* saying something."

7. See Reay (1970) for intriguing parallels in the use of outsiders at Borroloola.

8. See Myers and Brenneis (1984) for a fuller discussion of such issues.

9. Attempting to come to terms with this process in northern Australia, Sansom (1980) has called its result a "determination," reflecting how a group's "word" defines it as a social unit.

10. Anderson (1983) describes the importance Cape York people attribute to such relationships. They felt sorry for those who had no one to look after them: "Poor bugger, they got no boss."

11. A major problem in the articulation of black-white relations is the coordination of value. Whites and Aborigines do not really possess a shared system of equivalence. Strikingly, in fact, Pintupi are often uncertain about whether they have been "cheated." The issue is peripheral to the concerns of this chapter, but I have discussed it elsewhere (Myers 1980b).

References Cited

Anderson, Christopher
   1983 "Aborigines and Tin Mining in North Queensland: A Case Study in the Anthropology of Contact History." *Mankind* 13: 473–98.

Atkinson, Jane M.
   1984 " 'Wrapped Words': Poetry and Politics among the Wana of Central Sulawesi, Indonesia." In Brenneis and Myers, eds., 33–68.

Austin, J. L.
   1962 *How to Do Things with Words*. Cambridge: Harvard University Press.

Bailey, F. G.
   1969 *Strategems and Spoils*. New York: Schocken.

Balikci, Asen
   1970 *The Netsilik Eskimo*. New York: Natural History Press.

Barker, Graham
   1976 "The Ritual Estate and Aboriginal Polity." *Mankind* 10: 225–39.

Barnes, J. A.
   1962 "African Models in the New Guinea Highlands." *Man* 61: 5–9.

Barth, Fredrik
   1966 "Models of Social Organization." *Occasional Papers of the Royal Anthropological Institute*, no. 23.

Barwick, Diane
   1974 "And the Lubras Are Ladies Now." In Fay Gale, ed., 2d ed., 31–38.

Basso, Keith
   1984 " 'Stalking with Stories': Names, Places, and Moral Narratives among the Western Apache." In E. Bruner, ed., *Text, Play, and Story: The Construction and Reconstruction of Self and Society*. Proceedings of the American Ethnological Society.

Bates, Daisy
   1966 *The Passing of the Aborigines: A Lifetime Spent among the Natives of Australia*. Melbourne: Heinemann.

Bateson, Gregory
   1972 *Steps to an Ecology of Mind*. New York: Ballantine Books.
   1979 *Mind and Nature: A Necessary Unity*. New York: Dutton.

Begler, Elsie B.
   1978 "Sex, Status, and Authority in an Egalitarian Society." *American Anthropologist* 80: 571–88.

Bell, Diane
   1980a "Daughters of the Dreaming." Ph.D. diss., Autralian National University, Canberra.
   1980b "Desert Politics: Choices in the 'Marriage Market.' " In M. Etienne and E. Leacock, eds., *Women and Colonization*, 239–69. New York: Praeger.
   1981 "Women's Business Is Hard Work: Central Australian Aboriginal Women's Love Rituals." *Signs* 7: 314–37.

Bell, Diane, and Pam Ditton
  1980 *Law: The Old and the New.* Canberra: Aboriginal History (for Central Australian Aboriginal Legal Aid Service).
Berger, P., and T. Luckmann
  1967 *The Social Construction of Reality: A Treatise on the Sociology of Knowledge.* Garden City, N.Y.: Doubleday.
Bern, John
  1979 "Ideological Domination." *Oceania* 50: 118–32.
Berndt, C.
  1974 "Digging Sticks and Spears, or the Two-Sex Model." In F. Gale, ed., 2d ed., 39–48.
Berndt, C., and R. Berndt
  1945 "A Preliminary Account of Field Work in the Ooldea Region, South Australia." Sydney: *Oceania* bound offprint.
Berndt, R.
  1959 "The Concept of 'the Tribe' in the Western Desert of Australia." *Oceania* 30: 82–107.
  1970 "Traditional Morality as Expressed through the Medium of an Australian Aboriginal Religion." In R. Berndt, ed., 216–47.
  1972 "The Walmadjeri and Gugadja." In M. G. Bicchieri, ed., *Hunters and Gatherers Today,* 177–216. New York: Holt, Rinehart, and Winston.
  1975 "Territoriality and the Problem of Demarcating Sociocultural Space." In N. Peterson, ed., *Tribes and Boundaries,* 133–61. Canberra: Australian National University Press.
Berndt, R. (ed.)
  1970 *Australian Aboriginal Anthropology.* Nedlands: University of Western Australia Press.
Birdsell, Joseph
  1970 "Local Group Composition among the Australian Aborigines: A Critique of the Evidence from Fieldwork Conducted Since 1930." *Current Anthropology* 11: 115–42.
Bourdieu, Pierre
  1976 *Outline of a Theory of Practice.* Translated by R. Nice. Cambridge: Cambridge University Press.
Brenneis, Donald
  1984 "Straight Talk and Sweet Talk: Political Discourse in an Occasionally Egalitarian Community." In Brenneis and Myers, eds., 69–84.
Brenneis, D., and F. Myers (eds.)
  1984 *Dangerous Words: Language and Politics in the Pacific.* New York: New York University Press.
Buchler, Ira
  1978 "The Fecal Crone." In I. Buchler and K. Maddock, eds., *The Rainbow Serpent: A Chromatic Piece,* 119–212. The Hague: Mouton.
Burridge, Kenelm
  1969 *New Heaven, New Earth.* New York: Schocken.
Carnegie, David
  1898 *Spinifex and Sand.* London: C. Arthur Pearson.
Collier, Jane, and M. Rosaldo
  1981 "Politics and Gender in Simple Societies." In S. Ortner and H. Whitehead, eds., *Sexual Meanings,* 275–329. New York: Cambridge University Press.

Collmann, J.
1982 "New Thoughts on Perennial Issues." *Reviews in Anthropology* 9: 339–48.

Comaroff, J., and S. Roberts
1981 *Rules and Processes: The Cultural Logic of Dispute in an African Context.* Chicago: University of Chicago Press.

Davenport, William
1959 "Nonunilinear Descent and Descent Groups." *American Anthropologist* 61: 557–72.

Derrida, Jacques
1978 *Writing and Difference.* Translated by A. Bass. Chicago: University of Chicago Press.

Dixon, Robert
1971 "A Method of Semantic Description." In D. Steinberg and L. Jakobovitz, eds., *Semantics: An Interdisciplinary Reader in Philosophy, Linguistics, and Psychology,* 436–71. Cambridge: Cambridge University Press.

Douglas, Mary
1966 *Purity and Danger.* London: Routledge and Kegan Paul.

Dubinskas, F., and S. Traweek
1984 "Closer to the Ground: A Reinterpretation of Walbiri Iconography." *Man* 19: 15–30.

Duguid, Charles
1963 *No Dying Race.* Adelaide: Rigby.

Dumont, Louis
1965 "The Modern Conception of the Individual, Notes on Its Genesis." *Contributions to Indian Sociology* 8: 13–61.
1980 *Homo Hierarchicus: The Caste System and Its Implications.* Rev. English ed. Translated by M. Sainsbury, L. Dumont, and B. Gulati. Chicago: University of Chicago Press.
1982 "On Value." *Proceedings of the British Academy* 66: 207–41.

Durkheim, Emile
1912 *The Elementary Forms of the Religious Life.* Translated by J. Swain. New York: Free Press.

Dyson-Hudson, R., and E. Smith
1978 "Human Territoriality." *American Anthropologist* 80: 21–41.

Eliade, Mircea
1954 *Cosmos and History, or The Myth of the Eternal Return.* Translated by W. Trask. New York: Harper.
1973 *Australian Religions: An Introduction.* Ithaca: Cornell University Press.

Elkin, A. P.
1940 "Kinship in South Australia: General Survey and Summary." *Oceania* 10: 368–88.
1944 *Aboriginal Men of High Degree.* Sydney: Australasian Publishing Company.
1967 "Reaction and Interaction: A Food-Gathering People and European Settlement in Australia." In P. Bohannon and F. Plog, eds., *Beyond the Frontier: Social Processes and Social Change.* Garden City, N.Y.: Natural History Press.

Evans-Pritchard, E. E.
1937 *Witchcraft, Oracles, and Magic among the Azande.* Oxford: Oxford University Press.
1940 *The Nuer.* Oxford: Oxford University Press.

References Cited

Fingarette, Herbert

    1964 *The Self in Transformation: Psychoanalysis, Philosophy, and the Life of the Spirit.* New York: Harper Torchbooks.

Finlayson, H. H.

    1935 *The Red Centre.* Sydney: Angus and Robertson.

Frake, Charles

    1963 "Litigation in Lipay: A Study of Subanun Law." *Proceedings of the 9th Pacific Science Congress,* vol. 3.

    1974 "Plying Frames Can Be Dangerous: Some Reflections on Methodology in Cognitive Anthropology." *Quarterly Letter of the Institute for Comparative Human Development* 1 (3): 1–7.

Fried, Morton

    1967 *The Evolution of Political Society.* New York: Random House.

Fry, H. K.

    1933 "Body and Soul: A Study from Western Central Australia." *Oceania* 3: 247–56.

Gale, Fay (ed.)

    1974 *Women's Role in Aboriginal Society.* 2d ed. Canberra: Australian Institute of Aboriginal Studies.

Geertz, Clifford

    1973 *The Interpretation of Cultures.* New York: Basic Books.

    1975 "From the Native's Point of View: On the Nature of Anthropological Understanding." *American Scientist* 63: 47–53.

Giddens, Anthony

    1979 *Central Problems in Social Theory.* Cambridge: Cambridge University Press.

Glowcewski, Barbara

    1984 "Manifestations symboliques d'une transition économique: Le 'Juluru,' culte intertribal du 'cargo.' " *L'Homme* 23: 7–35

Godelier, Maurice

    1977 *Perspectives on Marxist Anthropology.* New York: Cambridge University Press.

Goffman, Erving

    1961 *Asylums.* New York: Doubleday.

Goodale, Jane

    1971 *Tiwi Wives.* Seattle: University of Washington Press.

    n.d. "Kaulong Gender." Manuscript.

Goodenough, Ward

    1955 "A Problem in Malayo-Polynesian Social Organization." *American Anthropologist* 57: 71–83.

    1969 "Rethinking Status and Role." In S. Tyler, ed., *Cognitive Anthropology.* New York: Holt, Rinehart, and Winston.

    1970 *Description and Comparison in Cultural Anthropology.* Chicago: Aldine.

Gould, Richard

    1969a *Yiwara: Foragers of the Australian Desert.* London: Collins.

    1969b "Subsistence Behavior among the Western Desert Aborigines of Australia." *Oceania* 39: 253–74.

Gregory, C.A.

    1982 *Gifts and Commodities.* London: Academic Press.

Hallowell, A. I.

    1955 *Culture and Experience.* New York: Schocken Books.

Hamilton, Annette
  1975 "Aboriginal Woman: The Means of Production." In J. Mercer, ed., *The Other Half: Women in Australian Society.* Hammondsworth: Penguin.
  1979 "Timeless Transformation: Women, Men, and History in the Australian Western Desert." Ph.D. diss., University of Sydney.
  1980 "Dual Social Systems: Technology, Labour, and Women's Secret Rites in the Eastern Western Desert of Australia." *Oceania* 51: 4–19.
  1981 "A Complex Strategical Situation: Gender and Power in Aboriginal Australia." In N. Grieve and P. Grimshaw, eds., *Australian Women: Feminist Perspectives*, 69–85. Melbourne: Oxford University Press.

Hansen, K., and L. Hansen
  1969 "Pintupi Phonology." *Oceanic Linguistics* 8: 153–70.
  1974 *Pintupi Kinship.* Alice Springs: Institute for Aboriginal Development.
  1978 *The Core of Pintupi Grammar.* Parts 1 and 2. Alice Springs: Institute for Aboriginal Development.

Haviland, John
  1979 "How to Talk to Your Brother-in-law in Guugu Yimidhirr." In T. Shopen, ed., *Languages and Their Speakers*, 161–239. Cambridge, Mass.: Winthrop.

Hayden, Brian
  1979 *Palaeolithic Reflections.* Canberra: Australian Institute of Aboriginal Studies.

Hiatt, L. R.
  1962 "Local Organisation among the Australian Aborigines." *Oceania* 32: 267–86.
  1965 *Kinship and Conflict: A Study of an Aboriginal Community in Northern Arnhem Land.* Canberra: Australian National University Press.

Hofstadter, Douglas
  1979 *Gödel, Escher, Bach: An Eternal Golden Braid.* New York: Basic Books.

Huntsman, J. W.
  1971 "Concepts of Kinship and Categories of Kinsmen in the Tokelau Islands." *Journal of the Polynesian Society* 80: 317–54.

Ingold, Tim
  1980 *Hunters, Pastoralists, and Ranchers: Reindeer Economies and their Transformations.* Cambridge: Cambridge University Press.

Irvine, Judith
  1979 "Formality and Informality in Communicative Events." *American Anthropologist* 81: 773–90.

Iteanu, André
  1984 "Levels and Convertibility." Manuscript.

James, William
  1884 "What Is an Emotion?" *Mind.*

Kaberry, Phyllis
  1939 *Aboriginal Woman, Sacred and Profane.* London: Routledge and Kegan Paul.

Kapferer, Bruce
  1976 "Introduction: Transactional Models Reconsidered." In B. Kapferer, ed., *Transaction and Meaning.* Philadelphia: Institute for the Study of Human Issues.

Kolig, Erich
  1979 "Djuluru: Ein synkretistichen Kult Nordwest-Australiens." *Baessler-Archiv,* neue folge 27: 419–48.

Lacan, Jacques
   1981 *The Four Fundamental Concepts of Psychoanalysis.* Translated by A. Sheridan. New York: Norton.
Leach, Edmund
   1958 "Concerning Trobriand Clans and the Kinship Category Tabu." In J. Goody, ed., *The Developmental Cycle in Domestic Groups.* Cambridge: Cambridge University Press.
Leacock, Eleanor
   1978 "Women's Status in Egalitarian Society: Implications for Social Evolution." *Current Anthropology* 19: 247–75.
Lederman, Rena
   1984 "Who Speaks Here? Formality and the Politics of Gender in Mendi, Highland Papua New Guinea." In Brenneis and Myers, eds., 85–107.
Lee, Richard
   1976 "!Kung Spatial Organization: An Ecological and Historical Perspective." In R. Lee and I. DeVore, eds., *Kalahari Hunter-Gatherers.* Cambridge: Harvard University Press.
   1979 *The !Kung San: Men, Women, and Work in a Foraging Society.* New York: Cambridge University Press.
   1984 *The Dobe !Kung.* New York: Holt, Rinehart, and Winston.
Lee, R., and I. DeVore
   1968 "Problems in the Study of Hunters and Gatherers." In R. Lee and I. DeVore, eds., *Man the Hunter.* Chicago: Aldine.
LeVine, Robert
   1973 *Culture, Behavior, and Personality.* Chicago: Aldine.
Lévi-Strauss, Claude
   1949 *Les Structures élémentaires de la Parenté.* Paris: Presses Universitaires de France.
   1962 *Totemism.* Chicago: University of Chicago Press.
   1963 "Structural Analysis in Linguistics and in Anthropology." In *Structural Anthropology*, 29–53. New York: Anchor Books.
   1966 *The Savage Mind.* Chicago: University of Chicago Press.
Levy, Robert
   1973 *The Tahitians: Mind and Experience in the Society Islands.* Chicago: University of Chicago Press.
Liberman, Kenneth
   1981 "Understanding Interaction in Central Australia: An Ethnomethodological Study of Australian Aboriginal People." Ph.D. diss., University of California, Los Angeles.
Lohe, M., F. W. Albrecht, and L. Leske
   1977 *Hermannsburg: A Vision and a Mission.* Adelaide: Lutheran Publishing House.
Long, J. P. M.
   1964a "The Pintubi Patrols: Welfare Work with the Desert Aborigines." *Australian Territories* 4 (5): 43–48.
   1964b "The Pintubi Patrols: Welfare Work with the Desert Aborigines—the Later Phases." *Australian Territories* 4 (6): 24–35.
   1971 "Arid Region Aborigines: The Pintubi." In D. Mulvaney and J. Golson, eds., *Aboriginal Man in Australia.* Canberra: Australian National University Press.

Lukács, G.
1973 *Marxism and Human Liberation: Essays on History, Culture, and Revolution.* New York: Delta Books.

Maddock, Kenneth
1972 *The Australian Aborigines: A Portrait of Their Society.* London: Penguin Press.
1981 "Warlpiri Land Tenure: A Test Case in Legal Anthropology." *Oceania* 52: 85–102.

Marshall, Lorna
1961 "Sharing, Talking, and Giving: Relief of Social Tensions among !Kung Bushmen." *Africa* 31: 231–49.

Martin, M. Kay, and Barbara Voorhies
1975 *The Female of the Species.* New York: Columbia University Press.

Marx, Karl, and Friedrich Engels
1947 *The German Ideology.* New York: International Publishers.

Mauss, Marcel
1904 *Seasonal Variations of the Eskimo: A Study in Social Morphology.* Translated by J. Fox. London: Routledge and Kegan Paul.

Meehan, Betty
1982 *Shell Bed to Shell Midden.* Canberra: Australian Institute of Aboriginal Studies.

Meggitt, M. J.
1962 *Desert People.* Chicago: University of Chicago Press.
1964 "Aboriginal Food Gatherers of Tropical Australia." In H. Elliot, ed., *The Ecology of Man in the Tropical Environment.* Morges: International Union for the Conservation of Nature.
1966 *Gadjari among the Walbiri Aborigines.* Oceania Monograph. Sydney: University of Sydney Press.
1972 "Understanding Australian Aboriginal Society: Kinship Systems or Cultural Categories." In P. Reining, ed., *Kinship Studies in the Morgan Centennial Year,* 64–87. Washington: Anthropological Society of Washington.

Meillassoux, Claude
1973 "On the Mode of Production of the Hunting Band." In P. Alexandre, ed., *French Perspectives in African Studies,* 187–203. London: Oxford University Press.

Merlan, Francesca
n.d. "Towards a Sociological Understanding of 'Mother-in-law' Speech Styles." Manuscript.

Morice, Rodney
1976 "Women Dancing Dreaming: Psychosocial Benefits of the Aboriginal Outstation Movement." *The Medical Journal of Australia* 2: 939–42.

Morphy, Howard
1977 " 'Too Many Meanings': An Analysis of the Artistic System of the Yolngu of Northeast Arnhem Land." Ph.D. diss., Australian National University, Canberra.
1984 *Journey to the Crocodile's Nest.* Canberra: Australian Institute of Aboriginal Studies.

Mountford, C. M.
1968 *Winbaraku and the Myth of Jarapiri.* Adelaide: Rigby.
1976 *Nomads of the Australian Desert.* Melbourne: Rigby.

References Cited

Moyle, Richard
    1979 *Songs of the Pintupi.*Canberra: Australian Institute of Aboriginal Studies.
Munn, Nancy
    1964 "Totemic Designs and Group Continuity in Walbiri Cosmology." In M. Reay, ed., *Aborigines Now.* Sydney: Angus and Robertson.
    1965 "A Report on Field Research at Areyonga." Australian Institute of Aboriginal Studies. Mimeographed.
    1969 "The Effectiveness of Symbols in Murngin Rite and Myth." In R. Spencer, ed., *Forms of Symbolic Action.* Proceedings of the American Ethnological Society.
    1970 "The Transformation of Subjects into Objects in Walbiri and Pitjantjara Myth." In R. Berndt, ed., 141–63.
    1973a *Walbiri Iconography.* Ithaca: Cornell University Press.
    1973b "Symbolism in a Ritual Context." In J. Honigrann, ed., *Handbook of Social and Cultural Anthropology.* Chicago: Rand McNally.
Myers, Fred
    1976 "To Have and to Hold: A Study of Persistence and Change in Pintupi Social Life." Ph.D. diss., Bryn Mawr College, Bryn Mawr, Pa.
    1979 "Emotions and the Self: A Theory of Personhood and Political Order among Pintupi Aborigines." *Ethos* 7: 343–70.
    1980a "The Cultural Basis of Pintupi Politics." *Mankind* 12: 197–213.
    1980b "A Broken Code: Pintupi Political Theory and Contemporary Social Life." *Mankind* 12: 311–26.
    1982 "Always Ask: Resource Use and Land Ownership among Pintupi Aborigines." In N. Williams and E. Hunn, eds., *Resource Managers: North American and Australian Hunter-Gatherers,* 173–96. Boulder: Westview Press.
    n.d. "What Is the Business of the 'Balgo Business'? A Contemporary Aboriginal Religious Movement." Manuscript.
Myers, Fred, and Donald Brenneis
    1984 "Introduction: Language and Politics in the Pacific." In Brenneis and Myers, eds., 1–29.
Nash, David
    1980 *A Traditional Land Claim by the Warlmanpa, Warlpiri, Mudbura, and Warumungu Traditional Owners.* Alice Springs: Central Land Council.
Nathan, P., and D. Japanangka
    1983a *Settle Down Country.* Alice Springs: Central Australian Aboriginal Congress.
    1983b *Health Business.* Richmond, Victoria: Heinemann Publishers.
Northern Territory Administration
    1920 Northern Territory Administration Annual Report.
    1935 Northern Territory Administration Report.
    1937 Northern Territory Administration Report.
    1938 Northern Territory Administration Report.
    1945 Northern Territory Administration Report.
    1946 Northern Territory Administration Report.
    1948 Northern Territory Administration Report.
    1956 Northern Territory Administration, Welfare Branch.
    1959 Northern Territory Administration, Welfare Branch.
    1961a "Finke River Mission, Hermannsburg, Central Australia." Northern Territory Administration, Welfare Branch.
    1961b "Pintubi Aboriginal Reserve." Northern Territory Administration, Welfare Branch.

1961c Northern Territory Administration, Welfare Branch, Annual Report.
1962 Northern Territory Administration, Welfare Branch, Annual Report.
1964 Northern Territory Administration, Welfare Branch, Annual Report.
1966 Northern Territory Administration, Welfare Branch, Annual Report.
1969 Northern Territory Administration, Welfare Branch, Annual Report.
1970 Northern Territory Administration, Welfare Branch, Annual Report.
1972 Northern Territory Administration, Welfare Branch, Annual Report.

Ortner, Sherry
1973 "On Key Symbols." *American Anthropologist* 75: 1338–46.

Panoff, Michel
1968 "The Concept of the Double Self among the Maenge of New Britain." *Journal of the Polynesian Society* 77: 275–95.

Peterson, Nicholas
1969 "Secular and Ritual Links: Two Basic and Opposed Principles of Australian Social Organization as Illustrated by Walbiri Ethnography." *Mankind* 7: 27–35.
1972 "Totemism Yesterday: Sentiment and Local Organization among the Australian Aborigines." *Man* 7: 12–32.
1974 "The Importance of Women in Determining the Composition of Residential Groups in Aboriginal Australia." In F. Gale, ed., 2d ed.
1975 "Hunter-Gatherer Territoriality: The Perspective from Australia." *American Anthropologist* 77: 53–68.
1983 "Rights, Residence, and Process in Australian Territorial Organization." In N. Peterson and M. Langton, eds., *Aborigines, Land, and Land Rights.* Canberra: Australian Institute of Aboriginal Studies.

Peterson, N., I. Keen, and B. Sansom
1977 "Succession to Land: Primary and Secondary Rights to Aboriginal Estates." In *Official Hansard Report of the Joint Select Committee on Aboriginal Land Rights in the Northern Territory.* Canberra: Australian Government Printer.

Peterson, N., P. McConvell, S. Wild, and R. Hagen
1978 *A Claim to Traditional Land by the Warlpiri and Kartangarurru-Kurintji.* Rev. version. Alice Springs: Central Land Council.

Petri, Helmut and G. Petri-Odermann
1970 "Stability and Change: Present Day Historic Aspects among Australian Aborigines." In R. Berndt, ed, 248–276.

Pink, Olive
1935 "The Landowners of the Northern Division of the Aranda Tribe, Central Australia." *Oceania* 6: 275–305

Pitkin, Hannah
1967 *The Concept of Representation.* Berkeley: University of California Press.

Radcliffe-Brown, A. R.
1913 "Three Tribes of Western Australia." *Journal of the Royal Anthropological Institute* 43: 143–94.
1930 "The Social Organization of Australian Tribes." *Oceania* 1: 34–63, 322–41, 426–56.

Read, Kenneth
1959 "Leadership and Consensus in a New Guinea Society." *American Anthropologist* 61: 425–36.

Reay, Marie
1970 "A Decision as Narrative." In R. Berndt, ed., 164–73.

References Cited 317

Ricoeur, Paul
  1970 *Freud and Philosophy: An Essay on Interpretation.* New Haven: Yale University Press.

Róheim, Géza
  1933 "Women and Their Life in Central Australia." *Journal of the Royal Anthropological Institute* 63: 207–65.
  1945 *The Eternal Ones of the Dream.* New York: International Universities Press.
  1950 *Psychoanalysis and Anthropology.* New York: International Universities Press.

Rosaldo, Michelle
  1973 "I Have Nothing to Hide: The Language of Ilongot Oratory." *Language in Society* 2: 193–223.
  1980 *Knowledge and Passion: Ilongot Notions of Self and Social Life.* Cambridge: Cambridge University Press.

Rose, Deborah
  1984 "Dingo Makes Us Human: Being and Purpose in Australian Aboriginal Culture." Ph.D. diss., Bryn Mawr College, Bryn Mawr, Pa.

Rose, F. G.
  1968 "Australian Marriage, Land-Owning Groups, and Initiations." In R. Lee and I. DeVore, eds.

Ryle, Gilbert
  1949 *The Concept of Mind.* New York: Barnes and Noble.

Sahlins, Marshall
  1968 "The Original Affluent Society." In R. Lee and I. DeVore, eds.
  1972 *Stone Age Economics.* New York: Aldine.
  1981 *Historical Metaphors and Mythical Realities: Structure in the Early History of the Sandwich Islands Kingdom.* Ann Arbor: University of Michigan Press.

Sansom, Basil
  1980 *The Camp at Wallaby Cross.* Canberra: Australian Institute of Aboriginal Studies.

Sapir, Edward
  1938 "Why Cultural Anthropology Needs the Psychiatrist." *Psychiatry* 1: 7–12.
  1970 *Culture, Language and Personality: Selected Essays.* Ed. by D. Mandelbaum. Berkeley: University of California Press.

Scheffler, Harold
  1965 *Choiseul Island Social Structure.* Berkeley: University of California Press.
  1966 "Ancestor Worship in Anthropology: Or Observations on Descent and Descent Groups." *Current Anthropology* 7: 541–51.
  1978 *Australian Kin Classification.* Cambridge: Cambridge University Press.

Scheman, Naomi
  1980 "Anger and the Politics of Naming." In S. McConnell-Ginet, R. Borker, and N. Furman, eds., *Women and Language in Literature and Society.* New York: Praeger.

Service, Elman
  1962 *Primitive Social Organization: An Evolutionary Perspective.* New York: Random House.

Shapiro, Warren
  1969 "Miwuyt Marriage." Ph.D. diss., Australian National University, Canberra.
  1971 "Patri-Groups, Patri-Categories, and Sections in Australian Aboriginal Social Organization." *Man* 6: 590–600.

1979 *Social Organization in Aboriginal Australia.* Canberra: Australian National University Press.

Sharp, R. L.
1934 "Ritual Life and Economics of the Yir-Yiront of Cape York Peninsula." *Oceania* 5: 19–42.

Shore, Bradd
1982 *Sala'ilua: A Samoan Mystery.* New York: Columbia University Press.

Silverstein, Michael
1976 "Shifters, Linguistic Categories and Cultural Description." In K. Basso and H. Selby, eds., *Meaning in Anthropology.* Albuquerque: University of New Mexico Press.

Simmel, Georg
1950 *The Sociology of Georg Simmel.* Translated, edited, and introduction by K. Wolff. New York: Free Press.

Solomon, Robert
1977 *The Passions: The Myth and Nature of Human Emotion.* Garden City, N.Y.: Anchor Books.

Spencer, Baldwin, and F. Gillen
1899 *The Native Tribes of Central Australia.* London: Macmillan.

Stanner, W. E. H.
1956 "The Dreaming." In T. A. G. Hungerford, ed., *Australian Signpost.* Melbourne: F. W. Cheshire.
1965 "Aboriginal Territorial Organization." *Oceania* 36: 1–26.
1966 *On Aboriginal Religion.* Oceania Monograph no. 11. Sydney: University of Sydney Press.

Steward, Julian
1955 *Theory of Culture Change.* Urbana: University of Illinois Press.

Strehlow, T. G. H.
1947 *Aranda Traditions.* Melbourne: University of Melbourne Press.
1965 "Culture, Social Structure, and Environment." In R. and C. Berndt, eds., *Aboriginal Man in Australia.* Sydney: Angus and Robertson.
1970 "Geography and the Totemic Landscape in Central Australia: A Functional Study." In R. Berndt, ed., 92–140.

Sutton, Peter
1979 "Wik: Aboriginal Society, Territory and Language at Cape Kerweer, Cape York Peninsula." Ph.D. diss., University of Queensland.

Thompson, E. P.
1979 *The Poverty of Theory and Other Essays.* London: Merlin Press.

Thomson, Donald
1964 "Some Wood and Stone Implements of the Bindibu Tribe of Central Western Australia." Proceedings of the Prehistorical Society 30: 400–22.
1975 *Bindibu Country.* Melbourne: Nelson Press.

Tindale, N. B.
1972 "The Pitjandjara." In M. G. Bicchieri, ed., *Hunters and Gatherers Today,* 217–68. New York: Holt, Rinehart, and Winston.
1974 *Aboriginal Tribes of Australia.* Canberra: Australian National University Press.

Tonkinson, Robert
1974 *The Jigalong Mob: Aboriginal Victors of the Desert Crusade.* Menlo Park, Calif.: Cummings.

1977 "Semen versus Spirit-Child in a Western Desert Culture." In L. R. Hiatt, ed., *Australian Aboriginal Concepts*, 81–92. Canberra: Australian Institute of Aboriginal Studies.

1978 *The Mardudjara Aborigines: Living the Dream in Australia's Western Desert.* New York: Holt, Rinehart, and Winston.

Turnbull, Colin

1961 *The Forest People.* New York: Simon and Schuster.

Turner, David H.

1980 *Australian Aboriginal Social Organization.* Canberra: Australian Institute of Aboriginal Studies.

Turner, Terence

1973 "Piaget's Structuralism." *American Anthropologist* 75: 351–73.

1979a "The Gê and Bororo Societies as Dialectical Systems: A General Model." In D. Maybury-Lewis, ed., *Dialectical Societies*, 147–78. Cambridge: Harvard University Press.

1979b "Kinship, Household, and Community Structure among the Kayapo." In D. Maybury-Lewis, ed., 179–217.

1980a "The Social Skin." In J. Cherfas and R. Lewin, eds., *Not Work Alone: A Cross-Cultural View of Activities Superfluous to Survival*, 112–140. Beverly Hills, Calif.: Sage.

1980b "Anthropology and the Politics of Indigenous Peoples' Struggles." *Cambridge Anthropology* (Winter).

1984a "Dual Opposition, Hierarchy, and Value: Moiety Structure and Symbolic Polarity in Central Brazil and Elsewhere." Manuscript.

1984b "Animal Symbolism, Totemism, and the Structure of Myth." In G. Urton, ed., *Natural Mythologies: Animal Symbols and Metaphors in South America.* Salt Lake City: University of Utah Press.

Turner, Victor

1967 *Forest of Symbols.* Ithaca: Cornell University Press.

1969a "Introduction." In R. Spencer, ed., *Forms of Symbolic Action.* Proceedings of the American Ethnological Society. Seattle: University of Washington Press.

1969b *The Ritual Process.* Chicago: Aldine.

1975 "Symbolic Studies." In B. Siegel, ed., *Annual Reviews of Anthropology.* Palo Alto, Calif.: Annual Review Press.

van der Leeden, A. C.

1975 "Thundering Gecko and Emu: The Mythological Structuring of Nunggubuyu Patrimoieties." In L. R. Hiatt, ed., *Australian Aboriginal Mythology*, 46–103. Canberra: Australian Institute of Aboriginal Studies.

Warner, W. Lloyd

1937 *A Black Civilization.* New York: Harper and Row.

Watson, James B.

1972 "Talking to Strangers." In S. Kimball and J. Watson, eds., *Crossing Cultural Boundaries.* San Francisco: Chandler Books.

Weber, Max

1947 *The Theory of Social and Economic Organization.* Translated by A. Henderson and T. Parsons. New York: Free Press.

Weiner, Annette

1976 *Women of Value, Men of Renown.* Austin: University of Texas Press.

1980 "Reproduction: A Replacement for Reciprocity." *American Ethnologist* 7: 71–85.

White, Isobel

1975 "Sexual Conquest and Submission in the Myths of Central Australia." In L. R. Hiatt, ed., *Australian Aboriginal Mythology*, 123–42. Canberra: Australian Institute of Aboriginal Studies.

1981 "Generation Moieties in Australia: Structural, Social and Ritual Implications." *Oceania* 52: 6–27.

Williams, Nancy

1973 "Northern Territory Aborigines under Australian Law." Ph.D. thesis, University of California, Berkeley.

1982 "A Boundary Is to Cross: Observations on Yolngu Boundaries and Permission." In N. Williams and E. Hunn, eds., *Resource Managers: North American and Australian Hunter-Gatherers*, 131–54. Boulder: Westview Press.

Williams, Raymond

1977 *Marxism and Literature*. Oxford: Oxford University Press.

Wittgenstein, Ludwig

1958 *Philosophical Investigations*. 3rd ed. New York: Macmillan.

Woodburn, James

1978 "Sex Roles and the Division of Labour in Hunting and Gathering Societies." Paper delivered at the 1st International Congress on Hunting and Gathering Societies, Paris, June 1978.

1979 "Minimal Politics: The Political Organization of the Hadza of North Tanzania." In W. Shack and P. Cohen, eds., *Politics in Leadership: A Comparative Perspective*. Oxford: Clarendon Press.

Yengoyan, Aram

1968 "Demographic and Ecological Influences on Aboriginal Australian Marriage Sections." In R. Lee and I. DeVore, eds., 185–99.

Index

Bands (con't.)
Organization, and groups, and
as communities)
distribution of large game
within, 75
membership of, 88, 94–96, 100–
102, 165, 167, 194, 195, 298n
movement of, 75, 77–89, 94–97,
101, 168, 257, 269, 270, 271,
292, 299n, 302n
relation to resources, 76–89, 94–
96, 100, 299n, 301n, 302n
sharing within, 75, 76, 107, 110,
115, 254, 278, 279
Barker, G., 128
Barnes, J., 72
Barth, F., 220, 292
Barwick, D., 308n
Basso, K., 289
Bates, D., 30
Bateson, G., 23, 105, 257
Begler, E., 308n
Bell, D., 147, 250, 252, 253, 300n,
303n, 308n
Berger, P., 241, 286
Bern, J., 308n
Berndt, C., 74, 75, 299n, 308n
Berndt, R., 29, 298n, 299n, 300n
Bestowal: 87, 170, 172–174, 195,
250, 276
and conflict, 161, 162, 172, 173
and male initiation, 231, 239
Birdsell, J., 18, 71, 72
Birth, 50
Boas, F., 13, 14
"Boss": 39, 40, 142, 222, 223, 243,
262–266, 269, 279, 282–285,
308n
and "looking after," 262–266,
269, 279, 282–285
Boundaries: 19, 43, 56, 73, 79, 89,
91, 93–96, 99, 100, 101, 155–
157, 167, 296, 297, 299n, 301n
and communities, 164–166
Bourdieu, P., 14, 96, 195
Brenneis, D., 221, 270, 304n, 308n
Broome, 268
Buchler, I., 217
Buck, B., 31
Burial, 132, 134, 303n
Burridge, K., 305n

Camp: as residential unit, 36, 42–
44, 54, 55
Pintupi ideas of (See also Ngurra,
as "camp"), 48, 54–57, 68, 88,
90, 92, 110, 128, 164, 300n
Carnegie, D., 30
Ceremonies: categories, 82, 85,
227. (See also Kurtitji;
Tingarri; Yarritjiti; Yilpintji;
Initiation, Male; Women)
decoration of body in, 66, 227,
230, 231, 300n
increase, 63, 300n, 301n
organization of, 149, 190, 202,
227, 233, 235, 237, 238, 267,
304n, 307n
origin of, 50, 51, 54
value of, 67, 118, 134
and social reproduction, 177,
178, 225–236
as gatherings, 45, 177, 230, 272,
307n
as medium of integration, 112,
149, 202, 234, 252, 253, 258,
259, 268, 269, 272
as symbolic action, 232, 234–238
Childhood: 107, 108, 110, 113–115,
171, 178, 179
and emotions, 107, 108, 112,
113, 171
Christianity, 269. (See also
Missions, Christian)
Circumcision, 61, 174, 231, 234,
236, 237, 239
Claims, 18, 22, 60, 113, 128, 133,
135, 137–143, 149, 155, 156,
158, 275, 276, 283, 295, 303n,
304n
Clark, B., 107, 110, 269
Clothing, 36, 39–41, 44, 233
Collier, J., 250, 251
Collmann, J., 127
Comaroff, J., 14, 292
Community Adviser, 263, 265,
267, 271, 283
Community Organization: 259,
260, 262–283, 285, 288, 291.
(See also Bands; Local Groups;
Settlement)
and ideology of, 270–282
and property, 263, 267, 268, 272,
273, 285

and representation (*See also*
Council, Village), 265–268, 280
Compassion: as emotion, 44, 62,
96, 99, 103, 107, 113, 115, 116,
118, 119, 125, 126, 160, 258,
264, 265, 266
as limit to autonomy, 115, 116,
119, 125, 266–269, 285
and authority, 125, 126, 266
and landownership, 144
Conception: 50, 107, 130, 131,
303n, 304n
and landownership, 129, 130,
131, 136–140, 142–144, 149,
152, 304n
Conflict, 16, 17, 38, 41, 81, 101,
142, 160–168, 170, 172, 173,
179, 258, 259, 262–264, 268,
269, 271–273, 289
Consensus, 125, 166, 255, 266, 270,
271, 273–276
Contact, white: 30–35, 37, 39, 53,
85, 299n
reasons for, 31, 34, 35, 39, 40
and work, 34, 37–41
Cooperation, 56, 73, 77, 104, 290.
(*See also* Production; Sharing)
Coresident, 16, 80–82, 87. (*See also*
Bands; "One-Countryman";
Residential Organization, and
groups)
Council, Village: 219, 261–268,
270–273, 277, 279, 285, 308n
legitimacy of, 262–268
and representation, 265–267,
308n
Councillor, Village: 221, 246, 262–
268, 272, 273, 285
cultural conception of, 262, 263,
265–268
Country (*See also* Ngurra;
Landownership): 48, 61, 66, 67
defined by The Dreaming, 48, 50,
53, 55, 57–69
esoteric knowledge of, restricted,
64, 67, 147, 149, 150, 157, 236,
245
identification with, 71, 91, 93–
95, 108, 117, 120, 128–145,
147, 151–153, 156, 158, 175,
176, 303n, 304n

knowledge of and ownership, 67,
68, 137, 149–152, 157
knowledge of and exchange, 221,
255
named, 50, 55, 57–60
resource use and individuals, 79–
102, 136, 155, 156
as code, 66, 67, 92
as connected, 50, 59–64, 69, 136,
155, 156
and boundaries, 91, 93–96, 140,
155, 156, 302n
as token in social process, 67, 68,
127, 128, 145, 146, 147, 150–
158, 221, 241, 255
as objectification of shared
identity, 134, 135, 144, 145,
155, 156, 158, 175, 176, 257

Davenport, W., 304n
Derrida, J., 302n
Death: 45, 56, 117, 118, 132–136,
167
as basis for claim to land, 132,
136–140
Decision-making: 246, 264–268,
270–276, 285, 287, 308n
and legitimacy, 265–271, 285
and compassion, 266, 269, 276,
285
DeVore, I., 19, 71, 258, 301n
Ditton, P., 308n
Dixon, R., 123
Docker River Settlement, 29, 45,
86, 99, 151
Douglas, M., 258
Dreaming, The (*Tjukurrpa*): 47–70,
86, 107, 118, 119, 125, 129,
130, 131, 138, 139, 141, 145,
149–152, 155, 156, 157, 166,
182, 221, 226, 241–243, 254,
255, 267, 270, 285–288, 297,
298n, 300n, 301n, 303n
and authority, 241, 247, 254,
255, 266, 267
and ceremonies, 51, 54, 66
and change, 52–54, 64, 66, 68,
267, 285
and identity, 50, 60, 66, 68, 109,
130–132, 143, 145, 148, 155,
221, 242, 255, 268, 285
and politics, 219, 220, 247

Dreaming, The (con't.)
  and revelation, 51, 53, 67
  and truth, 49, 67
  and value, 67, 68, 118, 119, 146,
    166, 220, 224, 238, 240, 242,
    243, 247, 254, 266, 288, 297
  as basis for landownership, 129–
    131, 136, 138–140, 142–144,
    149, 150, 152, 154–157, 262
  as model of life cycle, 241–243
  transcending relatedness, 119,
    125, 254, 255, 266, 297
Dreams, 51, 52, 67
Dubinskas, F., 302n
Duguid, C., 299n
Dumont, L., 69, 105, 220, 224, 288
Durkheim, E., 47, 220, 255
Dyson-Hudson, R., 96, 101, 302n

Ehrenberg Range, 28, 31, 84, 85,
    136, 137
Eliade, M., 225, 300n
Elkin, A. P., 30, 150, 181, 196–198,
    201, 210, 299n
Embarrassment (See Shame)
Emotions: and shared identity, 104,
    107, 113, 117–119, 121–124,
    162, 163, 269
  as cultural constructs, 18, 23,
    103–126, 253, 271, 302n
  as moral ideals, 116, 117, 172,
    253, 264, 269, 271
Equality, 70, 161, 170, 171, 203,
    215, 216, 224, 228, 229, 233,
    234, 240, 242, 243, 246, 247,
    254, 264–266
Estate, 59, 68, 128, 158
Ethnography, 12, 13, 14, 286, 292,
    293
Evans, E., 298n
Evans-Pritchard, E., 55, 300n
Exchange: 43, 75, 76, 104, 111,
    112, 163, 165, 170–177, 248,
    266, 290, 291, 305n
  equivalent, 173, 174, 211, 214,
    216, 234
  hierarchical, 173, 174, 211, 216,
    222, 223, 225, 236, 238
  and ceremony, 190
  and identity, 165, 173, 234, 236,
    239, 240, 245, 248, 266
  and social reproduction, 173,

182, 224, 239, 248, 305n
Exogamy, 71, 175–177, 190

Fauna, 26, 74
Fights: 81, 84, 86, 87, 112, 142,
    160, 161, 163, 169, 178, 253,
    264, 274
  as exchange, 171, 175, 214
Fingarette, H., 104
Finlayson, H., 75
Flora, 25, 26, 74
Food: foodstuffs, 74, 79, 80, 168,
    169, 301n, 302n
  distribution of, 43, 75, 76, 80,
    115, 190, 230, 235
  gathering, 43, 45, 74, 79, 80
  preparation, 74, 75
  rations, 34, 39, 40
  and whites, 39, 261
Frake, C., 14, 270
Freeman, D., 99
Fried, M., 99
Fry, H., 31, 183, 305n
Funeral Ceremonies (See also
    Yirkapiri), 133, 134, 200, 295

Geertz, C., 14, 104, 121, 109, 217
Generational Moieties: 177, 187,
    202–204, 214, 215, 217, 253,
    294
  and male initiation, 204, 229,
    231–235, 294
  and marriage, 204
  as reflection of regional system,
    203, 215, 217, 234, 294, 307n
Giddens, A., 14
Giles, E., 30
Gillen, F., 47, 228, 299n, 301n,
    303n
Glowcewski, B., 268
Godelier, M., 218
Goffman, E., 280
Goodale, J., 175, 303n
Goodenough, W., 191, 192, 200
Gordon Hills, 82, 94, 168
Gould, R., 57, 74, 75, 155, 299n,
    300n, 301n
Gregory, C., 305n
Grief (See Sorrow)

Haasts Bluff, 32, 33, 34, 36, 37, 39,
    40, 136, 137, 282, 299n

Reproduction, social (con't.)
267, 281, 288, 290–292, 295,
305n
and politics, 267, 281
and production of persons, 170,
173, 216–218, 221, 236, 243,
245, 254, 255, 264, 291, 305n
Residence: dwellings, 42, 43, 299n
marital, 42, 43, 56, 90, 110, 299n
bachelors, 42, 43, 56
women's camp, 42, 43, 212, 253
Residential Organization: choices
in, 43, 44, 82, 83, 88, 90, 97,
115, 270, 300n
internal spatial, 19, 27, 36, 42–
44, 86, 300n
and groups, conflicts within (See
also Bands, conflicts within),
160, 165, 252, 258, 268, 269,
274, 276
as communities, 164, 165, 259–
279, 290, 291, 296
Revenge Expedition (Warrmala),
62, 92, 93, 118, 160, 167–170
Ricoeur, P., 47, 302n
Roberts, S., 292
Róheim, G., 47, 108, 110, 180, 225,
247, 248, 287, 299n
Rosaldo, M., 47, 221, 250, 251, 270,
304n
Rose, D., 197
Rose, F., 219
Rubin, R., 302n
Ryle, G., 106

Sacred Objects, 59, 110, 118, 119,
134, 146, 153, 154, 166, 173,
174, 240, 245, 301n, 303n
Sacred Sites (Yarta yarta). (See also
Country; Landownership): 50,
58, 64, 66, 67, 78, 127, 128,
134–136, 150 153, 155, 166,
179, 203, 283, 294, 295
and exchange, 127, 151
and men/women, 64, 301n
knowledge of, 149, 150, 152
value of, 64, 66, 67, 118, 134,
149–151, 179, 283
visiting, 77, 97, 151, 183
Sahlins, M., 14, 291, 301n
San (!Kung), 43, 72, 289
Sandall, R., 304n

Sansom, B., 69, 127, 154, 156, 162,
274, 296, 301n, 305n, 308n
Sapir, E., 11, 14
Scheffler, H., 72, 197, 198, 303n,
305n, 306n
Scheman, N., 106
School, 37, 261
Self: concepts of, 104, 105, 120,
121, 124–126, 178, 302n
concepts of and political action,
265, 266, 269, 271, 272, 273,
297
selfhood, 18, 70, 104, 105, 107,
108, 124–126, 178, 241, 242
and autonomy, 107, 110, 122–
124, 265, 266, 269, 271
and identity with others, 108,
109, 115, 117–121, 178, 269,
271–273
Self-determination, Aboriginal, 21,
261, 277–284
Separatism, of Pintupi, 34, 36, 38,
40, 41, 259, 260, 270–275
Service, E., 72
Settlement. (See also Outstation):
21, 34, 36–38, 41, 45, 46, 53,
253, 257, 261, 262, 264, 265,
267–270, 272–284, 299n
facilities of, 33, 37, 41, 42, 261
living conditions in, 35, 36, 42,
43, 44, 261
and sedentarization, 34–38, 41,
133, 253, 261, 262, 268, 269,
275, 289
Sex, 112, 235, 237, 238, 250
Shame (Kunta): 100, 103, 112, 120–
125, 271
compared with Bali, 121
regulating shared identity and
autonomy, 120–124, 254, 271
and authority, 125, 126, 214
and disagreement, 144
and sacred objects, 122
and sex, 122, 123
and speech, 233, 271
and theories of conception, 123
Shapiro, W., 43, 175, 202, 295,
306n
Sharing: 44, 61, 76, 96, 115
as basis for conflict, 62, 115
of activity and identity, 164, 165,
177, 178, 233, 251, 268, 269

White, I., 250
White, R., 301n
Whites (*See also* Contact, white):
    Aboriginal relations with, 221–
    223, 246, 261, 263, 265, 267–
    269, 271–285, 293, 308n
    use of as outsiders, 276–285,
    308n
    Pintupi understanding of, 282–
    284
Williams, N., 295, 301n
Williams, R., 14, 242
Wilson, L., 39, 40
Wiluna Mission, 29, 44
Wittgenstein, L., 113
Women: 61, 64, 115, 146–148, 212,
    273, 277, 291, 294, 295, 298n,
    300n, 301n, 307n, 308n
    activities of, 43, 75, 76, 249, 277
    autonomy of, 249, 250, 277,
    307n, 308n
    importance of motherhood for,
    249, 251
    life cycle of, 90, 162, 212, 248–
    251, 298n
    restrictions on, 64, 66, 85, 93,
    226, 227, 229
    and marriage, 162, 248–251
    and ritual, 146, 147, 226, 227,
    249, 251, 301n, 308n
    and sexual politics, 248–252,
    308n

in male initiation, 230–232, 251
Woodburn, J., 291

Yarritjiti Ceremony, 226, 232, 235,
    251
Yawalyurru, 58, 61–63, 138, 139,
    141–144, 149–151, 282, 283,
    304n
Yayayi, 7, 21, 22, 28, 36, 42–46, 64,
    124, 135–138, 144, 150, 156,
    164, 173, 182, 196, 222, 243,
    245, 246, 249, 259, 260, 262–
    265, 283, 299n, 300n, 303n
Yengoyan, A., 299n
Yilpili (*See also* Ehrenberg Range),
    31, 84, 137
Yilpintji Ceremony, 226, 293; and
    sexual politics, 250
Yinyilingki, 7, 45, 156, 260, 264
Yirkapiri ("Mourners"). (*See also*
    Funeral Ceremonies;
    Initiation, Male), 200, 229–234,
    251
Yuendumu, 28, 33, 44, 45, 212,
    268, 293
Yulngu ("Murngin"), 197, 229, 295,
    303n
Yuti ("Visible"), 48–50, 69, 213,
    232, 243
Yutininpa ("Making appear"), 68;
    and procreation, 213

Smithsonian Series in Ethnographic Inquiry
Ivan Karp and William Merrill, Series Editors

Ethnography as fieldwork, analysis, and literary form is the distinguishing feature of modern anthropology. Guided by the assumption that anthropological theory and ethnography are inextricably linked, this series is devoted to exploring the ethnographic enterprise.

Advisory Board

Richard Bauman *(Indiana University)*, Gerald Berreman *(University of California, Berkeley)*, James Boon *(Cornell University)*, Stephen Gudeman *(University of Minnesota)*, Shirley Lindenbaum *(New School for Social Research)*, George Marcus *(Rice University)*, David Parkin *(University of London)*, Roy Rappaport *(University of Michigan)*, Renato Rosaldo *(Stanford University)*, Annette Weiner *(New York University)*, Norman Whitten *(University of Illinois)*, and Eric Wolf *(City University of New York)*.

Other Books in the Series:

Tsewa's Gift
Magic and Meaning in an Amazonian Society
Michael F. Brown

Barawa and the Ways Birds Fly in the Sky
An Ethnographic Novel
Michael Jackson

Independents Declared
The Dilemmas of Independent Trucking
Michael H. Agar

The Passion of Ansel Bourne
Multiple Personality in American Culture
Michael G. Kenny